The Na.

The Peoples of America

General Editors
Alan Kolata and Dean Snow

This series is about the native peoples and civilizations of the Americas, from their origins in ancient times to the present day. Drawing on archaeological, historical, and anthropological evidence, each volume presents a fresh and absorbing account of a group's culture, society, and history.

Accessible and scholarly, and well illustrated with maps and photographs, the volumes of *The Peoples of America* will together provide a comprehensive and vivid picture of the character and variety of the societies of the American past.

Already published

The Tiwanaku: A Portrait of an Andean Civilization
Alan Kolata

The Timucua
Jerald T. Milanich

The Aztecs
Michael E. Smith

The Cheyenne
John Moore

The Iroquois
Dean Snow

The Moche
Garth Bawden

The Nasca
Helaine Silverman and Donald A. Proulx

The Incas
Terence N. D'Altroy

The Nasca

Helaine Silverman and Donald A. Proulx

BLACKWELL
Publishers

The right of Helaine Silverman and Donald A. Proulx to be identified as authors
of this work has been asserted in accordance with the Copyright, Designs and
Patents Act 1988.

First published 2002

2 4 6 8 10 9 7 5 3 1

Blackwell Publishers Inc.
350 Main Street
Malden, Massachusetts 02148
USA

Blackwell Publishers Ltd
108 Cowley Road
Oxford OX4 1JF
UK

Library of Congress Cataloging-in-Publication Data has been applied for.

ISBN 0-631-16734-X (hardback); 0-631-23224-9 (paperback)

British Library Cataloguing in Publication Data

A CIP catalogue record for this book is available from the British Library.

Typeset in Sabon 11/13pt
by Graphicraft Limited, Hong Kong
Printed in Great Britain by TJ International, Padstow, Cornwall

This book is printed on acid-free paper.

To my mother, Edith Silverman, with love and gratitude
Helaine

To my wife, Mary Jean, the joy of my life
Don

Contents

Illustrations

Preface

Nasca is one of the most fascinating archaeological cultures of ancient Peru. Today its name engenders visions of beautiful polychrome painted pottery, grotesque human trophy heads, immense ground drawings, and sand-covered ruins. Among the public at large, Nasca is one of the most familiar of the great pre-Columbian cultures of the Americas because of its popularity with documentary film-makers. Yet scientific knowledge of Nasca is quite recent.

Our purpose in writing this book is to provide a comprehensive synthesis of scholarly knowledge about Nasca culture and society as it exists today. We seek to present the societal context for Nasca's material remains based on the history and results of archaeological investigations conducted over the course of the twentieth century.

The collaboration represented by this book has its origins in a meeting of the Society for American Archaeology held in 1974 when Donald Proulx was long beyond his doctoral dissertation on Nasca pottery and Helaine Silverman was just starting graduate school. We met in the symposium in which we both were participating and in which Silverman was presenting her first professional paper.

Both of us had become enamored with Nasca through its ceramic art. To this intense visual attraction we came to attach the intellectual questions that have guided our research over the years. In each of our cases, passion for Nasca began in the moldy basements of the anthropology buildings in which we had studied, Kroeber Hall at Berkeley for Proulx and Schermerhorn Hall at Columbia for

Silverman. Each of us had the distinct honor and challenge of working with material collected by pioneers in Andean archaeology, Max Uhle (Proulx) and William Duncan Strong (Silverman). Yet these collections were problematical in ways that forced our research in new directions. For Proulx, this developed into a lifelong study of the Nasca pottery style and its iconography in order to gain keener knowledge of the evolution of Nasca society and beliefs. For Silverman, it meant excavations at Cahuachi and, subsequently, fieldwork in the Pisco Valley in order to obtain new data. For both of us, extensive site survey in several valleys of the Río Grande de Nazca drainage has rounded out our distinct understandings of ancient Nasca society.

This book is the result of a true collaboration. We each affirm that this book could not – or not easily or happily – have been written without the assistance of the other. We have learned immensely from each other during the course of this collaboration. In terms of co-authorship we took different responsibilities and also made certain compromises on the more contentious issues that divide us. In the current book we have each spoken with our own voice, resulting in an internal dialogue readily apparent in the text and, indeed, explicitly signaled. We collaborated by writing different chapters and then extensively editing the manuscript, sending electronic files back and forth numerous times. Silverman appears as first author because of the greater number of chapters originally written by her. Chapter 10 remains her responsibility and she accepts the consequences for the speculation therein. Chapter 11 is based on Silverman's presentation at the 65th Annual Meeting of the Society for American Archaeology (Philadelphia, 2000).

Because of limitations on space we could not present all the figures and data backing up many of our statements and some of our longer arguments here. Readers are referred to Silverman's forthcoming book, *Landscapes of Meaning: Nasca Settlement Patterns in the Río Grande de Nazca Drainage, Peru* (University of Iowa Press, 2002) and to Proulx's almost completed book, *Nasca Ceramic Iconography* (working title).

Following Silverman (1993a: ix), except when quoting others, Nasca (with an "s") specifically refers to the famous archaeological culture dating to the Early Intermediate Period that is characterized by pre-fire slip painting of iconographically complex motifs. Nazca (with a "z") denotes the geographical area encompassed by the Río Grande de Nazca drainage, the specific river, the modern town, and all of the pre-Columbian and post-Conquest societies that existed in the drainage. Silverman has advocated this orthographic convention to avoid semantic confusion, although she recognizes that Menzel et al. (1964: 8) regard Nazca as a misspelling and Nasca as the historically correct form. Rostworowski (1993: 199) says that Nasca (with an "s") is closer to the Colonial Spanish pronunciation. She suggests that the word may have sounded like *Naschca*, similar to the *sch* sound in the name of the central coast Yschma polity.

We abbreviate the names of the time periods in the standard relative chronology for Peru as follows: Initial Period = IP; Early Horizon = EH; Early Intermediate Period = EIP; Middle Horizon = MH; Late Intermediate Period = LIP; Late Horizon = LH. Encompassing several named areas (Pampa de San José, Pampa de Nazca, Pampa de Socos, Pampa de Cinco Cruces, Pampa de Jumana, Pampa de Majuelos, Pampa de Los Chinos, Pampa de Las Carretas), here we refer simply to "the Pampa." Other abbreviations used are MNAAH for the Museo Nacional de Antropología, Arqueología e Historia in Lima; INC for the Instituto Nacional de Cultura; CIPS for the California Institute for Peruvian Studies.

Unless otherwise noted, all radiocarbon dates are presented uncorrected and uncalibrated.

All translations are by Helaine Silverman unless otherwise indicated.

Acknowledgments

Helaine Silverman: Writing this book has been one of the great pleasures of my academic career because of the opportunity and honor to collaborate with Donald Proulx whose work on Nasca art and society I admired as a graduate student and from which I have continued to benefit immeasurably as a professional. The collaboration is particularly poignant to me because it was Donald Proulx who, along with John H. Rowe, Dorothy Menzel, and the incomparable Lawrence Dawson, was so kind and encouraging to me long ago when, as a young graduate student, I began to work with William Duncan Strong's collections from Cahuachi. These generous colleagues facilitated my entry into the fascinating world of Nasca archaeology.

The fieldwork which underwrites various sections of this book was accomplished with the assistance of colleagues in Peru. I acknowledge with great thanks the professional help, insight, and kindnesses over many years of my Peruvian collaborators: Rubén García, Fernando Herrera, Josué Lancho Rojas, Bernardino Ojeda, Miguel Pazos, José Pinilla, and César Tumay.

Friends and other colleagues in Peru assisted me in countless ways during the years in which I was doing the research upon which this book is based. I remember with appreciation: Pedro Pablo Alayza, Susana Arce, José Canziani, Marta Tapía and Hernán Carrillo, Dante Casereto, Carmen Gabe, Benjamin Guerrero, Sonia Guillén, Pocha de Herrera, Peter Kaulicke, Krzysztof Makowski, Renate and Luis Millones, Pilar Remy, María Rostworowski, Idilio Santillana, Ruth Shady, Ana María Soldi, Oscar Tijero, Berta

Vargas, Lidia (Cuqui) de Velayos and the entire Velayos family, Rodolfo Vera, Adriana von Hagen, and Carlos Williams León.

I also acknowledge with appreciation the generous exchanges of information about Nasca that I have had with Anthony Aveni, David Browne, Patrick Carmichael, Anita Cook, Joerg Haeberli, Johny Isla, David Johnson, Josué Lancho Rojas, Giuseppe Orefici, Miguel Pazos, Ann Peters, Phyllis Pitluga, Francis (Fritz) Riddell, Katharina Schreiber, Ruth Shady, Gary Urton, John Verano, Dwight Wallace, and R. Tom Zuidema.

I have consistently received extraordinary institutional coopera- tion from the Instituto Nacional de Cultura in Lima and Ica, the Museo Regional de Ica, and the Museo Nacional de Antropología, Arqueología e Historia in Lima. To the directors and staffs of these great institutions I offer my thanks.

Doctoral fieldwork was funded by the Fulbright Program (1984– 5), the National Science Foundation (1984–5), and the Institute of Latin American Studies at the University of Texas at Austin (1983). Doctoral data analysis was supported by the Wenner-Gren Founda- tion (1985–6), the Organization of American States (1985), the Social Science Research Council (1985–6) and the National Sci- ence Foundation (1985). Post-doctoral fieldwork was funded by the National Endowment for the Humanities (1992), the National Geographic Society (1988–9), the USIA University Affiliations Program/Fulbright (1993–5), and the William and Flora Hewlett Foundation (1992) and the Tinker Foundation (1991) (both admin- istered through the Center for Latin American and Caribbean Studies at the University of Illinois at Urbana–Champaign). Post-doctoral data analysis was supported by the National Endowment for the Humanities (1992) and the University of Illinois at Urbana– Champaign. Leave time was generously provided by the University of Illinois at Urbana–Champaign. Fieldwork was conducted under the following permits: Resolución Suprema 165-84-ED, Resolución Suprema 226-88-ED, Resolución Suprema 282-89-ED, and Acuerdo Número 086-93-CNTCICMA/INC.

Donald Proulx: For me, this book is the culmination of almost forty years of research on the Nasca. Along the way, I have been indebted to many people and agencies for their inspiration, help, and financial assistance. Space does not permit me to acknowledge everyone, but the following people were especially influential in shaping my career. Lee Parsons, formerly assistant curator at the Milwaukee Public Museum, introduced me to Nasca when I was an undergraduate at the University of Wisconsin–Milwaukee and working part-time at the museum. The museum had just acquired the Malcolm Whyte Collection of pre-Columbian art, and I had the privilege of cataloging and researching part of the collection. This experience motivated me to go on to graduate school with a concentration in Peruvian archaeology.

I was fortunate to be admitted to the graduate program at the University of California at Berkeley where my mentor and friend, John H. Rowe, provided the intellectual and practical training I required to eventually achieve my goals. It was Rowe who first took me to Peru and introduced me to fieldwork and museum research in that country. The brilliant museum preparator at the Lowie (now Hearst) Museum of Anthropology, Lawrence Dawson, taught me how to analyze Nasca pottery and shared his vast knowledge of the style with me. Dorothy Menzel, conducting her own research in the museum at that time, gave me moral support and the benefit of her vast experience working with ceramics. Donald Collier of the Field Museum in Chicago allowed me full access to Kroeber's Nasca collections, which I used in my dissertation research.

Over the years many friends and colleagues have generously shared their own research and materials with me and have served as a sounding board for the exchange of ideas. These include Anthony Aveni, Ulf Bankmann, David Browne, Patrick Carmichael, Persis Clarkson, Vera Penteado Coehlo, Anita Cook, Lisa DeLeonardis, Christopher Donnan, Antonio Guarnotta, Joerg Haeberli, David Johnson, Sarah Massey, Stephen Mabee, Angelika Neudecker, Ana Nieves, Giuseppe Orefici, Tonya Panion, Anne Paul, Ann Peters, Francis Riddell, Richard Roark, Ann Pollard Rowe, Alan Sawyer, Katharina Schreiber, Gary Urton, John Verano, Dwight Wallace, Steven Wegner, and R. Tom Zuidema.

I want to single out my great respect for and the debt I owe to my co-author, Helaine Silverman, whose research at Cahuachi has revolutionized our view of Nasca society. Her extensive research on the south coast and her prolific output of publications has earned her the well-deserved reputation as the leading expert on Nasca culture. Our friendship and collaboration go back almost thirty years, and she has played a major role in shaping (and revising) my view of the Nasca.

A good portion of my Nasca research has centered on the formation of an archive of Nasca pottery modeled after the much more extensive Moche archive established by my good friend Christopher Donnan. The small collection of slides that began in my graduate school days has grown to a respectable collection of over 15,000 slides of more than 6,000 pots located in collections in the United States, Peru, Canada, Great Britain, Germany, France, and elsewhere. A list of all the curators who allowed me access to their collections would take several pages, so I will reserve individual acknowledgments for my upcoming book on Nasca ceramic iconography. However, I do now express my heartfelt thanks to all involved.

In Peru the following individuals have been instrumental in helping me to conduct the research reflected in this book: Jorge and Toni Alva, Susana Arce, José Cahuas Massa, Luis Jaime Castillo, Yolanda de Escobar, Henry Falcón Amado, Rubén García, Miriam Gavilán Roayzo, Fernando Herrera, Liliana Huaco Durand, Johny Isla, Federico Kauffmann Doig, Josué Lancho Rojas, and Miguel Pazos.

I wish also to acknowledge the loving support of my wife, Mary Jean Proulx, who unselfishly took care of our children while I was off working in Peru. More recently, she has visited Peru on two occasions and has always taken a deep interest in my work. She has put up with my occupation of our basement for a study and the many shelves of books throughout the house. She is also a critical proof-reader who has saved me from many embarrassments.

Lastly, I wish to acknowledge the financial support from the following agencies for the research reflected in this book: University of Massachusetts Faculty Research Grant (1966, 1985, 1988, 1990, 1992, 1996); the American Philosophical Society (1985); DAAD (Deutscher Akademischer Ausrauschdienst) Study Visit Grant (1988); NEH Travel to Collections Grant (1990); the H. John Heinz III Charitable Trust (1998); and the National Geographic Society (1998). My survey of the lower Nazca Valley was conducted under research permit Acuerdo 037G.D. No. 1170 (1998). I acknowledge with thanks the cooperation of the Instituto Nacional de Cultura in facilitating this fieldwork.

The authors wish to express special thanks to David M. Browne for his professional generosity and collegiality. He was the important initial impetus behind this volume. We also thank Steve Holland, the dedicated, superb technical draftsman and photographer in the Department of Anthropology at the University of Illinois at Urbana–Champaign, for his contribution to the book. We reiterate our appreciation to Joerg Haeberli, who has not only shared his vast knowledge of Nasca textiles, panpipes, and the far south coast with us, but also read various versions of relevant sections of the book and corrected them. Any remaining errors are solely our fault.

We acknowledge with many thanks the patience, superlative professionalism, and sympathetic understanding of our editor, Ken Provencher, as we brought this book to completion. We also thank Garth Bawden and Michael Moseley for their suggestions which helped us improve the book's content and style. We, of course, accept responsibility for its final form.

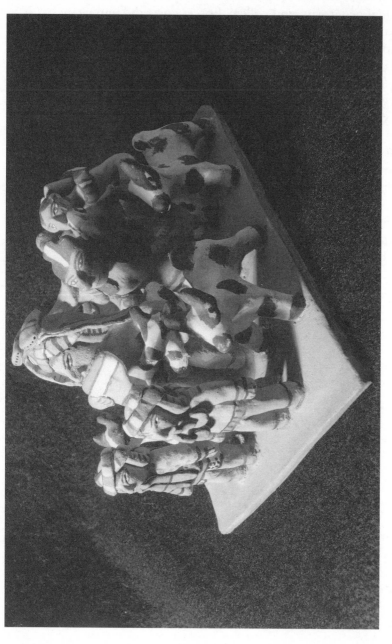

The unique, modeled, early Nasca scene published by Julio C. Tello in 1931. It depicts the procession of a finely dressed family. The father plays a large panpipe and two smaller ones rest on his head-covering. The mother carries two more panpipes, one in each hand. Parrots perch on the shoulders of the mother and another sits on the right shoulder of the daughter. The daughter carries a double-spout-and-bridge bottle in her left hand. The family is accompanied by four trotting dogs; another is held under the left arm of the father. The family may be going to Cahuachi (or another Nasca ceremonial center). Perhaps they are bringing the brilliantly colored birds to sacrifice, panpipes to play, and a fancy ceramic bottle to exchange or ritually consume (i.e. deliberately break). The tablet is in the collections of the Museo Nacional de Antropología, Arqueología e Historia in Lima, Peru. Size of the plaque to which the figures are affixed: 14.3 cm × 10.8 cm × 8 mm thick. Accession number 3/7778C-55308.

1

From Pots to People

Encountering Nasca

Nasca culture flourished in the Early Intermediate Period (ca. AD 1–700) in the narrow river valleys of the Río Grande de Nazca drainage and the Ica Valley in the midst of the arid south coast of Peru (figure 1.1). By the time of the Spanish conquest of the Inca empire in 1532, most traces of Nasca had long since disappeared, converting the once vibrant society into an archaeological mystery. Unlike the Moche culture of Peru's north coast with its huge adobe pyramids or the megalithic architecture of the Tiwanaku people of the Lake Titicaca region, early explorers and travelers found little of interest in the heartland of Nasca culture, although Luis de Monzón in 1586 (cited in Mejía Xesspe 1940: 569) did note the presence of ancient "roads" on the south coast (hundreds of years later these were rediscovered as geoglyphs).

Until the beginning of the twentieth century the only "excavations" conducted at Nasca sites were the illegal lootings of cemeteries by local *huaqueros* (grave robbers). Indeed, looting began at least as early as the nineteenth century since, by then, a small amount of Nasca pottery already had made its way into the collections of several European museums (Proulx 1968: 101). The most intense and damaging looting in the region, however, occurred in the twentieth century, following the onset of scientific archaeological excavations (Tello and Mejía Xesspe 1967: 156; Uhle 1914: 8).

Ancient Nasca culture was literally discovered by Max Uhle in Ica in 1901. Uhle, a German-born archaeologist, was working at

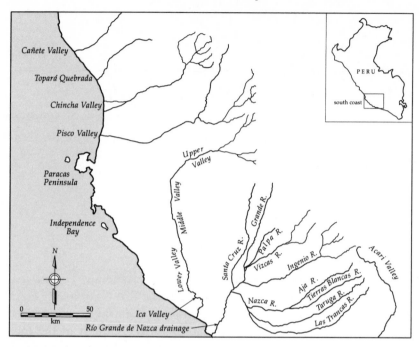

Figure 1.1   Map of the south coast of Peru.

the Museum für Völkerkunde in Berlin in the 1880s when he first saw several examples of exquisite polychrome pottery said to be from Peru. Fascinated by its beauty, Uhle began a decade-long quest to discover the source of these pots. His travels took him to various South American countries where he collected ethnographic and archaeological specimens for the Museum für Völkerkunde and later for the University of Pennsylvania Museum. In February 1901, Uhle realized his goal when he became the first person to scientifically excavate cemeteries containing Nasca polychrome pottery (for historical details, see Proulx 1970: 1–44). The location of these ancient graves was along the barren desert borders of the Hacienda Ocucaje in the lower Ica Valley on the south coast of Peru. Uhle sent the precisely provenienced grave goods to the University of California in Berkeley whose patron, Phoebe Apperson Hearst, had sponsored Uhle's project.

Uhle returned to the south coast of Peru in 1905 but did not excavate at this time. Rather, he purchased a large collection of pottery in the town of Nazca that had been looted from various sites in the Río Grande de Nazca drainage (Gayton and Kroeber 1927: 3–4; Uhle 1914). This collection also was sent to Berkeley and the pottery from Uhle's two south-coast trips form the core of the Hearst Museum's outstanding collection of Nasca pottery.

It is important to put Uhle's explorations and activities on the south coast in the larger perspective of what he was trying to accomplish in Peru (see Kroeber and Strong 1924: 97–8; Rowe 1962a: 398–9). Whereas, with few exceptions, nineteenth-century books on the ancient peoples of Peru attributed all ruins to the Incas, Uhle recognized that the people who made the exquisite Nasca pottery had lived long before the Incas. Since the time of Uhle's fieldwork, Nasca has occupied an important position in the development of Peruvian archaeology and our conceptualization of the kinds of societies that existed before the Incas. The history of the investigation of Nasca society reflects, in large part, the trajectory of the study of Peru's past and trends in archaeological research.

In the years following Uhle's discovery, knowledge of the attractive polychrome pottery became widespread as more specimens arrived in Europe. Thomas A. Joyce (1912) was the first scholar to use a color drawing – published as the frontispiece of his book on South American archaeology – to illustrate the beauty of the ware. Joyce (1912: 181) also seems to have been the first to use the term "Nasca Style" to describe this pottery. He elaborated further on the nature of the pottery in an article published in *The Burlington Magazine* (Joyce 1913a).

At the same time as Joyce, Henry Forbes (1913) published a short article on Nasca pottery. In it he illustrated in color eleven superb vessels from his own collection and described mummy bundles of this culture. It is unclear where Forbes obtained his information about Nasca mummy bundles but it could have come from an article by Uhle, also published in 1913. Written in German and while Uhle was living in Santiago, Chile, this article was Uhle's first major publication on his fieldwork in the Ica Valley, conducted twelve years earlier. In 1914 Uhle published an account in English of his discovery of the Nasca style and his chronology for the Ica Valley. In the same monograph, Edward K. Putnam (1914) described and illustrated a collection of ninety-four Nasca vessels at the Davenport Academy of Sciences. The pots had been purchased in Peru in 1911 by the Honorable C. A. Ficke, then president of that institution.

Ales Hrdlicka, a physical anthropologist, made two trips to Peru around this time, the first a brief survey in 1910 (see Hrdlicka 1911) and the second a three-month tour in 1913 which included visits to sites in the Acarí and Nazca valleys (see Hrdlicka 1914). Hrdlicka's objectives were "to determine, as far as possible, the anthropological relation of the mountain people with those of the coast; to make further studies regarding the distribution of the coast type; to determine the type of the important Nasca group of people; and to extend the writer's researches on Indian and especially pre-Columbian pathology" (Hrdlicka 1914: 2). Hrdlicka's research provided valuable insights into the form and variety of Nasca graves, the amount of looting in the area, and the range of grave goods being extracted by *huaqueros*. Hrdlicka was among the first to describe such important Acarí Valley sites as Chaviña and Tambo Viejo. He also contributed valuable information on Nasca practices of skull deformation and trephination (see discussion in chapter 4).

In 1915, Peruvian archaeologist Julio C. Tello conducted fieldwork in the Río Grande de Nazca region "with the purpose of studying the different classes of cemeteries there" (Tello 1917: 283). Tello recorded information on the shape, building material, and construction of the tombs as well as the orientation of the body and common grave goods. The frequent presence of trophy heads in the cemeteries interested Tello so much that they became the subject of his 1918 doctoral dissertation (see chapter 9). William C. Farabee, curator of the American collections at the University Museum in Philadelphia, spent one month in 1922 excavating sites in the Nazca Valley (see Mason 1926). Like Tello and other archaeologists at this time, Farabee's interest centered on cemetery excavation for the purpose of recovering fine grave goods, especially pottery.

Meanwhile, Alfred Louis Kroeber and his students at the University of California at Berkeley were analyzing Uhle's pottery collections from the many coastal valleys in which Uhle had worked, including Nazca and Ica. In the study of Uhle's materials from the Ica Valley excavations, Nasca did not figure exclusively but was one of several major pre-Columbian styles represented (Kroeber and Strong 1924). Furthermore, Nasca was not called Nasca but, rather, "Proto-Nazca as it has become customary to designate a very striking ware" (Kroeber and Strong 1924: 96; see Uhle 1913, 1914). The concept of proto-cultures had been coined by Uhle in his study of several of the ancient coastal cultures and, despite its connotation, referred to fully developed art complexes and societies (for example, Proto-Chimú: see Uhle 1998: 206). A later study, undertaken by Kroeber with Anna Gayton, dealt specifically with Uhle's Nasca pottery from Nazca and chronologically ordered the style into four sequential phases (see chapter 2). Diagnostic Nasca forms of pottery also were identified (see Gayton and Kroeber 1927).

Kroeber's experience with the Uhle collections convinced him of the importance of conducting new fieldwork because he was dissatisfied with the ceramic seriation he had worked out with Gayton. By obtaining a new sample of Nasca pottery from carefully controlled grave excavations Kroeber hoped to be able to substantiate or modify the Gayton–Kroeber sequence that had relied on pottery without grave and other definite local provenience (Gayton and Kroeber 1927: 4; see also Kroeber 1956: 330). In 1926 Kroeber conducted fieldwork in Nazca which he regarded as one of the most "strategic points of attack . . . because the several cultures already known from the Nazca region presented a problem of several cultures whose sequence had not been definitely determined" (Kroeber 1937: 127). For more than three months Kroeber excavated tombs, keeping a meticulous inventory of the grave associations of each burial and recording data on the burials themselves (see Kroeber and Collier 1998). In this fieldwork Kroeber was specifically more interested in "grave contents and interrelations of these as intact units than on settlements and buildings" for he thought that "Nazca ruins and structures are modest in comparison with the fine ceramics and textiles contained in Nazca cemeteries" (Kroeber and Collier 1998: 25). The importance of Kroeber's Nasca and Nazca work cannot be overemphasized. Kroeber (1928: 8–9) established a multi-phase chrono-stylistic sequence that ran from "Nazca A" to Inca. At the time, this was the "longest continuous [series] yet determined in Peru, possibly the oldest in absolute time, almost certainly as old as any yet resolved"

(Kroeber 1928: 9). Kroeber clearly articulated the goal of archaeological research at the time as chronology building on the basis of pottery collected through cemetery excavations; he eschewed settlement pattern archaeology. This perspective in Peruvian archaeology would not change till the Virú Valley project was conducted two decades later.

Tello returned to the Nazca region in 1926 and again in 1927. He specifically sought to excavate tombs whose contents would form collections for the Museo de Arqueología Peruana, some of which would be exhibited in Peru's pavilion at the Ibero-American Exposition in Sevilla in 1929. The nine months of fieldwork in 1927 resulted in the excavation of 537 tombs of which eighty pertained to "*Nasca clásico*" (early Nasca) and 176 to "*Chanka o Pre-Nasca*" (late Nasca) (Tello and Mejía Xesspe 1967: 147).

In 1932 the German archaeologist Heinrich Ubbelohde-Doering (1958; Neudecker 1979) traveled to the extremely arid and narrow Santa Cruz Valley in the northern Río Grande de Nazca drainage. His goal was to determine the kinds of graves in which Nasca pottery was found, the types of pottery that were found together and the kinds of weavings that were associated with the pots. He excavated about fifty graves, eight of which pertain to Nasca (see Neudecker 1979). He also excavated two Nasca graves at Cahuachi in the Nazca Valley (Ubbelohde-Doering 1958).

In so far as we know, the only fieldwork conducted in the following twenty years was a small excavation at Chaviña in Acarí in 1943 (see Lothrop and Mahler 1957). The situation changed dramatically in 1952, however, when William Duncan Strong (1957) undertook a major survey and excavation project in Ica and Nazca. It is important to remember that Strong had analyzed Uhle's pottery collections from Ica under the guidance of Kroeber when he was a college senior at Berkeley (see Kroeber and Strong 1924). Thus, Nasca was not unfamiliar to him.

Strong also had been a key participant in an important archaeological and interdisciplinary project in the Virú Valley on the north coast in 1946. In conceiving his south-coast project, Strong was influenced by the Virú Valley project's emphasis on settlement pattern archaeology. Strong (1957: 3) clearly described the primary purpose of his 1952 investigations as the determination of the temporal relationship between the Paracas and Nasca cultures and, concomitantly, the study of settlement patterns so as to "select the most promising sites for sondage." Strong (1957: 2) proposed to work by means of "detailed survey and stratigraphic techniques along the lines already inaugurated in Central and North Coastal Peru."

Strong chose to concentrate his efforts at Cahuachi because he believed he would get a deeply stratified sequence there. Thus, prior to excavation, Strong already was interpreting some of Cahuachi's architecture as "house mounds" in association with temples and cemeteries (see Strong 1957: table 1), implying that these mounds were formed by the sequential accumulation of domestic refuse and abandoned structures that then became stratified *in situ* over time. Strong's view was repeated by various scholars (for example, Matos 1980: 488; Rowe 1960: 41) and only came to be criticized when Silverman's (1993a *inter alia*) excavations at the site revealed that much of what Strong had interpreted as stratified habitation refuse was, in fact, construction fill for non-domestic mound architecture. What remains indisputable from Strong's (1957: 32) project, however, is his conclusion that "Cahuachi was the greatest, and probably the main capital site of the Nazca civilization in the time of its own peculiar highest florescence" which was the early Nasca period.

Strong (1957: 36–41) also excavated at Huaca del Loro in Las Trancas, the site which gave its name to the Huaca del Loro (Nasca 8) phase and culture (see Paulsen 1983; Silverman 1988b). In addition, Strong put in a stratigraphic trench at Estaquería, a few kilometers downstream from Cahuachi, in which he recovered sherds "which were mainly of Late Nazca (B) type but also included those of the Huaca del Loro culture of the succeeding epoch of Fusion. Earlier or later types were absent" (Strong 1957: 34). Strong (1957: 34) concluded that Estaquería "is really an extension of the Cahuachi site," a conclusion Silverman (1993a: ch. 5) has disputed.

In 1954–5 John H. Rowe (1956) directed a survey and excavation project that covered the vast southern portion of Peru. The overall purpose of this project was to establish relative chronological relationships among regions. The completion of a detailed chronology of the Nasca pottery style was assigned to Lawrence Dawson who had been working on a seriation since 1952 using Uhle's collections at Berkeley (Rowe 1956: 135, 146, 1960). In Peru,

Dawson continued to gather more data with which to further refine the sequence. At the same time, Dorothy Menzel and Francis Riddell conducted fieldwork in the Acarí Valley (Menzel and Riddell 1986; see also Rowe 1956, 1963). They identified important Nasca 3 and Inca occupations at Tambo Viejo, the largest and most complex site in the Acarí Valley. Rowe (1963: 11–12) identified Tambo Viejo, Huarato, Chocavento, and Amato as Nasca 3 habitation sites of an intrusive and fortified nature (see counterargument in Carmichael 1992; Valdez 1998). Rowe argued that early Nasca society had been organized as a small, militaristic empire led from a capital city at Cahuachi. According to him, the empire conquered Acarí before falling at the end of Nasca 3.

Rowe, Menzel, and Dawson returned to Peru a few years later under the aegis of the US government's Fulbright Exchange Program to carry out extensive and intensive investigations in Ica (see Menzel 1971; Rowe 1963; Wallace 1962). Their fieldwork provided important new information on the Nasca occupation of the valley, particularly during epoch 7 of the Early Intermediate Period (see Menzel 1971: 86–92). Concurrently, Wallace (1958, 1971, 1986; see also Menzel 1971) surveyed and conducted small-scale excavations in Pisco, Chincha, and Cañete, gathering important information on the Nasca-contemporary styles called Carmen and Estrella (see discussion in chapters 4 and 10; Silverman 1991: fig. 9.2). In 1975 Hans Disselhoff collected fragmentary cross-knit looped and embroidered textiles at Cahuachi. Unfortunately, the context of the finds and the nature of his work are unpublished other than mention in Eisleb's (1975: figs 127–9, 138, 139, 143, 145, 148a–b) catalog of ancient Peruvian art in the Museum für Völkekunde in Berlin.

Although the 1950s were characterized by excavation, the goal of Nasca research continued to be ceramic chronology. This focus continued in the 1960s, now in museum basements using extant collections. This endeavor was not meant to be an end in itself but rather a tool to be taken to the field so that contemporaneity and change in the archaeological record could be recognized, thereby opening up the possibility for diachronic interpretation of cultural process.

At Berkeley, Dawson finalized a nine-phase Nasca ceramic sequence using the method of similiary seriation by continuity of features and variation in themes (see Rowe 1959, 1960, 1961). At the same time, Kroeber (1956) revised the 1927 Gayton–Kroeber scheme, in reaction to seriations being worked out by Junius Bird at the American Museum of Natural History (unpublished) and Dawson at Berkeley. One of Rowe's students, Richard P. Roark (1965), examined the shift from the "monumental" style of Nasca ceramic iconography to the "proliferous" style. Roark identified a major iconographic change from religious themes to militaristic ones. Another Rowe student, Donald Proulx (1968), refined the seriation of phase 3 of the Nasca sequence and examined local and regional variation in Nasca 3 and 4 pottery from Ica and Nazca. Steven Wegner (1976), who also was a student of Rowe's, seriated Nasca 6 into three subphases. Dorothy Menzel (1977), Rowe's Berkeley collaborator, seriated Nasca 7 into three subphases and subdivided Nasca 8 into two subphases. Menzel (1964) dealt with Nasca 9 in her study of Middle Horizon pottery. Another of Rowe's students, Elizabeth Wolfe (1981), traced the evolution of the Spotted Cat and Horrible Bird on Nasca pottery.

Nasca pottery also was studied outside Berkeley. Silverman (1977) examined Strong's Nasca 2 material at Columbia University. She suggested a tripartite subdivision of this phase and made interpretive comments on the nature of the society that produced this ware. In a fascinating study undertaken for her MA degree at the University of Texas at Austin, Blagg (1975) recognized concurrent stylistic variation within the Nasca 5 phase (see chapter 2). In addition to these largely chronological studies, the investigation of Nasca iconography resumed (see chapter 6).

As museum research proceeded in the United States, Carlos Williams León and Miguel Pazos Rivera (1974) surveyed the Ica Valley from San José de los Molinos in the upper valley to the lower valley oases. This fieldwork, undertaken for Peru's Instituto Nacional de Cultura, resulted in an inventory of more than two hundred sites, including Nasca ones. Their report is a valuable, but unpublished, resource.

Archaeologists returned to the south coast in the 1980s because of a pressing need for primary (field-generated) data on Nasca social, political, and economic organization and cultural change. This focus represented a major shift in research orientation. It was born of the realization that the archaeological Nasca culture was an intellectual construct almost devoid of societal content (see Silverman 1993a: xi). The title of this chapter reflects the significance and importance of this change in Nasca research direction.

Working largely within a processualist paradigm due to necessity, scholars studied intra-site and inter-site settlement patterns and reconstructed ancient Nasca society on this basis. Sarah Massey (1986) concentrated on the Paracas and early Nasca occupations of the upper Ica Valley. Anita Cook (1999) and Lisa DeLeonardis (1991) investigated the occupation of the lower Ica Valley, recovering information on all periods of pre-Hispanic occupation but emphasizing, thus far, the Paracas data. In the Río Grande de Nazca drainage, Helaine Silverman (1993a) excavated at Cahuachi so as to assess its alleged urban character and role in Nasca society; she then surveyed the Ingenio Valley in an attempt to contextualize Cahuachi and recover more information on Nasca settlement and society (Silverman 1993b *inter alia*). More recently, Silverman (1997) excavated in the lower Pisco Valley in order to understand the Nasca-related Carmen occupation of that valley and to contextualize the Paracas Peninsula cemeteries. Since the early 1980s Giuseppe Orefici has excavated intensively and continuously at Cahuachi (Orefici 1987, 1988, 1992, 1993, 1996; see also Bueno Mendoza and Orefici 1984; Isla 1990) as well as conducting smaller and briefer excavations at other sites (see Isla et al. 1984). Johny Isla (1992) excavated habitation contexts at Usaca as part of Orefici's project. David Browne surveyed the Palpa, Vizcas and upper Grande valleys (Browne 1992; Browne and Baraybar 1988). Palpa is being restudied by Markus Reindel and Johny Isla (1999) in a project that includes major excavations. Katharina Schreiber (1998) surveyed the southern tributaries of the Río Grande de Nazca drainage including the Nazca Valley proper. She also has done a thorough study of Nazca's filtration gallery irrigation system (Schreiber and Lancho Rojas 1995). David Johnson (1999) is investigating Nazca's underground water supply and geoglyphs. Kevin Vaughn (1999) has just completed doctoral fieldwork at an early Nasca habitation site in Tierras Blancas; he is analyzing the data from the perspective of household archaeology, an innovation in south-coast archaeology overall because of the limited number of excavations in domestic contexts. Donald Proulx (1999c) surveyed the lower Nazca and Grande valleys. Patrick Carmichael (1991) reconnoitered the littoral zone between Acarí and the Bahía de la Independencia to ascertain if the frequent maritime iconography on early Nasca pottery was correlated with Nasca shoreline settlement. The California Institute of Peruvian Studies, directed by Francis Riddell, has been running a multi-year project in Acarí and Yauca, part of whose activities are generating valuable knowledge about Nasca on the far south coast (see, for example, Carmichael 1992; Kowta 1987; Menzel and Riddell 1986; Riddell 1985, 1986, 1989; Riddell and Valdez 1988; Valdez 1989, 1998).

Large numbers of Nasca habitation sites have been identified as a result of these surveys, whereas decades ago archaeologists complained about the lack of non-cemetery sites pertaining to Nasca culture. The recent projects also have identified a fair number of ceremonial sites in addition to Cahuachi, some quite impressive though none with Cahuachi's concentration of volumetric monumental architecture. Clearly, the chronology and collection-oriented goals of Nasca archaeology in the early twentieth century determined where archaeologists excavated and how they perceived the terrain around them.

Nasca and its Contemporaries

Nasca was one of many regional societies of the Early Intermediate Period. Among its contemporaries were Cajamarca and Recuay in the north highlands, Moche on the north coast, Lima on the central coast, and Pucara in the south highlands. In the foundational literature of the field, these societies were described as "Mastercraftsman Cultures" (see, for example, Bennett 1948: 6; Bennett and Bird 1964: 113–35), so-called because of their exquisite art styles. While the label "Mastercraftsman" is still appropriate – for no one can dispute the incredible aesthetic and technological quality of the pottery and textiles of many of these societies – it is also important to think of them in terms of "corporate styles." This is a term coined by Moseley (1992: 73) to refer to fine arts and crafts products "geared to serve corporate ends . . . aesthetic canons, design motifs, and iconography were dictated by the political and religious organizations supporting the artisans, commissioning their work, and controlling its distribution . . . characteristic of particular polities, religions, and organizations ... corporate symbolism." Moseley's appreciation of the political, social and economic aspects of craft production resituates the study of the Early Intermediate Period (EIP) societies as dynamic sociopolitical formations.

It is furthermore interesting that these EIP societies, which have been analytically sandwiched between others characterized by wide-spread shared cultural features (i.e. Chavín of the Early Horizon and Wari of the Middle Horizon), are not as regional or inward-looking as originally believed (see, for example, Bennett 1948: 6; Steward 1948: 104). Yes, it is certainly true that each EIP society is characterized by a pronounced territorialization: cemeteries, irrigation systems, well-developed settlement patterns, local art style. But already it is clear that Moche (see, for example, Bawden 1996; Castillo and Donnan 1994; Makowski 1994) and Nasca, at least, also manifest significant internal variation and outward pro-jection. Indeed, whereas archaeologists have tended to study Nasca from a regionally restricted perspective – the Ica Valley and the Río Grande de Nazca drainage – we argue that Nasca must be contextualized within the larger Central Andean area since various events and processes on the coast and throughout the highlands clearly affected Nasca society and Nasca affected them along several parameters over the many centuries of Nasca's existence. Furthermore, it has become apparent that within the Río Grande de Nazca drainage Nasca must be understood on a valley-by-valley and intra-valley basis so as to reconstruct each society comprising the archaeological Nasca culture. Clearly, all were Nasca in physical and material appearance (there were no non-Nasca people living within the Río Grande de Nazca drainage during the Early Inter-mediate Period). But Nasca was not a single, monolithically evolving culture.

The Relationship of People to Art Styles

So far we have said little about the people who produced the exemplary ceramics called "Nasca" beyond indicating the intellec-tual shift in research focus from chronology building to settlement pattern archaeology for the purpose of societal reconstruction. In the Central Andes, as in many other areas of the world, pottery styles have served as the primary means of identifying people or ethnic groups in the archaeological record as well as being the basis for the development of a relative chronology. The imputation of identity between pottery style and ancient ethnic group is based on a number of assumptions, some of which must be used with caution.

Pottery contains technological and symbolic elements, learned by enculturation and through conviction. Each society develops its own patterns of behavior, which are reflected in artifacts, including ceramics, and other aspects of material culture such as housing. Refining this normative view of culture is the knowledge that, at the same time, material culture can be deployed consciously, expressively, and "emblemically" by societies, groups within societies, and smaller divisions thereof down to the level of the family and individual. Furthermore, ideas can be borrowed from other ethnic groups. People can migrate to new locations. Ethnic identity is multi-dimensional; it is shifting and subjective; it is situationally subject to negotiation (for example, culture-differentiating barriers between individuals and between groups of varying inclusiveness can be raised and lowered selectively). All of this complicates the interpretation of style as a primary basis for the identification of group cohesiveness.

The reconstruction of a society that lacks any form of writing is particularly difficult. In the following chapters we attempt to "flesh out" a dynamic picture of Nasca ethnic identity and Nasca society based on preserved material culture and its patterns of distribution and also through the judicious use of ethnographic analogy, ethnohistory, and other techniques. Our conclusions will surely be modified as new field data become available in the future.

2

Emergence and Evolution of the Nasca Ceramic Tradition

This chapter has two related thrusts. In the first part we consider the Paracas origins of the Nasca pottery style. We also are concerned with Paracas culture as an antecedent for the development of Nasca culture, and Paracas society as this may evolve into Nasca. We emphasize that there are, in fact, several Paracas cultures, each located in a distinct part of the south coast, but interacting, and each with its own historical trajectory. The multiple manifestations of Nasca ultimately originate in this cultural and sociopolitical diversity.

In the second part of the chapter we present the development of the Nasca pottery style as it evolved from Paracas. We also explain how the changes perceived in it were translated into a relative chronological sequence. This relative chronology and an absolute chronological framework, suggested herein, are necessary for the rest of our treatment of Nasca society since, without a fine chronology, change in the archaeological record cannot be seen. But the Nasca chronologies – relative and absolute – are not without their problems.

The Paracas Antecedents of Nasca

Paracas is the name given to a south-coast culture whose most spectacular manifestations, arguably, are those excavated by Julio C. Tello in the late 1920s at a series of sites located at the neck of the Paracas Peninsula (see Tello 1959; Tello and Mejía Xesspe

1979). The sites consist of two spatially and chronologically discrete habitation areas (the Cerro Colorado habitation zone and the
Arenas Blancas habitation zone) and four cemeteries, each one more
spectacular than the next (Cavernas, Cabezas Largas, the funerary
nuclei of Arenas Blancas, and the great Wari Kayan/Paracas
Necropolis) (see discussion in Silverman 1991).

The material culture associated with the cemetery sites led Tello
to distinguish two archaeological Paracas cultures: Cavernas, earlier,
and Necropolis, later. The difference between the two cultures is
more than merely chronological, however. It appears that Cavernas
and Necropolis (the latter now called "Topará" with several phases
recognized in the late Early Horizon and early Early Intermediate
Period) material culture represents two distinct ancient societies
(see Lanning 1960; Peters 1997; Silverman 1991; Wallace 1986).
Cavernas is characterized by pottery painted with resinous polychrome organic pigments applied after firing (see, for example,
Donnan 1992: figs 54–8; Tello 1959). Necropolis/Topará is
characterized by very well-made, extremely thin monochrome
pottery (see, for example, Donnan 1992: fig. 64; Tello 1959) and
brilliant colored textiles bearing fantastically elaborate embroidered images (see Tello 1959: plates xiii–xvii, xxviii–lvii, lix–lxvi;
Paul 1990 *inter alia*). Cavernas people favored burial in deep,
bottle-shaped tombs. Necropolis/Topará people were buried amid
habitation remains, including of earlier people. Archaeologists are
still trying to understand the relationship between the Cavernas
and Necropolis people at Paracas as well as in the Pisco and Ica
valleys for at some sites the two societies appear to have co-existed
(Cook 1999; Peters 1987–8) despite Tello's clear evidence of
superposition at Cerro Colorado.

The name of the archaeological culture, Paracas, refers to it place
of discovery on the Paracas Peninsula. To differentiate the Paracas
remains of Ica from those of the Peninsula, the Ica Valley materials
are called by the style name "Ocucaje" (see Menzel et al. 1964).
Ocucaje pottery of Ica has been seriated into ten chrono-stylistic
phases, 1–10 (see Menzel et al. 1964). Ocucaje 8, 9, and 10 are
very well associated with habitation and other remains in the Ica
Valley (DeLeonardis 1991, 1997; Massey 1986). Phases 1 and 2
appear to lack reality (see discussion in Burger 1988; Donnan 1992:
fig. 59; García Soto and Pinilla Blenke 1995). Phase 3 corresponds

to the Chavin/Chavinoid phase represented at Karwa (see Burger 1988). Evidence for phases 4, 5, 6, and 7 is variable but extant (see Cook 1999; DeLeonardis 1991, 1997; Wallace 1962). The Paracas Cavernas remains from the Peninsula can be cross-dated to the later phases of the Ica Valley sequence. It is the Ica Valley that has the full Paracas stylistic, chronological, and settlement sequence, beginning several hundred years before the Cerro Colorado occupation.

It is commonly stated that the Nasca style developed smoothly out of Paracas by which is meant the Ocucaje style of the Ica Valley (see Menzel et al. 1964: 251–6). The evolution is phrased in terms of the technological shift in decoration from post-fire resin painting in Paracas pottery to pre-fire slip painting in Nasca (Menzel et al. 1964: 251). Nasca 1 continues to use incised lines to separate areas of color as is diagnostic of Paracas (see, for example, Donnan 1992: figs 71–5). There also are iconographic and formal continuities that can be traced in pottery such as the continued popularity of the double-spout-and-bridge bottle, musical instruments (pan-pipes, drums, trumpets), fish, killer whales, the human trophy head, fox, falcon and feline (see Menzel et al. 1964; Sawyer 1964).

The ceramic continuity between Paracas and Nasca in Ica is also a cultural one. There was no population break: Nasca people were the direct descendants of peoples already living in the valley. Indeed, paleobiological studies have produced independent confirmation of the continuity between the Paracas and Nasca peoples. "When the Nasca phase developed from the Paracas culture over a thousand year period, this cultural development did not result in a change in blood groups. The Huari and the Inca, however, were invaders who introduced genetic changes" (Allison 1979: 79).[1]

For as much continuity as there was between Paracas and Nasca, there were significant changes as well. The disappearance of the fancy grater bowl in Ica, where it was quite common (see Menzel et al. 1964), and in the Río Grande de Nazca drainage where it was less common (Silverman 1991), is a major discontinuity between Paracas and Nasca. Also, painted cloth mummy masks and ceramic masks (see Dawson 1979) disappeared in Ica after Ocucaje 10 and, to the best of our knowledge, never existed in the Río Grande de Nazca drainage.

In contrast to Ica, the Paracas antecedents to Nasca in the Río Grande de Nazca drainage are not well known in terms of settlement and pottery. Exciting new fieldwork by Markus Reindel and Johny Isla (1999) is updating Mejía Xesspe's (1976) references to Paracas pottery in Palpa, but their data are preliminary at the time of writing. The Early Horizon data of Katharina Schreiber are unpublished.

Let us first consider Cahuachi in the Nazca Valley. William Duncan Strong did not find a diachronically discrete Late Paracas occupation at Cahuachi (see Silverman 1993a: ch. 4). His few Late Paracas sherds (equivalent to Ocucaje 10 of the Ica Valley and the local late Early Horizon style called Tajo: see Silverman 1994a) occurred with Nasca 1 pottery. Orefici (1996: 174) reports Ocucaje 9 and 10 sherds in construction fills containing Nasca 1, 2, and 3 potsherds as well as a stratigraphic level with "a notable quantity of Paracas ceramic materials decorated with post-fire applied paint" along with other pottery types diagnostic of Nasca 1 (Orefici 1996: 179). However, Orefici (1996: 179) apparently has discovered a pure Ocucaje 10 tomb at Cahuachi. Silverman (1993a) did not find a discrete Late Paracas occupation at Cahuachi, though she reports a surface find of an Ocucaje 8 fancy grater bowl fragment (Silverman 1991: fig. 9.11).

For the Río Grande de Nazca drainage, Orefici (1996: 178) indicates the presence of Paracas material corresponding to Ocucaje 9–10 but he is not specific as to its frequency, nature, and provenience. Silverman (1994a) recovered some Ocucaje 8, 9, and 10 sherds during the Ingenio survey and several that may be either Ocucaje 3 or Ocucaje 8; note the bona fide Ocucaje 3 bowl fragment from the Nazca Valley published by Silverman (1991: fig. 9.10). Mejia Xesspe (1976) found more diagnostic Paracas pottery in Palpa than did Silverman in Ingenio. More recently, Reindel and Isla (1999) report the discovery of Middle Ocucaje phase Paracas pottery in Palpa at 3.5 m below the surface. The depth of this find has profound implications for the interpretation of the Early Horizon occupation of the Palpa Valley and, conceivably, the drainage. Reindel and Isla's (1999) data suggest that Paracas sites may be deeply buried and poorly represented on the surface. They conclude that a sparse Middle Paracas population took advantage of the Palpa Valley floor at this time, in addition to some sites located on valley hillsides. Silverman (1994a), too, has reported Paracas pottery on hillside sites in the Ingenio Valley. Both Silverman (1994a: Site 13) and Reindel and Isla (1999: figs 167, 168) report defensively located and walled hilltop settlements at this time. This suggests that the true density of Late Paracas sites in the Río Grande de Nazca drainage has not been perceived since defensive, walled sites should imply conditions of competition.

Essentially, Reindel and Isla and Silverman are reporting the same data but interpreting them differently. Reindel and Isla argue that there is significant evidence of Paracas occupation in Palpa (and see Mejía Xesspe 1976: 36, fig. 6). They see Paracas as the local style and culture of the Río Grande de Nazca drainage prior to Nasca. They are arguing that the pre-Nasca Río Grande de Nazca drainage people were culturally/ethnically Paracas.

In contrast, Silverman (1994a) interprets Paracas pottery as selectively introduced into the existing local (Tajo) context by means of a migration of Paracas people from the Ica Valley (see discussion in chapter 5). She downplays the importance of Paracas pottery at the few Ingenio Valley habitation sites with this material and notes the persistent co-occurrence of Ocucaje 10 with Nasca 1 (and see discussion of Cahuachi, above). Silverman (1994a: 366) concludes that Tajo did not provide sufficient antecedents for the stylistic (iconography and form) development of the Nasca 1 pottery style and the simultaneous rapid florescence of settlement.

While it is possible that the inhabitants of the different tributaries of the Río Grande de Nazca drainage participated differentially in the Paracas world with Palpa being more closely linked to Ica than Ingenio (for reasons to be determined), the data from Reindel and Isla's new work suggest that Silverman underperceived the nature and importance of Paracas in Palpa. If future excavations in the drainage recover the full complement of Paracas material culture (including the range of pottery shapes and ceramic iconography, the range of textile technology and associated iconography, and a continuous sequence from Ocucaje 3 through Ocucaje 10) and associated behavior (for example, mortuary patterns, civic-ceremonial sites) as manifested in the Ica Valley, scholars will have proof of a probably ethnically Paracas people in the Río Grande de Nazca drainage and the suggestion of an *in situ* development of Nasca 1 society from Paracas antecedents will be strengthened. Clearly, much more fieldwork is needed on the pre-Nasca occupation of the Río Grande de Nazca drainage and its significance for the evolution of Nasca society.

Historical Review of Nasca Relative Chronologies

Soon after the discovery of the Nasca style two stylistic variants were recognized: a more naturalistic, representational mode (figure 2.1) and an abstract one (figure 2.2) (Tello 1917; Uhle 1914: 9). Uhle (1914: 9) described the differences between the two modalities in these terms:

> It is easy to distinguish certain varieties among specimens of pottery of the same culture. Some will show a greater variety of colors, others are plainer; some show severe outlines in their figure designs, while others are marked by a free and flowing treatment, which often degenerated into a mass of meaningless staff or arrow-like points and scrolls around the original nucleus of the design. It appears that those designs which are distinguishable by the more severe treatment of the figure ornament in unison with the richest harmony of its coloring, must be considered as representing the earlier type.

Figure 2.1 Naturalistic, representational, "monumental" style of Nasca pottery (*photo*: Helaine Silverman).

Figure 2.2 Abstract, conventionalized, "proliferous" style of Nasca pottery (*photo*: Helaine Silverman).

Clearly, Uhle thought that representational or referential iconography preceded conventionalized designs. This decision was based on Uhle's belief in the existence of a law of artistic development from realism to abstraction (see Rowe 1960: 29). Tello (1917, 1940), on the other hand, erroneously argued that conventionalized Nasca pottery (his "pre-Nasca") preceded the referential corpus (see also Rosselló Truel 1960). This is interesting because Tello (1928) correctly argued that Paracas culture gave rise to Nasca. Yacovleff (1932b) also offered a stylistic developmental ordering of Nasca art and concluded, like Uhle before him, that Nasca art evolved from representational motifs to abstract ones.

In an attempt to deal in a more systematic way with the internal chronology of the Nasca style, Gayton and Kroeber (1927) devised a quantitative method of ordering which they considered suitable for collections of unassociated pottery such as that purchased by Uhle in Nazca and curated at Berkeley. By correlating frequencies of specific designs and color combinations with shape categories

(Gayton and Kroeber 1927: fig. 2; Kroeber and Collier 1998: fig. 90), two major substyles (designated A and B) were identified, separated by an intermediate phase (X). They subsequently defined a tentative fourth phase, Y, representing "a late or decaying form of styles A-X-B, in which occasional A-X-B traits persisted, more were degenerate, still others were altered so as to be virtually new" (Gayton and Kroeber 1927: 30). Kroeber (1928: 8) emphasized that the Gayton–Kroeber position was the exact opposite of Tello's. Kroeber referred to the "apparent impasse" that both had reached because "lack of objective data forced subjective interpretations which were contrary according to observer. The design sequence was actually read forward by one student, backward by another" (Kroeber 1928: 8). But Kroeber (1928: 8) knew that Wari (then called Tiahuanaco) had to be more recent than Nasca. He argued that one group of Nazca pottery, Y, sometimes occurred in association with "Highland designs of Tiahuanaco character." This Y group, therefore, had to be terminal Nasca. Gayton and Kroeber then reasoned that since Y is more similar to B than to A, B had to be closer to Y and therefore the correct direction of the Nasca sequence would have to be from representational to abstract or A to B. This is what Tello had inverted as "Pre-Nazca" to "Nazca." It was a brilliant deduction and anticipated the guidelines of Rowe's (1959, 1960, 1961) method of similiary seriation which orders objects according to closest resemblances working away from known end points (see below). From the beginning, then, we see that researchers recognized the existence of two modes of portrayal in Nasca art and tried to order them chronologically. In the absence of stratigraphy, however, all positions in the debate were speculation. This is the situation that prompted William Duncan Strong's fieldwork at Cahuachi and that is evidenced by the title of his 1957 monograph.

In a series of articles written in the late 1950s and early 1960s John Rowe described a non-typological and non-quantitative method of ceramic analysis called "seriation by continuity of features and variation in themes" or "similiary seriation" (see Rowe 1959, 1960, 1961; see discussion in Silverman 1993a: 35–7). Similiary seriation is based on the assumption that, "within a given cultural tradition, change in culture in general and change in style in particular are both usually gradual processes" (Rowe 1961: 326).

Table 2.1 Dawson's sequence compared to other relative chronologies proposed for the Nasca style

Stylistic strains	Dawson's phases	Sawyer's phases	Kroeber (1956) phases	Gayton and Kroeber (1927) phases
Disjunctive	9	Nasca–Wari	Coast Tiahuanaco	Y–3
				Y–2
	8		Y	Y–1
Proliferous	7	Late Nasca	B	B
	6			
Transitional	5	Middle Nasca	AB	X
Monumental	4	Early Nasca	A	A
	3			
	2			
Proto-Nasca	1	Proto-Nasca		

The general principles underlying this form of seriation go back to the nineteenth century and were first used by John Evans in 1849 to arrange a series of British coins chronologically (Rowe 1961: 326). General Alfred Lane-Fox Pitt-Rivers, who was one of Britain's leading excavators and an innovator in typological analysis, also wrote an early article, in 1875, on the technique (see Rowe 1961: 326).

The similiary technique was brilliantly developed and applied to Nasca pottery by Lawrence Dawson, then a young student and ceramicist at the University of California at Berkeley. Dawson's chronological seriation was based on ordering by continuity of features and themes. Dawson took these general principles and modified them to address the specific nature of Nasca pottery including the complex mythical designs. Each trait, whether a portion of a larger design such as a particular form of mouth mask on a mythical creature, or a specific cup bowl shape, was seen as representing part of a continuum through time. Each individual vessel contains specific traits of drawing and shape representing an association of contemporaneity at a particular point in time. The greater the number of traits on a single vessel, the more precise the chronological order can be. Dawson worked away from the pottery styles of two known ends, Paracas of the Early Horizon and Wari of the Middle Horizon and created nine chronological-stylistic phases, Nasca 1–9 (table 2.1; see layout of complete seriation in Silverman 1993a: figs 3.2–3.8; see also Blagg 1975; Pezzia 1969: 129–40; Proulx 1968, 1983; Roark 1965; Rowe 1960). Various phases of the Nasca sequence were subsequently further refined into subphases, as indicated in chapter 1.

Nasca 1 ("Proto-Nazca") and Nasca 2 ("Cahuachi Polychrome") were recognized by Strong (1957) at Cahuachi. Rowe's (1960: 29) term, "monumental," described the variety or modality of Nasca art that exhibits relatively realistic designs (Uhle's representational). The term specifically referred to Nasca 3 and 4 pottery (Rowe 1960: 41; figure 2.3 top), roughly equivalent to Gayton and Kroeber's Nazca A. Nasca 5 is transitional between monumental and proliferous (see Blagg 1975; Roark 1965; figure 2.3 middle), but should not be confused with Gayton and Kroeber's Nazca X which has no self-defining property but, rather, mixed vessels of various phases. Rowe used the term "proliferous" for the more conventionalized motifs having volutes, rays, and points (also recognized by Uhle; figure 2.3 bottom). Proliferation began on certain "Bizarre Innovation" pottery of Nasca 5 (Blagg 1975; Roark 1965: 26; see below under "Nasca 5") and is characteristic of Nasca phases 6 and 7 (Rowe 1960: 41); it corresponds roughly to Gayton and Kroeber's Nazca B. Nasca 7, a crucial phase for understanding the events of the Middle Horizon, remains very poorly known because it is unpublished. Nasca 8 was first defined by Strong (1957) who called it Huaca del Loro after the type site (see also Silverman 1988b); Dawson has called Nasca 8 "Disjunctive" (Proulx 1968: 1); it more or less corresponds to Gayton and Kroeber's Nazca Y.

It is important to indicate that the Berkeley seriation method operates at the level of the *style*, but Blagg (1975: 6) cogently argues that the Nasca style is, in fact, composed of seven styles. Blagg accepts the validity of the two major styles, *monumental* (essentially Nasca 3 and 4) and *proliferous* (essentially Nasca 6 and 7). In addition she recognizes: "proto-Nasca" (lumping Nasca 1 and 2; we believe that Nasca 1 should be kept separate), "conservative monumental" (Nasca 5 in the style of earlier monumental pottery), "progressive monumental" (Nasca 5 with particular changes, yet still within the canons of monumental portrayal), "bizarre innovation" (Nasca 5 with highly abstracted designs; these lead into the full proliferous strain of Nasca 6; see Roark 1965: 25–6), and a "Nasca–Wari decadent style" (Nasca 8/Loro and Nasca 9).

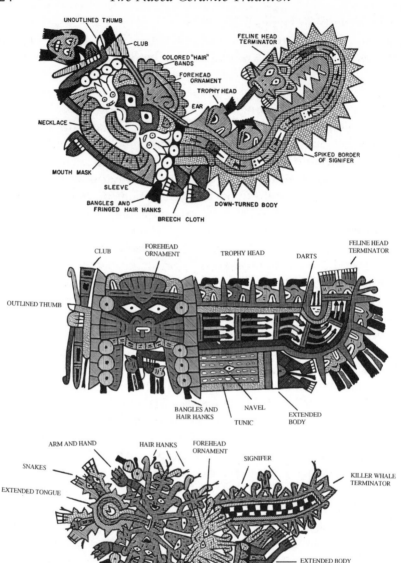

Figure 2.3   The fine differences in Nasca 3, 5, and 6 images (top to bottom) of the Anthropomorphic Mythical Being. Recognition of these kinds of variations over time in complex ceramic iconography permitted Lawrence Dawson to do a similiary seriation of the Nasca style (Nasca 3: Proulx 1968: fig. 19; Nasca 5: Roark 1965: fig. 40; Nasca 6: Roark 1965: fig. 62).

The Nasca Ceramic Phases
of the Berkeley Relative Chronology

Nasca 1

Nasca 1 slip paints were thick and applied unevenly to the vessel surfaces. The thick slip paints often crackled during firing, a trait also present on many Nasca 2 pots. In general, Nasca 1 pottery was decorated in only two or three colors. Red slip already was known from antecedent Paracas pottery and white slip had been introduced in Ocucaje 10 from the Topará Tradition with which Late Paracas and Nasca 1 people were in contact (Menzel et al. 1964). Thus, the shift to slip painting in Nasca 1 was not unheralded. Over time more colors were added to the palette. The jet black pigment of Nasca 1 was seldom duplicated in intensity in later phases. The surfaces of Nasca 1 pots are typically marred by fire clouds, differing surface colors, and other forms of uneven firing.

Based on the collections from his excavations at Cahuachi, Strong defined the following Nasca 1 ("Proto-Nazca") types: Cahuachi Polychrome Incised and Modeled Thin (Strong 1957: figs 7f, g, 10a–i), Cahuachi Polychrome Incised and Modeled Thick (Strong 1957: fig. 10j), Cahuachi Stylus Decorated (Strong 1957: figs 7a–c, 9g–i) and Cahuachi Polished Black Incised (Strong 1957: fig. 9a–f). Among the common and/or diagnostic decorated forms of this Nasca 1 pottery are modeled double-spout-and-bridge bottles such as those which portray fruit in a basket (de Lavalle 1986: 119), human effigy bottles (Donnan 1992: fig. 74; Lapiner 1976: fig. 473) including fisherman effigies (de Lavalle 1986: 120 bottom), single and composite modeled bird bottles (Lapiner 1976: fig. 475; Larco Hoyle 1966: cover), jars (Donnan 1992: fig. 75) and slip-painted and incised bowls (Strong 1957: fig. 10c). Panpipes (see, for example, Purin 1990: fig. 138), trumpets, and ceramic drums (Lapiner 1976: fig. 466) are a major vehicle for mythical iconography (see, also, the geometrically decorated Nasca 1 panpipes in Purin 1990: fig. 137). But this polychrome slipped and incised material is actually rare in the archaeological record. Most Nasca 1 pottery is fine plainware. These vessels are undecorated, thin-walled

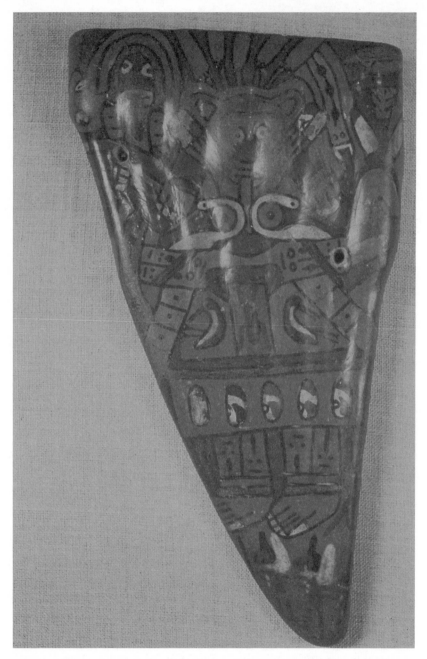

Figure 2.4   Nasca 2 panpipe in the Joerg Haeberli Collection. The iconography of this panpipe was the index-type for Lawrence Dawson's definition of Nasca 2 (*courtesy*: Joerg Haeberli).

bowls that may be shallow or deep, incurving, straight-sided or carinated; some derive from Ocucaje 10 antecedents and others are closely related to contemporary Chongos forms. Interestingly, fine plainware is present at Cahuachi though it was not reported by Strong (see Silverman 1993a: 250–1, figs 16.34–16.37). Fine plainware is abundant at habitation sites.

The range of vessel shapes in Nasca 1 is limited. For instance, in Donald Proulx's archival sample of sixty-nine Nasca 1 pots, over half (52 percent) are modeled bottles, usually in the form of a human effigy.

Nasca 2

Strong (1957: fig. 11) discriminated a ceramic phase between "Proto-Nazca" (Nasca 1) and full-blown "Early Nazca" (i.e. Nasca 3 at Cahuachi) that he called "Cahuachi Polychrome" (Strong 1957: 25, fig. 11; see also Silverman 1977). According to Strong (1957: 25), Cahuachi Polychrome is characterized by shapes that are more similar to Proto-Nazca than Early Nazca. The bottle is the dominant vessel shape in the Nasca 2 ceramic corpus (Parsons 1962: 149). Some double-spout-and-bridge bottles continued to have caps (Parsons 1962: 149), a trait derived from Nasca 1, itself influenced by the Topará Chongos phase (via Ica, we presume). Effigy bottles constitute 20 percent of Proulx's archival sample for this phase; capped double-spout-and-bridge bottles constitute another 20 percent; globular bottles are 15 percent of the sample. Bowls of various form constitute 17 percent. Nasca 2 effigy jars and ceramic musical instruments (drums, trumpets, panpipes) are well known.

It is important to realize that Strong's Cahuachi Polychrome does not constitute the entire corpus of Nasca 2 pottery. In fact, there is considerable iconographic complexity in the Nasca 2 style as seen, for instance, in the Haeberli Panpipe, an extraordinary panpipe of unknown provenience that Lawrence E. Dawson used as the basis of his definition of this phase (figure 2.4), and the Bernstein Drum (figure 2.5). A greater number and variety of natural and supernatural motifs are found on Nasca 2 pottery than Nasca 1. Natural iconography includes warriors, animals, plants,

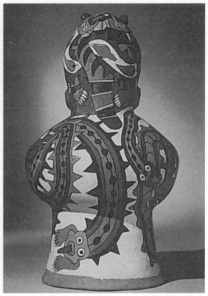

Figure 2.5   Nasca 2 drum. Originally known as the Guggenheim Drum and published by Sawyer (1968: 403), this ceramic masterpiece is now in the David Bernstein Collection, DB Fine Arts, New York City (*courtesy*: David Bernstein).

fish, and birds. Among the supernatural personages are new varieties of the Anthropomorphic Mythical Being (AMB), the Trophy Head Taster, the Mythical Killer Whale, Mythical Spotted Cat and a Mythical Harvester whose face is painted with colored dots (see illustrations in chapter 6). Whereas incised lines separated areas of slip color on Nasca 1 pottery (which is a direct link to Paracas antecedents), in Nasca 2 painted black lines were used or there was no outlining at all (as in the Cahuachi Polychrome type).

Nasca 3

Nasca 3 is a turning point in the evolution of Nasca iconography. By this time Nasca pottery was technologically competent and aesthetically superb. Proulx (1968) has emphasized the homogeneity of Nasca pottery in Ica and Nazca at this time.

Many new mythical creatures appeared. The Nasca 3 iconographic world is inhabited by a number of supernaturals such as the AMB (figure 2.3 top), Spotted Cat, Mythical Harvester and Serpentine Creature (see illustrations in chapter 6). The Horrible Bird and Mythical Harpy are introduced in this phase (see illustrations in chapter 6). In addition, there is a profusion of natural representations – human figures, plants, animals, fish, birds, reptiles. There also is an explosion of geometric motifs in Nasca 3: double spirals, triangles, nested rectangles, step-frets, multi-colored wavy lines, split diamonds, and chevrons. Although black, red, and white predominate as the favorite color combinations, many other colors are used in the designs. The double-spout-and-bridge bottle was the most popular vessel form in this phase, comprising fully 21 percent of all vessels in Proulx's sample. In addition, the cup bowl, which would become quite popular in Nasca 4, was introduced in Nasca 3, accounting for 15 percent of Proulx's sample (see Proulx 1968: figs 3, 4).

Nasca 4

Nasca 4 is not an innovative phase. Few changes in overall designs occur (i.e. Nasca 3 motifs continue in Nasca 4), although many more vessels have geometric designs with black or red (dark) backgrounds rather than the more common white background found in phase 3. One of the few new motifs to appear in Nasca 4 is an Anthropomorphic Monkey (see chapter 6; figure 2.6). Whereas Nasca 3 potters painted their motifs with a free-flowing manner of expression, Proulx (1968: 95) has observed that most Nasca 4 motifs are painted using the principle of modular width by which the visual field is conceived of in horizontal panels of equal width. To maintain the desired width additional lines often were drawn as fillers.

There are very few new shape categories in Nasca 4. Most vessel forms were present in the previous phase, although frequencies of vessel categories change. Cup bowls (for example, Proulx 1968: plate 7a) become the most frequent shape in the Nasca 4 decorated ceramic inventory, comprising 30 percent of Proulx's sample. Double-spout-and-bridge bottles decline in popularity to 14 percent.

Figure 2.6   The Nasca 4–5 Anthropomorphic Monkey (Blasco Bosqued and Ramos Gómez 1986: figs 335–7).

Figure 2.7   Seated, fat, naked woman. Tattooed or body-painted mythological designs decorate the genital area and buttocks (Seler 1923: fig. 208).

Nasca 5

Nasca 5 was a time of great iconographic innovation (see discussion in chapters 6 and 10). The number of painted human representations on pottery increased dramatically. Notable are the large, hollow figurines or jars in the form of a naked woman whose thighs, buttocks, and pubic areas were decorated with elaborate designs of supernatural themes such as the Killer Whale and Rayed Faces (figure 2.7). Decorative bands of multiple female faces, the Anthropomorphic Mythical Killer Whale, Fan-headed Mythical Killer Whale and Winged Mythical Killer Whale also were introduced at this time. The abbreviated "Bloody Mouth" form of the Mythical Killer Whale has a sudden and short-lived popularity in Nasca 5 times (figure 2.8). The Harvester, a male figure wearing a conical hat and carrying or emanating plants, is almost exclusively restricted to Nasca 5. The Anthropomorphic Monkey is also

Figure 2.8   The "bloody mouth" form of the Killer Whale (Roark 1965: fig. 45).

associated with agricultural plants or trophy heads; it reaches its apogee in Nasca 5 but is not a very prevalent theme (Proulx 1989a). The Nasca 5 Anthropomorphic Monkey is quite different from the Mythical Monkey or Affendämon (Ape Demon) that is almost exclusively restricted to Nasca 7. A new form of AMB appeared in Nasca 5, characterized by a body composed of darts (figure 2.3 middle).

There also was great innovation in vessel form in Nasca 5. The goblet shape, female figurines, effigy bottles and jars were introduced. In Proulx's Nasca 5 sample, vases are the most frequent shape category representing 25 percent of the vessels. The double-spout-and-bridge bottle continues to decline in popularity, now being only 8 percent of Proulx's sample.

Nasca 6

Just as Nasca 3 was the high point of the monumental mode of Nasca art, Nasca 6 is the apogee of the proliferous school and, some would say, of the Nasca potters' art. Nasca 6 pottery has few equals in terms of stylistic complexity (the experiment with bizarre innovation had ended and the artistic rules for iconographic depiction were again standardized; intricacy of the proliferous mythical motifs; profusion of colors; symbolic content) and technological proficiency (mastery of slip painting, fine control of the firing of the vessels).

Figure 2.9   Nasca 6 Jagged Staff God (Ubbelohde-Doering 1925–6: fig. 5).

Evolving from Nasca 5 antecedents, vases represent 30 percent of Proulx's archival sample of Nasca 6 pottery. Other forms are so numerous that no other single shape category dominates. There are large double-spout-and-bridge bottles, head-and-spout bottles, flaring bowls, jars (including head jars) and a few single-spout bottles, effigy bottles, flasks, face-necked bottles, and figurines. An early precursor to the Nasca 7 (and Nasca 8) goblet originates in Nasca 6 in small numbers.

A veritable flood of new motifs was painted on Nasca 6 pottery although many of these derived from earlier prototypes. Thus, there were new varieties of the AMB. Also, the Mythical Killer Whale remained important and various AMB's were shown with Killer Whale characteristics (this is important given Yacovleff's [1932b] classic study that identified the killer whale as the principal supernatural creature of the Nasca pantheon). The Jagged Staff God (figure 2.9) appeared but was short-lived, being restricted to Nasca 6. Certain previously common Nasca icons disappeared from the pottery. These include the Spotted Cat, Mythical Spotted Cat, Horrible Bird, Harvester, Harpy, and Serpentine Creature.

Roark (1965) observed that the shift from monumental to proliferous depiction was radical and involved a new emphasis on militaristic themes. In Proulx's sample, there are 220 examples of trophy heads as the primary motif and clearly they reached their height of popularity in Nasca 6. Many effigy bottles portray warriors holding trophy heads in their hands (for example, de Lavalle 1986: 136 top right). Scenes of warfare are common. At the same time, the number of vessels exhibiting plants, animals, bird, fish, and reptiles declines significantly.

Nasca 7

Proulx (1994) describes Nasca 7 as a period of rapid innovation and change. He observes that a number of major, traditional shape categories seem to end abruptly at the end of phase 7A: the tall vase, tall head jar, the head-and-spout bottle, and the collared bottle. New vessel forms in Nasca 7B/C are the result of outside influence. For instance, the cumbrous bowl may be from some adjacent highland area (Ayacucho? Lucanas?) or from further south along the coast; Nasca 7 B/C cumbrous bowls have a conical profile and are interior decorated, particularly the upper rim. Moche is the source of what appears to be the most significant influence on the Nasca 7 style (Proulx 1994). The face-necked bottle and bottle with a single long tapering spout attached to the body by a handle are Moche introductions. Moche iconographic influence is clearly seen in the running position of warriors, a concept of motion alien to the Nasca style, as well as a "feather staff" carried by these figures and the use of floating fillers (see Proulx 1994: fig. 11). Also foreign to the style is the depiction of terrain which is painted between the outstretched legs of these running warriors. Proulx (1989a) also suggests an origin of the Mythical Monkey (see figure 2.10), a new mythical creature, in the Moche Moon Animal, itself derived from Recuay (see Bruhns 1976).

Few Nasca 6 iconographic motifs of supernaturals continued in Nasca 7, and iconographic emphasis shifted to the Mythical Killer Whale. In phase 7, the attached bodies (torso, legs, and so on) of various types of AMBs disappeared. Thus, earlier varieties of the AMB were replaced by an abbreviated form called "fan-headed" because the post-cranial body is replaced by an elaborate proliferous head ornament (figure 2.11).

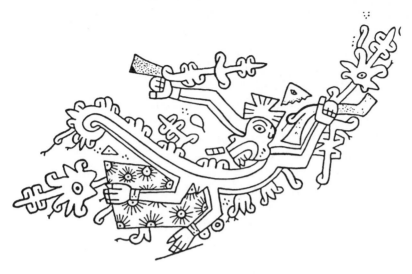

Figure 2.10 Nasca 7 Mythical Monkey or Affendämon (Ubbelohde-Doering 1925–6: fig. 22).

Figure 2.11 Nasca 7 Fan-headed Anthropomorphic Mythical Being (Della Santa 1962: fig. 71)

Nasca 8/Loro

In 1952 William Duncan Strong (1957: 36–41, figs 15, 17) identified a distinct ceramic corpus during his excavations at the Huaca del Loro site in Las Trancas. Strong (1957: 40) also excavated graves with this material in his Burial Area 4 opposite Cahuachi. At

Cahuachi itself this material has been found by Ubbelohde-Doering (1958), Orefici (see Carmichael 1988) and Silverman who discovered a large corpus of the material in a ritually entombed room at the site (see Silverman 1988b, 1993a: ch. 13, figs 13.15–13.36).

Strong (1957: 40) regarded this pottery as so different from the late Nasca material to which it was related that he coined a new style name, Huaca del Loro, after the type-site; today that style is called "Loro" for short. Its distinct character had already been recognized by Kroeber, prior to Strong's discovery of the Huaca del Loro site, when he and Gayton seriated the Uhle materials (Gayton and Kroeber 1927: 26, 27; Kroeber 1956: 375).

Nasca 8/Loro is radically different from the preceding Nasca phase, despite influence and continuity from it. Silverman (1988b *inter alia*) has argued that Nasca 8 is not, properly speaking, a Nasca phase. She highlights significant differences between Nasca 8/Loro and Nasca 7 and 9 pottery (see Silverman 1988b: 25; also see Proulx n.d.). Nasca 8/Loro pottery, in general, lacks polished surfaces, is a thicker, heavier ware, and has a reduced number of colors; vivid polychromy is abandoned. Double-spout-and-bridge bottles and panpipes do not characterize Nasca 8/Loro, although drums are known. Heavy shapes such as cumbrous bowls (anticipated in the cumbrous bowl of Nasca 7B/C) and a deeper bowl of spherical form (the most frequent shape in Proulx's sample, representing 21 percent of the corpus) appear. Face-necked bottles (with and without connecting handles), incurving vases with round bottoms, jars of various sorts (high-collared, flaring collared, effigy, head, necked, low-collared, neckless) and other forms (effigy bottles, head-and-spout bottles, bottles with a long spout and handle, bottles with short spouts, a flask) also are introduced or popularized. Some Nasca 8/Loro pottery is resist-painted with a fugitive, black, organic pigment. Resist is used to create simple decoration such as medallions. There is a preference for banding geometric designs in horizontal panels. Geometric designs such as step-frets, dominoes, zigzags, chevrons, and crosses are common. Complex, supernatural iconography is lost or is highly abstract and limited.

The majority of Nasca 8/Loro motifs are geometric (38 percent in Proulx's sample) or geometric abstractions of earlier motifs such as trophy heads, the Killer Whale, and the Mythical Monkey. Geometric motifs predominate in the offering corpus from the

Room of the Posts (Silverman 1993a: ch. 13). Proulx's sample includes human representations. These may take the form of face-necked jars with painted vestiges of hair, arms, and legs on the body of the vessel, or they are effigy vessels. These humans lack the detail and quality of painting seen in the earlier phases, but it is significant that Nasca 8/Loro people placed so much emphasis on the human form.

Nasca 9

Nasca 9 is Chakipampa, a Wari rather than Nasca product (see Knobloch 1983: 308). We do not consider it further.

Absolute Chronology

Rowe (1967) recognized two distinct patterns in radiocarbon dates from the south coast when these first became available. The discrepancy between the two scales ("long" and "short") is particularly pronounced for Nasca phases 1 through 4. These inconsistencies may be explicable by several arguments. First, whereas the original relative chronology had epochs one hundred years in length, it is clear that some ceramic phases were longer or shorter than others (for example, Proulx 1968: 99–100), and some may even be contemporary. Second, archaeologists may have interpreted regional differences in ceramic style as chronological. The geographical complexity of the Río Grande de Nazca drainage and the likelihood of pots moving out of their original locus of manufacture (for a variety of reasons) strongly suggests that regional variation must be taken into consideration in understanding style and chronology. Third, what has been interpreted as chronological also may be the expression of family or social group styles. Fourth, functional differences – particularly in so far as the pottery was used in ritual – also may have been interpreted as chronological.

Since Rowe's (1967) article was published, more radiocarbon measurements for various of the Nasca ceramic phases have become available (see Silverman 1993a: table 3.1; Ziólkowski et al. 1994). The published dates for the early Nasca phases appear inconsistent. We use the consistent dates of the Chavín de Huántar absolute chronology as our chronological control.

Chavín influence on the immediately pre-Nasca Paracas pottery and textiles of Ica probably began during the expansive Janabarriu phase, dated to 390–200 BC (Burger 1981). This is the final and maximal phase of the Chavin style that came to an end with the intrusion of Huarás white-on-red ceramics (Burger 1981: 595). Even if Ica potters developed their own local canons of representation upon initial reception of Chavín ideas (see Wallace 1991: 104–8) rather than remaining in contact with Chavín de Huántar (see Menzel et al. 1964; Rowe 1962b), the post-Chavín Paracas or Ocucaje 8 style cannot have coalesced much earlier than 200 BC.

Taking into account the field reality of Ocucaje 8, 9, and 10 (see, Cook 1999; DeLeonardis 1991), and the development of Nasca 1 from Ocucaje 10 antecedents (see Menzel et al. 1964: 251), it is highly unlikely that Nasca 1 can be earlier than the final century of the first millennium BC. Nasca 1 also can be cross-dated to the Pucara style of the Lake Titicaca Basin on the basis of Pucara's use of incised lines to separate areas of slip-painted color (see Rowe 1971: 118). Radiocarbon dates from strata of pure Pucara refuse date to approximately 150 BC–AD 100 (see Ziólkowski et al. 1994). These dates also support the suggestion that Nasca 1 dates to this period of time.

We suggest that Nasca 2 dates to around AD 100–200, Nasca 3 to AD 200–400, and Nasca 4 to AD 400–500. Independent corroboration for this time-frame also comes from the Cabezas Achatadas cemetery in Camaná where Disselhoff (1969) obtained three (uncorrected) radiocarbon dates for early Nasca-associated pottery and textiles (see chapter 4): AD 95 ± 95, AD 145 ± 85 and AD 420 ± 70.

Happily, the radiocarbon dates for the later Nasca phases form a consistent series. Nasca 5 is dated to AD 525 ± 90 (Strong 1957: table 4), Nasca 7 to AD 576–696 (Lothrop and Mahler 1957: 47), and Nasca 8 to AD 830 ± 80 (Silverman 1993a: table 13.2) and AD 755 ± 80, 756 ± 90, 985 ± 70 and 1055 ± 70 (Strong 1957: table 4; see comments in Silverman 1993a: table 13.1; Ziólkowski et al. 1994). In addition, McEwan (1996: fig. 12) publishes four fragments of the same Nasca 6 bowl from his excavations at Pikillacta.[2] According to his radiocarbon dates for the site, the Nasca 6 pottery must date to between AD 600 and 900. Based on the Nasca radio-carbon dates, we would argue for a date at the earlier end of his radiocarbon sequence (and see Silverman 1988b, 1993a: table 3.1).

Nasca archaeology is in dire need of a consistent series of phase-by-phase radiocarbon dates. This will be possible only with more excavation, ideally at habitation sites. It is a secure chronology that will let us see the "punctuated changes" (Pauketat 1998: 54) neces-sary for doing a theoretically informed archaeological ethnography of the ancient Nasca.

3

Life in the Desert

At first glance, the desert environment in which the Nasca flourished would not appear to be propitious for the rise of a complex and prosperous society. Indeed, Kosok (1965: 51) aptly described the Grande river system as composed of "minute, isolated valleys that lie scattered over one of the world's driest deserts." But writing only decades after the Spanish conquest of Peru, the chronicler, Pedro Cieza de León, described Nazca in the following terms.

> [O]ne walks toward the beautiful valleys and rivers of Nazca. In past times these were well populated, and the rivers irrigated the valleys' fields in a well ordered manner . . . And because these valleys are so fertile, as I've said, a great quantity of sugar cane has been planted in them, and other fruit that is taken to sell in the cities of this realm. (Cieza de León 1973: 185)

Writing several decades after Cieza de León, Felipe Guaman Poma de Ayala (1980: 983, numbered illustration 1043) depicted the Spanish town of Nazca in a setting of vineyards and stated that Nazca produced the best wine in the realm, comparable to that of Spain. He also said that Nazca had *"abundancia y poca agua"*, both abundance and scarcity of water.

Ica, too, was verdant and fertile into the early Colonial Period with plentiful wine (some of it exported to other parts of Peru), all manner of fruit, and a wealth of bread, maize, meat and fish (Guaman Poma de Ayala 1980: 961). Yet, Ica's environment was precarious. Cieza de León wrote:

[O]ne goes to the refreshing valley of Ica, which isn't less large or populated than the others. A river runs through it which, in some months of the year . . . has so little water that the inhabitants of this valley really feel its lack. When Ica was in its prosperous prime, before it was conquered by the Spaniards, when it enjoyed the rule of the Incas, among the many canals that irrigated this valley there was one larger than the rest that descended in a most remarkably ordered way from the highlands and was like the river. Now, in these times, when water is lacking and this big irrigation canal is in ruins, along this same river people excavate large pits and the water remains in them and the people drink from them and from them the people have extended small irrigation canals to water their fields . . . In this valley there are great forests of algorrobales and many fruit trees . . . and deer, doves . . . and other game. (Cieza de León 1973: 184–5)

Nasca people made the most of their desert setting. Clearly, the situation in the past was better than it appears now. Yet human society was subject to the same recurrent climatological and geological phenomena as those in effect today. In this chapter we look at climate and ecology as a basis for understanding the evolution and many aspects of the organization and ideology of Nasca society.

Overview

The river valleys of coastal Peru are circumscribed by the Pacific Ocean to the west, the Andean highlands to the east, and desert to the north and south. The coastal rivers originate in the highlands as a result of summer (December–March) rainfall. Surface water is the result of runoff from the mountains. It is this runoff that fills the rivers and flows down to the ocean.

The Grande and Ica rivers, which were the heartland of Nasca culture, are special because they do not have the classic, wide, inverted V-shaped delta with rich alluvial deposits that is typical of most of Peru's other coastal river valleys. Rather, the Grande and Ica rivers arrive at the Pacific Ocean shore as mere trickles of water after having passed through narrow canyons. Although the mouths of the Ica and Grande rivers are less than 20 km apart and within eyeshot on a clear day, inland the river valleys diverge greatly (figure 1.1). Agricultural land is not continuous in the lower valleys but, rather, is confined to oases. The best and largest tracts of agricultural land in both river systems are located substantially inland from the shore because of the lack of a true delta.

The Río Grande de Nazca drainage system is furthermore exceptional on the Peruvian coast because it is formed of many affluents with only one outlet to the sea – the Grande River itself (figure 1.1). The multi-tributary configuration of the Río Grande de Nazca drainage exists because uplift in previous geological times blocked the access to the sea of the Grande's affluents. Thus, the Río Grande de Nazca drainage is configured like the fingers of a hand joined at the wrist, with narrow ranges of hills separating one valley from the next. Each of the ten discrete river valleys (Santa Cruz, Grande, Palpa, Vizcas, Ingenio, Aja, Tierras Blancas, Nazca, Taruga, Las Trancas) comprising the drainage has its own distinct headwaters in the rugged highlands. Actually, the Nazca River proper does not have headwaters since it originates in the junction of the discrete Aja and Tierras Blancas rivers, which have their own headwaters.

The Grande, Ingenio, Palpa, Vizcas and Nazca rivers are considered the only "real" rivers of the Río Grande de Nazca drainage because the other tributaries of the system are a series of little, narrow *quebradas* (gulleys, washes, ravines), such as Atarco, Carrizal and Usaca, that drain into the Nazca River and have surface water only intermittently in accordance with summer rains (see ONERN 1971a: 181). Within the drainage, the north–south distance between rivers is well over 50 km and the east–west length of individual valleys may be as great or greater. Inter-valley connections are shortest via the foothills located at or near the valley necks, rather than along the coast.

Referring to the largely inland development of Nasca agriculture and society and its ecological setting, the great geographer–historian, Paul Kosok (1965: 50), observed that the Nazca region "is not strictly coastal . . . It is even less Sierra. Indeed, its character includes elements of both." Kosok (1965: 50) aptly described Nazca as a "peculiar transition zone," pointing out that the Río Grande de Nazca drainage "forms the beginning of an increasingly elevated series of intensively cultivated branch valleys of the western

semi-Sierra region which extends southeast towards Arequipa."
He also noted that the Nazca region "has always been the natural
southern coastal entrance into the southern Sierras proper – connecting this section of the Coast with Ayacucho, Abancay, Cuzco
and even Lake Titicaca" (Kosok 1965: 50). The veracity of Kosok's
assertion is seen in similarities between Pucara and Nasca 1 pottery
(see Rowe 1971).

The Ica Valley is remarkable in its own right, too. Unlike the vast
majority of Peruvian coastal rivers which run east–west, the Ica
River, which is 220 km long, makes a sharp turn south at its valley
neck and from that point runs almost due north–south to its mouth.

Ecology

The area in which Nasca culture developed is classified ecologically
as a "sub-tropical desiccated desert" (ONERN 1971a, b). The
desert character of the Nasca region is demonstrated by meteorological records. For instance, the average rainfall in the Ocucaje
Basin in the lower Ica Valley is only 0.3 mm per annum (ONERN
1971b: 42). Yet, as along the rest of the Peruvian coast, relative
humidity is quite high, averaging 70 percent and at times reaching
100 percent, particularly in the winter, though without rain. It is
appropriate to refer to the Peruvian coast as a maritime desert.

Smaller units of ecological significance to the ancient Nasca
people can be recognized within the overall classificatory designa-
tion of "sub-tropical desiccated desert." They are the following:

chala: the pre-mountain zone that occurs, on average, below approximately 500 m above sea level and extends to the seashore.
The *chala* was a major venue for agricultural settlement for all
pre-Columbian people.
littoral: the narrow strip of seashore including the mouths of the
rivers.
yunga: the narrow, sunny, dry, and hot *quebradas* above the *chala*
from approximately 500 to 2300 m above sea level. The *yunga* is
characterized by a rapid ecological transition up toward the
highlands. The *yunga* also was a major settlement zone in all
ancient time periods.

lomas: winter fog meadows. The pre-Columbian inhabitants of the Río Grande de Nazca drainage and Ica Valley could have taken advantage of these winter fog meadows located in pockets in the upper valleys of the rivers and at places along the littoral. The *lomas* would have been valuable as camelid pasturelands in the past.

Pampa Galeras: an area of high pasturage (*puna*) located at more than 4,000 m above sea level above Tierras Blancas in Lucanas Province between Tambo Quemado and Puquio. Pampa Galeras today is home to thousands of vicuña and other altiplano wild-life. It is possible that in the past other members of the camelid family, such as the wild guanaco, were present there.

oases: the small fertile basins of the lower Ica and Grande valleys.

Constraints and Solutions for an Agricultural Society

Kroeber (1944: 25) observed that the amount of cultivable land in the Ica Valley and Río Grande de Nazca drainage was quite limited. A government survey revealed that only 12,920 ha of land were under cultivation in the Río Grande de Nazca drainage thirty years ago (ONERN 1971a). Kroeber (1937: 227) estimated that approximately 20,000 ha of land in the Ica Valley were irrigated in 1921. In our opinion, Kroeber (1944: 25) was correct when he said that "however dense the population, it could never have been very great absolutely."

All of the tributaries of the Río Grande de Nazca drainage suffer frequently from scarce water and a variable water regime. Modern observations indicate that in their middle portions, the rivers carry surface water only two years out of seven (Schreiber and Lancho Rojas 1995: 231). When water does flow, the volume is far below that of other valley systems further to the north. Within the Río Grande de Nazca drainage, the southern tributaries of Aja, Tierras Blancas, Nazca, Taruga and Las Trancas have the least amount of water. "The Aja River . . . has an average annual flow of only 30.27 million cubic meters of water, compared to 198.05 million cubic meters of water that flow down the Río Grande" (Schreiber and Lancho Rojas 1995: 231). Clearly, surface water is and was insufficient; drought exacerbated the situation.

Because each of the constituent rivers of the Río Grande de Nazca drainage has its headwaters in a different part of the adjacent highlands, the rivers usually do not charge at the same time during the summer rains. Furthermore, a northern valley in the drainage might receive more or less rain-fed irrigation water than a valley to the south, and vice versa. Such a predictably unpredictable situation could have fostered inter-valley relationships of cooperation as a way of spreading risk; it also could have promoted competition among communities for scarce water resources.

In addition to its multiple tributaries, the Río Grande de Nazca drainage is unusual because two different water regimes operate: a northern one of surface water which produced a more or less standard coastal irrigation system, and a southern one whose characteristic scarcity of surface water was resolved in the past through the construction of an ingenious system of underground canals or galleries that tapped subsurface water and surface leader canals and reservoirs from which fields were irrigated (González García 1978; Mejía Xesspe 1940; Rossel Castro 1977; Schreiber and Lancho Rojas 1995; Silverman 1993a: 3, 8–11). Colloquially, the system is called "*puquios*" and some scholars favor this name (see Schreiber and Lancho Rojas 1995). However, Rostworowski (1998a: 144) presents persuasive lexical evidence indicating that the man-made galleries were known as *huncólpi* in ancient times rather than *puquios* (*pukyu, pucyo, puyo, pukio*). A *pukio* is actually a natural spring or source of water. We refer to this irrigation system as filtration galleries, the earlier name in the archaeological literature.

A typical filtration gallery consisted of several parts (figure 3.1). A horizontal tunnel or "gallery" was excavated laterally until it intersected the underground aquifer. The walls of the tunnels were lined with river cobbles without the use of mortar, and, at the uppermost end, the water filtered between the stones into the gallery (Schreiber and Lancho Rojas 1995: 234). The roof of the gallery was constructed from either dressed stone slabs or from wooden logs, the latter having to be replaced at regular intervals (Schreiber and Lancho Rojas 1995: 234). Most of these excavated tunnels were relatively narrow, generally less than one square meter. Other galleries appear to have been constructed by digging an open trench and then filling it in after building the walls and ceiling

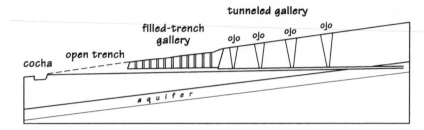

Figure 3.1   Plan of a filtration gallery (after Schreiber and Lancho Rojas 1995: fig. 3).

of the conduit (tunnel) at the bottom. These tunnels were generally of greater height (about 2 m) than those made by tunneling through deeper levels to reach the water source. The length of these galleries was quite variable, ranging from a few meters to as long as 372 m.

Spaced above the galleries at varying intervals (between 10 and 30 m apart) are funnel-shaped holes, or *ojos* ("eyes"). The opening of the conical *ojos* can be as wide as 15 m on the surface of the ground, narrowing down to a meter or two at the bottom. Several of the *ojos* have been reconstructed in recent years to include spiral, cobble-stone ramps leading to the bottom, such as those now visited by tourists at Cantalloc in the Nazca Valley (figure 3.2).

Each major filtration gallery could have several dozen *ojos*. These *ojos* had several functions. They provided air and light as workers built the underground system. They also served as entrances to the galleries for annual cleaning of the irrigation system – a task which continues today. (In creating and maintaining these *ojos* care had to be taken to ensure that debris did not wash down the sides of the pit and fill the water in the tunnel.) And they provided access to the water in the tunnels and thus could be used as wells.

The lower end of the filtration gallery system consists of open trenches which emerge from the tunnels allowing public access to the water for drinking, bathing, washing clothes and, of course, channeling it for agricultural purposes. These trenches are V-shaped, often with terraced sides lined with river cobbles that form retaining walls. The bases of these trenches can be as narrow as a meter and as wide as 10 m at surface level (Schreiber and Lancho Rojas 1995: 234). In the Nazca Valley, ten of the filtration galleries are open trenches for their entire lengths, indicating that the water

Figure 3.2 An *ojo* of a filtration gallery near Cantalloc in the Nazca Valley (*photo*: Helaine Silverman).

table is relatively close to the surface in these locations (Schreiber and Lancho Rojas 1995: 234). Some of these open trenches can be quite long. A trench at Achako in the Nazca Valley is over 1 km in length, while many others are at least 500 m long. Many of the open trenches empty into small reservoirs, or *cochas*, which serve as wells and as distribution points for directing the water into irrigation canals (*acequias*).

There are thirty-six filtration galleries still functioning in the Río Grande de Nazca drainage today: twenty-nine in the Nazca Valley, two in the Taruga Valley, and five in Las Trancas (Schreiber and Lancho Rojas 1995: 234). There appear to have been more in the past, perhaps as many as fifty, but these have been altered or destroyed. There is considerable debate over the age of the filtration galleries. Barnes and Fleming (1991) argue that they are post-Columbian and were created by the Spanish. The fact that filtration galleries are not mentioned by the early Colonial traveler, Pedro Cieza de León, is cited by them as strong evidence that the filtration galleries did not exist in the mid-1500s. In contrast, Schreiber and Lancho Rojas (1995) argue that there is little documentary evidence for the attribution of filtration galleries to the Spanish. They indicate that Barnes and Fleming fail to mention that Cieza de León did not personally travel on the south coast of Peru, was never in Nazca, and could not have had the opportunity to observe the filtration galleries. We note that Rostworowski (1998b: 144) says that the earliest reference to the filtration galleries is by the Spaniard, Reginaldo de Lizarraga, writing in 1605, who witnessed the cleaning of the components of the entire filtration gallery system during the dry season.

Schreiber and Lancho Rojas (1995) also indicate that they have found Middle Horizon and Late Intermediate Period artifacts on the surface of berms left behind from the construction of the filtration galleries at Anglia, Achako, Agua Santa, Soisonguito, Pangaraví, and Santa María. This suggests a pre-Columbian age for the filtration galleries. Furthermore, they note that domestic occupation in the water-scarce areas of the southern tributaries, which today have filtration galleries, began in Nasca 5 times, suggesting that this is when the filtration gallery system was invented. Like Schreiber and Lancho Rojas, we reject a Colonial Period construction date for the filtration galleries and find Barnes and Fleming's

(1991) argument specious. We are convinced that the filtration galleries are pre-Hispanic and, in all likelihood, were invented by Nasca people.

Ica's hydrology also involves surface and subsurface water resources. Although Ica is a fertile valley, it is also one of the drainage system's most chronically water deprived. Craig and Psuty (1968: 60) found that the volumetric discharge of the Ica River is so variable that "it is best characterized as an intermittent stream." Of particular note, however, are the springs or seeps of groundwater and a high water table in the lower valley. This explains the dense pre-Hispanic settlement pattern in the oases (Cook 1999; Uhle 1914: 5–6). Cook (1999: 65) specifically notes that prior to the expansion of irrigation and cotton agriculture in the twentieth century, the lower valley oases were covered with an impenetrable growth of canes, reeds, rushes, shrubs, and hard grass. There is also water at less than 2 m below surface near the seashore (Engel 1981: 18), but Patrick Carmichael's (1991) survey of the south coast littoral strip did not reveal evidence of significant Nasca occupation (see below).

Natural Catastrophes

The Central Andes are subject to major climatic perturbations. The greatest of these is the famous El Niño/Southern Oscillation (ENSO). El Niño is an anomalous displacement of the icy cold Humboldt Current off Peru's coast such that warm equatorial waters intrude (Macharé and Ortlieb 1993: 36). El Niño is a recurrent and capricious phenomenon, aptly described by Fagan (1999: 51) as "a chaotic pendulum, with protean mood swings that can last months, decades, even centuries or millennia."

The warming change in water temperature is enough to kill many endemic cold water fish and mollusc species. El Niño is manifested on land by unusually high temperatures accompanied by massive rainfall on the normally arid coast. There are devastating river floods and hillside *huaicos* (debris or mud flows). On the south coast, the most recent El Niño, in 1998, triggered massive flooding and *huaicos*. The Ica River overcharged its banks, depositing a layer of mud across the city of Ica. In the Río Grande de

Nazca drainage, water coursed across the Pampa, destroying some of the geoglyphs. El Niño has been in existence for at least five thousand years (Fagan 1999: 53). Therefore, the signatures and effects we see today are surely the same as those that occurred in Nasca times. Today's ENSO is scientifically understood and predictable, though unavoidable. El Niño was surely perceived as an awesome event in the past.

Other climatic perturbations in the Andes include recurrent droughts. Two occurred in the sixth century AD and would have affected Nasca society. One is dated to AD 540–560; it was followed by an extreme drought between AD 570–610 during which there was a 20 percent drop in precipitation from the mean (Thompson et al. 1985: table 1). Peru also suffers from frequent large-magnitude earthquakes. The south coast has often been affected by these. Furthermore, it is not uncommon for a severe El Niño to be preceded by an earthquake (Moseley et al. 1992).

Orefici (1990: 116) has argued that cyclical catastrophic rains and associated *huaicos* (by implication, El Niño) prompted five episodes of total remodeling of Cahuachi's temples and the rebuilding of other constructions. He interprets the collapse of a monumental wall at one large mound as the result of tremendous water pressure inside the building pushing out (Orefici 1990: 116–17). He claims that similar events occurred elsewhere at the site between the second and fourth centuries AD, during the apogee of the ceremonial center. In contrast, in her (admittedly small-scale) excavations at Cahuachi, Silverman (1993a) did not find evidence of massive water movement and associated destruction. Also, all of the molluscan taxa from Silverman's excavations at Cahuachi are native to the cold waters off the south coast; the only exception is Spondylus which is known to have been an object of long-distance trade and exchange (see Rodríguez de Sandweiss 1993: 298).

Moseley et al. (1992: 209, 212) caution that terrain-inscribing ENSO events are exceptionally rare in the archaeological record. The dramatic climatological events over two hundred years which Orefici (1990) posits for Cahuachi should be visible elsewhere on the south coast and beyond. We are not aware of these conditions for the stipulated time-frame, though this may be due to lack of excavation data. However, even brief and not necessarily heavy

episodes of rain in Nazca could have destabilized adobe constructions because of prior accumulated stresses from tectonic activity.
And even if these events were local rather than ENSO-produced,
clearly Nasca society was coping with a dynamic climate. Moseley
(1987, 1997) has argued that recurrent major climatic perturbations
created a punctuated equilibrium or punctuated change in the
development of Andean civilization just as climate change affects
people everywhere. "Andean civilization did not arise or mature
under a constant climatic regime" (Moseley 1987: 8). Alternating periods of drought, flood, and benign conditions were the
normal state of affairs and presented opportunities and challenges
to the inhabitants of the south coast, just as they did to all Andean
people (see, for example, Moore 1991; Moseley 1987; Nials et al.
1979).

On independent evidence it can be shown that ancient Nasca
groups coped with varying degrees of foresight and success to
repetitive episodes of excessive rain and earth movements. Whereas
at Cahuachi architectural preparation appears to have been minimal, in Nasca 3 times the inhabitants of an Ingenio Valley site
constructed a massive 35-m long wall of rocks and boulders across
the path of a *huaico* to prevent potential damage to the site from
new *huaicos*. And at another Ingenio Valley site, a major wall was
reoriented away from its sharp right angle to create a deliberate
barrier against *huaicos* common in the adjacent *quebrada*. In fact,
rock from subsequent *huaicos* is visible up against the outer side of
this wall so the design was successful.

Grodzicki (1990: 97) reconstructs a catastrophic river flood and
heavy rains around AD 600 which he claims to be the result of
another El Niño. He says the event severely damaged adobe constructions at Cahuachi and probably affected the valley fields. But
by this time Cahuachi had ceased to function as the great early
Nasca ceremonial center. Aerial photographs of Cahuachi (see, for
example, Silverman 1993a: figs 5.1, 5.2) show repeated water flow
through the site that damaged walls after the site's period of maintenance. In contrast, Georg Petersen (1980), a geologist, has hypothesized that the demise of Nasca culture was due to the pressure
of an advancing desert. Clearly, more geological work is necessary
in Nazca and full publication of data is crucial.

The Subsistence Economy

Nasca subsistence was based largely on agriculture. Nasca iconography and excavated remains indicate that Nasca people had a varied diet. This included high carbohydrate seed crops such as corn or maize (*Zea mays*), peanuts (*Arachis hypogaea*), jack beans (*Canavalia ensiformis*), squash (Cucurbita), Lima beans (*Phaseolus lunatus*), and kidney beans (*Phaseolus vulgaris*); high carbohydrate root crops such as achira (*Canna edulis*), sweet potatoes (Ipomoea), manioc (*Manihot utilissma*), jíquima (*Pachyrrhizus tuberosus*), yacon (*Polymnia sonchifolia*), and many varieties of potatoes (Solanum); and fruit such as the hot chili pepper called ají (*Capsicum frutescens*), pacae (*Inga feuillei*), lúcuma (*Lucuma obovata*), avocado (*Persea americana*), huarango pods (*Prosopis chilensis*), guava (*Psidium guajava*), and pepino (*Solanum muricatum*) (see Isla 1992; O'Neale and Whitaker 1947; Silverman 1993a: ch. 20; Valdez 1994: 677). Nasca art depicted many of these agricultural plants, notably achira, bean, ají, jíquima, lúcuma, maize, pepino, yuca (figure 3.3; see O'Neale and Whitaker 1947).

Agricultural technology

The Nasca had to rely on annual flooding of the rivers, natural springs, and the filtration galleries in order to practice agriculture in the desert. An irrigation infrastructure (maximum elevation canals, feeder canals) must have existed in the northern drainage where filtration galleries do not exist. But the elements of such a system have not been identified, probably because the narrowness of arable tracts of land in the Nasca territory required their reutilization and/or destruction by later peoples. As noted above, filtration galleries exist and are still in use in the southern tributaries.

Pointed wooden digging sticks (see Silverman 1993a: 280–1, figs 19.16, 19.17) appear to be painted on Nasca pottery (see, for example, Townsend 1985: fig. 6) and textiles (see, for example, Sawyer 1979: fig. 17 right). Ground stone tools for food preparation (grinding slabs, rockers, or handstones) are occasionally observed on the surface of Nasca sites (see, for example, Silverman 1993a: fig. 19.27).

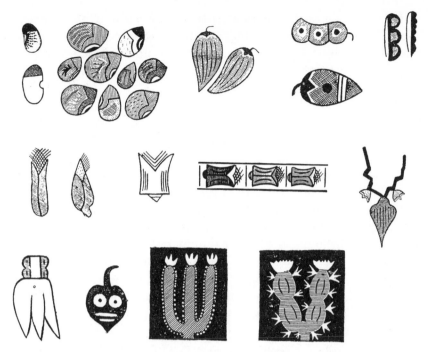

Figure 3.3 The major edible plants of the Nasca, as seen in ceramic iconography (Seler 1923; Yacovleff 1933).

The Nasca irrigation system required maintenance as do contemporary canals in traditional Andean communities. Based on ethnographic analogy, we assume that there was some water distribution decision-making entity and that water rationing was conditioned as much by the actual differential growth requirements of particular plants as by the pressure of interest groups within the community (see Mayer 1985: 61–3, 70–4). Certainly, the community must have been united to defend its rights to water and land *vis-à-vis* other communities. Based on the relationship between irrigation canals and social territories known to have existed elsewhere on the Peruvian coast (see, for example, Netherly 1984; Rostworowski 1978: ch. 2; Sherbondy 1982), it is reasonable to think that canals and social groups were coterminous among the ancient Nasca. Thus far, there is no evidence that the irrigation system of an entire valley or several valleys functioned as a single geo-social-political system.

Labor organization is another aspect of farming technology. Nasca settlement patterns indicate that the labor force lived in immediate proximity to its fields. Ceramic and textile iconography depicts male farmers. Women must have been involved in field work as well.

Locally grown industrial (non-food) crops

Cotton was a key industrial product in ancient Nasca society (and is a key commercial crop in the valleys today), vital for community self-sufficiency. Cotton fiber composed the majority of fibers in Nasca textiles (Phipps 1989). Nasca ceramic art illustrates cotton nets used in fishing (for example, Lapiner 1976: figs 511, 512) and cotton nets are known from excavation at Cahuachi (O'Neale 1937: plate lxvg, h; Orefici 1993: fig. 122 *inter alia*; Silverman 1993a: 272, fig. 18.22). The only technological description of these is provided by Lila O'Neale who analyzed Kroeber's textile materials from his Nazca Valley project. O'Neale (1937: 202) identifies "the two simplest methods of constructing this type of fabric: knotless netting, or half-hitching, the coil without the foundation of basketry; and the netting with simple or finger knot." Meshes are about a half-inch square and the cotton cord is described as coarse. Non-edible plants such as cane, totora reeds, and junco also were used for utilitarian purposes such as matting. Gourds also were a major non-edible agricultural product. Gourds were both an important utilitarian object as well as a major vehicle for iconographic expression (see, for example, Kroeber and Collier 1998: fig. 70; de Lavalle 1986: 182 center; Silverman 1993a: figs 19.20–19.22).

Coca is known to be and to have been a valued commodity and fundamental element of social and political life in the Andes (Allen 1988; Murra 1980). Coca leaf should have been locally available in the *chaupiyunga* (middle *yunga*, 500–1000 m above sea level) areas of the various tributaries (see Rostworowski 1989a, b *inter alia*). This variety of coca, *Erythroxilum novogranatense var. trujillemse*, is distinct from that of the jungle and was recognized as such in pre-Columbian times (see Rostworowski 1998b: 135–6; see also Towle 1961: 58–60).

We infer coca's use in Nasca society from painted coca bags and modeled bulging cheeks on late Nasca male effigy figures (for example, de Lavalle 1986: 140). There is also iconographic evidence that women chewed coca leaf (see Reinhard 1992: fig. 8). Coca's use may have been controlled by males with the socially aggrandizing benefits its redistribution would bring. Orefici (1993: color fig. 34) illustrates a textile artifact identified as a coca bag (*"chuspa"*), which he dates to Nasca 8/Loro. The only archaeological context of coca leaf at a Nasca site of which we are aware is evidence recorded by Helaine Silverman at an early Nasca site in the middle Grande Valley. There, coca leaves were observed adhering to a loose adobe on the site surface. If Nasca 8/Loro is considered to be Nasca, then Ubbelohde-Doering's (1958) discovery of coca leaves in his type-phase tomb at Cahuachi also may be included in this discussion.

The hallucinogenic San Pedro cactus (*Trichocereus pachanoi*) was a wild plant of major ritual significance to the ancient Nasca. Its preparation as a brew in pots should be detectable by residue analysis.

Marine resources

We referred above to Carmichael's (1991) survey and to the fact that he found no evidence of permanent Nasca littoral sites. Nevertheless, the Nasca exploited marine resources. Archaeologists have recorded abundant shell, fish bones, and nets on the surface of various inland Nasca habitation sites (see, for example, Proulx 1999c). At Cahuachi, Helaine Silverman recovered remains of a fish known locally as *"anaque"* or *"cachema"* (*Cynoscion analis*), the popular *"corvina"* (*Sciaena gilberti*), and the *"coco"* (*Paralonchurus peruanus*), along with other members of the families *Sciaenidae* and *Clupeidaie* (see Rodríguez de Sandweiss 1993).

Nasca people also hunted or scavenged sea mammals such as seal, otter, and whale to judge from ceramic iconography (Buse n.d.). Donald Proulx has seen "fisherman bottles" that depict men straddling what appear to be inflated skin boats while catching fish in nets. The inhabitants of lower valley oases probably were making the short trek to the seashore to obtain marine products and exchanging these with people living further inland.

Insight into ancient Nasca maritime practice can be inferred from Marcus's (1987: 9) observations of contemporary Cañete fishermen. They recognize three basic types of coastal habitats: *peña* or the rocky cliffs that plunge into the sea including sea caves and small offshore islands, *costa* or the stretches of cobble or gravel beach, and *playa*, the sandy beaches. Each of these ecological niches has a slightly different mix of fish, molluscs, and mammals. The *peña* zone supports a number of shellfish including periwinkles, limpets, mussels, chitons, sea snails, the abalone-like chanque, and the acorn barnacle. Among the fish in this zone are the grunt, the pintadilla, and the scaled blenny along with varieties of drum. The *costa* zone is home to the robalo, drums, lorna, and bonito. The *playa* zone contains polycheate worms, euphausiids, and coquina clams, along with two types of crustaceans, the mole crab and the burrowing shrimp. Corvina, one of the best-selling fish in today's marketplace, is found in this zone along with lorna, mismis, ayanque, and the left-eye flounder. Various forms of sharks, rays, and skates complete Marcus's list. Sandweiss (1992: table 36) provides a list of the thirty most common fish species in the Pisco area, closer to the Nasca heartland.

Whale ivory was occasionally carved by late Nasca people to make figurines (for example, Morris and von Hagen 1993: fig. 76) and hand grips for spear throwers (Lothrop and Mahler 1957: 42, plate xx). Whale bone must have been obtained by scavenging along the shore.

Animal resources

Camelids were a key animal resource for the ancient Nasca; the llama is well known on the coast despite its highland origin (see Shimada and Shimada 1985). Camelid wool was dyed for use as threads in embroidery and it was used in the structure of fabrics, such as warp-faced constructions (O'Neale 1937; Phipps 1989). Its abundance surely correlates to the availability of the raw material. Llamas also were used for sacrifice and feasting at Cahuachi (for example, Orefici 1993; Silverman 1993a: 199, 202, 209, 301, 304, 305; Strong 1957: 31; Valdez 1994) and were consumed at habitation sites (Isla 1992: 150). Llamas also would have been important as beasts of burden for the caravans used in any long-distance enterprise. The age and sex ratios of camelid remains in Nasca archaeological contexts imply local husbandry (see Valdez 1988). Such husbandry possibly took place in the *lomas* (Valdez 1994: 677; see also Orefici 1993: 43, 92 who identifies both llama and alpaca). Some ceramic iconography depicts scenes of humans holding tethered and, therefore, domesticated camelids, presumably the llama (see, for example, Carmichael 1988: plate 26; Disselhoff 1966: 98; Purin 1990: fig. 149).

Scenes of camelid hunting (of guanaco?) also were painted on Nasca pottery (for example, Eisleb 1977: fig. 207; Kroeber and Collier 1998: figs 259, 272) and may refer to real events that happened in a *puna* such as Pampa Galeras and/or in the *lomas*. Various Nasca pots depict hunters using obsidian-tipped spears and spear throwers against camelids (see, for example, Eisleb 1977: 207; Kroeber and Collier 1998: fig. 259). The archaeologically recovered technology used in hunting does not appear to differ significantly from that portrayed on painted scenes of Nasca warfare: spear throwers, wooden spears, clubs, slings with projectile stones, and knives/points (especially of obsidian). Bolas (weights tied to cords to snare the legs of animals) also seem to have been used in hunting, but the iconography depicts them as a series of stones aligned along a single cord rather than on multiple cords (the traditional form).

The guinea-pig was another important animal resource in ancient Nasca society. Silverman (1993a: 168) recovered a sacrificial cache of at least twenty-three guinea-pigs at Cahuachi. Isla (1992: 150) reports guinea-pig in habitation contexts at Usaca. Further excavations in domestic contexts should reveal their abundant consumption.

Non-edible animals were of great interest to the Nasca as well. Nasca potters portrayed terrestrial animals such as dog, fox, pampas cat, mice, and monkey. The local desert fox is well known from Nasca pottery, particularly as a ceremonial headdress (for example, Proulx 1983: catalogue fig. 122; Sawyer 1964: 292, fig. 9e–j). Monkeys appear in painted form (for example, de Lavalle 1986: 146 bottom; Proulx 1983: catalogue fig. 104). The Nasca represented a range of birds on their pottery (condor, cormorant, falcon or hawk, "forest bird," great egret, hummingbird, Inca tern,

Figure 3.4   Some of the principal birds depicted in Nasca ceramic iconography (Gayton and Kroeber 1927; Seler 1923; Yacovleff and Muelle 1934).

parrot, pelican, and the white-collared swift, *Steptoprocne zonarius albicincta*, which is the famous *"vencejo"*) (figure 3.4). Brilliantly colored bird feathers were used in ritual attire (for example, Kroeber and Collier 1998: 79, 259, fig. 73 ; Orefici 1993: 42; Strong 1957: 31). Dogs and parrots (see the modeled plaque illustrated by Tello 1931) may have been pets among the Nasca.

A variety of amphibians (frog, lizard, tadpole, others) and reptiles (snakes) are represented in Nasca iconography but their role, if any, in the diet is unknown. Insects (spiders, others) also were painted. It is possible that their role was symbolic, representing the beginning of the annual flow of water (in the case of frogs, toads, and polliwogs) or protectors of the crops from predators (snakes and lizards).

Non-subsistence Activities

Fancy pottery production

Nasca was a complex society with a rich material culture within which pottery figured prominently. It is reasonable to think that there was craft specialization in Nasca society, for the ceramic iconography can be so complex and beautifully painted, and the technical quality of the pottery is so high, including the obtaining and mixing of slip pigments, that it seems plausible that only a knowledgeable as well as talented artist could produce this material. However, ethnography teaches us that extraordinary pots can be produced by part-time potters (for example, the Canelos Quichua case: see Whitten and Whitten 1988).

Arnold (1985: 90) has explicitly argued that the environment and geographical setting of Nazca – away from the coastal strip in an area with constant sunshine and little rainfall – provided the ideal conditions for the development of full-time, year-round ceramic specialization leading to the complex Nasca pottery tradition. However, unambiguous evidence of specialized Nasca pottery production has not been forthcoming. Pottery production sites – as these are known, for instance, for Wari (for example, Anders et al. 1998; Pozzi-Escot 1991) and Moche (for example, Russell et al. 1994a, b) – have eluded Nasca archaeologists. At Cahuachi the evidence for pottery production consists of miscellaneous fragments of red pigment and pigment-stained rocks, spatulas, and fine-haired objects that could be paint brushes (Orefici 1993: 100, figs 118, 119; Silverman 1993a: 277, fig. 19.9 *inter alia*: compare to the pottery-painting tools found at Maymi, see Anders et al. 1998: 11). Petersen (1980: 12) reports that in 1970 he discovered alongside a temple at Cahuachi "a quantity of earthy, dark and brick-red colors; ochres [mineral of clay and ferric oxide] that evidently were used for decorating the pottery. Some ash stains and fragments of vegetable charcoal indicated, perhaps, the places where pottery was fired." Kroeber (Kroeber and Collier 1998: 259) also has reported a lump of gypsum useful for polishing, sandstone useful as an abrasive, hematite pigment and a quartz pebble with hematite adhering to one face. But these objects are not found concentrated in a particular area as would be seen in workshop conditions.

Potters plates should be prima-facie evidence of pottery production, even in the absence of craft markers such as wasters, calcined deposits, and production tools. Potters plates have been recorded by Orefici (1993: fig. 117, provenience not given) and by Isla (1992: 143) at habitation sites. Helaine Silverman recovered fragments of potters plates on the surfaces of seven Nasca sites in the Ingenio and middle Grande valleys. Three or four of these are habitation sites, one is a cemetery, and one site's function is obscured by a later occupation.

Thus, while it can be expected that pottery production was occurring at Cahuachi and there is physical evidence in support of this proposition, it is also possible that Nasca people, especially after the decline of Cahuachi, were making pottery in their villages on an individual basis. We also make this argument based on the widespread distribution of fine Nasca pottery at habitation sites of all periods, in addition to the ubiquitous presence of pottery at cemeteries and civic-ceremonial sites. Indeed, symbol-bearing pottery was a key element of Nasca daily life throughout the life-span of this society. Fancy pottery may have been exchanged throughout the drainage with Cahuachi perhaps being the primary vehicle of its movement in early Nasca times as is suggested by the pottery being carried by a family on the modeled plaque illustrated by Tello (1931). At present we favor the notion that most Nasca pottery production took place in the valley floor at the clay source and adjacent to the water and fuel necessary for production (see Arnold 1985: 20). Such loci are probably unrecoverable today due to the intervening centuries of alluvial deposition.

Clay was a cheap raw material for the ancient Nasca people and pots are abundant in the archaeological record. Nevertheless, repair holes are frequent (see, for example, Silverman 1993a: 260–1, fig. 17.5). We are considering the dual possibilities that repair indicates the value of pots in Nasca society in terms of their symbolic content/prestige/life histories (see Silverman 1993a: 335) and that there was a real economic cost of fuel needed for firing which would have made pot conservation pragmatically worthwhile and desirable.

High-tech provenience characterization of a large sample of Nasca pottery from various sites and phases may be able to resolve this continuing conundrum in south-coast archaeology unless, of course, the clay beds selected for the raw material have the same compositional signature throughout the drainage. Vaughn and Neff's (2000) neutron activation study of potsherds from an early Nasca domestic site in Tierras Blancas indicates that painted vessels form a single group, whereas there is variability in the chemical composition of plainware.

In addition, we must consider the musical instruments made of pottery: panpipes, drums, and trumpets. So adept were the ceramicists who produced Nasca panpipes that Bolaños (1988: 107) has suggested that these were not the musicians themselves, but a different group of specialists in Nasca society. Independently, Haeberli (1979) demonstrates that over the course of the many centuries represented by the ceramic phases of the panpipes there is a scale based on a common basic frequency interval. Pitch was standardized and most Nasca panpipes were tuned to gapped scales. This involved selecting a Nasca scale frequency or tone as the keytone, followed by choosing specific frequencies from the Nasca scale. But evidence for a system of standardized keytones has not been discovered. For Haeberli, this indicates that "different musicians and/or communities had their instruments tuned to their scales." The continued study of panpipe technology could help archaeologists identify the communities constituting the larger Nasca society.

Domestic and fancy textile production

Based on ethnographic analogy, ordinary cloth for personal/family use was probably made by women at habitation sites. They would have spun cotton and wool thread and woven the textiles. Ceramic spindle whorls (reutilized sherds with a central hole) are occasionally found on the surface of Nasca habitation sites; presumably excavation would reveal their widespread occurrence.

Textiles were traditionally made on a backstrap loom (see illustrations in Donnan 1976: fig. 47; Guaman Poma de Ayala 1980:

191, 193). From early Nasca contexts at Cahuachi, Strong (1957; see also Phipps 1989) and Silverman (1993a: figs 19.12–19.15) found wooden weaving implements such as shuttles, heddles, and a comb in addition to needles, spindles, whorls, cotton balls, and abundant thread (see also Pezzia 1969: 142–3). Silverman (1993a: fig. 13.37) also recovered four bundles of tied canes in the Room of the Posts at Cahuachi, which she identifies as portable backstrap looms; these date to the Nasca 8/Loro ritual interment of the room.

Sawyer (1997) has identified early Nasca textile samplers. He says that these indicate the organization of fine textile work as well as status differences in Nasca society. He argues that strong similarities in image renderings across samplers indicate that "Nasca iconography was under the strict control of the religious hierarchy" and he posits a workshop situation (Sawyer 1997: 72, 76). He suggests that apprentices copied the experienced hand of an expert embroiderer and that these motifs decorated garments worn by low-ranking members of Nasca society. Indeed, Sawyer (1997: 76) argues that Nasca needlework projects were so complex and labor-intensive that they eventually overwhelmed the capacity of "embroidery workshops." Such a workshop may have existed at Cahuachi at a small mound excavated by William Duncan Strong in 1952 that was subsequently bulldozed (see discussion in Silverman 1993a: 52, 64). At this locus, Strong (1957: 28) recovered "numerous cloth fringes and other unworn fragments from beautifully woven and colored embroideries as well as other textile types . . . fine pieces were so abundant . . . that it seems possible that these structures [a series of heavy walls, perhaps used as walks, and a series of well-constructed nicely finished wattle-and-daub walls and floors] were used particularly by weavers." This context dated to Nasca 2. The abandonment of the facility may be evidence of the shift to the ceramic medium in Nasca 3 times that various scholars have recognized.

Other evidence of textile production has since been discovered at Cahuachi, though none as compelling as Strong's. Silverman (1993a: figs 18.4, 18.6–18.15) recovered scores of three-dimensional textile figures that would have been attached to bands and sewn on to base cloths, possible needles (Silverman 1993a: fig. 19.12), a wooden comb (Silverman 1993a: fig. 19.13), and other weaving implements (Silverman 1993a: fig. 19.15). Orefici (1993: fig. 129) speculates that an offering of magnesium sulphate in a Nasca pot had an original use as a mordant for textile dyes. Orefici (1993: color figure 32) also illustrates a comb for textile production.

Nasca textiles were made using a wide range of techniques that are fairly well defined in the literature. Among these techniques were interlocking warp and weft (Rowe 1972; see also O'Neale 1937: plate xxxix), needle-knitting or the cross-knit loop stitch used to produce extraordinary three-dimensional textiles (Lothrop 1964: 198–9), plainweave (O'Neale 1937: 206), double cloth (O'Neale 1937: plate xliia), gauze (O'Neale 1937: plate xli), tapestry (O'Neale 1937: plate xxxviii), and plaiting (O'Neale 1937: plate xlii). Plainweave textiles could be superstructurally decorated by magnificent embroidery (see Sawyer 1997; see also O'Neale 1937: plates lv–lx), brocade (O'Neale 1937: plate xxxiii, l), three-dimensional tabs and figures (for example, Gundrum 2000; Haeberli 1995; O'Neale 1937: plate lxi–lxiii), and painting (for example, Sawyer 1979). Both Orefici (1993: plate 35) and Strong (see Phipps 1989: 232) have recovered examples of tie-dye, a rare decorative technique in Nasca textile art that is over-represented in the literature because of its striking appearance.

Color in Nasca textiles was due to naturally occurring differences of pigmentation in cotton and camelid wool (with colors ranging from white to beige to brown to black) as well as to the dyeing of wool fiber. Phipps (1989: 176–94) identifies mineral pigments made of oxides, hydroxides, and carbonates of copper, iron, and manganese; these were used with a binding medium. Some of these coloring agents are locally available (for example, tannins for browns, cochineal insects on cactus for carmine red, indigo for violet blue), whereas others required travel out of the local and even ethnic/macro-social group region. For instance, Phipps (1989: 180, 225) suggests that a cinnabar (mercuric sulfide ore) colorant on Nasca textiles from Cahuachi may only have been available at the headwaters of the Pisco River in Huancavelica. If this was the ancient source, we probably would be seeing the coveted color moving down the Pisco Valley, across the foothills to the upper Ica Valley, and from there being traded and exchanged. Purple was obtained from the excretion of shellfish such as *Perumytilus purpuratus* and *Concholepas concholepas*; these shells are known at Cahuachi (see Rodríguez de Sandweiss 1993).

The issue of pigment source is also critical for understanding the slips applied to Nasca pottery in terms of their organizational (economic, political, social) implications. Clearly, pigments and dyes were valued in Nasca society. Although the ancient Nasca were able to supply their basic necessities in the immediate vicinity, other desired non-subsistence goods must have implicated complex inter-societal mechanisms and labor mobilizations.

Metallurgy

Gold is locally available in the Río Grande de Nazca drainage but it was extremely laborious to obtain under artisanal conditions. This may explain why Nasca gold artifacts are rare in museum and private collections and even rarer in recorded tombs (see Carmichael 1988: 304–5). At least through 1993 Giuseppe Orefici had reported no gold from Cahuachi. Continued and new fieldwork by others in the Río Grande de Nazca drainage may change the appreciation we present here.

Some scholars say that the Nasca used copper (see Carmichael 1988: 304–5, 498–9) and copper does exist geologically in the Río Grande de Nazca drainage (ONERN 1971a: 74). However, Heather Lechtman (personal communication, 2000) indicates that she has never seen any copper artifacts with Nasca provenience. She believes that this metal was not used by Nasca people. This matter requires further study.

Long-distance Exchange or Procurement

Nasca people had the ability to be self-sufficient in their valleys. But self-sufficiency is a cultural perception. As is and was the case with so many other peoples around the world, the Nasca eagerly sought foreign goods for the prestige their distant source would imply and/or because a foreign good was demonstrably better along some parameter than a local equivalent. In addition to tangible items that could be claimed or negotiated in distant lands, intangibles, including stylistic influence, were also exchanged (for a powerful discussion of this general anthropological issue, see Helms

1979, 1988). The quintessential long-distance goods in the Central Andes were obsidian and Spondylus. Both were present in Nasca society and we turn to them now.

Obsidian

Archaeologists working in Peru have been extremely interested in obsidian since Burger's (1984; Burger and Asaro 1977) pioneering work in the sourcing of Central Andean obsidian and his demonstration of the multi-faceted significance of its different patterns of distribution (see, for example, Burger 1984; Burger et al. 1998a–c; see also Browman 1998). In the Ingenio Valley, obsidian is present on the surface of eighty-one Nasca sites/sites with Nasca occupations of all phases, some of which are geoglyphs and cemeteries. Obsidian is also known to occur at a probable early Nasca site in Las Trancas where it is sourced to Quispisisa (see Burger and Asaro 1977: 307–8). Obsidian is also present at Cahuachi (see, for example, Silverman 1993a: 160, fig. 19.26, table 19.3; Valdez 1994: 677). Massey (1986: 254) reports obsidian in association with Nasca 1 occupations in the upper Ica Valley, and Burger and Asaro (1977: 308) report the use of Quispisisa obsidian at San José de Cordero which is said to have a Nasca 7 occupation.

During her survey of the Ingenio Valley, Helaine Silverman observed a greater surface density of obsidian at upper-valley sites than lower down, but not all upper-valley sites have obsidian on their surfaces and when it does occur it may be much lighter in density. There appears to be a significant drop-off in obsidian density below 675 m above sea level. The obsidian recorded consisted of large and small flakes, projectile points, the occasional knife and scraper, nuclei, and worked obsidian whose function is unknown. These artifacts represent all stages in the lithic production process (for example, core, debitage, finished products, reuse). Silverman identifies one site in the middle Ingenio Valley as a possible Nasca lithic workshop. In addition to these quotidian uses, obsidian also played a major ritual role in Nasca society as the material from which ceremonial knives, probably used in human decapitation, were made (see, for example, Silverman 1993a: fig. 19.25; see also Yacovleff 1932b: figs 3, 5).

The Quispisisa obsidian source is located near Huanca Sancos in Ayacucho, in the *puna* production zone at 3780 m above sea level, above a river tributary draining into the Pampas River (Burger and Glascock 2000). The location was readily accessible to Nasca people. For instance, from the uppermost Ingenio Valley the route to the source involved crossing only a 2-km stretch of *puna* to reach a tributary that descends directly into the Huanca Sancos Valley. Only some 15 km of this route would have been at or slightly above 4,000 m above sea level. Different Nasca societies may have developed their own routes to obtain obsidian.

Identifying the routes by which coastal people may have arrived at the Quispisisa source, however, leaves unanswered the important question of protocol governing exploitation of the source (see discussion in Burger and Asaro 1977: 315–18). Although archaeologists do not yet know how Quispisisa obsidian arrived at coastal Nasca sites (by what route, who organized the trip, who effected the trip, etc.), clearly – in the Ingenio Valley, at least – obsidian was not uncommon in Nasca times. Furthermore, Nasca people appear to have been deliberately choosing obsidian from the Quispisisa source in Huanca Sancos over the Pampas source of obsidian at Jampatilla in the Carahuarazo region. The Nasca decision appears topographically understandable because the Pampas source is more distant and more difficult of access than Huanca Sancos, notwithstanding the Nasca sherds present in the Carhuarazo Valley (as noted by Schreiber 1992: 139, 227). More research on obsidian in Nasca society is needed.

Spondylus

There is yet more to learn about *Spondylus pictorum*, a thorny oyster whose bi-valve shell is colored brilliant red on the outside and yellow/white inside. Spondylus is the luxury good *par excellence* in the Central Andes. Ethnohistoric documents and archaeological contexts indicate its extremely high symbolic value for thousands of years among Central Andean societies (see Davidson 1982; Murra 1975; Paulsen 1974).

The Nasca Anthropomorphic Mythical Being wears a necklace of Spondylus or Spondylus may alternate with mother-of-pearl plaques (for example, Proulx 1968: figs 18, 19). Occasionally, human males are shown with a Spondylus necklace as part of their elite or ritual attire (for example, de Lavalle 1986: 123), or they may wear a mother-of-pearl necklace without Spondylus (for example, Donnan 1992: fig. 74). Actual Nasca Spondylus artifacts are known (see, for example, Proulx 1996: plate 20; Richardson 1994: 97), but Spondylus is rare in the Nasca archaeological record and these objects usually lack provenience or it is unstated (for example, Orefici 1993: fig. 109). Silverman (1993a: fig. 13.8) recovered twelve small pieces of Spondylus in the clean sand fill covering a niche in the east wall of the Room of the Posts at Cahuachi, hence in a Nasca 8/Loro context. On survey, she recorded Spondylus shell on the surface of eight multi-component sites whose main occupation may be Nasca or may be later.

Hardships of the Desert

The desert environment of the south coast has created an ideal context for the natural mummification of bodies buried in the dry sand. These human remains provide archaeologists and physical anthropologists with a wonderful source of information about ancient disease, pathologies, and injuries as well as data about burial and other religious practices. We know that life was tough in the desert. The ancient Nasca commonly suffered from a variety of indigenous diseases, including tuberculosis, malaria, respiratory diseases, and gastrointestinal diseases caused by parasites, worms, and bacterial infections (Allison 1979). Allison (1979: 77) reports that 50 percent of all children died before the age of 10, and only 27 percent of the survivors lived past 40 years. These figures are not too different from statistics on rural populations in the early part of the twentieth century, prior to the development of antibiotics and improved medical technology and services. Yet within these biological parameters and the physical environment described above, the Nasca people developed the culture and technologies with which to create one of the most extraordinary societies of ancient Peru.

4

We, the Nasca

We do not know what the Nasca called themselves, though world-wide it is common for societies to refer to themselves as "people" in the sense of "we are the human beings." Archaeology demonstrates that the Nasca were a people who recognized themselves as such and others as outsiders. Nasca people shared a particular culture and consciously and strategically deployed cultural signatures of Nasca identity redundantly across multiple domains in Nasca society. In this chapter we consider the shared material, intangible, and corporeal features and practices that define the cultural identity of the Nasca people and their territory. These include: physical appearance and distinctive cranial deformation; language; pottery, textiles, and other media manifesting a very specific supernatural iconography and style, form, and technology of representation; the style and technology of architecture and particular patterns in the use of space; specific burial patterns; headhunting and a diagnostic method of preparation of the decapitated head; and geoglyphs, to name the most obvious. As we shall see in chapter 5, particular sites also were important to Nasca cultural identity, among which Cahuachi, the great early Nasca ceremonial center, was pre-eminent.

Lest our discussion be considered a "trait list," we emphasize that this book seeks to explain how the many spheres of Nasca culture and society developed and interacted through participatory human activity. Once there is a better household basis to Nasca archaeology, we will be able to understand Nasca identity not just normatively but also dynamically as personal and group daily practices responding to and creating historical contingency with cultural continuities and discontinuities.

Physical Appearance

The Nasca, like other pre-Columbian peoples, were physically similar to the Asiatic peoples of Siberia and Mongolia, with whom they are thought to share a common ancestry. Certainly, the facial characteristics of ancient Nasca people – well preserved in tombs and beautifully rendered on pottery – support this interpretation. The Nasca had high, padded cheekbones, an epicanthic fold of the eyelids, "shovel-shaped" incisor teeth (a concave depression in the back of these teeth), and straight black hair. Andean people are short. In his study of the Quechua Indians of the Cuzco area, Ferris (1916: 80) reported an average height for males of 5 feet 1 inch, with women on average slightly smaller. The ancient Nasca also were short. Allison (1979: 77) states that the height of the people of Nazca has not changed appreciably since pre-Columbian times and that "[m]odern rural inhabitants of mixed blood are still about the same size as their Indian ancestors."

In addition to their somatic features, Nasca people also manipulated their physical appearance through frontal-occipital cranial deformation, which created a skull that was unnaturally elongated and flat across the forehead (see Browne et al. 1993: fig. 11).[1] Nasca people with characteristically deformed skulls are commonly portrayed in ceramic effigies of both sexes (see, for example, de Lavalle 1986: 126, 128 left, 129 top left, right, 183 left middle). The headdresses of the two boys and man on the famous Tello (1931) ceramic plaque show that Nasca headdresses were accommodated to the culturally manipulated form of the head. Cranial deformation was accomplished by binding a cushion to an infant's forehead and a board to the back of the head (Orefici 1993: fig. 133; Weiss 1962: fig. 3, plate ii). Sloan Williams (personal communication, 2000) indicates that frontal-occipital cranial deformation is divided into two types, erect and oblique, which implies the use of different deforming devices.

Although scholars call the practice of skull manipulation "cranial deformation," Weiss (1972: 166) makes the very important

point that "for those who used the cranial bone-altering implements, these were formers, not deformers." Cranial deformation
formed the child into a social being in its own society and permanently marked him/her as such. Nasca cranial deformation is a
dramatic example of the situational manipulation of ethnic identity. As Emberling (1997: 307) has observed, "ethnic groups marked
by (culturally defined) physical characteristics would be the least
flexible of all." Clearly, Nasca people specifically identified themselves and recognized each other by particular physical attributes,
both permanent (cranial deformation) and impermanent (such as
language and dress which, nevertheless, were characteristic; see
below).

The actual distribution and frequency of cranial deformation in
Nasca society has not been determined but it appears to have been
common (see, for example, Browne et al. 1993; Coehlo 1972;
Silverman 1993a: 220). In Carmichael's (1988: 183) sample of 102
skulls from Nasca burials, 68 percent were artificially modified.
But the fact that the practice was not universal must be significant,
though the significance remains to be determined.

Trephination is the removal of one or more sections of bone
from the cranium while the person is still alive. Trephination is
very well known on skulls attributable to the Paracas Cavernas
and Paracas Necropolis cultures of the Paracas Peninsula, Pisco,
and Ica (see Pezzia 1968: 93–4; Tello 1928: 688–9; Weiss 1953:
14, 1958: 525, plate xvii). Some people died as a result of the
operation. Remarkably, others lived as evidenced by healed bone
(closure). According to Allison and Pezzia (1976), nine skulls in the
Museo Regional de Ica indicate that trephination was practiced by
the ancient Nasca people. However, Sloan Williams, a physical
anthropologist at the University of Illinois–Chicago (UIC), has told
us that she has not seen any evidence of trephination on skulls
recovered by Alfred Louis Kroeber from Nasca sites in the Nazca
region (these remains are curated at the Field Museum of Natural
History in Chicago). Nor has Kathleen Forgey, also at UIC,
observed trephination on skulls in other Nasca collections that
she has studied. Helaine Silverman is hesitant to assert the existence of trephination among Nasca people. Donald Proulx feels that
trephination was practiced at this time. Further study will resolve
this issue.

Language and Cognition

Information about the aboriginal languages of south coastal Peru is recoverable to a certain time depth through information contained in Spanish documents and by linguistic reconstruction, toponymy (the study of place names), and patronymy (the study of personal surnames). However, it is important to bear in mind that the Nasca language cannot be directly recovered in the archaeological record because the ancient Nasca did not write and the ethnically Nasca people had disappeared hundreds of years before the Spanish arrived on the scene (see chapter 11), though it is possible that their language could have continued.

Linguistic reconstruction can provide important insights into the past which fieldwork has the possibility of testing through the use of other markers of social identity such as pottery and architectural style, as well as food preference and burial pattern, among others. On the other hand, there is not a one-to-one correlation between language and ethnicity and we must not necessarily assume that linguistic variation correlates positively with variation in material culture. Nor can we assume that the language(s) spoken on the south coast at the time of the Spanish Conquest were spoken a thousand years earlier or with the same distribution. We also need to be aware of the precariousness of glottochronological dates and the fact that there are changes in the meanings of words. There also has been long-term toponymic change so we must avoid picking and choosing place names.

Nevertheless, a plausible linguistic reconstruction for Nasca can be suggested. Max Uhle, who began his career in philology, recognized two language strata in Ica.

> The older geographic names in the valley of Ica and lower down on the river belong, so far as we can see, to at least two different languages. One of these is Quechua, the other older. We count among geographical terms of Quechua provenience the following: Chirana, Huacachina, Chulpaca, Tinguina (?), Comatrana (?), Callanga (?). Among those of an older origin would be: Ica, Lujaraca, Tajaraca, Ocucaje, Oyujaya, Cachiche, Tate. (Uhle 1924: 130–1)

Subsequently, Tello and Mejía Xesspe (1979: ch. 2) gave extended treatment to the indigenous languages of the south coast.

Like Uhle, they also recognized the existence of pre-existing non-Quechua languages on the south coast, specifically "Akaro" which corresponds to Kauki and Jaqaru (Tello and Mejía Xesspe 1979: 8, 29). They speculated that Akaro was the language of the Paracas, Nasca, and Chincha cultures (Tello and Mejía Xesspe 1979: 10, 12).

We believe that the older language of Ica was, indeed, a member of the Jaqi/Aru language family (see Hardman de Bautista 1978; Torero 1975). Jaqi/Aru languages were spoken in the South Andes and extended north into the highlands of the valleys of the Department of Ica and in Ayacucho almost up to the border with Huancavelica. What remains to be explained is why there are no pre-Quechua place names in the Río Grande de Nazca drainage (or none of which we are aware) whereas they exist in Ica.

The suggestion that Paracas/Nasca peoples spoke an Aru language, of which Aymara in the southern highlands is a relative, is particularly appealing because of the similarities Chávez and Chávez (1975) have shown between the altiplano's Yaya-Mama Tradition and Paracas pottery of Ica and the ceramic parallels noted by Rowe (1971) between Pucara and Nasca 1. Interestingly, too, Weiss (1953: 16) states that the "Paracas cranial deformations – although by their form members of the coastal group – by the devices that produced them must be grouped with the annular types used by the Aymara in the highlands."

The existence of surface and subsurface water resources in the Río Grande de Nazca drainage and Ica Valley (see chapter 3) should have implicated a vocabulary of spatial terms, probably involving concepts such as: at, near, far and very far from the surface; located to a certain direction of something else; moving slowly or fast, steadily or intermittently; straight and curving; upriver and downriver; on the horizon; fractured terrain and unbroken flat plain; and so on. These terms would have had to have been an integral, inextricably linked component of the Nasca cultural-cognitive system and absolute geographical world.

Nasca Dress

Dress in the Andes was the paramount ethnic signifier (Rodman 1992: 318). The characteristic clothing and ornaments worn by the

Nasca can be reconstructed from iconographic representations on their pottery (see, for example, Tello's modeled scene) and from artifacts (for example, Horié 1990–1; Rowe 1990–1). O'Neale (1937) has described in detail distinct Early Nasca garment types and associated accessories as these are known from Kroeber's excavations. These items of dress included mantles, tunics, turbans and turban bands, headcloths, headbands, loincloths, slings, pads, and fringes. Although most people probably went barefoot, leather sandals have been found in some Nasca cemeteries.

Attributes of Sex and Gender

The representation of genitalia and breasts only appear on naked figurines in Nasca art (see, for example, Lothrop and Mahler 1957: plates viii, ix). The iconographic identification of the sex of an individual can also be based on secondary evidence such as clothing, hair style, and occupation. But in some cases it is impossible to ascertain.

Depictions of women are absent in Nasca ceramic art until phase 5 when they suddenly become a major theme. Nasca women wore their hair longer than men, either braided or loose; they are portrayed with long tresses reaching midway down the back, while in the front the hair frames the face and falls part way down the breast on either side with bangs over the forehead. Sometimes women adorned their hair with feathers or gold plumes. The main item of clothing worn by females is an ankle-length mantle, which is most often shown wrapped around the body, sometimes fastened with a pin. When drawn on a ceramic vessel, these mantles served as the background for mythical creatures who are drawn on top of them. Beneath the mantles women seem to have worn a long tunic, probably consisting of two rectangles of cloth sewn together to form the tubular garment. The major difference between male and female tunics is the length, with some of the later female examples extending to the ankles. Headcloths were sometimes used.

Although females may be depicted with facial painting or tattoos, the majority are not. On the other hand, women commonly display tattoos on their arms, and, especially in the case of Nasca 5 and late Nasca figurines, on their thighs, buttocks, and surrounding the genital area (see figure 2.7). Most of these tattoos are of

Figure 4.1   Nasca male with moustache and goatee; note decapitated human heads (*photo*: Helaine Silverman).

supernatural themes such as killer whales and rayed faces. Actual tattoos have been preserved on the arms of mummified bodies found in Nasca tombs.

Nasca men wore a loincloth (see de Lavalle 1986: 164 bottom) and tunics with a vertical neck slit and vertical slits for the arms (see de Lavalle 1986: 115; Rickenbach 1999: color plate 155). Ordinary tunics were made of plainweave cloth with single-color sections of blue, gold, grey, green, pink, and red. Men used turbans which they held in place with headbands and/or their slings (see Rickenbach 1999: color plate 152). Sometimes they wore headcloths over these. Farmers wore conical hats which were stitched up the front side (see Rickenbach 1999: color plates 185, 186). Men's hair could be short or long and braided. Ceramic representations suggest that males used a wide variety of painted or tattooed facial designs, especially among warriors. Although body hair was usually sparse on Native Americans, some Nasca men are portrayed with thin moustaches and/or goatees (figure 4.1). Males have a much wider range of headgear than females, apparently reflecting the occupation of the wearer as warrior, farmer, fisherman, or shaman. Tassels, feathers, and other appendages are often attached to these headpieces. Fancy dress for men included "elaborate ensembles of broad collar, sleeved shirts, and fancy skirts" (Sawyer 1979: 137). Men wore necklaces composed of rectangular pieces of Spondylus shell, gold earrings, gold mouthmasks, gold forehead ornaments, and feline or fox headdresses. Colored bird feathers or gold plumes sometimes were incorporated into headdresses. These items of clothing were symbols of religious deference and ritual authority.

Both men and women wore earrings, square or rectangular in shape, sometimes made of Spondylus shell, and attached to the ear lobes with loops of string.[2] Other shell jewelry is known (de Lavalle 1986: 129 right; Proulx 1996: plate 20; Richardson 1994: 97; Silverman 1993a: figs 19.1, 19.2) but, overall, jewelry is rare.

Early Nasca Textile Tradition

There was an early Nasca textile tradition, elements of which may have begun as early as Nasca 1, particularly as seen in the three-dimensional borders attached to plain cotton cloths (for example,

Sawyer 1975: fig. 124). The early Nasca textile tradition is comprised of painted cotton textiles, plainweave cotton ground cloths to
which three-dimensional cross-knit looped tabs and pendant figures
are attached, so-called "flounces" and borders of cross-knit looped
bands with structurally attached tabs and three-dimensional figures,
and embroidered textiles. Other kinds of Early Nasca decorated
textiles are known (see O'Neale 1937; Orefici 1993: figs 33–5;
Phipps 1989; Silverman 1993a: ch. 18). Sawyer (1997) identifies an
elaborate Nasca 2 needlework textile style. Fancy Nasca 3 textiles
seem to be rare and most Nasca 3 textile iconography appears
simple (for example, O'Neale 1937: plate lviii) compared to that
decorating pottery.

Nasca Pottery Tradition

As previously indicated, the Nasca pottery tradition evolved out of
antecedent Paracas. The two traditions are distinguished on the
basis of the notable substitution of pre-fire slip painting for the
earlier post-fire resin painting.

Interestingly, Nasca potters conceived of the vessel surface in
a manner totally unlike the "child's coloring book" conception
in our own society. Rather than filling in color within an outline,
the Nasca potter applied color to areas and subsequently outlined
these colored areas with a black line thereby creating a crisp image.
We regard this feature as a key element of Nasca cognition as well
as ceramic technology. Perhaps the artist wanted to avoid bleeding
of colors from the wet medium of slip (a pigment suspended in a
clay solution) prior to the first firing: application of slip within a
slip outline would result in dissolution of the fine line border.
Alternatively, subsequent outlining of areas of color may have
permitted correction of minor errors that occurred as the slip
pigment was applied. This painting process is confirmed in an
unfinished bowl in the collections of the Krannert Art Museum at
the University of Illinois (Sawyer 1975: fig. 136).

Nasca Musical Tradition

Panpipes, drums, and trumpets made of clay were a key element
of ritual and Nasca cultural identity (see discussion of musical

instruments in chapters 6 and 8). Nasca music has been studied by Bolaños (1988), Haeberli (1979), and Rossel Castro (1977: ch. 11) among others. We know what sounds could be physically produced on these instruments but not, of course, how they were arranged into compositions.

Headhunting

The taking and subsequent manipulation of the human head was a very important Nasca custom (see chapters 9 and 10). The trophy head is a major element of Nasca iconography (see, for example, Blasco Bosqued and Ramos Gómez 1991; Proulx 1971; Tello 1918) and actual trophy heads are very well known in the archaeological record (see, for example, Browne et al. 1993; Coehlo 1972; Silverman 1993a: ch. 15). The characteristic manner of head preparation makes these objects unambiguously identifiable as Nasca (see Silverman 1993a: figs 15.1, 15.2). The issue, of course, is whether these heads had corresponded to Nasca people in life.

All trophy heads found in Nasca archaeological contexts are treated identically. There is a large hole in the foramen magnum at the base of the skull in order to remove the brain (see Browne et al. 1993: fig. 13). There is a small hole in the frontal bone (see Browne et al. 1993: fig. 12) in order pass through the carrying cord which can be tied around a piece of wood on the interior of the skull (figure 4.2). Where conditions of preservation are good and the flesh is preserved, the lips are sealed with cactus spines (Silverman 1993a: figs 15.1, 15.2). The scalp may exhibit deliberate cut marks. The jaws are lashed together (figure 4.2). The cheeks and eye sockets may be stuffed with cotton. When cranial deformation is present, it is Nasca in style (Verano 1995: 218; see Browne et al. 1993: fig. 11), presumably marking the identity of the decapitated individuals as Nasca.

Geoglyphs

Although other Andean people, including other south-coast people, are known to have made geoglyphs, no ancient society did so with the intensity of the Nasca. Geoglyph-making must be considered a key arena of Nasca self-expression. We discuss geoglyphs at length in chapter 7.

Figure 4.2   Nasca trophy head showing carrying cord tied around a crosspiece of wood inside the head (Feature 21 at Cahuachi; see Silverman 1993a: 220). The mandibles are lashed together and the cheeks are stuffed with cotton cloth. Note the enlarged foramen magnum.

Spatial Parameters of Nasca Cultural Identity

In the preceding sections of this chapter we have suggested those material features – recoverable and not – that define Nasca cultural identity. We define the Nasca heartland as the Río Grande de Nazca drainage because no other Early Intermediate Period (EIP) style competes with Nasca and Nasca is the sole style and already quite complex in Nasca 1 times (e.g., Strong 1957: fig. 10). But what about the Ica Valley where the Nasca style was first identified?

All phases of Nasca pottery are also found in the Ica Valley (see Menzel 1971; Menzel et al. 1964; Pezzia 1968; Proulx 1968; Williams León and Pazos Rivera 1974). However, there is Topará influence and, possibly, actual Topará pottery, corresponding to the Chongos phase during EIP 1 (for example, Sawyer 1966: 96) and the Campana phase during EIP 2 (see Massey 1986, 1992). But Nasca 1 and 2 pottery, devoid of Topará influence and developed from local Paracas antecedents, is well known and well represented in Ica. Ica's Nasca 3 pottery is fully Nasca with shapes and design themes almost identical to those of the Río Grande de Nazca drainage (Proulx 1968). Nevertheless, Proulx (1968: 96) argues that there was an initial stimulus from Nazca-Nasca in EIP 3 because prior to this time slip-painted pottery was rare in Ica; this is a point for further fieldwork and study. From Nasca 3 times on, there is no doubt about the exclusivity and florescence of Nasca pottery in Ica.

One of the pressing issues in Andean archaeology is definition of the geographical extent of the Nasca cultural identity beyond Ica and its political correlates. In this section we critically examine the data for the presence of Nasca remains to the north (Paracas Peninsula, the Pisco, Chincha, and Cañete valleys, and valleys further north), south (Acarí and valleys further south) and east (the highlands) of the Nasca heartland. We will show that to the north and south of Ica–Nazca there is a dropping off of Nasca pottery in terms of quantity, diversity, and exclusivity. The data show a clinal distribution of the Nasca pottery style on the south coast and into the far south coast and central coast (figure 4.3). Societies interacting with Nasca from either side of its core territory were markedly different from Nasca and from each other (see figure 4.4 for the locations of the coastal valleys of Peru referred to in the following sections).

The issue of Nasca remains at Paracas Peninsula sites

Textiles from the several burial grounds at the neck of the Paracas Peninsula that were excavated by Tello (1959; Tello and Mejía

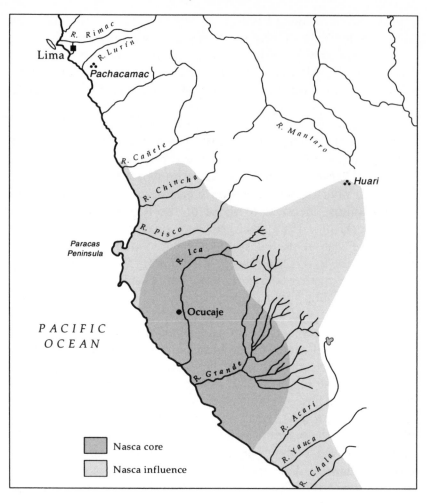

Figure 4.3 The Nasca core and periphery in terms of the distribution and influence of Nasca pottery.

Xesspe 1979 *inter alia*) have been referred to as "Paracas 9," "Paracas 10," "Nasca 1," and "Nasca 2" (see Dwyer 1971; Lanning 1967: 122), implying that there was evolution within a single cultural tradition whose heartland was Ica and Nazca. However, Lanning's (1960) and Wallace's (1986) research on the early pottery styles of the south coast clearly demonstrated that the well-made, thin-walled, oxidized, plain or red-slipped or white-slipped

Figure 4.4   Map of Peru with major coastal valleys indicated.

monochrome pottery that is associated with the spectacularly embroidered and complexly figured polychrome Paracas Necropolis textiles is Topará.

No Nasca pottery was recovered at the Peninsula by Tello (1928: 687; see also Tello 1959; Tello and Mejía Xesspe 1979). Although

Engel (1966: fig. 60 b, c, d; see also Lanning 1960: 465) states that he found Nasca pottery in the Arena Blanca habitation zone, analysis of his material reveals that he mistook Chongos and Carmen materials for Nasca 1 and Nasca 3 respectively.

Nasca remains and Nasca influence in Pisco

To the best of our knowledge, there have been no reports of slip-painted and incised Nasca 1 pottery (Strong's "Cahuachi Polychrome Incised Thick" and "Cahuachi Polychrome Incised and Modeled Thin" types) in Pisco. This is very important because this is the ware that carried complex Nasca iconography. However, a group of Nasca 1 concave-sided bowls with sharp basal angles and thin-walled concave bowls without polychrome slip is quite similar to Chongos pottery found with many of the Paracas Necropolis burials (Menzel 1971; compare Wallace 1986: fig. 3 and Silverman 1997: figs 8, 10 to Silverman 1993a: figs 16.5–16.10, 16.34–16.37; see also Strong 1957: figs 7A–E, 9, 10F) and present at sites in Pisco, Chincha, and Cañete (see Silverman 1997: fig. 8; Wallace 1986). As Menzel (1971: 116–18) has indicated, Topará and Nasca 1 peoples must have been in close contact with each other. But the EIP 1 occupation of Pisco is not Nasca; it is Chongos, a Topará phase (see Wallace 1986).

Similarly, the EIP 2 occupation of Pisco is Campana, the final Topará phase (see Menzel 1971: 120–1; Wallace 1986), not Nasca. To the best of our knowledge, Nasca 2 pottery (corresponding to Strong's 1957: fig. 11 "Cahuachi Polychrome" type and to more iconographically complex Nasca 2 material) has not been reported from Pisco, although slight Nasca 2 influence has been rarely observed by Helaine Silverman in pottery from the Alto del Molino site; Peters (1997: 552, fig. 7.43) also reports a sherd from a mound at the same site with a painted design "in a style firmly associated with Nasca 2." These examples may be evidence of the beginning of the end of the Topará ceramic tradition and may indicate a different form of engagement between Topará and Nasca societies than that which characterized these societies in EIP 1. Additionally, it must be noted that in Silverman's (1997: 454) excavations at Alto del Molino, EIP 2/Campana strata were not encountered.

Rather, there was a hiatus in occupation between the sub-*huaca* Chongos occupation and the Carmen occupation of the *huaca*.

Alto del Molino was a splendid Carmen civic-ceremonial center in EIP 3, with several *huacas* and an extensive habitational settlement between them. The site could have been as large as 88 ha. Just the portion of Huaca 2 still preserved (see Silverman 1997: figs 6, 11, 12) reveals architecture as complex as that found at Cahuachi. Huaca 2 was built of massive chambered fill and dedicated, minimally, by four burials. The mound had a monumental central staircase whose passageway originally was painted with fine polychrome murals replicating the designs on Carmen pottery. This staircase led to the summit of the mound on which there was perishable architecture. There was at least one other staircase on the north side of the mound. There were large courts and small rooms. And there are other Carmen mounds at the site waiting to be excavated (if they have not been destroyed).

Furthermore, Alto del Molino was not alone in the Pisco Valley in EIP 3. Minimally, it was contemporary with the large (15 ha but long destroyed) agglutinated habitation site at Dos Palmas further up the valley (see Rowe 1963: plate i), the site that gave the pottery style its local name, and with Wallace's (1971: 82–3) site PV58-2. These sites were located at the neck of the Pisco Valley, probably to control irrigation water to the lower valley. This also was the point at which a route of easy crossing between Pisco and Ica was located.

The EIP 3 Carmen style of Pisco emerged as the synthesis of former Topará canons and Nasca input (see Menzel 1971: 121–4; Rowe 1963: 11; Silverman 1997; Wallace 1971; see illustrations in Engel 1966: 214, 215). After centuries of Topará monochromy, the Carmen style of EIP 3 is considered to mark a strong break from the preceding Topará ceramic tradition. Nasca influence on Pisco's Carmen pottery style is seen in Carmen's pre-fire slipped polychromy (up to eight discrete colors: white, black, red, yellow, purple, brown, orange, and gray), panpipes, double-spout-and-bridge bottles, and certain iconographic motifs (for example, birds, fish, plants). But the Carmen style is highly original in its manner of representation. Complex supernatural iconography is rare in Carmen, at least from the perspective of the Alto del Molino collections, and, when present, it is a reinterpretation of Nasca ideas (see Panion 1997: 46). Thus far, Carmen pottery in Pisco appears to be distributed throughout the valley and the style is homogeneous. Furthermore, "no one group of Carmen ceramics from a specific site appears to be more Nasca than another" (Panion 1997: 48, 49).

Menzel (1971: 121–2) states that the Carmen style of Chincha and Cañete is virtually identical to Pisco's, though with a more restricted design vocabulary (exclusively geometric). Silverman (1997) argues that Pisco is the origin place of the Carmen style because the Pisco variant is more varied than that of Chincha or Cañete. The greater range of Carmen pottery in Pisco is probably due to Pisco's geographical proximity to Nasca populations living in the upper Ica Valley with whom, Silverman (1997: 456) suggests, they were in contact.

Peters (1997) argues that a Nasca 3 state invaded Pisco and put an end to the Paracas Necropolis/Topará tradition. Panion (1997: 48) has considered the possibility of a Nasca colonization in Pisco, among other scenarios offered, based on actual Nasca sherds around Tambo Colorado (see Engel 1957). We acknowledge that it is possible that there were Nasca people resident within the Pisco Valley to judge from pure Nasca 3 gravelots that have been recorded there (see Peters 1997).

However, Helaine Silverman maintains her position (see Silverman 1997) that, despite the lacunae in knowledge about EIP 2 Campana society in Pisco and evidence of Nasca influence on Carmen pottery, Carmen's complexity should not be attributed to a Nasca invasion for Pisco has a long, preceding occupational history with notable cultural complexity, particularly in the Chongos phase. Silverman argues that Carmen society in Pisco was complex and had its own florescence with major civic-ceremonial architecture such as the *huacas* at Alto del Molino (Silverman 1997), and high population levels as evidenced by a florescent settlement pattern and densely agglutinated sites such as Dos Palmas (see Rowe 1963: plate 1; see also Wallace 1971). She believes that it behooves us to understand the endogenous factors in the rise and configuration of Carmen, in addition to Pisco's relationship to Chincha, before looking for outside bearers of civilization.

Silverman proposes that the Carmen–Nasca 3 relationship was one of peer polity interaction:

Pisco's acceptance, adoption and adaptation of Nasca ceramic technology and its embedded ideology may have visibly, pragmatically
signalled Pisco's conscious lessening of its own cultural markers of
social identity . . . so as to facilitate the intersocietal interaction with
Nasca peoples . . . Carmen is not the result of a Nasca conquest of
Pisco . . . and was, instead, an autonomous society (or group of
culturally affiliated societies) in a landscape of similarly complex
polities on the south coast. (Silverman 1997: 455–6)

The relationship between the Carmen and Nasca people must have
been complicated and negotiated. It looks as though Carmen society picked and chose what it wanted from Nasca. The full context
and nature of Nasca–Carmen interaction remains to be elucidated
through more fieldwork in the upper Ica Valley and throughout the
Pisco Valley.

The Estrella pottery style evolves from Carmen, but with new
iconographic input from Nasca (Menzel 1971; Wallace 1958: 45–
7). Phase 4 of the Estrella sequence has a very tight association with
Nasca 7 trade sherds and Nasca 7 is far more abundant in Pisco
than Nasca 4, 5, and 6 sherds. Menzel (1971: 128) identified
Estrella and Nasca 7 sherds in the same discrete strata in Ica. Nasca
7 pottery in Estrella contexts is identical to Ica Valley Nasca 7.
Only physical-chemical analysis and more fieldwork will be able to
determine if we are dealing with trade pieces, excellent copies, or
the product of colonization. Certainly, the influence of Nasca 7 on
Estrella speaks to enduring ties between the upper valleys of Pisco
and Ica, as suggested earlier, and Menzel (1971: 128) emphasizes
that Estrella and Nasca 7 exerted mutual influence on each other.
But there is no doubt that the two styles represent separate spheres
of sociopolitical integration, albeit with intersocietal contact.

Nasca in Cañete

Kroeber's (1937: plates lxx–3, 4, lxxiii–4, lxxvii–2) discovery of
Nasca 7 trade sherds and a panpipe fragment in a "Middle Cañete"
occupation of the great Cerro del Oro site are still without local
context. At this point it is impossible to say if the sherds arrived
down-the-line, passing first through Pisco and Chincha, or by some
direct contact of which we have no other record.

Nasca and the central coast

Still further north it is interesting to consider that the polychrome
Lima style replaced the arguably Toparoid Miramar style at more
or less the same time or slightly after the Carmen emergence on
the south coast (see Patterson 1966: table 1). Given the previous
episodes of contact between the south coast and central coast (see
Silverman 1996b), it is not unreasonable to suggest that Lima's
polychromy derived from the south. It is well known that Lima
Interlocking motifs subsequently appear on Nasca 5 and 6 pots
(for example, de Lavalle 1986: 165 top right). If and how Lima
Interlocking jumped over Cañete, Chincha, and Pisco remains to
be investigated.

Nasca and the north coast

There is influence of the Moche style on Nasca 7 pottery (see
Proulx 1994). Most of the Nasca 7 pottery with Moche influence
has a provenience in the southern tributaries of the Río Grande de
Nazca drainage. No reciprocal Nasca influence is observable on
Moche pottery. Moche influence is strong enough to suggest that
Nasca potters saw Moche pots up close. No direct terrestrial evidence of contact between the two peoples is known. By virtue of
the distances involved, we assume that Moche (and Lima) contact
with Nasca people was by sea and that Moche contact with Nasca
involved the former's displacement south, rather than vice versa,
because the Moche were proficient mariners and because there is
no evidence of Nasca seafaring. Furthermore, Carmichael's (1991)
littoral survey confirms the inland agricultural orientation of the
Nasca. Except for Moche stylistic influence, other Moche objects
have not been found on the south coast and Nasca objects have not
been found on the north coast (or the central coast for that matter).
The issue of Nasca–Moche contact is all the more perplexing
because Haberland (1958; see Proulx 1994: 93) indicates that the
Moche objects reported to be from guano deposits on the Chincha
Islands (Kubler 1948) actually came from Macabí Island, halfway
between the Chicama and Moche valleys. Contact would not re-
quire the establishment of a settlement, much to the detriment of

later archaeologists. Clearly, more investigation of the Moche–Nasca connection is needed.

Nasca remains in the Acarí Valley

John Rowe (1963: 11–12) proposed that a Nasca 3 state, led from the allegedly urban capital site of Cahuachi, created a small militaristic empire on the south coast of Peru through territorial conquest. He interpreted Tambo Viejo (see Valdez 1998: fig. 3) in the Acarí Valley as a Nasca 3 site unit intrusion, and interpreted Amato, Huarato, and Chocavento as other, smaller, Nasca 3 settlements (see Valdez 1998: fig. 5). For Rowe, the most notable feature of these sites was their "fortification walls" (see Valdez 1998: figs 6–9). He believed that the rapid rise and fall of these Acarí sites were causally attributable to the decline of Cahuachi and the collapse of a short-lived Nasca 3 state.

Recently, Rowe's reconstruction of Acarí has been challenged by Carmichael (1992) and Valdez (1998) on the basis of their new investigations conducted under the auspices of the California Institute for Peruvian Studies (CIPS). Carmichael and Valdez both argue that the Nasca style is limited in occurrence in Acarí. Furthermore, Carmichael (1992: 6) argues that the walls at the alleged Nasca 3 sites lack features typical of defense and that their function at these sites remains open to speculation. Let us review their arguments.

The EIP 1 occupation of the Acarí Valley is poorly known. According to Valdez (1998), it is not Nasca. The EIP 2–3 occupation of Acarí is manifested by a local style called "Huarato" (Valdez 1998).[3] Nasca 2 pottery appears to enter the Acarí Valley at this time but the vehicle for it is not understood. Although there is fine Nasca 3 pottery at several sites in the Acarí Valley (including those originally noted by Rowe), Carmichael (1992) and Valdez (1998) argue that Nasca 3 is not intrusive in Rowe's (1963) sense of an invasion or conquest. Rather, they have determined that Nasca pottery occurs in limited frequency and that Nasca is not the local, indigenous style of Acarí.

There is more Nasca pottery at Tambo Viejo, the largest site in the valley, than at other contemporary Acarí sites. For Valdez (1998), this suggests strongly that that site's residents were the dominant agents of contact with Nasca and that the use or manipulation of Nasca pottery was strategized. He contends that Huarato people had differential access to Nasca pottery which was an exotic and, therefore, valuable good. Valdez (1998: 176–7) argues that access to Nasca pottery could have been gained through direct contact with Nasca people by means of Huarato participation in pilgrimage to Cahuachi during which other esoteric knowledge could have been obtained. But given the absence of complex supernatural iconography in the Nasca 3 corpus from Acarí and given the rarity of panpipes and double-spout-and-bridge bottles in Acarí, we think that other possible scenarios can be suggested to account for early Nasca pottery in the valley without the direct involvement of Huarato people in the Nasca religious cult. These alternative explanations include down-the-line trade and direct trade and exchange. If Huarato people did go to Cahuachi, we think that they were being motivated less by and/or participating differently in the cult celebrated there than were the people of the Río Grande de Nazca drainage. Thus far, there is no ceramic evidence of the presence of Huarato people at Cahuachi and no evidence that Huarato people maintained a temple/shrine at Cahuachi as has been hypothesized for the Río Grande de Nazca people and, possibly, those of Ica (see Silverman 1993a: ch. 22, fig. 16.52).

As indicated above, complex Nasca iconography does not occur in Acarí. Perhaps it was eschewed by the Huarato people because it was incomprehensible to them and/or inaccessible if Nasca pots were made, used, and exchanged among Nasca peoples and Huarato people were excluded from this network because they were not Nasca. Perhaps, instead, Huarato people took advantage of other opportunities presented by the congregation of multitudes at Cahuachi such as being able to establish social ties and exchange or trade their goods for lesser Nasca products such as attractive but simply decorated Nasca bowls and cups used at the ceremonial center. Or perhaps Huarato people did not travel to Cahuachi at all but, rather, to what for them were the outskirts of Nasca territory – Las Trancas – and there engaged in exchange, established and lubricated social ties, and obtained Nasca pottery that was then brought back to Acarí.

As to what the Acarí people could have been trading, perhaps the "what" is not as important as the "why." Nasca people had access to obsidian and maritime products (to name only the most obvious exchange/trade-prone goods documented in the archaeological record) without need of Acarí middlemen. But perhaps the object of long-distance trade was inter-ethnic contact to establish reciprocal ties that could be activated in times of need (including non-subsistence need) and stress (especially climatic) – that is, risk management.[4] A 1692 document cited by Neira Avendaño (1990: 63) says that the Acarí Valley was rich in *lomas* pasturelands for three or four months of the year and that there also were *lomas* between Nazca (i.e. Las Trancas) and Acarí. Such extensive *lomas* might have provided the Acarí people with the ability to care for herds of camelids of vital importance to the Nasca people. Or perhaps people of both valleys met in these intermediate *lomas*, thereby establishing contact and negotiating rights to strategic *lomas* resources.

There is a significant decline in occupation in the Acarí Valley after EIP 3. Only a small amount of Nasca 4 pottery is known, having been recently identified at Coquimbo and Tambo Viejo (Valdez 1998: 119; compare to the earlier statement of Riddell and Valdez 1988: 96). Little is understood about EIP 4 society in Acarí. The nature of EIP 5 society in Acarí is unknown.

EIP 6 is a time of new, although still apparently limited, settlement in the Acarí Valley following the previous abandonment of sites. Some Nasca 6 pottery is said to exist at Gentilar, Cancino, the cemetery at Chaviña, and a cemetery at Tambo Viejo (Riddell and Valdez 1988: 98). The relationship between Nazca-Nasca and Acarí was re-established and reworked or renegotiated in EIP 7. There is major Nasca influence in the Acarí Valley in EIP 7–8 and actual Nasca 7 pottery was found at the rich Chaviña cemetery (Lothrop and Mahler 1957), the Chaviña fishing village (Valdez 1990: 27–8), the inland settlement at Gentilar (Valdez 1989), La Oroya (Salguero Jara 1989), Cancino (Valdez 1989: 30), Tambo Viejo cemetery, and Amato (see summary in Kent and Kowta 1994). However, the Acarí Valley was not subject to Nazca at this time (nor was it in previous times as has been discussed above). There is no evidence of:

any Nazca Valley-based political structure or intervention . . . there is little to suggest any polity organized beyond a local village level. Such villages were few at the time. The only one excavated was Gentilar . . . [which] consisted of some 25–30 quincha houses in no apparent pattern, spread out along a low ridge . . . No evidence exists for a centralized community structure. Nor were there any differences among the houses in terms of size or function. (Kent and Kowta 1994: 120)

Kent and Kowta (1994) have identified a distinct EIP 8 pottery style with strong similarities to Nasca 8/Loro pottery in the Río Grande de Nazca drainage. We think that these Acarí people were in contact with the Nasca people living in the closest valley to the north, Las Trancas, where Huaca del Loro is located.

Nasca remains south of Acarí

Nasca pottery is rare south of Acarí; the valleys of the far south coast have their own independent ceramic styles. Interestingly, though, two of the Nasca pots Max Uhle (1914: 3) saw as a young man working in the Museum für Völkekunde in Berlin were catalogued (VA 7827, VA 10967) as having far south-coast proveniences, from Arica and Chala respectively. If the proveniences are correct, the Arica pot would be the southernmost piece of Nasca pottery. In addition, there are notable similarities between early Nasca cross-knit looped textiles from the Río Grande de Nazca drainage and textiles found in far south-coast valleys.[5] Looters are now flooding the illegal antiquities markets with Nasca-like cross-knit looped textiles from the Ocoña, Majes–Camaná, and Quilca–Sihuas–Vitor valleys.[6] Cross-knit looped textiles may occur as far south as Omo in the Moquegua Valley. In this section we consider the reported Nasca remains in the far south-coast valleys.

In 1972 Máximo Neira Avendaño and Hermann Trimborn conducted excavations at Pampa Taimara, near Chala (Neira Avendaño 1990: 97). The site is located at 200 m above sea level on a *meseta*, about 4 km inland from the sea, above/east of what would later be the extensive Inca ruins at Quebrada de la Vaca. The site's inhabitants would have had access to a tiny area of arable land. Neira Avendaño (1990: 96–9) reports the discovery of Nasca 6, 7, 8/Loro and 9/Chakipampa sherds. The pottery is apparently associated with five refuse mounds that are attributed to Nasca rather than a local culture. The archaeological deposit is said to have been "*revuelto*" or mixed up without an orderly stratification, possibly explaining the association of multiple phases of Nasca pottery.

While in Nazca recently, Proulx was shown two Nasca 7 pots which are said to have an Ocoña Valley provenience. Ocoña is immediately north of Camaná.

In 1965–6 Disselhoff (1969) excavated 135 burials at the Cabezas Achatadas ("flattened heads") cemetery in Camaná, at the mouth of the Majes River, some 300 km south of Nazca. Disselhoff's burials included three headless mummies and what he described as a trophy head. In addition, Disselhoff (1969: 390) speculated that the style of cranial deformation at the cemetery could relate to Nasca or be "a fashion of the time." Disselhoff also recovered various examples of superb, richly colored, cross-knit looping. There are bean-shaped tabs and fringed borders in the form of human figures and trophy heads (see color illustrations in Sawyer 1997: figs 127, 128, 130). These bear an incontrovertibly close relationship to materials from the Nasca heartland, including textile fragments that have been excavated at Cahuachi (see, for example, Silverman 1993a: figs 18.5–18.11, 18.13; see also O'Neale 1937: plate lxi, lxii; Phipps 1989: 673, 674, 684, 688, 693, 707 *inter alia*). Disselhoff also recovered an embroidered textile with birds that alternate in vertical orientation and are clearly Nasca-like (compare to O'Neale 1937: plate xliiie, lviic, lxiif, h). He was perplexed by the "absence of any genuine Nasca ceramics at the same time that there is an abundance of fine polychrome textiles" (Disselhoff 1969: 390). According to Proulx, Disselhoff did not realize that his figure 4a was indeed an early Nasca-style vessel (a collared jar with a series of step-frets painted below the broken collar), though the quality of the painting is not up to classic Nasca standards.

The distance involved between Camaná and the Río Grande de Nazca drainage and the apparent leap-frogging over Acarí are perplexing. Two explanations can be proposed for Disselhoff's textile materials: either far south-coast people invented the cross-knit looping technique and its iconography which they somehow diffused north to Nasca territory where these textiles evolved, or the technique and iconography diffused southward, possibly skipping the intervening valleys. Disselhoff (1969: 389) himself regarded his textile remains as less accomplished than their Nasca cohort and concluded that they had been made locally. Joerg Haeberli (personal communication, 2000) emphasizes that cross-knit looping is already present on the far south coast in his Siguas 1 phase dating to the late Early Horizon. Furthermore, for Haeberli, "the numbers alone of textiles in discontinuous double interlocking warp and weft between Siguas 1 (many, complex) and the south coast (few) suggest a flow northward." But, as Haeberli recognizes and advocates, more data are need.

Recently, Donald Proulx had the opportunity to study slides of material observed by Joerg Haeberli at the La Chimba cemetery in the Sihuas[7] Valley, immediately south of Camaná. Proulx identifies one fragmented bowl as Nasca 3 in style and shape, though unique in iconography. He concludes that this piece may be a locally made imitation of true Nasca ware. In addition, three effigy vessels, said to come from the Sihuas Valley, date to Phase 3 in the Nasca ceramic sequence. Two of the three pots depict farmers, their heads covered with traditional white hoods and flaps extending down the back. Their faces are painted with multi-colored spots as may have been the Nasca custom during harvest festivals. In their hands they hold various plants. The third effigy vessel portrays a male, possibly a warrior, whose head is wrapped with multiple slings that extend down the back. Proulx's analysis suggests that one of the effigy farmers is a local imitation because of a number of unusual traits in addition to the standard Nasca ones. The other farmer effigy could well be a trade piece; analysis of the vessel's paste will be critical in determining its point of origin. The male warrior has enough unusual elements to argue for a local manufacture in Sihuas.

Joerg Haeberli has photographed another seven Nasca-style vessels said to have a Sihuas region provenience. Three of the vessels are Nasca 3 trade pieces: one double-spout-and-bridge bottle and two bowls. There is also a Nasca 5 or 6 proliferous bowl with unusual aspects suggesting local manufacture in Sihuas, a Nasca 6 vessel with an unusual modeled house on the top portion also suggesting local manufacture, a unique Nasca 6 or 7 human effigy vessel, and a Nasca 7 goblet that could well be an import from the Nasca heartland.

Yet further south, Goldstein (2000: 347) has recorded fragments of a Nasca flaring bowl from a site in the Moquegua Valley. The pottery was found in association with Pucara pottery. Goldstein (2000: 354, fig. 15) also has found early Nasca-style textile fragments at several Moquegua habitation sites and cemeteries, also in association with Pucara textiles in the same habitation sites and cemeteries.

The prehistory of the poorly known far south-coast valleys constitutes an exciting research agenda in and of itself. Determination of the nature, context, direction, and mobilization of Nasca–far-south-coast interaction make it even more exciting. Certainly the abundance of Nasca-like textiles and the rarity of Nasca and Nasca-related pottery suggests that textiles were easier to transport – but for what reason? At this point it appears that exotic elements were likely status or prestige items for elite members of local communities. Down-the-line trade without direct inter-ethnic contact, direct contact between Nasca and far south-coast peoples, and actual Nasca colonies on the far south coast all have to be considered, bearing in mind that the scenario appears to vary over time.

Nasca and the highlands

There was some kind of interaction between Nasca people and those living in the highlands to the east. Schreiber (1992: 139, 227) reports rare examples of Nasca ("especially Nasca phase 4") potsherds in the Carhuarazo Valley. Lidio Valdez (personal communication, 2000) has generously informed us that some hundred fragments of Nasca 4–6 pottery have been found by a colleague of his during excavations as Viscapalca, at the headwaters of the Pampas River, in the puna! This sample of Nasca pottery is actually greater in number than that which Valdez knows from Acarí.

Paulsen (1983) and Knobloch (1983: 289–316) argue vigorously that there was significant contact between Nasca 7 society and Huarpa people of highland Ayacucho based on certain ceramic iconography. Knobloch (1983) has identified specific Nasca 7 features on Huarpa pottery of Ayacucho: Nasca 7 spirals, hooks, and dots appeared on Huarpa 2 pottery and Nasca red was adopted by Huarpa 3 potters to create polychrome, whereas earlier Huarpa pottery was a black and white bichrome style (see Paulsen 1983; compare, for example, Benavides Calle 1971: plate 6a, and de Lavalle 1986: 168 bottom left/top panel). Nasca 7 pottery also received or adopted ceramic traits from the Huarpa culture of Ayacucho: background stippling of design areas, a shift from white to darker backgrounds (red or black), black line spirals attached to vertical bars, and special patterns of zigzag lines (see Knobloch 1983; Paulsen 1983). Minor elements in each style are involved and the connection appears to be one of mutual influence.

People Again

One of the key issues in contemporary archaeology is the recognition of cultural identity in the material record. This topic began its modern iteration with the foundational volumes edited by Shennan (1989) and Conkey and Hastorf (1990), the latter including revisions of several previously published important articles on style and ethnicity (see Sackett 1990; Wiessner 1990). Over the past decade the archaeological literature on ethnicity has mushroomed, with major contributions by Emberling (1997), Jones (1997), and Stark (1998) to name only the most obvious. All of the current literature ultimately traces its intellectual lineage to Barth's (1969) influential work on ethnic groups and boundaries. Indeed, Emberling (1997: 295) notes that some anthropologists speak of the study of ethnicity in terms of a BB (before Barth) and AB (after Barth) divide.

   In this chapter we have situated ourselves in the AB period. We have considered the first two of four identifiable aspects of ethnogenesis: the origin and maintenance of an ethnic group; the final two aspects, transformation and disappearance, are considered in chapter 11. We have argued that the Nasca actively constituted themselves as such through a specific material culture and its associated social, technological, and ideological behavior. All too often archaeologists talk about the distribution and diffusion of material traits, particularly ceramic ones, as if pots walked of their own accord. We have emphasized Nasca intersocietal interaction as this was facilitated or inhibited by particular markers of Nasca cultural identity. It is in this context that we return to Michael

Moseley's formulation of corporate styles, mentioned in chapter 1. We are in agreement with Moseley (1992: 74) who indicates that the "corporate styles generally spread as far as their supporting reciprocity systems reached." And we note Moseley's (1992: 74) important warning that:

> stylistic unity at the corporate level had little relation to ethnic homogeneity or cultural cohesion at the folk level . . . change in corporate style and replacement of one by another did not necessarily reflect population change or the replacement of one ethnic group or cultural group by another. Conservative folk styles were more sensitive indicators of population dynamics, but these traditions also changed without entailing ethnic change.

Clearly, a challenge for Nasca archaeologists now and in the near future is to determine the relationship between pottery style and cultural identity. Provenience sourcing and iconographic distribution studies of Nasca pottery, combined with the analysis of other aspects of material culture, will enable us to refine our current largely monolithic understanding of the Nasca people.

5

The Inhabited Landscape

In 1953 Gordon R. Willey published *Prehistoric Settlement Patterns in the Virú Valley, Peru*, a book that remains, after almost fifty years, one of the landmarks in the history of archaeology. In that classic work Willey explicitly detailed and exemplified the concept and field strategy that enabled him to trace some three thousand years of cultural development in one particular valley on Peru's north coast. Willey's guiding framework was "settlement patterns," defined by him as "the way in which man disposed himself over the landscape on which he lived" (Willey 1953: 1). Willey argued that settlement patterns are the most profitable approach to understanding the "structure and function of ancient societies" because they reflect "community life . . . the natural environment, the level of technology on which the builders operated, the various institutions of social interaction and control which the culture maintained . . . [They are] directly shaped by widely held cultural needs" (Willey 1953: 1). Generations of archaeologists around the world have followed Willey's model, using settlement patterns to interpret social, political, economic, ritual, and environmental organization, particularly when supplemented by excavations at a range of sites, from the level of household to grand pyramid.

In this chapter we consider the sites of the ancient Nasca people as these have been revealed by various surveys and excavation projects. We begin with Cahuachi, the greatest of the Nasca sites, and go on to consider the other ceremonial centers, settlements, and cemeteries that comprised the inhabited world of the ancient Nasca (figure 5.1). We then analyze these data diachronically

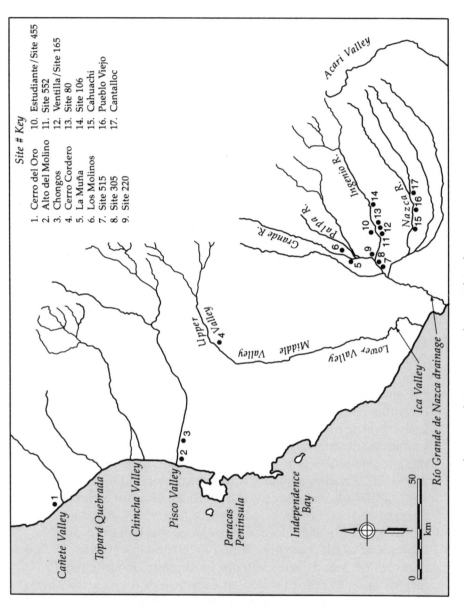

Figure 5.1 Location of principal Nasca sites discussed in the text.

Site # Key

1. Cerro del Oro
2. Alto del Molino
3. Chongos
4. Cerro Cordero
5. La Muña
6. Los Molinos
7. Site 515
8. Site 305
9. Site 220
10. Estudiante/Site 455
11. Site 552
12. Ventilla/Site 165
13. Site 80
14. Site 106
15. Cahuachi
16. Pueblo Viejo
17. Cantalloc

so as to trace the changes that occurred in Nasca settlement over time.

Cahuachi

Cahuachi is located on the south bank of the Nazca River, in a narrow section of the valley at approximately 365 m above sea level, at a point where subterranean water emerges to the surface. Cahuachi extends in length for some 2 km and covers approximately 150 ha. The site is elaborated over a series of brown, barren, hill-covered river terraces just above the valley floor and beneath the Pampa de Atarco (Silverman 1993a: fig. 5.2). Millenniums of wind erosion have flattened the tops of the hills and eroded their sedimentary strata, thereby giving the hills a naturally truncated, pyramidal appearance. These hills form the core of the majority of artificial constructions at the site (see Silverman 1993a: figs 5.2, 5.4–5.6, 5.8–5.10, 5.13, 5.19, 5.20, 5.24, 5.26, 5.27, 5.30, 5.31). Cahuachi's mounds face north to the Pampa, where the greatest concentration of geoglyphs is located. One of the great trans-Pampa lines runs between Cahuachi and the Ingenio Valley (see Silverman 1990a: fig. 2). Several lines in a geoglyph complex on the Pampa de Atarco, behind Cahuachi, point directly at the site's major architectural features (Silverman 1993a: fig. 22.2).

Cahuachi has been known in the archaeological literature since early this century but only Alfred Louis Kroeber, alone among the early investigators, perceived the spatial and temporal extent of Cahuachi, the unusual nature of Cahuachi's monumentality, and the site's uniqueness in Nasca society (see Kroeber and Collier 1998: 75). Kroeber's understanding of the site on the basis of his 1926 fieldwork was confirmed by William Duncan Strong's 1952 project.

Rowe (1963) canonized Cahuachi in the literature as a key example of south-coast urbanism. But Silverman's (1988a, 1993a) excavations found little evidence in support of Strong's (1957) identification of house mounds at Cahuachi or Rowe's assessment of the site as urban. Missing from the archaeological record at Cahuachi in Strong's, Orefici's and Silverman's excavations are extensive zones of dense, permanent habitation and quotidian activity areas corresponding to epoch 3 of the Early Intermediate Period, Cahuachi's apogee. Furthermore, the deposits identified by Strong and accepted by others as stratified midden appear to be construction fills used for creating volumetric, non-residential, ceremonial mounds. Strong did, however, discover a Nasca 1 habitation locus and a probable Nasca 2 textile-working district. Therefore, archaeologists need to elucidate what caused the atrophy of Cahuachi's early domestic activities in favor of the hyperdevelopment of its ceremonial aspects to the point that, by epoch 3 of the Early Intermediate Period, Cahuachi had become the greatest Nasca ceremonial center with apparently few permanent residents (for example, as opposed to the processes of urban growth around ceremonial foci described by Wheatley 1971).

Approximately forty mounds occupy only some 25 ha of the estimated 150 ha of Cahuachi (figure 5.2). However, the non-volumetric or "open space" between Cahuachi's mounds is carefully constructed. The site is formed by a pervasive and repetitive pattern of modified natural hills (the semi-artificial mounds) in direct association with naturally and artificially bounded open spaces (three-sided and four-sided enclosures or *kanchas*) that extend over the site (Silverman 1993a: ch. 6). This is the mound-and-*kancha* pattern. Silverman (1990b, 1993a) argues that the large ground-level plazas were places of congregation. She explains the lack of standardization in the mounds at Cahuachi as the result of their construction by discrete social groups in accordance with the amount of labor available to them, in addition to those mounds at the site's center – the central acropolis – that appear to have been the focus of pan-Nasca devotion and expressive ritual.

Based on the material evidence revealed by survey and excavation at the site and the comparison of these patterns with the remains generated during a modern Catholic pilgrimage at a sanctuary in Ica, Silverman (1990b, 1993a, 1994b) concludes that during its Nasca 3 apogee Cahuachi functioned as an empty ceremonial center. She suggests that Cahuachi's mounds were built and modified during pilgrimage episodes by the different social groups constituting the Nasca nation and that the ritual objects and domestic materials within the construction fills (ceramic plugs, possible spindle whorls, and other textile-related implements, plain gourds, plainweave textiles, miscellaneous threads and cords, plant

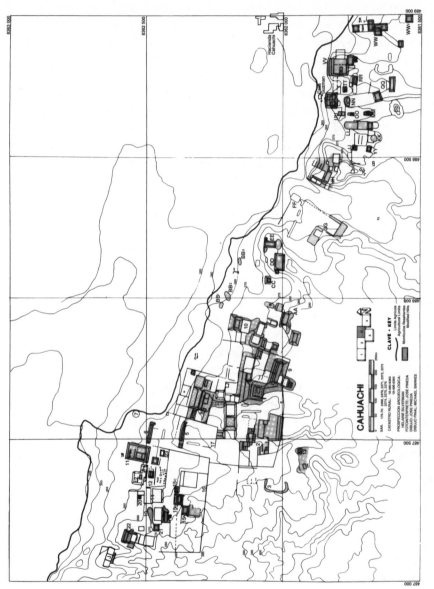

Figure 5.2   The central and eastern zones of Cahuachi.

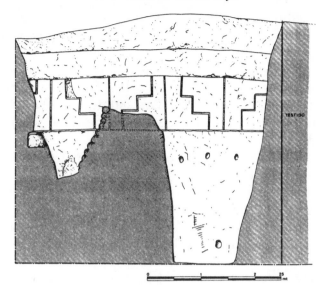

Figure 5.3   The north face of the Step-fret Temple on Unit 10 at
Cahuachi (Orefici 1988: 201).

and malachological remains, and so on) were generated during
frequent pilgrimage episodes and festive occasions at the site, during which time they were swept up to be included in the fills as
well as being deliberately placed (Silverman 1988a, 1990b, 1993a,
1994b). Some mounds, such as Strong's Great Temple, were Nasca-
inclusive temples, whereas others were maintained by particular
social groups (perhaps *ayllus*: see Silverman 1990b, 1993a: 309–
12). She proposes that one small mound, called Unit 19, is such an
"*ayllu*-maintained" mound with its own temple (the Room of the
Posts) and related special purpose areas, including burial chambers
(see Silverman 1993a: chs 12, 13). Because the size of recovered
plainware vessels far exceeds the needs of single families for cooking and storage, Silverman suggests their use in supra-family feasting (see Silverman 1993a: figs 16.25–16.28, 16.30).

Silverman's determination that Cahuachi was not an urban site
is supported by Giuseppe Orefici's seventeen years of excavation at
the site which further demonstrate its hyperceremonial nature. For
example, Orefici (1987: cover; figure 5.3) has discovered a "Step-
fret Temple" (so-called because of a mud frieze decorating its north

face). Dated to Nasca 1, this is the earliest ceremonial structure thus far identified at Cahuachi; surely there are other Nasca 1 ceremonial constructions waiting to be unearthed. The Step-fret Temple shows that Cahuachi was a sacred site from its earliest Nasca occupation. This, of course, raises the question of the factors at play in the seemingly dramatic shift from the Early Horizon (Tajo and/or Paracas) to Nasca 1 social formation (see Silverman 1991, 1994a).

On the floor of one of the agglutinated rooms on the north-east side of Strong's Great Temple (Unit 2), Orefici discovered a cache of hundreds of broken panpipes (personal communication; see *Life Magazine*, December 1999, pp. 96–7). These rooms may have stored the ritual paraphernalia used in ceremonies as well as been facilities for the curation of damaged and obsolete symbolically charged objects. Strong (1957: 31) already had recovered ritual paraphernalia from the Great Temple, including fine pottery, colored feathers, and llama remains suggestive of sacrifice and feasting. Silverman's (1993a: chs 16–21) small-scale excavations also produced a bounty of ritual paraphernalia, including hundreds of panpipe fragments, pyro-engraved gourds, elaborate textile fragments, offerings of feathers and shell, offerings of maize, caches of petrified wood and huarango fruit, a stone vase fragment, and various other items.

Orefici also excavated the burial of more than sixty sacrificed llamas in an area immediately south-east of Unit 19, and he has recovered the remains of at least 154 adult and sixty-five young camelids in construction fill in ceremonial mounds (see Valdez 1988). The animals appear to have been sacrificed and consumed in ceremonial episodes (Valdez 1988: 34, 1994: 677). Silverman (1993a: 199, 202, fig. 14.16) excavated a llama burial (Burial 10) on Unit 19, though it dates to after Cahuachi's Nasca 3 apogee. A llama leg was recovered from one of the deep prepared cylindrical shafts on Unit 12B, presumably the remains of a sacrifice (Silverman 1993a: 68).

Although Valdez (1988) reports the remains of only three guineapigs in his analysis of Orefici's faunal material, clearly guinea-pig was a ceremonial food and ritual offering at Cahuachi (see Silverman 1993a: 168). Valdez (1994) identifies a *pachamanka* (earth oven) at Cahuachi. The stone-and-mud-lined pit contained corn, beans, sweet potatoes, manioc, achira, jíquima, ají, and camelid bones, all resting on achira leaves below which were charcoal and wood. This context is also highly suggestive of ceremonial feasting of the kind that would occur at a ceremonial center and pilgrimage place. Few vessels appropriate for food storage are reported. This suggests only a limited need to store large quantities of food for long periods at Cahuachi. This, too, supports the pilgrimage model of the site.

On Unit 10, Orefici has uncovered a maze of rooms and corridors, with repeated architectural modifications (accesses blocked, rooms filled in). The architecture of Unit 10 is much like Unit 19, a mound that is empirically demonstrated to be ceremonial rather than domestic in nature (see Silverman 1993a: chs 12, 13).

Cahuachi's hyperceremonial nature is also demonstrated by its unusually high proportion of iconographically elaborate pottery (Silverman 1993a: tables 16.1–16.4). Interestingly, though, other than Strong's textile-working area, neither Orefici nor Silverman has evidence of major craft activity at the site. Although Orefici (1987: 7) reports finding an oven which he associates with ceramic production, he has not yet found any firing areas or wasters. His other evidence for the potter's craft consists of pigments and fine-haired paintbrushes (Orefici 1993: fig. 119, see also fig. 118). Silverman (1993a: figs 19.4–19.10) recovered these same kinds of artifacts in her excavations. Both projects have recovered abundant textile remains as well as artifacts related to textile manufacture (see Orefici 1993: fig. 129, plates 29, 32; Silverman 1993a: figs 19.12–19.15). Yet neither project has found a production locus such as the probable textile-working complex discovered by Strong (1957: 28, fig. 5B, C).

We see, then, that Cahuachi was a large, non-urban site replete with pyramids, temples, plazas, ritual offerings, sacred paraphernalia, and burials. Cahuachi's architectural elaboration constructed sacredness over sacredness. A conjunction of factors explains why Cahuachi is where it is and, concomitantly, what it is. Cahuachi is a site of natural *huacas* and these naturally truncated hills were artificially modified into pyramid mounds. Cahuachi is a place where subsurface water "magically" comes to the surface. And Cahuachi is connected to and on the edge of the Pampa which played an integral ritual role in Nasca society.

Other Nasca Ceremonial Centers

In the literature there are only sketchy mentions of ceremonial sites other than Cahuachi and most of these are quite unimpressive compared to it. Nasca civic-ceremonial sites appear to occur only below 600–700 m above sea level. Schreiber (1999: fig. 11.7) identifies an "Early Nasca platform mound–cemetery complex" at Pueblo Viejo. Kroeber (Kroeber and Collier 1998: 42) recorded the existence of an adobe structure at Ocongalla Zero. At Cantalloc, Kroeber found an early Nasca "cluster of [adobe] walls suggest[ing] a low pyramid . . . the structure was complex and had been much worked over, so that nothing decisive eventuated" (Kroeber and Collier 1998: 71). At Soisongo A, Kroeber recorded:

> two small pyramidal structures . . . The smaller pyramid, or Mound X . . . is an 8-m-sq mass bounded by an adobe wall averaging 1 m or more in height and filled mainly with gravel . . . together with layers of maize straw [*chala*]. The wall was built of wedge-shaped adobes set on their base ends . . . The larger rectangular Mound Y . . . is 20 m east–west by 12 m north–south, plus an 8 × 6-m annex extending out. (Kroeber and Collier 1998: 62)

There are no reports of Nasca civic-ceremonial architecture south of the Nazca Valley except for the Nasca 8/Loro type-site of Huaca del Loro in the Las Trancas Valley.

The architecture at Nasca ceremonial centers shares features of construction. These physical features were key elements of Nasca spatial organization and religious behavior. They are cultural signatures of Nasca, elements of its grammar of the built environment, and crucial diagnostics of the Nasca landscape, indeed, of "Nascaness." The maximal expression of these features occurs at Cahuachi. This supports the identification of Cahuachi as the cumulative and collective representation of the people/social groups who worshiped/paid homage there (see Silverman 1990b, 1993a: 309–12). Among these features are:

- The pervasive terracing of naturally truncated hillsides as an energetically and materially cheap manner of achieving the impression of monumental architecture.

- The common flattening and clearing of hill summits to create special-purpose non-domestic space.
- The frequent association of mounds with patios and plazas on and below them.
- The use of a *chala* (corn husk) fill (sometimes composed of bundles or packets of *chala*) to raise a mound.
- *Chala* fill and other construction fill can contain significant amounts of fancy Nasca pottery and organic remains (see, for example, Kroeber and Collier 1998: 42 for Ocongalla Zero, also Cax; compare to Silverman 1993a: figs 4.7, 4.8, 5.15, 5.28).
- The occasional use of *huarango* posts placed at intervals in *chala* fill (a feature which Silverman [1993a: 65, fig. 5.11] has explained as structural support to disperse the weight of the fill).

Some of the early Nasca civic-ceremonial sites in the drainage have associated domestic occupations whose residential area varies in size from small to substantial. In addition, Nasca civic-ceremonial sites were desirable places for burial. For instance, early Nasca burials were placed in and around the Cantalloc complex. We know from Cahuachi that burials at a ceremonial center could be earlier than, contemporary with, and later than the civic-ceremonial foci (see Silverman 1993a).

Nasca Village Sites

Despite his extensive fieldwork in the Río Grande de Nazca drainage, Tello (1959: 60) observed few ancient habitation sites, monumental buildings, or ceremonial mounds in comparison to cemeteries which he regarded as "very rich, abundant and illustrative in so far as tombs and their contents are concerned." Kroeber was similarly unimpressed with Nasca habitation sites. Referring to the limited amount of arable land in Ica and Nazca, he concluded that "however dense the population, it could never have been very great absolutely" (Kroeber 1944: 25). Robinson (1957: 13) stated that "cemeteries were predominant" among the sites he visited during his survey in the Río Grande de Nazca drainage. And Strong (1957: table 1) recorded no Nasca habitation sites during his south-coast reconnaissance other than "house mounds" at Cahuachi and the

"Late Nazca" occupation at Chaviña in Acarí. In contrast, recent surveys conducted in the Río Grande de Nazca drainage have identified hundreds of Nasca habitation sites (see Browne 1992; Browne and Baraybar 1988; Proulx 1999c; Schreiber 1998, 1999; Silverman 1993b; see also Isla 1992; Isla et al. 1984) and scores are known in Ica (Massey 1986; Williams León and Pazos Rivera 1974). The discrepancy is surely due to research focus, fieldwork methodology, and the misinterpretation of looted site surfaces (the looting of burials placed within architecturally modest habitation sites convey the impression that the sites are mortuary rather than domestic).

Nasca habitation sites were self-sufficient, with easy access to irrigable agricultural land. There was a keen Nasca interest in the upper valleys of the tributaries of the Río Grande de Nazca drainage (see, for example, Schreiber 1999: fig. 11.7). This is explicable by the readily available and easily exploitable water there, both as seasonally charged flood water and as *pukios* (natural springs; see chapter 3). Interestingly, though, the Nasca people of the Río Grande de Nazca drainage were not overly interested in the valley necks in contrast to the major early Nasca occupation of the neck of the Ica Valley (see Massey 1986).

By preference, Nasca people established their habitation sites on appropriately sloped hillsides of the valleys. Using naturally occurring field stone, they created terraces that expanded horizontal surfaces; on these terraces they constructed houses of perishable materials (see Williams León 1980: fig. 3.8). Other geo-topographical settings also were used. For instance, there are habitation sites in the upper Ingenio Valley located in the mouths of *huaicos* where the naturally occurring boulders were used as the prime building material. In the wide middle Grande Valley there was a distinct settlement preference for the raised terraces of the east side of the valley over the flat land on the opposite bank in addition to whatever sites may have existed in the valley bottom and been subsequently destroyed. There was an area of significant Nasca occupation in the vicinity of Coyungo in the lower Grande Valley (Proulx 1999c). Nasca people must have taken advantage of the high water table of the oasis-like Ocucaje and Callango basins in the lower Ica Valley and established settlements to judge from the many recorded burial sites there (see, for example, Proulx 1970).

Sites of adobe and *quincha* (wattle-and-daub walls) are characteristic of the lower Ica and lower Grande valleys (see, for example,
Proulx 1999c). The scarcity of Nasca habitation sites of all phases
on both sides of the lower Ingenio Valley and in the middle Ica
Valley (see Williams León and Pazos Rivera 1974) is probably due
to site burial by alluviation and site destruction by industrialized
farming.

Bearing in mind that there has been virtually no excavation at
Nasca habitation sites, it nevertheless appears from survey that
most of these were small, measuring less than one hectare to only
several hectares in size. In Palpa, Nasca habitation sites range in
size from 0.25 to 8 ha in Nasca 1 and Nasca 2, 0.25 to 6 ha in
Nasca 3, 0.5 to slightly under 3 ha in Nasca 4 and Nasca 6, 0.25 to
8 ha in Nasca 5, and from just over 1 ha to a little more than 2.5 ha
in Nasca 7 (Browne 1992: gazeteer). Massey's (1986: tables 4.4–
4.6) Ica Valley data show Nasca site sizes that range from 0.5
to 18 ha in Nasca 1, 1 to 18 ha in Nasca 2, and 0.5 to 25 ha in
Nasca 3–4 (which she lumps).

As seen in Massey's data (1986: 184), within this size range in
the upper Ica Valley, undifferentiated habitational architecture is
found at sites as large as 15 ha in size ("large nuclear village") but
"specialized architecture and elite residences" may be present at
much smaller sites. Similarly, some large terraced hillside habitation sites in the Río Grande de Nazca drainage are undifferentiated,
such as Site 220 in the lower Ingenio Valley which measures 9.6 ha.
On the other hand, small habitation sites may have internally
differentiated architecture. A good example is Estudiante/Site 455
in the middle Ingenio Valley. It is a single component Nasca 1 site
that measures 4 ha but has two sectors of finely executed planned
architecture amid the other ordinary hillside terraced habitation
architecture of the site (figure 5.4). Very large sites may be internally differentiated with habitation, civic-ceremonial features and/
or cemeteries and/or geoglyphs. The clearest example of this is
the multi-component Ventilla/Site 165 in the middle Ingenio Valley
(Silverman 1993a: 324–7, fig. 23.2).

Specific material features link some of the valley sites to Cahuachi.
For instance, petrified wood found on the surface of Site 87 in the
upper Ingenio Valley may associate the inhabitants of that village
to Unit 19 at Cahuachi where a cache of size-graded petrified wood

Figure 5.4 Estudiante/Site 455 on the north side of the middle Ingenio Valley. Ground-level view of Sector A, a planned architectural unit of finely built, bilaterally symmetrical field-stone terraces located in between areas of ordinary field-stone terraces (*photo*: Helaine Silverman).

was found (see Silverman 1993a: 281, fig. 19.18). Fine Nasca 1 blackware is also present at Site 87, a pottery type well known from Cahuachi, including Unit 19 (see, for example, Orefici 1993: 29, fig. 139; Silverman 1993a: 231, fig. 16.4; Strong 1957: fig. 9).

Nasca Cemeteries

We consider cemeteries to be part of the inhabited landscape and are especially interested in how cemeteries were arranged, where they were located with regard to habitation, ceremonial, civic, defensive, and other categories of sites, what other factors may have intervened in the choice of cemetery location, and so on. We are challenged in some of our interpretations by the fact that Nasca cemeteries are looted (were they intact, they might be imperceptible on the surface) and, as indicated above, looting may be obscuring the primary habitation function of many sites.

Apparently, the Nasca located discrete cemeteries anywhere, though by logical preference they placed cemeteries off the potentially flooded valley floor. Cemeteries also were associated with habitation sites where burials were placed in and around domestic contexts or in separate facilities adjacent to the habitation area. Burials also were made at civic-ceremonial sites, both in cemeteries at these sites and within their architecture. In the case of a few specific burials dating to Nasca 5, mortuary facilities appear to have been sited in association with culturally valued, naturally occurring, and artificial features such as water and geoglyphs (for example, La Muña in the Palpa Valley, Site 81 in the middle Ingenio Valley). Rarely, Nasca cemeteries were separated from other functional areas at sites by physical features such as walls.

In the Río Grande de Nazca drainage, burials of all Nasca phases are known but they vary in distribution. In the Ingenio Valley, for instance, Nasca 1 burials were virtually unrecognized in the upper valley despite the widespread presence of Nasca 1 habitation sites. In the middle Grande Valley there is a preference for the east side of the valley for burial location as well as for habitation sites. Nasca 2 and Nasca 3 mortuary sites are well spaced and distributed throughout the Ingenio Valley; again in the middle Grande Valley there is a preference for the east side. Nasca 4 burials are present throughout

Figure 5.5 The site of La Muña, at the confluence of the Palpa and Grande rivers (*photo*: Donald Proulx).

the Ingenio Valley, well spaced and distributed. There is one Nasca 4 mortuary expression on the west side of the middle Grande; all other Nasca 4 burials in the middle Grande appear to be restricted to the east side of the valley. There is a florescent Nasca 5 cemetery distribution throughout the Ingenio Valley and on both sides of the middle Grande Valley. Whereas there are few Nasca 6 and even fewer Nasca 7 habitation sites in the Ingenio Valley and middle Grande Valley, there is a significant distribution of mortuary sites for both these phases including burials on both margins of the middle Grande. Nasca 8/Loro burials are rare but known in the Ingenio Valley. The temporal and spatial distribution of Nasca burials in the Ingenio–middle Grande area corresponds well to published Nasca burials from elsewhere in the drainage and Ica (see Carmichael 1988: appendix 1; Proulx 1970; Strong 1957).

Nasca cemeteries vary internally and among each other. La Muña is the greatest known Nasca burial site (see Reindel and Isla 1999; Rossel Castro 1977). The site is composed of building complexes that extend over several hundred meters along the valley hillsides as well as a discrete necropolis with special mortuary architecture (figure 5.5). Burial chambers are up to 13 m deep and measure some 40 × 40 m at the upper range of their size.

In the Ingenio Valley, shallow, circular, and irregular unprepared pits were the most common Nasca burial form identified. Evidence of urn burials was occasionally observed. Also recognized were prepared tombs. Mortuary architecture at these sites could consist of simple field stone-lined pits covered by stone slabs (these are also known in the upper Ica Valley: see Massey 1986: 323) and adobe- or stone-lined shafts of varying depth with and without *barbacoas* (tomb roofs composed of superimposed *huarango* logs and lashed canes). Rarely, chambered architecture was observed; this could be constructed of adobe or field stones set in mud mortar. At Usaca, Isla (1992) noted burials in urns, burials in pits excavated into a thick stratum of clay which were covered by a *barbacoa*, and burials in *barbacoa*-covered circular pits against whose slightly inclined sides field stones were set in mud. Carmichael (1988) analyzed data from Río Grande de Nazca drainage Nasca burials that had been excavated by William Farabee, Alfred Louis Kroeber, and Giuseppe Orefici. His sample shows these same practices.

Nasca burials from Cahuachi conform to various of the burial patterns described above and also had different configurations. Kroeber (Kroeber and Collier 1998), Strong (1957) and Silverman (1993a: ch. 14) have reported Nasca 3 burials from mound contexts at Cahuachi. Kroeber's Unit A burials encompassed cists with and without *barbacoas* as well as urn burials; he found several similar burials in open areas (see analysis in Silverman 1993a: 210–13; and original data in Kroeber and Collier 1998). Silverman's Unit 19 burials are cylindrical cists covered with fine *barbacoas* (see Silverman 1993a: figs 14.2, 14.3, 14.5–14.13). A looted urn burial also was observed (Silverman 1993a: fig. 14.4). Strong found one burial (his Burial 8) in a 70-cm wide circular shaft under the corner of two massive conical adobe walls in Cut 3 on Unit 6. This burial may have been dedicatory for the architecture above it. Strong (1957: fig. 4) also discovered Nasca 5 and 6 burials in two cemetery areas between mounds at Cahuachi. Burials in these areas included circular pits without *barbacoas*, circular and oval shafts (some having rough adobe walls) with fine *barbacoas*, a rectangular cist with fine adobe walls and a large *barbacoa*, rectangular cists with plastered walls but no roof, and urn burials.

Data on Nasca burials in Ica are more limited. Nasca 1 burials from Ocucaje are known to include roofed cist tombs with fine walls of adobe or laced cane, urn burials, simple shaft graves covered with a *barbacoa*, and shallow pits (Carmichael 1988: 385–92). Uhle's Nasca 3 and Nasca 4 tombs at Ocucaje were typically deep pits covered with *barbacoas*; in some cemeteries he observed chambers with rough adobe walls (Uhle 1913, 1914; see Proulx 1970). Williams León and Pazos Rivera (1974) note numerous Nasca cemeteries in their Ica inventory that are associated with other site functions such as habitation and civic-ceremonial sectors.

The Nasca Occupation of the Río Grande de Nazca Drainage

Nasca 1

Although there is a domestic occupation associated with the monumental one at Cahuachi, Cahuachi already was in a physical and conceptual class by itself in Nasca 1 times by virtue of its unique (as currently known) volumetric architecture (the Step-fret Temple) and abundance of highly elaborate slip-painted and incised pottery.

Nasca 1 appears full blown and as a veritable demographic explosion in those valleys for which detailed published information is available (Palpa, Ingenio). There is a significant Nasca 1 occupation in Palpa with a range of site sizes (Browne 1992; Browne and Baraybar 1988). Cerro Carapo (Browne et al. 1993: figs 1, 2) is a particularly large hillside settlement. Several of Palpa's Nasca 1 sites have civic-ceremonial architecture and there is a dense concentration of civic-ceremonial and domestic occupation at Llipata. In Ingenio, Nasca 1 habitation sites vary by size, but size does not necessarily correlate with internal site differentiation as discussed above. Most Nasca 1 habitation sites are undifferentiated and equivalent: large or small, they consist of uniform remains, usually field-stone terraces. At some Nasca 1 habitation sites there were encapsulated civic-ceremonial features such as a small mound or a cleared surface, but these do not necessarily correlate with size and appear to have served the resident population only. A handful of Nasca 1 habitation sites in Ingenio, however, show internal differentiation of architecture or architecture that is significantly different from that present at the majority of other Nasca 1 habitation sites. Examples are Estudiante/Site 455 and Ventilla/Site 165, noted above.

In addition to habitation sites, the Nasca 1 landscape also was composed of cemeteries, civic-ceremonial sites, and geoglyphs. Some civic-ceremonial sites appear to lack associated habitation zones, others have minor ones, and at others both functions appear to be well represented. The well-developed Nasca 1 occupation of the Río Grande de Nazca drainage provides a congruent context for the major artistic and architectural florescence documented at Cahuachi in Nasca 1 times. However, we have indicated above that the conditions leading to this dramatic expansion of population and cultural complexity remain to be explained. Silverman (1994a: 378) hypothesized that Paracas people from Ica migrated to the Río Grande de Nazca drainage (at least to the northern valleys for which there are good data) in order to account for the dense and highly articulated Nasca 1 settlement pattern. But she did not consider the further ramifications of such a migration in terms of its effects on the remaining population in Ica, relationships between people of Ica and the Río Grande de Nazca drainage, or on the development of Nasca culture and the growth of socio-political complexity in the drainage, particularly in so far as Cahuachi is concerned. Other issues we would suggest for examination are whether the entire Río Grande de Nazca drainage "became Nasca" at the same time following the Early Horizon Paracas–Tajo occupation, and whether there was intra-drainage variation during the Early Horizon (for instance, we are unaware of the presence of Paracas pottery in Taruga and Las Trancas, the southernmost tributaries of the Río Grande de Nazca drainage).

Nasca 2

There is a dense occupation of the Río Grande de Nazca drainage in Nasca 2 times. Habitation sites of varying size and configuration, cemeteries, civic-ceremonial sites, and geoglyphs have been identified.

By or in EIP 2, the ceremonial function of Cahuachi appears to have overtaken its domestic aspect. As Cahuachi is thus far known, the only evidence of habitation comes from Strong's apparently special-purpose, textile, craft-residential locus. The abundant Nasca 2 pottery at the site indicates that construction of ceremonial architecture was expanding. Strong determined that the Great Temple (Unit 2) began to be constructed at the end of this phase. Nasca 2 panpipes and drums are well known at Cahuachi and in museum collections (see figures 2.4 and 2.5). Taken together, these data indicate that the Nasca religious cult was growing. However, iconographically complex Nasca 2 pottery was not widely distributed at habitation sites. Rather, most Nasca 2 pottery appears to conform to Strong's (1957) "Cahuachi Polychrome" type. Fancy textiles may have had a wider distribution besides occurring at Cahuachi (see Sawyer 1997).

There are somewhat fewer Nasca 2 habitation sites in the Ingenio–middle Grande region than existed in EIP 1. Browne (1992: 79) sees some reduction of settlement in Palpa in Nasca 2 times though he cautions that this may be due to sample bias. Schreiber (1999;

Schreiber and Lancho Rojas 1995) reports numerous habitation sites, mostly small villages, located in the zones of infiltration and upper portions of the Aja and Tierras Blancas valleys during her "Early Nasca" period which lumps Nasca 2, 3, and 4. Carmichael (1991: 9–10) recorded at least three sites with Nasca 2 occupations in the lower Grande valley.

Most Nasca 2 habitation sites are simple domestic settlements of varying size. A few sites manifest intra-site stratification with better and poorer areas of habitation. It is also appropriate to speak of inter-site stratification. Ingenio's Site 106 can serve as an example. As a major Nasca 2 complex, Site 106 consisted of a large hill that functioned as a *huaca* (figure 5.6). On this hill there are associated habitation zones conforming to standard Nasca field-stone masonry terraces. There appears to be a walled ditch running along the west side of the hill. The Site 106 *huaca* is reminiscent of Unit HH at Cahuachi (see Silverman 1993a: 81, fig. 2.4) in that it is a large bilobal or U-shaped hill that was modified to become impressive civic-ceremonial architecture. Around the Site 106 *huaca* are a cluster of other habitation zones, geoglyphs, and cemeteries with Nasca 2 occupations. At the habitation sites there are better and less well-constructed habitation terraces; walls demarcate certain habitation areas. There is also a self-contained area of unlooted stone-lined storage pits. Cemeteries contain unprepared cists, prepared cists, and special mortuary chambers.

Nasca 3

The Nasca 3 landscape of the Río Grande de Nazca drainage was highly differentiated. In addition to habitation sites of varying size and configuration, there were many cemeteries, civic-ceremonial sites, and geoglyphs. Nasca 3 was the apogee of Cahuachi (see Silverman 1993a; Strong 1957). Coeval with the stunning expansion of building at the site, fine decorated Nasca pottery was abundant throughout the Río Grande de Nazca drainage and in Ica as well.

In Palpa, Browne (1992: 79) observed that "no particular domestic site is predominant in terms of scale or special architecture." In Ingenio most Nasca 3 habitation sites were undifferentiated and

Figure 5.6 Site 106, looking south at the great bilobal hill *huaca* (*photo*: Helaine Silverman).

redundant: large or small, they consisted of uniform remains such as terraces, though a few had simple encapsulated civic-ceremonial features. Ventilla/Site 165, however, was a major habitation site at this time with a high degree of intra-site stratification. Schreiber (1999: 167) reports that in the southern tributaries, "Early Nasca" (i.e. Nasca 2, 3, and 4) people "lived in small scattered villages in the Andean foothills . . . villages were located only in those portions of the valleys with reliable sources of water." In the lower Grande Valley, Carmichael (1991) recorded several small and large villages with burials.

Many civic-ceremonial sites functioned in Nasca 3 times in addition to Cahuachi. Schreiber (1999) indicates the existence of two small "platform mound and cemetery complexes" at Pueblo Viejo and Cantalloc. In the lower Grande Valley, Carmichael (1991) recorded a small site with platforms of bundled vegetal material (as at Cahuachi) and another ceremonial center with burials. In the Ingenio and middle Grande valleys several civic-ceremonial centers appear to reach their apogee in Nasca 3 or to have been important sites at this time. In Palpa, Browne (1992: 79) observed that in Nasca 3 times "sites of civic-ceremonial character assume a more prominent position in the hierarchy of site functions." Similarly, Reindel and Isla (1999), who lump Nasca 2 and 3 together, see a "clear settlement hierarchy" of two levels in Palpa. There are the simple settlements that Browne also observed and, at Los Molinos, impressive civic-ceremonial architecture which Reindel and Isla (1999: figs 171, 173) interpret as "a planned settlement with monumental [adobe] architecture . . . walls that are almost one meter thick extend over long stretches in a right-angled pattern. Long stepped walkways provide access to large spaces situated atop terraces. The terraces cover the lower area of the valley slope upon which the settlement is situated." They call these remains "great enclosures, palaces, residences . . . where the representatives of power lived" and simple perishable architecture of reed huts lay on the periphery of this central area (*El Comercio*, September 21, 1999, p. A10; Reindel and Isla 1999). Importantly, the construction techniques and formal and spatial organization of the architecture of Los Molinos (see Reindel and Isla 1999: fig. 171; figure 5.7) are readily comparable to those seen at Cahuachi (compare with Orefici 1993: fig. 83; Silverman 1993a: figs 12.6, 12.34).

Figure 5.7 The site of Los Molinos, Palpa Valley (*photo*: Donald Proulx).

Nasca 4

On the basis of his examination of William Duncan Strong's pottery collections, Rowe (1963) argued that Cahuachi was abandoned in Nasca 4 times. However, Silverman (1993a: ch. 13, figs 13.40, 13.41) has demonstrated that the Room of the Posts at Cahuachi cannot be earlier than Nasca 4. Therefore, some ceremonial construction continued at Cahuachi in Nasca 4 times. Nevertheless, as the Room of the Posts was being built, other areas of that same mound were being taken out of circulation through the blocking of accesses, the annulment of passageways, and the laying of fills (see Silverman 1993a: ch. 13). Thus far, no Nasca 4 burials are known from Cahuachi. Post-apogee offerings, including trophy heads, were left in these abandoned architectural contexts beginning in Nasca 4 times.

The dramatic decline of monumental civic-ceremonial architecture at Cahuachi after Nasca 3, and the apparent cessation of construction at the site after Nasca 4, are paralleled to a significant degree in settlement patterns throughout the drainage. For instance, the important site of Los Molinos was abandoned after Nasca 3 (Reindel and Isla 1999) and only one sector of the great Ventilla/Site 165 habitation center was occupied in Nasca 4. Nasca 4 sites are significantly reduced in number, size, and complexity from the preceding Nasca 3 phase.

Browne (1992: 80) offers two plausible explanations for the significant change on the landscape: sample bias or a classificatory problem (i.e. that Nasca 4 is a stylistic but not a chronological division). Silverman (1993b: 113–14) also has considered the possibility that Nasca 4 lacks chronological reality even though the Room of the Posts was built in Nasca 4 times (Silverman 1993a: figs 13.40, 13.41). One of the few excavated Nasca habitation sites, Marcaya, in the Tierras Blancas Valley, dates to this phase (see Vaughn 1999). Thus, the settlement pattern changes in Nasca 4 times appear to be very real.

Nasca 5

The Nasca 5 landscape was once more highly differentiated with habitation sites of varying size and configuration, cemeteries, civic-ceremonial sites, and geoglyphs. At Cahuachi the latest evidence of architectural modification comes from Unit 19 and corresponds to a final floor laid in a room atop the mound; a small pit was excavated into this floor into which a trophy head was deposited (Silverman 1993a: fig. 12.18), arguing for the abandonment of the room. Nasca 5 also may be when panpipes and other motifs were traced on the west and south walls of the Room of the Posts (based on the iconographic similarity of a traced rayed face on this wall to painted rayed faces on Nasca 5 pottery: see Silverman 1993a: 180, compare fig. 13.10 drawing/bottom right image to Roark 1965: fig. 49/main image). Also, Nasca 5 and 6 burials were placed in cemeteries in open areas *between* mounds (Strong's Burial Area 1: see Strong 1957: 32, 34, figs 4, 13C–E, 14B, D, E, G–J; Silverman 1993a: ch. 14,) in contrast to the Nasca 3 apogee pattern of burials *on* mounds. Cahuachi was no longer functioning as a great civic-ceremonial and pilgrimage center.

Habitation sites flourished in the drainage in Nasca 5 times. There were scores of large and small habitation sites, most of which consisted of field-stone terraces. Encapsulated civic-ceremonial features at the habitation sites are not significant beyond the immediate local level.

In addition to ordinary habitation sites in the Ingenio Valley, Ventilla/Site 165 may have reached its greatest size at this time. It had ordinary habitation areas within walled enclosures and civic-ceremonial areas that included mound construction. There also were civic-ceremonial centers in Ingenio and the middle Grande Valley. Most of these are characterized by architectural compartmentalization (rooms) rather than volumetric mass (mounds), although some enclosures, terraced hillside faces, flattened summits, and mounds that were functioning in earlier Nasca times also appear to have been used in Nasca 5.

In Palpa, various habitation sites were abandoned and others relocated (Browne 1992; Reindel and Isla 1999). Reindel and Isla (1999) correlate the Nasca 4–5 decrease in settlement with the emergence of a few, larger sites in Nasca 5. Interestingly, almost none of the civic-ceremonial sites functioning in Nasca 3 times was occupied in Nasca 5 times (Browne 1992). Rather, several of the Nasca 3 civic-ceremonial sites became burial grounds, such as Los Molinos. La Muña became the most important Nasca 5 site in the valley and was one of the most important sites in the drainage at this time. It had major civic-ceremonial architecture in addition to its mortuary aspects. We are in profound agreement with Browne (1992: 80) who realized that the changes in settlement pattern in Palpa were tremendously significant – evidence of "a major change in the structure of social relations." We return to this issue in chapter 10.

Schreiber and Lancho Rojas (1995: 249–51) report that in EIP 5 settlement of the middle sector of the Nazca Valley occurred for the first time and:

> the middle Taruga Valley includes a very large Nasca 5 site, and several major Nasca 5 sites were established in the middle Las Trancas Valley as well . . . It is interesting that while people were moving down into the middle valley, others were moving farther up-valley in Nasca 5. New and larger settlements were established at elevations above 1,050 m asl in the Aja Valley, and above 1,150 m asl in the Tierras Blancas Valley.

Schreiber and Lancho Rojas (1995) attribute the dramatic shifts in settlement pattern in the southern tributaries to the opening up of the filtration galleries which would have provided irrigation water to these water-poor stretches. Such an economic intensification could have been provoked by population increase and/or by the sixth century AD droughts that are documented by Thompson et al. (1985). Schreiber (1999) reports no Nasca 5 civic-ceremonial centers in the southern tributaries.

Late Nasca/Nasca 6 and 7

Roark (1965: 60) interpreted the relative rarity of Nasca 6 vessels in his sample (Nasca 6 is less than half of the Nasca 5 sample) as signifying that Nasca 6 "occupied a shorter span of time than did Phase 5." This may explain why so few Nasca 6 habitation sites are known.

In the Ingenio–middle Grande region Nasca 6 habitation sites are rare and none appears to be of notable size or complexity. The most important aspect of the Nasca 6 settlement pattern in

Ingenio–Grande and for the drainage overall is the disappearance of Ventilla/Site 165 as such; only one small area of the site is
occupied in Nasca 6 times. The dramatic changes in the pattern of
habitation sites is repeated at civic-ceremonial sites. Thus, the collapse of Ventilla/Site 165 appears to have affected the adjacent Site
80, a formerly great civic-ceremonial center. The Nasca 6 presence
at Site 80 is minor and restricted to geoglyphs and the artificially
modified north face of a hill.

The Nasca 7 settlement pattern in Ingenio–Grande also is
extremely limited. Only a handful of habitation sites had Nasca 7
occupations; three civic-ceremonial sites continued to be used, and
Nasca 7 potsherds were found on the surface of a few geoglyphs. In
the lower Grande, Carmichael (1991: 9–10) recorded only one site
with a Nasca 7 occupation.

In the Palpa Valley, Browne (1992: fig. 8) recorded 30 percent
fewer Nasca 6 sites than existed in Nasca 5; none of the Nasca 6
occupations is the principal one. According to Browne (1992), the
decline in occupation in parts of the Palpa Valley is so pronounced
by Nasca 7 that almost all settlement is confined to the west bank
of the upper valley. In contrast to Browne, Reindel and Isla (1999)
observed a slight increase in the number of Nasca 6–7 sites over the
Nasca 4–5 pattern. They argue that their late Nasca sites are larger
than in the previous phases, with a greater number of residents,
and that various late Nasca sites present evidence of greater construction planning. At present it is impossible to reconcile the
divergent views of Browne and Reindel and Isla concerning late
Nasca settlement in Palpa except to note that Reindel and Isla have
lumped contiguous phases (Nasca 4–5, Nasca 6–7) and the field
methodologies of the two projects varied. We state our belief that
these data are not necessarily contradictory but, rather, may indicate strongly varying local responses to the unstable sociopolitical
and climatic milieu.

For Late Nasca times in the southern tributaries, Schreiber and
Lancho Rojas (1995: 249–51) observe:

> a complete change from the pattern of numerous small villages seen
> in Early Nasca times to a pattern characterized by a limited number
> of very large towns. In the middle Nasca Valley there is a cluster of
> one large and two small sites; in the upper Tierras Blancas there is a

similar cluster. In the middle Taruga Valley growth of the large Nasca 5 site to cover some 16 hectares made it the largest site in the region in Late Nasca times. In the middle Las Trancas Valley several large villages were occupied in the Late Nasca period. Our data indicate that the Late Nasca period was a time of population aggregation and increased sociopolitical complexity.

Nasca 8/Loro

In Ingenio, the decline in settlement that began in Nasca 6 and intensified in Nasca 7 reached its maximum in Nasca 8/Loro times. In Ingenio, no Nasca 8/Loro habitation sites have been identified nor has Nasca 8/Loro been recovered from geoglyphs. Nasca 8/Loro sites are unreported from Palpa (Browne 1992). Rather, the known (reported) Nasca 8/Loro sites in the drainage are cemeteries, the ritual entombment context of the Room of the Posts at Cahuachi (Silverman 1988b, 1993a: 79, ch. 13; Strong 1957), and the major civic-ceremonial sites of Huaca del Loro, Tres Palos II, and Estaquería. Nasca 8/Loro is prevalent and significant in the southern tributaries compared to its presence in the northern valleys.

Nasca Settlement and Society

We have written this chapter from the perspective that the Nasca occupied and created a sociophysical world in which time, space, and place were a process. The landscape was gendered and animated by *huacas* and myths of creation (see, especially, Salomon 1991). In addition to the culturally constructed, naturally given features of the valleys, the built environment encompassed architecture ranging from the humblest walls of habitation sites to adobe mounds at ceremonial centers and great markings on the desert. Water was all important to human life and it is also likely that irrigation networks created and reflected social space.

Nasca settlement patterns formed a coherent, environmentally responsive, environmentally manipulative, and ideologically based system encompassing social, economic, political, and religious landscapes. The social landscape ranged from geographically proximal kin to other Nasca people defined as outsiders with whom battles were conducted and trophy heads taken. The economic landscape was organized around village-based agriculture and the greater distances traveled to accommodate other quotidian and the prestige aspects of the economy. The sacred landscape was dominated by Cahuachi and there probably was a ritual geography (i.e. non-physically constructed) that organized and oriented human settlement and movement around non-conventional sites such as Cerro Blanco, a huge sand-covered mountain that is one of the outstanding topographical features of the Río Grande de Nazca drainage (see discussion in chapter 8). The political landscape varied over time from periods of greater integration, as when Cahuachi was functioning, to later periods of significant factional competition. Cemeteries could have been an important feature of the inhabited landscape if the Nasca dead were an active part of the living world as was the case elsewhere and at other times in the Central Andes (see, for example, the Huarochirí Manuscript; Isbell 1997).

6

Symbolic Expressions of the Natural and Supernatural World

Nasca pottery occupies a particularly prominent place in the annals of ancient Peruvian art as one of the most beautiful art styles ever produced at any time, anywhere. But it is important to indicate that this material was not regarded by its manufacturers and users in the past as the isolatable, exhibitable objects of today's art world. Rather, that which is typically called "pre-Columbian art" was, in its time, a magnificent, rich corpus of material culture that expressed and fulfilled many nuanced roles in society in overlapping social, economic, political, and ritual contexts.

The Nasca invested immense effort in the manufacture of fine pottery. It is truly ubiquitous in the archaeological record and was the premier vehicle of Nasca symbolic expression. Nevertheless, the meaning and role of pottery in the ancient Nasca world are not well understood, despite the efforts of several generations of scholars. In this chapter we examine the intellectual history of the study of Nasca art and its manifestations across media. We consider intersecting issues such as craft production, status and social reproduction, legitimation of authority, and religious beliefs and interpret these as interconnected fields of cultural production and meaning.

Historical Background

Most scholars are unaware that it was chronology-obsessed Max Uhle who, in *Die Ruinenstaette von Tiahuanaco . . .*, written with

Alphons Stübel (1892), initiated the systematic study of ancient Andean religion using ethnohistorical and archaeological data to identify the principal divinities of the pantheon. Yet, ironically Uhle, who was so enamored of the Nasca pottery style that he painstakingly tracked down its origin, was little interested in Nasca imagery. Rather, it was Thomas Joyce who made one of the first attempts to interpret Nasca iconography. Joyce used as his database a collection of thirty-four Nasca vessels that had been acquired by the British Museum. In a brief article published in 1913, Joyce argued that the mythical creatures depicted on Nasca pottery could be deciphered as humans dressed in costumes which represented the totemic clan-ancestor in animal form (Joyce 1913b: 113). The basis for his interpretation appears to have been his familiarity with chroniclers such as Garcilaso de la Vega who described the use of animal costumes by the Incas in their rituals to portray the ancestors of their *ayllus*. Using ethnographic analogy, Joyce suggested that the depictions on Nasca vessels could be interpreted in a similar manner. He was the first to use the terms "mouthmask," "tunic," and "cloak" to describe the apparel worn by these figures.

In the United States, Edward K. Putnam became interested in Nasca pottery as a result of its presence in a collection of over four hundred Peruvian objects in the Davenport Academy of Sciences in Iowa. These had been acquired in Peru and examined by Max Uhle, then the Director of the National Museum in Lima. Putnam (1914) classified the themes present on the Nasca pots into several categories: animal figures (into which he also lumps other naturalistic forms such as birds, plants, fish, and so on); figure pots (head jars, effigy forms); rows of faces; human monster figures (of which he describes six variations, labeled A through F); and miscellaneous forms. Putnam's taxonomy was limited by the size of the sample and by his own views of the nature of the art. In his study Putnam attempted little analysis of his own; rather, he cited Joyce's (1913b) interpretations with which he was familiar. Like Joyce (1912, 1913a, b), Putnam argued that many of the Human Monster Figures "may be nothing more than men in the dress of a bird, or of a serpent, or a centipede, or a scorpion, or some other animal" (Putnam 1914: 26). On the other hand, he suggested that "others might perhaps be called animals with men's heads" (Putnam

1914: 26). In the same volume containing his study, Putnam also published an introductory essay about Nasca by Max Uhle (1914).

The first comprehensive work on Nasca iconography was written by the German Americanist, Eduard Georg Seler. Seler's greatest achievement was the publication of a five-volume work entitled *Gesammelte Abhandlungen zur Amerikanischen Sprach- und Altertunskunde* [Collected Papers on American Linguistics and Archaeology] which appeared between the years 1902 and 1923 in Berlin. This magnum opus consisted mainly of Seler's studies of Middle American writing and calendrical systems and contained excellent drawings taken from the codices and monuments of that region. Eduard Seler's interest in ancient religions and his familiarity with the large collection of Nasca vessels in the Museum für Völkekunde in Berlin led him to attempt a study of the iconography present on the Nasca pots. In Volume 4, Seler (1923) published "Die buntbemalten Gefässe von Nasca im südlichen Peru und die Hauptelemente ihrer Verzierung" [The polychrome painted pottery from Nasca in southern Peru and the main elements of its decoration].

Seler was the first scholar to attempt a systematic classification of the major mythical motifs in the Nasca style. He identified the following themes: (1) the Spotted Cat, bearer of the resources of life, (2) the Cat Demon, (3) the Cat Demon as a Bird, (4) the Bird Demon, (5) the Jagged Staff Demon, and (6) other Vegetation Demons. In addition, he also described representations of humans, including trophy heads, animals, plants, and other objects. Although we now use different terms for these motifs, have added new ones, and distinguish a multitude of varieties, Seler made major inroads into the understanding of Nasca art. He correctly observed that Nasca religion, as seen through the symbolism of its art, focused on crop fertility. What he failed to note was the strong military component in the Nasca art style and the relationship of warfare and the taking of trophy heads to fertility. Yet this should not detract from the pioneering contributions of this great scholar. Today, the greatest value of Seler's study lies in the series of over four hundred drawings (many of them roll-outs) of the motifs on the vessels. These drawings constitute a major corpus of Nasca iconography for the specialist and are still widely reproduced in almost every work dealing with the subject, including this book.

Another important pioneer in the study of Nasca iconography was Eugenio Nicandrevich Yacovleff. Yacovleff was born in Russia and studied at the Agricultural College in Moscow where he became interested in botany and geology. He emigrated to the Americas, planning to go to California to grow fruit (Anonymous 1934: 324). Apparently, his ship stopped at Callao on the way and Yacovleff decided to stay in Peru. Soon after he arrived, he became affiliated with the National Museum and was a regular contributor to its journal, *Revista del Museo Nacional*. Yacovleff combined his scientific knowledge with ethnographic sources and contemporary evidence to produce a better understanding of the iconography represented on Nasca pottery.

Yacovleff's (1931) first article, "El vencejo en el arte decorativo de Nasca" [The *vencejo* in Nasca decorative art], examined the representations of the bird called *vencejo* (swift) (see figure 3.4 top middle). His subsequent study of falcons, condors, and other raptorial birds (Yacovleff 1932b) was more ambitious. He cross-culturally examined the representations of these birds, both naturalistic and mythical, in the major pre-Columbian art styles of Peru, including Chavin, Nasca, Moche, Wari, and Inca. Not only was Yacovleff able to differentiate the different species of birds by their markings, but he attempted a cultural interpretation of their significance, often using the writings of Spanish chroniclers such as Cobo and Cieza de León. Yacovleff's recognition of falcon eye markings on Nasca head jars, for example, led him to argue that warriors painted their faces with falcon marks to symbolize the arrogance, strength, and swiftness of this creature (Yacovleff 1932b: 50). In another study, "La jíquima, raíz comestible extinguida en el Perú" [Jíquima, an extinct edible root in Peru], Yacovleff (1933) identified the tuber represented on many Nasca pots as the jíquima plant, an edible root that was widely distributed and used in pre-Columbian times. This article goes much further in its iconographic reach, identifying many of the other plants represented on the pottery (see figure 3.3) and showing the plant associations of various Nasca mythical beings.

Perhaps Yacovleff's most important and, at the same time, most speculative article was his treatise, "La deidad primitiva de los nasca" [The primitive deity of the Nasca] (Yacovleff 1932a). In it he argued that the most important of the mythical creatures depicted in Nasca art was the Killer Whale (*Orcinus orca*) (see figure 6.1a). Yacovleff astutely recognized that Killer Whale traits were used in conjunction with other Mythical Beings, including those that were associated with plants and warfare. His most controversial argument was that the Mythical Killer Whale was gradually endowed with the features of the agricultural deity reflecting the gradual change in the society from primitive fishermen[1] to agriculturalists (Yacovleff 1932a: 148). His arguments were in direct contrast to the position of the leading Peruvianist of that period, Julio C. Tello (1923: 204, 585, 590), who argued that the feline, specifically the jaguar, lay at the roots of Nasca religion and art.

Yacovleff and Muelle's (1932, 1934) fieldwork and research on Paracas also provided insights into Nasca. They saw specific similarities between the "semi-naturalistic" style of Paracas Necropolis textiles (i.e. the Block Color style) and Nasca pottery (Yacovleff and Muelle 1934: 145, fig. 29). They believed that this pointed to a close relationship between the two. They also highlighted particular dissimilarities that provided a means for disentangling their genetic relationship.

Yacovleff and Muelle (1934: 147) demonstrated the origin and evolution of certain motifs on Nasca pottery. They also argued that because Nasca iconography developed on spherical pots, certain adjustments were made to the figures portrayed so as to accommodate them (appropriately in terms of the cultural sensibility of that society) to the vessel surface. Yacovleff and Muelle (1934: 148, 150) also concluded that Nasca ceramic art influenced Paracas Necropolis textile art rather than vice versa because, among other observations, they noted various errors[2] in the Paracas Necropolis portrayal of different species of birds that were inexplicable as a lack of opportunity to observe the correct situation in nature.

Following Yacovleff's premature death in 1934 the iconographic study of Nasca ceramic art lay largely dormant until 1959 when K. H. Schlesier (1959) published an imposing study of Nasca iconography entitled "Stilgeschichtliche Einordnung der Nazca-Vasenmalereien Beitrag zur Geschichte der Hochkulturen des Vorkolumbischen Peru" [Historical-stylistic classification of Nasca vase painting: a contribution toward the history of high cultures in pre-Columbian Peru]. It is most notable for its excellent illustrations of almost 250 Nasca vessels from six German museums, many of which had not been published before.

Schlesier was especially interested in the trophy head, a theme first treated by Tello (1918). Schlesier argued that Nasca religion was focused on the worship of the skull and trophy heads and that warfare was important. Much of Schlesier's interpretation of Nasca religion centered around his belief that there was a basic similarity or identity between many of the gods found in Nasca art and those nature gods that were present in Mesoamerica such as the rain god, earth god, moon god, clouds, and so on. His study included illustrations of Mesoamerican deities seen in the codices, and he attempted to understand the meaning of symbols in Nasca art by their similarity to better known icons in Mesoamerican art. Schlesier's speculative interpretation also may have been influenced by his familiarity with Seler's writings. And like Yacovleff, Schlesier realized that Nasca mythical beings changed over time. Schlesier also independently distinguished what Rowe (1960) called the monumental and proliferous strains of Nasca pottery.

Sawyer (1964) examined the continuous development of Paracas pottery's feline, fox, falcon, killer whale, and trophy head motifs in Nasca ceramic art. The greatest continuities he demonstrates are for the feline (compare his fig. 6n, o to his fig. 7b, c), fox (compare his fig. 8i, j to fig. 9e, g) and killer whale (compare his fig. 12b to 12c). A major issue to be resolved is if there is enough iconographic continuity between Ocucaje 10 pottery and textiles and the Nasca 1 pottery style to account for the subsequent development of Nasca iconography, or whether Nasca received input from the Block Color imagery of the Paracas Necropolis textiles, or whether there was a highly developed early Nasca textile style whose iconography was transferred to Nasca pottery and, if so, what were the origins of this textile style.

Since the early 1960s there has been an increased interest in the iconographic analysis of Nasca art (for example, Allen 1981; Blagg 1975; Blasco Bosqued and Ramos Gómez 1980, 1986, 1991; Carmichael 1988, 1994; Eisleb 1977; Morgan 1988; Proulx 1971, 1983, 1989a–c, 1991, 1994, 1996; Ramos Gómez and Blasco Bosqued 1977; Roark 1965; Sawyer 1962, 1964, 1966; Townsend 1985; Zuidema 1972 *inter alia*). These studies range from catalogs of iconographic motifs to sweeping reconstructions of the under-lying structural system of Nasca social and political organization.

Nasca Pottery as a Window on Society

Jackson (2000: xiv) has perceptively observed that "[i]n a complex society that has no phonetic script, visual representation takes on particular importance. Imagery and other visual agents work in concert with oral communication to simultaneously record and transmit the society's ideology and values." Symbolic images and the particular objects they "decorate" can legitimate and mark different kinds of authority (for example, political, religious) and roles (for example, age-based, gendered). They can constitute assemblages for the celebration and perpetuation of particular occasions such as funerary or ceremonial. And they can indicate various kinds of symmetrical and asymmetrical economic relation-ships involved in production and exchange.

We know that Nasca pottery was not made for exclusive use in mortuary contexts because many vessels show evidence of previous use and broken pieces of Nasca fine ware may show repair (see, for example, Silverman 1993a: fig. 17.5). We also know that the pots were not exclusively for use at ceremonial centers for they are widely distributed at Nasca habitation sites. Nor is their presence at these habitation sites only the result of *in situ* burials for fine Nasca pottery occurs at unlooted and, presumably, cemeteryless habitation sites (see also Isla 1992: 148). In his study of Nasca burial patterns, Carmichael (1988) convincingly demonstrated that the distribution of Nasca pottery was unrestricted in society. Thus, the two independent data sets confirm each other.

Silverman (1993a: 303–4) has argued that, with the growth of Cahuachi as the great early Nasca ceremonial center, there arose an increased need for ritual vessels: fine pottery was specifically produced for use in Nasca ceremony and as a result (ritual con-sumption) much was broken (deliberately and accidentally) and so entered the archaeological record. Most iconographic innovations appear to begin in the Río Grande de Nazca drainage (Proulx 1968), perhaps confirming and affirming the significance of Cahuachi and Nazca's importance. Proulx (1968: 71) argues that there was less stylistic variation in the Río Grande de Nazca drainage than in the Ica Valley, even though in Nazca there are some ten tributaries (it will be important to test this contention against the recently collected survey data). Proulx (1968: 71) argues that this situation indicates greater centralization in Nazca than in Ica.

The Nasca double-spout-and-bridge bottle actually was a bottle, though its original contents are unknown; residue analysis might be able to provide some clues. One double-spout-and-bridge bottle illustrated in the literature still has its cotton-wad stopper in place (Parsons 1962: 149 bottom right).

The cup bowl was surely a ritual drinking vessel. Silverman has directly compared a broken fine goblet from Cahuachi to drinking glasses broken on the plaza of the shrine of the Virgin of the Rosary of Yauca, in the nearby Ica Valley, during the annual pilgrimage festival (Silverman 1993a: 224–5, fig. 12.11). Decorated bowls and dishes were used by Nasca peoples, presumably in ceremonial feasting (see, for example, Strong 1957: 31). Occasionally, the literature mentions that an object painted on a Nasca vessel was found in that vessel, such as ají peppers (for example, Isla 1992: 127). In other words, fine Nasca pottery constituted the "tools" for ceremonial feasting and drinking. The imagery on these vessels enhanced and may have referred to their situational use.

Head jars (for example, Kroeber and Collier 1998: fig. 154; de Lavalle 1986: 130, 131; Silverman 1993a: fig. 16.19) begin at the end of Nasca 3. Proulx (1968: 92) states that head jars are found only in the Nazca Valley (i.e. not in Ica). Head jars may have substituted in graves for real human heads lost in trophy head-taking (see Kroeber and Collier 1998: 118; see, especially, de Lavalle 1986: 145 top right). In Carmichael's (1988: 314) sample of burials, head jars were present in sixteen graves of which only two contained headless bodies.

Musical instruments (panpipes, drums, trumpets) were used in Nasca ritual (for example, Carmichael 1988: plates 27, 29; de Lavalle 1986: 142 top left; Tello 1931). Pottery panpipes, in particular, are common at ceremonial centers, cemeteries, and habitation sites (see examples in Benson and Conklin 1981: 69; Bolaños 1988; Lapiner 1976: fig. 528; Purin 1990: figs 137, 138; Rossel Castro 1977: ch. 11). Panpipes also are depicted in painted (see, for example, Carmichael 1988: plate 29; de Lavalle 1986: 142 top left) and modeled form (Tello 1931) on other pottery vessels giving us insight into how they were used in Nasca society. Pottery trumpets (for example, de Lavalle 1986: 134 bottom right; Purin 1990: fig. 134) are known but are not common. We suspect that their rarity in the archaeological record is due to their pattern of breakage which may be inhibiting their accurate identification. Ceramic drums are very well known. Just like drums today, Nasca ceramic drums required a skin membrane to be stretched over the body of the instrument. A Nasca ceramic drum at the Museo Regional de Ica (DA-3651) still has a well-preserved skin membrane covering its mouth and tied around with cord. Some drums bear the most complex iconography of the Nasca style (see, for example, de Lavalle 1986: 134 upper right, 135; figure 2.5). As a point of interest we note that the Spanish chroniclers mention that the Incas sometimes made drums out of the skins of their defeated enemy.

Various kinds of hand-made female and male solid ceramic figurines were produced by Nasca potters. Few pottery figurines have been found in context by archaeologists, although they are well illustrated in the literature. Yet enough are reported to indicate that they had varied contexts. Lothrop and Mahler (1957) obtained three ceramic figurines in late Nasca burials at Chaviña in Acarí. Kroeber (1937: plate lxx–3, 4) collected two Nasca 8/Loro figurine fragments from two different tombs at Cerro del Oro in Cañete. Strong (1957: 40) reports fragments of twenty-two figurines from the temple and room fill as well as refuse deposits at Huaca del Loro in Las Trancas; these appear to date to Nasca 8/Loro. A broken figurine was found on the surface of the Lower Eastern Rooms at the base of the small Unit 19 mound at Cahuachi (Silverman 1993a: 260, fig. 17.1).

According to Morgan (1988: 327), small, standing female and male figurines appeared at the end of Nasca 3. They continued through Nasca 5. At the end of Nasca 5, larger, seated female figurines were introduced along with a few larger standing male figurines. These continued through Nasca 7. Seated female figurines survived into Nasca 8/Loro but almost all standing figurines disappeared. They were replaced by large, stylized figurines with modeled heads, typical Nasca painted faces, and stylized tapered bodies devoid of arms and legs (see, for example, Parsons 1962: 147 top right; Sawyer 1975: fig. 154). Parsons (1962: 147) has suggested that these could have served as grave markers given their easily implanted form.

Without the indication of genitalia, it is difficult and, indeed, risky to attribute biological sex to these figurines. Roark (1965: 27, 31) considered the absence of facial hair to be a possible female indicator in his comments on the so-called "girl faces" and "woman form bottles." Female figurines are always naked and are better identified by their plaited hair coming over the shoulders and down the back, exaggerated buttocks, rounded abdomens (alluding to pregnancy?), and vaginal slit (not always present) (see Spielbauer 1972: 22). In addition, effigy bottles of obese naked women – with and without painted body designs (for example, Kroeber and Collier 1998: fig. 254; de Lavalle and Lang 1978: 68, 69; Lapiner 1976: fig. 509) – are a hallmark of Nasca 5 pottery. Male figurines have genital bulges (see Spielbauer 1972: 20). Males may be painted wearing ponchos, a head covering, a short loincloth, and a large shell pendant hanging from a string tied around the neck or in some combination of the preceding (see, for example, Lothrop and Mahler 1957: plate ix–b). In Morgan's (1988) sample, 80 percent of the figurines studied were identified as female and 20 percent as male.

Morgan (1988) has observed that the minimally adorned appearance of these figurines contrasts with the multitude of well-attired humans, human deity impersonators, and mythical beings depicted in Nasca pottery. She suggests that the figurines "may picture humans, functioning in a ritual context related to a specific cult or deity" (Morgan 1988: 330). She refers to them as "propitiatory offerings" (Morgan 1988: 343) and suggests that there was a concern with the fertility of the sea rather than human fecundity and the renewal of plant, animal, and water resources in the arid desert regime of the south coast. She posits a shift of religious beliefs toward marine fertility at the end of Nasca 5 (Morgan 1988: 342).[3]

The Nasca carved killer whale or sperm whale teeth (whale ivory) into small human figurines; these are rare (see Lapiner 1976: figs 505–8). Horié (1990–1) and Rowe (1990–1) have published a group of cloth figurines – all without context and provenience. Silverman (1993a: fig. 18.3) recovered a cloth figurine in association with other miniature objects in a Nasca 3 burial at Cahuachi. The function of these is unknown.

Nasca pottery depicts adult members in many roles, occupations, and activities. The overwhelming majority of males fall into two major occupational/social categories: farmers and warriors. Early Nasca farmers are quite naturalistic in their depiction; they hold either plants or agricultural digging sticks in their hands. They wear minimal clothing, often only a loincloth and a distinctive conical cap with flap extending down over the back of the neck for protection against the sun (Blasco Bosqued and Ramos Gómez 1980: plate xxxiii–2; Eisleb 1977: fig. 211). Their portrayal is congruent with their toil in the hot desert climate of the south coast of Peru. There are also modeled vessels depicting elaborately costumed males holding agricultural plants (for example, de Lavalle 1986: 123).

Warriors form the other major category of male representations in Nasca ceramic art. In the early phases of Nasca pottery, warriors are nearly always depicted in a frontal, full-face manner displaying facial painting and holding weapons in their hands (Lapiner 1976: fig. 491). Warriors are more elaborately clothed than farmers. They wear both a tunic on the upper portion of the body and the traditional loincloth. Headdresses range from slings wound around the head in the turban-like fashion seen on modeled vessels (Blasco Bosqued and Ramos Gómez 1991: figs 416–22) to more standardized caps portrayed on the painted types (Blasco Bosqued and Ramos Gómez 1991: fig. 383). Weapons include clubs, spears and spear throwers, and slings. By Nasca 5, warriors painted in profile become the dominant type (Blasco Bosqued and Ramos Gómez 1991: fig. 383). These figures exhibit many of the same characteristics as earlier warriors with several exceptions. Military paraphernalia becomes more and more elaborate through time. Feather staffs (Blasco Bosqued and Ramos Gómez 1991: fig. 385) and elaborate clothing mark the later phases.

Individual portraiture depicts men as warriors/chiefs (de Lavalle 1986: 136 top right, 137 top left), warriors/chiefs with scraped knees (de Lavalle 1986: 124, 125), coca chewers (de Lavalle 1986: 140 top right, bottom), llama herders (Carmichael 1988: plate 26), almost naked men (de Lavalle 1986: 128 left, 129 right), and musicians (de Lavalle 1986: 132, 133, 142 top left) among others. Men also are depicted carrying a load of pots on the back (Rickenbach 1999: fig. 135). Men also dress up in the costume of supernaturals or are those supernaturals (for example, de Lavalle 1986: 122). Men also participate in ritual life by means of dance and music (for example, Morris and von Hagen 1993: fig. 77). Seated human males (Menzel et al. 1964: 254) may wear fox skin headdresses (Kroeber and Collier 1998: 126, 173, plate 8); these individuals have prestige by virtue of their position and accoutrements. Some portrait bottles depict finely clothed human males in association with trophy heads (see, for example, de Lavalle 1986: 136 top right); these men are clearly being shown in positions of power. Rarely, women may be depicted in comparable regalia and posture, but without the trophy head associations (see de Lavalle 1986: 136 top left).

Nasca pottery gives few clues as to the range of women's activities in this society (see chapter 3). Pregnant women are depicted (de Lavalle 1986: 126). There are several modeled Nasca vessels graphically depicting scenes of childbirth. Other modeled vessels have rare depictions of women carrying burdens on their backs, leading llamas by ropes (Purin 1990: fig. 149), and either cooking or preparing *chicha* in a group (Lumbreras et al. 1975: fig. 110). As mentioned in chapter 3, women most likely played as important a role as men in agricultural activities, but the ceramic art tells us little. Nor do we see the depiction of weaving even though this was an important activity (by way of comparison, see the women working in the Moche textile workshop scene published by Donnan 1976: 47).

Scenes of interactive human life are not common in Nasca ceramic art, and Nasca pottery provides little indication of the full range of cultural activity in society. Motifs in which people interact include farmers (de Lavalle 1986: 168 bottom), fishermen (de Lavalle 1986: 120 bottom; Lapiner 1976: fig. 512), warriors in battle and taking trophy heads (de Lavalle 1986: 147; Lapiner 1976: fig. 491), and very rare burial and/or ancestor worship scenes (Carmichael 1988: plates 28, 29). It is interesting that few family groups and no children are seen in the art except on the famous Tello (1931) procession piece. Erotic scenes are present in Nasca pottery (for example, de Lavalle 1986: 180; Kauffmann-Doig 1981: plate xxxiii; Lapiner 1976: fig. 501), but are much rarer than in contemporary Moche art and, indeed, may reflect influence from the Moche area in the latter part of the sequence.

The Supernatural World

Donald Proulx (1983, 1989c, 1991 *inter alia*) has sought to decode, classify, and interpret the major themes in Nasca art utilizing the thematic approach advocated by Panofsky (1955) and successfully applied by Donnan (1976 *inter alia*) to Moche art, ancient Peru's most representational style. Like Yacovleff, Proulx has recognized that Nasca mythical beings can be identified by consistently recurring combinations of design elements. Nasca supernatural iconography was accretive and mutational. Nasca "deities" or "mythical creatures" can consist of multiple combinations of elements which produce a wide range of forms. Proulx observes that many Nasca motifs are the product of a combination of a seeming infinite number of symbolic elements which make it difficult to identify any motif as "standard." In all, approximately thirty major motifs in Nasca ceramic iconography can be identified and refined into approximately two hundred "sub-varieties." The principal supernatural themes are the Anthropomorphic Mythical Being (AMB) (figure 2.3), Harpy (figure 6.1b), Horrible Bird (figure 6.1c), Mythical Killer Whale (figure 6.1a), Mythical Spotted Cat (figure 6.1d), Serpentine Creature (figure 6.1e), Harvester (figure 6.1f), Hunter (figure 6.1g), Jagged Staff God (figure 2.9), and Mythical Monkey (figure 2.10). A supernatural being and/or the human being who portrayed it could have aspects or "grammatical modifiers." Thus, the AMB could be represented with lizard attributes (Townsend 1985: fig. 19), Mythical Killer Whale attributes (Proulx 1989c: fig. 27c), *vencejo* attributes (Proulx 1989c: fig. 26a), or others. Perhaps these different configurations refer to particular mythological stories and different actions of the supernatural beings which were then enacted by their human agents (and see Proulx 1989c: 145). Let us look at a few of the mythical creatures in more detail.

The term "mythical creature" is applied to any anthropomorphic animal or human with special characteristics that suggest it is supernatural. These traits might include the presence of a mouthmask, forehead ornament or Spondylus shell necklace, special facial painting, or ritual clothing among others. The most frequently encountered "mythical creature" in the early part of the

(a)

(b)

(c)

(d)

(e)

(f)

(g) (h)

Figure 6.1 (a) Mythical Killer Whale (Yacovleff 1932a: fig. 2i);
(b) Harpy (Roark 1965: fig. 43); (c) Horrible Bird (Seler 1923: fig. 115);
(d) Mythical Spotted Cat (Seler 1923: fig. 8); (e) Serpentine Creature
(Yacovleff 1933: fig. 1f); (f) Harvester (Sawyer 1979: fig. 17); (g) Hunter
(Roark 1965: fig. 65); (h) "Masked Dancer" or Standing
Anthropomorphic Mythical Being (Seler 1923: fig. 27c).

Nasca ceramic sequence is the AMB. This term applies to a variety
of semi-human masked creatures with feline attributes commonly
found on double-spout-and-bridge bottles, cup bowls, and less
frequently on other vessel shapes. The AMB had its roots in Paracas
textile art and persisted in the Nasca style through Nasca 6. The
AMB has a human body clothed with shirt and breechcloth and is
depicted wearing a distinctive mouthmask and forehead ornament.

Seler (1923) called the AMB the "cat demon," arguing that it
was primarily an animal form with human characteristics. Blasco
Bosqued and Ramos Gómez (1980), on the other hand, label it as a
"fantastic human," emphasizing its human qualities and suggesting that the representation is that of a human with supernatural
animal characteristics. Supporting this view are the actual gold
mouthmasks and forehead ornaments that are known in museums
and private collections (see, for example, Lothrop 1937). For
Helaine Silverman, these real objects suggest that Nasca males

(presumably), perhaps shamans or ritual dancers, sometimes dressed in impersonation of these mythical beings. Townsend (1985) specifically identifies the AMB as a masked ritual performer. Nevertheless, archaeologists have not documented Nasca graves in which the deceased individuals possess the same ritual paraphernalia as that shown in art (in contrast to Moche burials at Sipán and San José de Moro: see Alva 1994; Donnan and Castillo 1992). Donald Proulx believes that the majority of the depictions of the AMB are symbolic representations of sacred and powerful forces, with only a few representing costumed humans.

In the earliest Nasca phases the most common form of AMB is drawn horizontally around the circumference of a double-spout-and-bridge bottle or vase (figure 2.3). The body either can be extended or downturned; a club is usually found in one hand and a human trophy head in the other. A cloak or "signifer" extends from the back of the creature's head. The signifer is usually spiked along its border, with trophy heads or plants present between its projections. The terminator or end of the signifer can take many forms, including a feline head and paws, a bird, animal, fish, or plant. The term "signifer," as used by Roark (1965), suggests that this element of the motif may have been used to denote the character or identity of the particular variation painted on the vessel, much like Christian saints can be identified by their associated elements in western art. Other forms of the AMB include a front-facing standing variety, more human-like in appearance, holding a club and trophy head in his hands (figure 6.1h). An avian variety with outspread wings is portrayed eating a human trophy head (Seler 1923: figs 72–6), while yet another avian variety is depicted in the more conventional form of a masked human with wings attached to his body (Seler 1923: figs 85, 86).

As noted in chapter 2, Nasca 5 was a period of great experimentation and innovation in the Nasca pottery style. Among the new innovations taking place at this time is a great increase in military themes. This includes a new variety of AMB, usually drawn horizontally around the periphery of a vessel, which has spears (or "darts") extending from both its head and arms as well as being appended to its body (figure 2.3 middle). The Mythical Monkey also has a military aspect (see figure 2.10): a running stance (like Moche warriors), objects held in the hands which may be stylized weapons

Figure 6.2 Example of a figure in the Bizarre Innovation style (Roark 1965: fig. 48).

and/or trophy heads, and combat engagement with ordinary human beings; it is also associated with plants (see comments below).

In Nasca 5 fully half of the ceramic iconography is mythical (Blagg 1975: 37). About 10 percent of all Nasca 5 pots are rendered in the Bizarre Innovation style which is used only for mythical subjects. The Bizarre Innovation is characterized by extreme abstraction (figure 6.2).

The Mythical Killer Whale, representing the most powerful creature of the sea, nevertheless appears to be of secondary importance to the AMB. Like the AMB, it has its origins in Paracas art. The creature is depicted naturalistically in Nasca 1 with the exception of the human arm extending from its ventral side. Soon, however, Mythical Killer Whales are depicted holding knives or human trophy heads in their anthropomorphized hands; this association with trophy heads and blood continues through the entire ceramic sequence. In Nasca 5 radical changes take place in the depiction of some of the Mythical Killer Whales. An abbreviated form appears, representing a frontal view of the creature's head characterized by open jaws and a patch of blood (symbolizing a trophy head). Roark (1965) coined the term "Bloody Mouth" for this variant form (see figure 2.8). The Bloody Mouth is most prevalent in Nasca 5 but continues into Nasca 6; in Nasca 7 and 8 it is replaced by a profile form with a jagged-toothed jaw. In the meantime, Killer

Whale attributes are attached to the AMB in the form of signifers which terminate in the form of a killer whale tail.

The Horrible Bird (figure 6.1c) is an anthropomorphized raptorial bird, probably a combination of condor and hawk, representing one of the most powerful forces of the sky. In the earliest Nasca ceramic phases the Horrible Bird is depicted as a naturalistic predator, often shown eating human body parts. Beginning in Nasca 3, the motif becomes anthropomorphized with the addition of human legs to the creature. Its form becomes more stylized with a long, white-tipped beak clutching a human trophy head, and wing panels which also depict trophy heads. Even more variations with "bizarre innovations" are seen in Nasca 5, when the Horrible Bird reaches its apogee. The motif suddenly and inexplicably disappears at the end of Nasca 5; there are no Horrible Bird representations in the proliferous strain.

Another bird-like mythical creature has been given the name Harpy after a similar form found in ancient Greek art. The Harpy (figure 6.1b) has a human head and an avian body. The head, crowned by two or three black lobes, often has hawk markings around the eyes and a protruding tongue. Black "hair hanks" cascade from either side of the head. Like the Horrible Bird, the Harpy's wing panels often depict human trophy heads. The Harpy has a short life in the pottery style, beginning in Nasca 3 and reaching its height in Nasca 5, after which it disappears from the repertoire.

The Mythical Spotted Cat (figure 6.1d) can be traced back to its naturalistic prototypes in the Paracas style. Once identified as a river otter or "*gato de agua*" by Valcárcel (1932), it is now clear that this image represents a small local feline known as the pampas cat (*Lynchailurus colocolo, Felis colocolo*), characterized by semi-lunar pelage markings, striped tail, and small ears separated by a "cap." Beginning in Nasca 2, a mythical version with mouthmask appears, and in Nasca 3 plants are attached to the body, a feature which links this creature to agriculture and fertility. The Spotted Cat becomes more angular in Nasca 4, and hawk markings are often found on the eyes. Like the Horrible Bird, the Mythical Spotted Cat virtually disappears at the end of Nasca 5.

The Serpentine Creature (figure 6.1e) is composed of a snake-like body with a human or feline head attached, sometimes wearing a mouthmask. This mythical being seems to be associated with vegetation and fertility. Its origins go back to Paracas textiles on which representations of the creature are found as appendages or streamers attached to the AMB. The Serpentine Creature is a common theme in Monumental Nasca art, but the motif disappears during Nasca 5.

Another new motif, that emphasizes the concept of fertility, is a creature known as the Harvester (figure 6.1f), which is present in both secular and mythical forms. The Harvester represents a farmer, wearing a conical "dunce" hat that is stitched up the front, and at the rear has a cloth flap that covers the back of the neck. The Harvester is depicted in a frontal position with hands outstretched to the sides and holding plants. The vast majority of the Harvester representations are found in Nasca 5, after which time they quickly and completely disappear from the style. Earlier modeled effigy forms of the Harvester are found in Nasca 2 and 3, where it is recognized by spotted facial painting and the painted plants held in the hands (see Blasco Bosqued and Ramos Gómez 1991: fig. 350). A Mythical Harvester, also associated with agricultural plants, is distinguished by the presence of "supernatural" traits, such as Spondylus shell necklaces, painted or spotted faces, and mouthmasks (Proulx 1983: 95, 1989c: 150; Townsend 1985: fig. 7).

The Hunter (figure 6.1g) appears in Nasca 6 and, with few exceptions, appears to be restricted to that phase. The Hunter is a warrior drawn horizontally on the surface of vases and double-spout-and-bridge bottles with the head always pointing to the left. We are considering this a mythical representation because of the homogeneous manner in which he is depicted and his association with trophy heads. Unlike other mythical beings, the Hunter's mouth is open, displaying a row of teeth. A Z-shaped red stripe of facial painting extends from the warrior's pointed nose, curving beneath the creature's eye. The head is covered with a rounded black cap or helmet decorated with an "X" design over a horizontal bar. The figure's shirt is decorated with representations of human trophy heads. A loincloth with elaborate ties covers his lower body. In his right hand, which appears to emerge from the back of his head, he holds a spear thrower. His left hand, which extends forward beyond his head, is grasping a highly abstracted staff decorated with quartet rays (see Roark 1965: fig. 34c for examples). Small tufts of human hair attached to this rayed band, however, reveal that the creature is indeed holding a group of trophy heads. This is made more emphatic by the realistic depiction of trophy heads in bands both above and below the figure. Like the Nasca 5 AMB with a multitude of spears attached to its body, the Hunter reflects the emphasis on militarism in Nasca 5, 6, and 7 and symbolizes the importance of headhunting in Nasca society.

The Jagged Staff God (figure 2.9) is a minor mythical creature that is also found mainly in Nasca 6, although its origins may go back to Nasca 5. Unlike the Hunter, the Jagged Staff God is more variable in appearance. He is usually depicted facing frontally, sitting with crossed legs. The head of the creature is highly elaborated with flutes and volutes protruding from the top; often a tongue emerges from the creature's mouth. Invariably, this mythical being holds staffs with jagged rays in both hands. Hair hanks attached to the staffs suggest that these, too, may represent symbolic trophy heads.

The Mythical Monkey or Affendämon was first illustrated by Seler (1923: fig. 254; figure 2.10). It was initially characterized as a "jumping" or "springing" demon, but later was referred to as a masked demon in an ape or monkey mask. Found primarily in Nasca 7, the Mythical Monkey is a very distinctive motif consisting of the sinuous body and curled tail of a monkey surmounted by a very distinctive head. This head, often turned 180 degrees to look backward toward its tail, has a mouth filled with jagged, bucked teeth, quite unlike the teeth of a naturalistic monkey and more like the jaws of a killer whale. A small pug nose rises above the mouth area. A single eye, eyebrow, and curled ear are found near the top of the head. On its head the Mythical Monkey wears a hat or forehead ornament. Its hands grasp proliferous staffs which may represent plants or perhaps weapons.

Although this Mythical Monkey may, as suggested earlier by Ubbelohde-Doering (1925–6) and Schlesier (1959), be associated with agricultural fertility and/or water, there is also a military aspect to the figure. The creature has the same running stance seen in warrior representations in Nasca 7 as well as a plethora of "fillers" or elements which surround the body. Many of these floating elements appear to be missile stones or spears, also seen in

Figure 6.3 Decapitated Mythical Monkey (Ubbelohde-Doering 1925–6: fig. 23B).

representations of warriors. This method of portraying motion in the figures as well as the use of floating fillers is new to the Nasca style in phase 7. The source of these innovations may be contact with the contemporaneous Moche culture of the north coast. Indeed the Mythical Monkey figure itself, which appears so suddenly in the iconography, may be derived from the so-called Moche "humped animal" or "moon-animal" (Bruhns 1976).

In Nasca 7 another variety of the Mythical Monkey appears, the Decapitated Mythical Monkey (figure 6.3). This creature is usually painted in a solid black color on a white background, its back and tail arched upward, and its headless neck pointing into the ground, much like an ostrich. Human trophy heads are often represented on the pot, and occasionally the decapitated head of the mythical monkey itself. Also commonly drawn on the vessel are a series of circular elements with a central dot, much like an eye, but often with lines radiating out from beneath them. Like its more complete counterpart, the Mythical Monkey, this creature seems to be more closely associated with symbols of warfare and decapitation. For example, the symbols for earth or terrain are seen between its legs, much in the same way that human warriors are depicted in the art. By the end of Nasca 7, the Mythical Monkey and the Decapitated Mythical Monkey are replaced by a circular decapitated head with jagged teeth which seems to have been derived at least partly from these more naturalistic forms. In Nasca 8/Loro, these decapitated heads are commonly depicted in the art.

Baroque elaboration of minor motifs such as mouthmasks and forehead ornaments characterizes the art of the proliferous strain (figure 2.2). These took on a life of their own with the further addition of series of chained heads, rays, and volutes. By Nasca 6 the proliferation of the style was complete. The human elements of the AMB and representational features of other main figures became subordinate to the proliferated minor themes. Thus, the proliferated AMB lost the traditional human/feline form of its head which now assumed a variety of configurations – some with feline traits, while other forms have large, grotesque eyes on a yellow or black background, which appear to symbolize the Mythical Killer Whale in form. At the same time, the outstretched human body is retained, but the signifer is reduced to bars with volutes and scrolls. It appears that the head of the creature has now taken on the function of the signifer of earlier AMBs in defining the nature of the particular varieties. Further abbreviation of the AMB occurs in Nasca 7 when the human body is eliminated entirely and replaced by a large fan-shaped element (figure 2.11). Emphasis now is entirely on the head which symbolizes the whole creature.

Throughout the Nasca sequence the tongues of mythical creatures have great importance, often physically connecting one element of a design with another (Rossel Castro 1977: fig. 28; Ubbelohde-Doering 1931: table iii), though the meaning is unknown. In other cases a tongue-like element, emanating from the mouth, is widened to form a field depicting a variety of themes, from polliwogs to human farmers (see, for example, the Haeberli Panpipe in figure 2.4) and other figures (see Ubbelohde-Doering 1931: table iv). Rayed faces, some trophy heads, the Harpy, and many other creatures are routinely displayed with extended tongues.

In the so-called "disjunctive strain," corresponding, in the Berkeley relative sequence, to Nasca 8/Loro and Nasca 9, the Nasca style disintegrates into a series of geometricized symbols. Many of these "geometric designs" are abstracted abbreviations of mythical creatures or their various parts, now virtually unrecognizable to the untrained eye. Much work needs to be done in order to sort out the major themes remaining in the style. Crude, face-neck jars appear in the style along with other "foreign" elements. At the time this art was produced, the south coast of Peru was being strongly influenced from the Ayacucho area in the highlands, a reversal of the situation in Nasca 7 for some scholars (for example, Knobloch 1983; Paulsen 1983). The significant foreign influence and extreme alteration of the Nasca style in its disjunctive phases probably reflects the end of Nasca sociopolitical and ideological coherence – the collapse of Nasca civilization (see chapters 2 and 11).

Other Images

There is a class of motifs that contemporary scholars interpret as geometric (Blasco Bosqued and Ramos Gómez 1980: ch. 3; see, for example, Eisleb 1977: figs 152–7, 159–81), though the work of Whitten and Whitten (1988) with contemporary Ecuadorean pottery shows that overtly geometric motifs may have very complex supernatural references. In addition, objects such as panpipes (de Lavalle 1986: 132, 133), spears and spear throwers (Eisleb 1977: figs 206, 207; Purin 1990: fig. 148), clubs (Seler 1923: fig. 137), and slings (Purin 1990: fig. 146) also were painted on Nasca pots. This iconography remains to be fully studied.

Approximations of Nasca Meaning

Nasca art was a multi-vocalic system of complex visual representation in which certain images were meant to evoke multiple meanings. For instance, the fox was both an animal common in the Nasca natural world and, drawing an analogy with Inca practice, associated with the harvest and agricultural rituals (see Zuidema 1983). The pampas cat probably thrived on the south coast prior to intensive agriculture and dense human settlement (see Peters 1991: 275) and is depicted in Nasca art in realistic form and as the Spotted Cat (see Proulx 1983, 1991; Wolfe 1981). The swift/vencejo feeds on insects, particularly those that hover near water, and therefore may have been used by the ancient Nasca people to locate sources of water and served as a symbol of water and fertility (see discussion in Yacovleff 1931; Silverman 1996c). Cacti grew in the

desert and San Pedro cactus was the source of a potent hallucino-
gen. And so on.

Scholars differ on their interpretation of the ultimate frame of
reference of Nasca ceramic imagery. Donald Proulx argues that
Nasca art portrays naturalistic representations of subjects in the
real world as well as a plethora of supernatural or sacred motifs.
Peters (1991: 311; see also Yacovleff and Muelle 1934) has concluded that Nasca ceramic and textile art "depicts useful plants
and animals and the primary human activities of natural resource
extraction. It emphasizes fish and fishing, agriculture, and the creatures – especially the birds – of field and forest." Carmichael (1992)
argues that the entire text of Nasca art refers to the supernatural
world, whether overtly mythical beings or seemingly naturalistic
animals and humans are being represented. Regardless, Nasca art
indicates a major societal concern with agricultural fertility.

Proulx (1968) observed that 19 percent of the pots in his Nasca
3–4 sample are decorated with mythical iconography, 47 percent
are naturalistic, and 34 percent are geometric. The frequency of
iconography in the early Nasca pottery excavated by Silverman
(1993a: table 16.8) at Cahuachi yielded a similar result: 22 percent mythical, with naturalistic and geometric evenly splitting the
remainder. Less than 20 percent of monumental iconography in
Blagg's (1975: 19) Nasca 5 sample was mythical in nature.

On the basis of survey data, archaeologists know that decorated
Nasca pottery is unrestricted in *distribution*, occurring at habitation sites of all sizes. But we do not know – for lack of adequate
ceramic analysis – if sherds with mythical iconography replicate
the *frequency* pattern observed in burials and at Cahuachi, or if
such pottery was more (or less) common. This issue bears on the
function of the fine ware as well as its production and, possibly,
control. In addition to survey data, excavation at habitation sites will
give us a better understanding of the use of fine ware and possibly
significant distribution of iconography according to archaeological
contexts. Nevertheless, the presence of fine ware and panpipes at
habitation sites suggests that artifacts necessary for participation in
the cult were not restricted to the Nasca elite and/or the ceremonial
centers.

Major differences in male costume appear to be associated with
occupation/activity rather than rank though, clearly, males of significant status are portrayed on late Nasca pottery. Indeed, ceramic

art vividly reveals that the locus of authority in Nasca society underwent a major shift between early Nasca and late Nasca times. In the early Nasca phases individuals clothed in the symbols of their deities dominate the representational landscape. Academic consensus appears to favor the interpretation that *early* Nasca trophy head-taking was conducted by supernaturals and their impersonators as a fertility–sacrifice ritual related conceptually to beliefs about ancestors. It is this highly ritualistic aspect of early Nasca iconography that Roark (1965) contrasted with expressions of militarism in the *late* Nasca style and which we see as individualizing aggrandizement by human male actors within the context of a factionalized landscape (see also Browne et al. 1993; Silverman 1993a: 215–17). In late Nasca times human males portray themselves in positions of power without supernatural allusions.

Nasca Pottery Production and Technology

Nasca pottery was painted with a rich, varied palette of some fifteen slip pigments. These include a very diagostic purple-red in addition to varying tones of white, black, orange, gray, red, purple, yellow, and brown. Eleven different colors could be applied to a single vessel. These vessels are typically highly polished. The Nasca repertoire of shapes includes various kinds of dishes, bowls, vases, jars, and the hallmark double-spout-and-bridge bottle (Gayton and Kroeber 1927: fig. 2; Proulx 1968: figs 1–16; Roark 1965: plates 1–3, 7–16).

The potter's wheel did not exist in pre-Columbian America. Nor did Nasca potters use molds, although these existed in other ancient societies of the Central Andes such as Moche. The technology of Nasca ceramic production was simple (except for panpipes: see below) but efficacious. Given the truly extraordinary quality of Nasca pottery and its characteristic iconographic complexity, it is fascinating and perplexing to note the lack – at least thus far – of pottery workshops and corresponding elite patronage as these have been documented in other societies, particularly Moche (see, for example, Jackson 2000; Russell et al. 1994a, b).

The actual manufacture of vessels was rapid when done by a practiced hand. Nasca pots were created by hand coiling, paddling, and drawing (Carmichael 1986, 1998). Often, a ceramic potters plate (see chapter 3) or the base of a gourd was used to form the base of the vessel and give the vessel stability as it was shaped. As a result of using these objects in the forming process, Nasca vessels have a characteristic round bottom and may have the dimple of the gourd's interior base. Carmichael (1986) has determined that the technology of forming pots was quite stable over time. In contrast, the technology of slip painting and panpipe manufacture were dynamic. We will talk first about slip painting.

The initial use of slip painting was truly a phase of experimentation. The early slips were thick and applied unevenly to the vessel surfaces. Furthermore, whereas in antecedent Paracas pottery the resin pigments applied to a vessel surface after firing had no reason to change color, great must have been the surprise of early Nasca potters as their slip pigments changed color in firing or even burnt up. The switch from resin pigments to slips resulted in the loss of certain Paracas colors such as green. It took time for Nasca potters to learn what changes would occur in slip color during firing. Eventually they developed a vibrant, multi-colored palette of their own.

Nasca 1 pottery was decorated in a limited number of slip colors. Donald Proulx specifically notes that Nasca 1 pottery has a jet black pigment, seldom duplicated in intensity in later phases. In addition, orange, red, maroon, white, and gray were used, though most Nasca 1 vessels were painted in only two or three colors. Red slip already was known from antecedent Paracas pottery and white slip had been introduced in Ocucaje 10 from the Topará Tradition with which Late Paracas and Nasca 1 people were in contact (Menzel et al. 1964). Thus, the shift to slip painting in Nasca 1 was not unheralded. Proulx has observed that the surfaces of Nasca 1 pots are typically marred by fire clouds, differing surface colors, and other forms of uneven firing. In firing the thick slips often crackled, a trait also present on many Nasca 2 pots.

By Nasca 3 slip painting and firing had been perfected. The thickness of the paints is even in consistency. However, burnishing lines, though less visible to the naked eye, can still be seen on many vessels when lighting is optimal.

In Nasca 5 a white slip paint becomes the preferred background color on a majority of vessels to the exclusion of red or black which were commonly found on pots of earlier phases. Horizontal banding in various colors encircles many phase 5 vessels. A new pigment color is found for the first time as well. It is a blue/gray tint that sometimes contains small reflective particles whose source may be a mineral called specular hematite. Nasca 5 is the time period when Nasca artists also paint complex designs in black outline form without adding the normal polychrome spectrum to the composition (for examples, see de Lavalle 1986: 137 bottom left; Rickenbach 1999: color plates 121, 126, 128). This innovation seems to be related to the wide range of experimentation taking place in this transitional phase.

In phases 6 and 7, Nasca polychrome painting reached its peak of technological perfection, both in the number and quality of the slip paints and the wide variety of vessel forms. Contact with distant cultures such as Moche in phase 7 led to the introduction of new shapes and design features. By phase 8, or what we are calling the Loro style, the Nasca style was transformed into something quite different as a result of new cultural influences from the highlands. The quality of the pottery changes dramatically and recognizable Nasca iconography disappears.

Pottery panpipes are a Nasca cultural diagnostic and here, too, we see change over time. Haeberli (1979) and Bolaños (1988: ch. 3) distinguish between two kinds of panpipes on the basis of morphology: those derived from Paracas antecedents have knobby jointed tubes; the others have straight tubes. The two types of tubes differ in acoustical characteristics (Joerg Haeberli, personal communication, 2000). The two kinds are contemporary in Nasca society and knobby jointed tubes are found through Nasca 7 (see, for example, Haeberli 1979: fig. 2). Interestingly, it is the Nasca panpipes of Paracas shape that usually bear the most complex slip-painted imagery (see, for example, Benson and Conklin 1981: 69; Purin 1990: fig. 138; figure 2.4). The Nasca-Nasca straight-tube panpipes tend to be slipped monochrome, bichrome, or trichrome, or have geometric designs (see, for example, Bolaños 1988: 57–9; Haeberli 1979: fig. 1; Purin 1990: fig. 137).

Modern replication of ancient techniques

Today, local potters in Nazca replicate ancient techniques with excellent results. Potters mix a fine-textured clay with a coarser one. As the vessel is formed, the potter strives to maintain even wall thickness and hand smoothes the walls so as to work out air bubbles that would cause the vessel to crack during firing. Once the vessel is formed, it is removed from its supporting base.

In the next stage of replicative pottery production the vessel is scraped smooth with small wooden and/or shell tools. Then two layers of a protective self-slip undercoating are applied to seal the clay. Each layer is left to dry in the hot Nazca sun. Once these two layers have been absorbed, the entire vessel surface typically is covered with colored slip that will serve as the base color for the vessel. Several layers of this slip may be applied; each is left to dry in the sun.

Then the painting of the design begins. Using different ground mineral pigments the palette of slip paints is created: the iron oxides such as hematite and limonite for red, yellow, and brown; kaolin for white; carbon or manganese oxide for black. Designs are painted with brushes just like the ones archaeologists recover from sites: small wooden handles to which human hair is tied forming flexible bristles (see, for example, Silverman 1993a: 277, fig. 19.9). After the colors are applied, the design areas are outlined with fine black lines. The individual colors are allowed to dry before the next slip is applied.

After the vessel is completely painted it is left to dry to a leather-hard state as a fuel of charcoal is heated to red-hot. Vessels are placed in the bottom of a circular kiln made of clay bricks. The pots are covered with slabs of baked clay to prevent the hot char-coals from touching the vessels and to allow oxygen to combine freely with the clay vessels (i.e. the vessels are fired in an oxidizing atmosphere). Then charcoal is placed on top of the baked clay slabs. First a layer of cold charcoal is laid down, then the red-hot fuel. This permits the cold charcoal to gradually absorb heat and thereby produce a slow, even fire. After twelve hours the vessels are removed. The final procedure is to polish the pots with small stones lubricated with naturally occurring facial oil. This polishing can produce a surface so lustrous that the pots appear to be glazed.

Nasca Textiles

Textiles were important as symbol bearers. Early Nasca textiles are famous for their intricate cross-knit looped decoration (see, for example, Haeberli 1995; Silverman 1993a: figs 18.4–18.11, 18.13).

Cross-knit looping is rare in late Nasca times but it is known: at Chaviña two doll heads in cross-knit looping were found (see Lothrop and Mahler 1957: plate xviiic, d). In addition, the Nasca excelled at the technique known as discontinuous single inter-locking warp and weft, particularly during Nasca 2 (see Rowe 1972). This technique continued to be used through Nasca 9 (Joerg Haeberli, personal communication 2000).

Orefici (1993: color plate 33; see also Discovery's 1999 tele-vision documentary, "Peru's City of Ghosts"; see also *Life Maga-zine*, December 1999, pp. 96, 97) has recovered textile fragments at Cahuachi that are virtually identical in technique and icon-ography to pieces in Sawyer's (1997: figs 68, 69, 115) Nasca 2 Cabildo gravelot and other unprovenienced embroidered and cross-knit looped and tabbed material. These textiles bear complex icon-ography. And, indeed, Sawyer argues that there is a largely unknown corpus of elite Nasca 2 embroidered textiles whose imagery was transferred to Nasca 3 pots when sumptuary embroidered textile production became perceived as too time-consuming and was abruptly abandoned, resulting in the kind of textiles (the Nasca 3 textiles) recovered by Kroeber, Strong, Silverman, and Orefici at Cahuachi. As indicated earlier, Strong's (1957) textiles from the alleged workshop at Unit 7 (resident textile workers in the service of the cult at Cahuachi) should be Nasca 2 based on the associated ceramic remains. Silverman (1993a) has attributed the shift in medium (from textile to pottery) of ideological expression to the growth of the cult at Cahuachi and the need for ritual pottery in the inclusive ceremonies performed there.

Sawyer (1979, 1997) argues that early Nasca textiles were made for interment in burials and, in rare cases such as the Brooklyn Museum Textile (see Gundrum 2000; Haeberli 1995) and Göteborgs Etnografiska Museum Textile (see Paul 1979), as ceremonial cloths, perhaps wall hangings. Sawyer (1979: 129) suggests that because of their lack of mordant the painted textiles (see Sawyer 1979: figs 3, 4, 6–8, 10, 13–16, 23, 25) could not be washed and there-fore were made only for exhibition and burial. Clearly, other Nasca textiles were garments used in life, for instance the embroidered shirt published by O'Neale and Whitaker (1947) and the garments identified by O'Neale (1937) as mantles, loincloths, tunics, turbans, and bands.

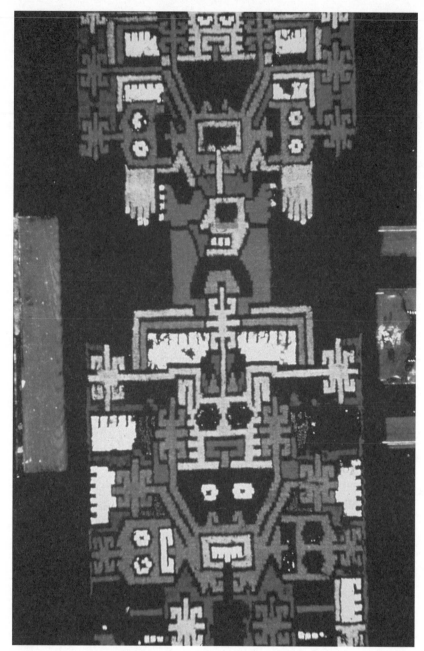

Figure 6.4 Nasca 6 textile with geometricized motif (Brooklyn Museum; *photo*: Donald Proulx).

The most famous of the painted textiles deal with agricultural fertility and portray farmer figures in human garb (Sawyer 1979: figs 14–16, 18, 20) and deity-imitating costume (Sawyer 1979: figs 23, 25) in association with agricultural plants. Apparently contemporary with these "harvest festival" textiles is the embroidered shirt with crop-bearing figures published by O'Neale and Whitaker (1947). Sawyer (1979: 141) speculates that this shirt may have been worn by a functionary presiding at these ceremonies. Nasca 5 painted textiles have smaller and more densely spaced motifs in comparison to earlier Nasca painted textiles.

Phipps (1989: 298) has observed that in later Nasca "there is an increasing number of textiles which exhibit design and iconographic imagery constructed with woven and yarn-manipulated techniques." Slit tapestry textiles are quite common. Many of the Late Nasca textiles have geometricized (because they are structurally created) proliferous-style designs (for example, Anton 1987: fig. 71; de Lavalle 1986: 54, 55; de Lavalle and Lang 1980: 79, 81; figure 6.4).

Gourd Carving

The carving and pyro-engraving of gourds is an ancient art form in the Andes. On the south coast it was well developed among Paracas people (for example, Lapiner 1976: fig. 217) prior to Nasca. It is well known in Nasca (Lapiner 1976: fig. 489; de Lavalle 1986: 182 middle; Orefici 1993: fig. 108; Silverman 1993a: 181–4, figs 19.21, 19.22). The AMB figures prominently among the Nasca pyro-engraved motifs. Kroeber and Collier (1998: fig. 70) illustrate an early Nasca carved gourd decorated with a finely costumed human playing a panpipe and possibly holding a gourd rattle. Animals also are shown (Orefici 1993: fig. 108 center). Valdez (1998: fig. 27) illustrates a pyro-engraved gourd decorated with Nasca 3 birds that was recovered in Acarí. There are also pyro-engraved rattles (Silverman 1993a: fig. 13.38). In addition, appropriately shaped unmodified or cut gourds were ubiquitous, serving a variety of uses as domestic containers of varying size and form.

Featherwork

We believe that featherworking (feathered textiles, feathered adornments) was rare in ancient Nasca society till the period of Nasca–Wari contact. Nevertheless, actual feathers are documented in Nasca archaeological contexts. Strong (1957: 31) recovered bird plumage from his excavations on the Great Temple at Cahuachi. Phipps (1989: appendix vii) specifically notes two examples of feather textiles in Strong's collections from Cahuachi. Silverman (1993a: 272, fig. 18.24; see also Silverman 1993a: fig. 19.3) reports a surface find from Cahuachi of a fragment of a colorful feathered textile. O'Neale (1937: 202) cites one example of feather-adorned textile art in Kroeber's collections from Cahuachi, a band with bright yellow feathers that would have been applied to the textile garment. Orefici (1993: 141) recovered a whole guacamayo (a tropical forest bird with brilliantly colored feathers) as an offering at Pueblo Viejo (Orefici 1993: fig. 31); we do not know if he has recovered feathered textiles.

In our opinion, none of the extraordinary feather art (tunics, shirts, mantles, pectorals, carrying bags, hats, headdress, "decorative" panels, fragments of larger pieces) illustrated by de Lavalle (1986) is recognizably Nasca in style and none of these pieces has a known association with Nasca pottery. Furthermore, some items clearly are Middle Horizon in date, pertaining to Wari contact with the south coast (for example, de Lavalle 1986: 112, 113); some pieces are later still. We are uncertain of the authenticity of a feathered basketry crown attributed to Nasca culture by Benson and Conklin (1981: 74–5; compare to Sawyer 1997: fig. 26, said to be from Ocucaje but without reported ceramic association) and we note the comment that "the gold elements appear to be recent additions."

Stone Carving

Nasca artists carved stone beakers. Some are plain (Silverman 1993a: fig. 19.23) and others, such as the Tello (1940) stone vase, are inscribed with elaborate supernatural iconography (see also

Orefici 1993: fig. 167). The Tello stone vase is a tall, cylindrical vessel engraved with two virtually identical anthropomorphic figures, each one in profile with upturned frontal head. The figures wear tunics and loincloths. Running down their backs is a serrated serpent that is probably the figures' tails. The same motif issues from each mouth as a tongue. Each mouth is surrounded by a mouthmask and the whiskered appearance of these, plus the shape of the figures' heads, ears, eyes, and hands (paws, unclawed), suggest a feline aspect such as the Spotted Cat, although these anthropomorphic figures do not possess the Spotted Cat's other defining features (see Wolfe 1981). One figure holds a forehead ornament, the other a stylized human head or strung pendant. The legs are depicted as serpent bodies with heads that end at the ankle. The feet are thumbed and rest on an annular ring carved with a continuous step-fret band.

Iconographically and stylistically the Tello stone vase has similarities to the anthropomorphic feline imagery on Paracas Necropolis Mummy Bundle 378-mantle 17 (see Paul 1990: plate 13), which is dated to EIP 1B, and to Sawyer's (1997: figs 30, 31, 46) Cabildo sampler figure E3, which Sawyer attributes to Nasca 2. It is very close to a carved stone bowl fragment recovered by Orefici (1993: fig. 167) on the surface at Cahuachi. So, clearly, fancy stone vessels were being carved in early Nasca times.

Late Nasca people carved small (approximately 20 × 35 cm), highly stylized and abstract, sexless, statuettes from a locally available white calcareous rock (see, for example, Sawyer 1975: fig. 155). Helaine Silverman distinguishes two types. Type A has a disproportionately large head, slit eyes, slit mouth, projecting nose, and tapering body (figure 6.5). Type B is more schematic, being essentially an elongated cone with the barest indication of a face (figure 6.6).

Metallurgy

Nasca craftsmen made gold forehead ornaments, gold mouthmasks and other gold items of personal adornment such as head plumes, bracelets, earrings, pendants, clothing plaques, pectorals, and, remarkably, spear throwers (for example, de Lavalle 1986: 184–91;

Figure 6.5 Type A stone sculpture found on the surface of Site 296A2 in the middle Grande Valley. Note the plainweave cloth adhering to the surface, suggesting that originally it had been clothed (*photo*: Helaine Silverman).

Figure 6.6 Type B stone sculpture found on the surface of Site 256 in the lower Ingenio Valley (*photo*: Helaine Silverman).

Lothrop 1937; Proulx 1996: plate 21; Tello 1923: figs 84, 85). Kroeber, for instance, found a thin, trapezoidally shaped, hammered gold sheet "stamped with a monster head and with four small holes for attachment" in his Burial 17 at Majoro Chico A which dates to Nasca 4 (Carmichael 1988: 498; Kroeber and Collier 1998: 51). Proulx (1996: plate 21) illustrates a pair of bird-like creatures, possibly the "Trophy Head Taster," depicted on gold cut-outs that were carefully hammered to almost uniform thinness. Some gold objects – such as mouthmasks and forehead ornaments – are identical to their representation in pottery (for example, Lothrop 1937: plates xxxi–xxxiii) and some gold objects themselves bear themes of the ceramic iconography (see, for example, Lothrop 1937: plates xxxvi–f, xxxvii). However, in comparison to the glorious metallurgical crafts of contemporary Moche artists on the north coast (see, for example, Alva 1994), Nasca goldwork is technologically and artistically modest.

Spear-thrower Hooks

The Nasca carved elaborate spear-thrower hooks (hand grips). These could be made of sandstone (Orefici 1993: fig. 168) or of whale bone (de Lavalle 1986: 183 bottom; Lothrop and Mahler 1957: plate xx).

Prospects for the Study of Nasca Art

The study of pre-Columbian art of the Central Andes is an underdeveloped field. Kubler (1990: 32) attributes this situation to the co-evolution of New World archaeology and anthropology. Yet, it is this social science grounding that can give the study of pre-Columbian art its greatest intellectual strength, providing a human and social context for the art and enabling significant understanding of the cosmological, symbolic, ideological, and sociopolitical systems represented in it. Indeed, art is culture. It encompasses all of the intersecting domains that can be suggested for any society: cognitive, communicative, ecological, economic, environmental, ethnic, geographical, psychological, social, technological, temporal, and, of course, it is an aesthetic medium. A particularly important recent theoretical development in the field of ancient Peruvian art is the view that art may be empowering; that is, that the use of certain objects enhanced and confirmed the power of elite individuals (on the role of metallurgy see, for example, Burger 1988: 129–31; Lechtman 1984; Shimada 1981), or may reflect changes in the structure of power within an ancient society (see, for example, Browne et al. 1993; Cook 1992b). We suggest that the biggest obstacle faced by scholars of pre-Columbian art in the Andes is the lack of iconographically detailed pre-Contact manuscripts and the rarity of early post-Conquest illustrated indigenous documents. Furthermore, the Andean ethnohistoric literature overwhelmingly concerns the late pre-Hispanic highland Inca, whereas many of the iconographically richest materials of ancient Peru were produced centuries before on the coast.

Silverman (1996a) has identified an early "Peruvian School" of art historical studies whose members were concerned with several subjects that are central in Andean iconography: sacrifice, propitiation of nature, initiation, ritual, shamanism, and power. Contemporary scholars, too, are necessarily concerned with these domains, as well as others. Thus, whereas the Peruvian School was concerned, for instance, to identify the gods of the ancient Andean pantheon, today's scholars apply ethnographic, ethnohistoric, and archaeological data to their "readings" of ancient art and seek to discern in its motifs and structure the nature and organization of the producer societies. Recent approaches to ancient Andean art are guided by the recognition that religion was not a separate realm of life but rather that religion and social, political, and economic life were embedded. There is now what we can call a holistic approach to the study of Peru's pre-Hispanic art.

Although Moche art has received the most attention (see discussion in Silverman 1996a: 16–19), the art of Peru's other great "Mastercraftsman" (for example, Bennett and Bird 1964) cultures, especially Paracas and Nasca, has received new attention over the past twenty years from art historians and archaeologists. As we have indicated in this chapter, Nasca art has been studied from explicitly stucturalist (for example, Zuidema 1972) and thematic (for example, Proulx 1989c *inter alia*) perspectives. Other scholars have tackled particular iconographic themes. We noted, for instance,

Townsend's (1985) identification of the Anthropomorphic Mythical Being in Nasca iconography as the portrayal of a masked and costumed ritual performer. The meaning of the common trophy head theme in Nasca art is also a current matter of interpretation (for example, Browne et al. 1993; Carmichael 1994; Proulx 1971, 1989b; Silverman 1993a: ch. 15; see, too, Tello 1918). What is needed now is a systematic, collaborative, frontal attack on this huge, varied, and iconographically rich corpus, such as enviably exists for Moche. Like Moche art (for example, Bawden 1996: 117–33; Castillo 1989; Jackson 2000), Nasca art can be regarded as a text. The objects and symbolic images on them should be amenable to translation and interpretation. Continued iconographic decipherment and contextualization of this rich material culture[4] will lead to a greater understanding of Nasca cosmology, worldview (the conception of the proper structure of human society and humanity's place in nature), political ideology and political economy, social and ritual practice, and sociopolitical organization.

Beyond the agenda for art studies proposed above is our view that landscape, too, is art and artifact, the result of human creativity in all of its many dimensions. In addition to the primary economic focus on the landscape, scholars have recently emphasized its sacred aspects. It is this perspective that takes us to the next chapter dealing with the great geoglyph-marked landscape of the ancient Nasca.

The Geoglyphs of the Río Grande de Nazca Drainage

The sloping desert plain between the Nazca and Ingenio valleys covers approximately 220 sq km. It is known as "the Pampa." Traced on the surface of the Pampa is a vast complex of intricately superimposed lines, geometric forms, and representational figures executed at huge scale (see illustrations in Bridges 1986: 9, 12–31; Kosok 1965: ch. 6; figure 7.1). These markings are colloquially known as "The Nazca Lines" and technically as "geoglyphs" (ground drawings). Geoglyphs are also present on the hillsides of the valleys of the Río Grande de Nazca drainage (see Silverman 1990a; Silverman and Browne 1991) and on smaller pampas in and between valleys (for example, the Cresta de Sacramento in the Palpa Valley: see Reindel and Isla 1999; Pampa de Piedras Gordas between the Ingenio and Grande rivers: Rossel Castro 1977: 198–200, fig. 44b). Geoglyphs are known outside the drainage as well (for example, Cook 1992a writing about Ica; Rosselló Truel 1978 writing about the central coast). In this book we are concerned mostly with the Río Grande de Nazca and there, clearly, the profusion of geoglyphs, particularly the lineal ones, is an indication of their tremendous importance in Nasca society.

The Factual History of the Geoglyphs

The history of scientific research and interpretations about the Nazca Lines has been comprehensively reviewed in several publications

Figure 7.1 The geoglyph-marked Pampa. In the center: the portion of the Pampa above the south side of the middle Ingenio Valley, more or less from Quebrada El Fraile west almost to the PanAmerican Highway. Around the center image: some of the major biomorphic figures on the Pampa (*photo*: Servicio Aerofotográfico Nacional).

(see Aveni 1990a; Morrison 1978, 1987; see also Reinhard 1988: 9–11). Here, therefore, we summarize only the high points.

In 1926 Alfred Louis Kroeber (Kroeber and Collier 1998: 39, 41, figs 9, 10; also see Morrison 1987: 13) drew what may be the earliest plans of Nazca's geoglyphs and noted that they were made by removing surface rock. He described "ray roads" radiating out from "islandlike rocky knolls," what today are called ray or line centers (for example, Aveni 1986, 1990b; see Rossel Castro 1977: plate xvii). He speculated that they may have been used for religious processions or games (Kroeber and Collier 1998: 42). At about the same time, Toribio Mejía Xesspe observed long lines, trapezoids, and several zigzags on the hillsides of various valleys of the Río Grande de Nazca drainage and on the Pampa. He interpreted these markings as "*seqes*" (*ceques*) or "religious roads" (Mejía Xesspe 1940: 565–9).

Paul Kosok, a professor of history at Long Island University and brilliant scholar of the comparative study of civilizations, may have heard Mejía Xesspe's presentation at the 27th International Congress of Americanists in Lima in 1939 (upon which Mejía Xesspe's 1940 publication was based; see Morrison 1987: 27). Certainly, the geoglyphs were already being discussed in the circles in which Kosok was moving in Lima (Morrison 1987: 25, 27).

On a return trip to Peru in 1941 Kosok traveled to Nazca to view the markings first-hand. It was during this trip that Kosok happened to observe the sun setting over the end of one of the lines on the Pampa (Kosok 1965: 52; Morrison 1987: 29, 32–3). He concluded that the geoglyphs had served as an ancient calendar and that the lines pointed to the position of the sun at different times of the year or pointed to various stars or constellations. Kosok (1965: 49) characterized the markings on the Pampa as "the largest astronomy book in the world."

Kosok's enthusiasm for the geoglyphs was so great that he recruited Maria Reiche, a German mathematics teacher who already had interest in Peru's past, to continue his investigation of the markings (Kosok 1965: 53; see also Morrison 1987: 28–9). Reiche devoted the remainder of her long life to their study from Kosok's astronomical perspective (Kosok and Reiche 1947, 1949; Reiche 1951, 1958, 1968, 1973, 1974, 1976 *inter alia*). Unlike her mentor, who also had observed geoglyphs on the valley slopes and noted their proximity to habitation sites (see Kosok 1965: fig. 1 caption), Reiche concentrated on the Pampa, thereby decontextualizing the geoglyphs from the ancient societies that had produced them. She accepted and expanded Kosok's (1965: 52) hypothesis that the geoglyphs "had some connection with early calendrical and astronomical observations," an idea which had "suddenly struck" Kosok rather than being formulated on the basis of trial-and-error observations.

The astronomical theory states that the Pampa geoglyphs graphic-ally recorded an astronomical calendar necessary to the function-ing of the seasonal agricultural economy of the ancient people. This calendar is said to be composed of sight lines marking the position of the sun at the solstices and equinoxes, the appearance and disappearance of important stars, and constellations such as the Pleiades; the figures would correspond to the constellations. The astronomical theory has been effectively debunked by astron-omers Gerald Hawkins (1969) and Anthony Aveni (1990a, b). Basically, an alignment between a celestial object and a ground marking is statistically insignificant because countless stars are visible in the clear night sky at Nazca. Furthermore, any astronom-ical theory of the Nazca Lines would have to take into account Andean southern hemisphere astronomy which is based on dark cloud animal constellations (for example, Urton 1981) rather than the connect-the-stars zodiacal constellations of the European northern hemisphere sky (see Pitluga 1999).

It is clear from their history of research that the geoglyphs did not create the sensation among professional archaeologists that they were later to have among the public at large when they gained world attention through their popularization by Erich von Däniken in the late 1960s (see below) and documentary television and print media's fascination with the persona of Maria Reiche. Few archaeologists (for example, Horkheimer 1947) interested themselves in the geoglyphs between the time of their "formal presentation" by Mejía Xesspe and the arrival of archaeologists on the scene in the 1980s as the south coast once more became a major focus of fieldwork (see discussion in chapter 1; and see below).

The "Mythological" History of the Geoglyphs

Perhaps no "ancient mystery" has attracted as much sensational attention as the Nazca Lines. Over the years many speculative explanations have been proposed for the function of the geoglyphs. The most notorious among these was put forth by Erich von Däniken (1969, 1970, 1980 *inter alia*) in the many editions of his best-selling book, *Chariots of the Gods?* (see also the eponymous popular television program and von Däniken's August 1974 interview in *Playboy* magazine; see, too, WGBH/Nova's 1979 program, "The Case of the Ancient Astronauts"). In these, von Däniken propounds the extraterrestrial origin of various world civilizations (see also von Däniken 1972). Von Däniken (1970: 33) argues that the geoglyphs of Nazca "were laid out according to astronomical plans" and could have been "an airfield . . . built according to instructions from an aircraft." He says their purpose was "to say to the 'gods' [extraterrestrials in the space ships]: 'Land here! Everything has been prepared as you ordered." He claims that enormous drawings on hillsides "were undoubtedly meant as signals for a being floating in the air." Von Däniken states that the geoglyphs have such immense scale that they are only understandable as a response to aerial viewing. Von Däniken (1998) has recently reiterated and refined his extraterrestrial views in a new volume, *Arrival of the Gods*. We quote below the main points of his argument.

[T]here were once gigantic space cities which orbited the earth . . . From these space-towns various types of aircraft . . . visited the earth. One of these landed in the Nazca region. Of course it needed no runway, and anyway, no one would yet have made one. Why should a contingent of extraterrestrials land in the arid and inhospitable region of Nazca? Because the area is chock-full of minerals . . .
. . . The landing created a trapezoid surface on the ground. The trapezoid is broadest where the landing craft put down, and narrowest where the eddies of air made least impact on the ground. From distant hills and mountains the native Indians watched the activities of the strangers with fear and astonishment. Human-like beings with golden, shimmering skins walked around, bored holes in the ground, gathered rocks and did unknown things with strange tools. Then one day there was a thunderous noise. The Indians rushed to their observation posts and saw the 'heavenly chariot'

ascending into the sky. That was the beginning of Nazca as a place of pilgrimage. It was now 'holy ground'. The gods had been there! Yet the gods soon returned, this time with other heavy chariots . . .

. . . At one spot the gods laid a narrow, coloured tape on the ground and bent it into a zigzag line. It contained landing and take-off information . . . as on an aircraft carrier . . . Finally the gods placed huge geometric patterns on the mountain summits, which served as landing orientation . . . All this activity may have lasted weeks or months . . . At last peace returned to this region. The gods had departed and taken all their equipment with them . . . Nothing was left apart from a few trapezoid shapes on the ground and a broad track with a snakelike line underneath it. And two or three strange rings on a few hilltops . . .

[The native population made geoglyphs in order to induce the gods to return.] . . . In all directions there arose lines and trapezoid surfaces as one tribe tried to outdo another. They all slaved away in the blessed hope that the gods would return and reward them for their dedicated service . . .

. . . Being inquisitive, as people are, small groups kept coming back to this mystical place . . . The priests gave the order and people obeyed. Nazca became a place of worship . . . Years and decades passed . . .

. . . The toil in the desert was seen as a kind of "sacrifice." . . . The more impressive an earth marking appeared, the greater would be the gods' reward . . . It was a particularly impressive invitation to the heavenly ones to land here rather than on a competitor's territory . . .

. . . The cat's-cradle network of lines also proves that many generations laid down signs that were different from their forefathers', often over the top of previous markings . . .

. . . this all beg[a]n because of prehistoric flights . . . The figures on the mountain slopes make this clear – beings emanating rays, figures which point to the heavens with one arm and to the earth with the other . . . drawings and figures are orientated to the sky. There is even an "aeroplane model" scraped out of the ground at Nazca – a "bird" with rigid wings . . . But where did these gods come from? . . .

. . . If we just replace the little word "gods" with "extraterrestrials" we've finally hit the nail on the head. (von Däniken 1998: 138–50, 162)

In addition to maintaining his position on the extraterrestrial origin of the geoglyphs, in his new book von Däniken (1998: 93) now informs us that archaeologists have not recognized the actual remains of the extraterrestrials: skulls exhibiting cranial deformation "are not of earthly origin." Or, he later suggests, the deformed skulls also could have been copied from the appearance of the gods (von Däniken 1998: 144).

Von Däniken (1998: 94) characterizes the work of archaeologists who have studied the geoglyphs as "fantasies." He sneers that scholars' "scientific explanations are just unsubstantiated, piecemeal hunches" (1998: 95) and "a catalogue of academic garbage" (1998: 124). He conflates the writings of archaeologists and autodidacts, castigating all for publishing material "riddled with repetitions and claptrap, as well as intentional distortions and falsehoods" (1998: 103). He also bombasts "scientific TV programmes [which] are concocted from such old wives' tales, then distributed world-wide and shown to young people in school" (1998: 103–4). In place of the explanations of archaeologists, von Däniken (1998: 104) offers, in his words, "unproven assumption."

Other interpretations of the Nazca Lines, though erroneous, seek to contextualize the geoglyphs within ancient Nasca society rather than the heavens. Not believing in extraterrestrials, Jim Woodman (1977) argued that the ancient Nasca people themselves made and viewed the giant markings from the air by means of "ancient airships superbly crafted of native materials." Woodman built a hot-air balloon of cotton fabric with a passenger-pilot gondola made of reeds from distant Lake Titicaca to "prove" his point. Of course, although the ancient Nasca people made excellent cotton textiles, there is absolutely no empirical evidence that they ever used them in the manner proposed by Woodman. Nor is there any evidence of reeds from Lake Titicaca in any Nasca archaeological deposit thus far excavated. Nor is there evidence that Nasca people ever saw reed boats. We also note Rossel Castro's (1977) incorrect idea that the geoglyphs were remnants of cultivated fields, and Stierlin's (1983) faulty suggestion that the cleared areas served as giant textile workshops. Other examples could be provided but these should suffice.

Archaeologists working in the Central Andes should have had the proverbial field-day with the more egregious of the pseudo-scientific theories about the Nazca Lines. But archaeologists directed their energies toward science, not refutation of the absurd (see Cazeau and Scott 1979; Feder 1990; Harrold and Eve 1987). Archaeologists did not comprehend the harm the willful appropriation and misrepresentation of the past could cause to the profession and to the Peruvian nation. Rather, archaeologists have continued to write scholarly articles only for scholarly audiences. We, the authors of this book, ashamedly include ourselves in this elitist group. The professionalization of archaeological knowledge has left the explanation of ancient mysteries, such as the huge markings on the desert plain at Nazca, open to interpretation and misuse by all. Minimally, we hope that this chapter and this book will prove to the reader that the geoglyphs and all the other great works of Nasca society were made by the ancient people, were the result of a long process of *in situ*, authochtonous cultural development, and are fully congruent with what is known about pre-Columbian civilization in the Andes overall.

Forms of Geoglyphs

There are some thirty *biomorphic* figures on the Pampa. Twelve can be seen around the center image in figure 7.1. Moving clockwise from the top left corner and using the common nomenclature they are: Flower, Monkey, Crooked Neck Bird, Killer Whale with Trophy Head, Hands, Dog, Radiating Hooks, Spider, Killer Whale with Obsidian Knife, Huarango Tree, Whale, and Hummingbird. Other figures on the Pampa include: Condor (Morrison 1987: 42), Pelican (Reiche 1974: 78 top left), at least six other Birds (for example, Bridges 1986: 17, 19; Reiche 1974: 38–9), Lizard (Reiche 1974: 37), Another Animal (Reiche 1974: 38–9/box 26), Fan (Morrison 1987: 69 top right), Nasca 5 Rayed Face (Morrison 1987: 29), Tuber (Morrison 1987: 111), Tupu (Reiche 1974: 108), an almost Obliterated Figure covered by subsequent trapezoids (Morrison 1987: 100), Forehead Ornament (Morrison 1987: 60 top left), Pinwheel (Reiche 1974: 107), Unnamed (Reiche 1974: 88), and other Indistinguishable Figures (see Reiche 1974: 38–9/ box 1).

The so-called Astronaut or Owl Man (Bridges 1986: 12) is a highly divergent figure in the Pampa corpus. It covers some 30 m on the slope of a hill on the Pampa. It can, however, be compared to a small figure from Palpa (see Reindel and Isla 1999: fig. 181, bottom row, second from right). Until recently, it was thought that animal/human geoglyphs were restricted to the Pampa. However, Reindel and Isla (1999: figs 177, 178, 181, 182) illustrate several small anthropomorphic, human and animal figures on the mesa above Sacramento in the Palpa Valley. Given the smaller size of these valley geoglyphs and the difficulty of seeing them at ground level, it is likely that others exist in other valleys, but have not been identified.

Geometric geoglyphs include spirals (Morrison 1987: 102; Reiche 1974: 14), zigzags, triangles (Bridges 1986: 9), trapezoids (convergent sides; Bridges 1986: 13), quadrangles (Bridges 1986: 24; Morrison 1987: 106), and *campos barridos* or great square and rectangular cleared fields (Silverman 1990a: fig. 10). Geometric figures can be simple or composite (see Aveni 1990b: fig. ii.11; Morrison 1987: 118, 119; Silverman 1990a: fig. 13). Other geometric and combination geoglyph forms are well known in the valleys such as the "yarn and needle" at Cantalloc near the town of Nazca (Bridges 1986: 16, 21; Reiche 1974: 27), another possible "yarn and needle" (see Silverman 1990a: fig. 14) and spirals with lines and trapezoids (Silverman 1990a: fig. 13) in Ingenio, and the impressive complex of lines, trapezoids, spirals and zigzags above Sacramento in the Palpa Valley (see Reindel and Isla 1999: figs 176–80; see also Bridges 1986: 20).

The *lineal* geoglyphs *per se* consist of long lines of unvarying width (single lines, multiple parallel lines) (Aveni 1990a: fig. I.1c, d, I.5; Morrison 1987: 39 top, 67 bottom left; Reiche 1974: 110). Line widths can be as narrow as 10 cm and as wide as at least 1.2 m. Also included in the concept of lineal geoglyphs are ray centers (see Aveni 1986; Kroeber and Collier 1998: figs 9, 10; Morrison 1987: 116; figure 7.2).

Technology

A small number of geoglyphs were made by an additive technique involving the piling up of surface rock to create the design; these are the earliest geoglyphs and are Paracas in style and date (see figure 7.3). The vast majority of geoglyphs on and off the Pampa

Figure 7.2   A ray center on the Pampa (*photo*: Helaine Silverman).

were made by a subtractive technique; all known Nasca geoglyphs
are subtractive.[1] It is with these markings that we are concerned in
this chapter.

The technology of subtractive geoglyph-making was actually
quite simple. It involved removing (by hand, by sweeping) the
dark, angular rocks covering the Pampa surface so as to reveal the
underlying unoxidized, lighter-colored subsurface. The lithic detritus
was then placed as a border around the cleared area forming a
kind of berm. On incomplete geoglyphs rocks can be seen piled up
in the middle of the cleared space or along its sides, waiting to be
placed as edging, each pile possibly corresponding to a worker (see
Morrison 1987: 68 bottom, 69 top, 124; National Geographic
Society 1992: 146–7; Silverman 1990a: fig. 6). This rock border
can range in height from a few centimeters to a meter (Aveni

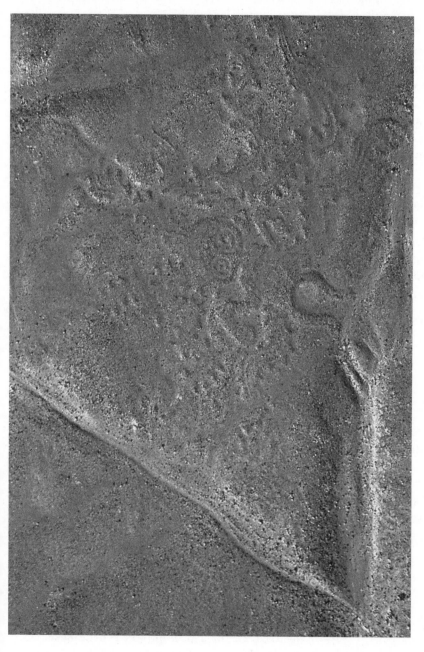

Figure 7.3 A complex figure on the Pampa in the late Paracas style made by the additive technique (*photo*: Helaine Silverman).

1990a: 5–6). The geoglyphs are visible because of the contrast between their dark outlines and cleared interiors.

The physical construction of the individual geoglyphs was not a monumental task (see, for example, Morrison 1987: 55 top photograph) and did not produce volumetric architecture. However, the technology of the geoglyphs – whether biomorphs (life forms: plants, animals, humans) or lineal – is precise. Clearly, coordinated organization of labor is implied; that is, someone or some group was in charge of their elaboration. Depending on the nature of the culturally important information reflected and recorded in the geoglyphs (see below), those members of society directing their elaboration may have been able to control and play the situation to their advantage.

The scale of the figural geoglyphs could be two hundred times as large as the model used (Reiche 1973: 9). For instance, the Crooked Neck Bird is 285 m long; the Lizard is 188 m long; the Monkey is 90 m long; the Hummingbird is 50 m long. Several replicative experiments have demonstrated how the long straight lines, large spirals, and huge figures could have been made without the benefit of aerial overview or sophisticated instrumentation to compensate for the visual distortion at ground level caused by their vast scale (see, for example, Aveni 1990a: 23–5, fig. 1.9; Morrison 1978: 43 top; National Geographic Explorer's TV documentary, "Mystery of the Nazca Lines", October 18, 1987). Straight lines probably were laid out by sighting through or along wood posts and pulling cotton string along the sight line to delineate a geoglyph edge; large figures could have been amplified from textile-based warp and weft grids staked on the ground; spirals and the curved portions of figures may have been achieved by running string around a wood stake compass to create the arc segments using a standardized unit of measure (see discussion in Reiche 1973: 12; see illustration in National Geographic Society 1992: 146–7).

Chronology

The vast majority of geoglyphs on and off the Pampa were made by Nasca people and date to all of the Nasca phases on the basis of their associated surface pottery and iconography shared with Nasca pottery (Isbell 1978; Reindel and Isla 1999; Silverman 1990a). These iconographic parallels are particularly strong with the early Nasca ceramic phases (see, for example, Hadingham 1987: 77–9; W. H. Isbell 1978; Reinhard 1988: 36–53; versus Morrison 1978: 79).

Even though the superposition of lineal geoglyphs over manifestly Nasca figural geoglyphs is readily apparent on the Pampa (Bridges 1986: 14, 23; Reiche 1974: 1, 2; Reindel and Isla 1999: fig. 176), the data gathered by Silverman and Browne (Silverman 1990a; Silverman and Browne 1991) and Reindel and Isla (1999) show an overwhelming association of all kinds of geoglyphs (lines, geometric forms, representational figures) with Nasca culture. Silverman and Browne (1991; see also Silverman 1992b) recovered very limited evidence of geoglyph manufacture and use in subsequent time periods, and Reindel and Isla (1999) found no evidence of post-Nasca geoglyphs in Palpa. In contrast, Clarkson (1990: 170), whose project was conducted on the Pampa, argued that most of the lineal geoglyphs on the Pampa were post-Nasca in date. We emphasize our disagreement with Clarkson because the valley geoglyphs encompass all of the types found on the Pampa (although valley figures are much smaller in scale) yet are predominantly and often exclusively associated with Nasca potsherds. This is not to say that there are no Late Intermediate Period (LIP) geoglyphs, for indeed there are. One of the most impressive geoglyph fields is located in the Ingenio Valley at the base of a great LIP habitation site and LIP pottery covers the ground markings (see Silverman 1990a: 448, fig. 17). David Johnson (personal communication, 1998) has observed lineal geoglyphs in association with LIP sites such as Cerro Colorado in the lower Nazca Valley. But, clearly, the apogee of geoglyph elaboration is associated with Nasca people.

Current Scholarly Knowledge and Interpretations

The modern era of geoglyph studies has involved fieldwork by astronomers (Aveni 1986, 1990b; Pitluga 1999), anthropologists (Reinhard 1988, 1992; Urton 1982, 1990), and archaeologists (Browne 1992; Clarkson 1990; Reindel and Isla 1999; Silverman 1990a; Silverman and Browne 1991). Research has emphasized both the geoglyphs on the Pampa and the geoglyphs off the Pampa. Most of the theories which have resulted are viable and mutually complementary. All of us explicitly see the geoglyphs as an important and complex indigenous cultural expression requiring contextualization in ancient society.

Pampa perspectives

Aveni (1986, 1990b: 111–12) has emphasized the symbolic, ritual, and social aspects of the geoglyphs, particularly the radial arrangement of lines on the Pampa. He recognizes a similarity to the ceque system of the Incas and compares the geoglyphs to a "highly ordered hierarchical cosmographical map, a mnemonic scheme that incorporated virtually all important matters connected with the [ancient] world view" (Aveni 1986: 37). We agree. Though not volumetric architecture, the geoglyphs created a highly structured, built environment.

Zuidema (1982: 428) argues that the *huacas* of the *ceque* system and *huacas* in general represented the distinct sociopolitical units that worshiped there; each *ayllu* or social group was responsible for its *huaca* and was, concomitantly, related to a *ceque*. Following the *ceque* analogy, Aveni also sees the geoglyphs being used as places of convergence and important places of worship or sacrifice. Each Nasca group made and was related to its geoglyphs. A group may have produced many geoglyphs over its life-span. We also highlight the inseparable concept of space–time implicated in the *ceque* system and suggest that there was an integral temporal parameter to the Pampa. Geoglyphs were surely made and used at ritually prescribed times of the year and, as such, marked time and through their use were a form of lived time.

Aveni (1986: 39) also thinks the geoglyphs were walked. Similarly, and based on analogy with the ethnographic Qoyllur R'iti pilgrimage, Silverman (1990a: 453) has suggested that they were "danced and tranced" into existence (see below). Thus, some scholars feel strongly that the geoglyphs were dynamic rather than static ritual venues.

Clarkson's (1990) investigations on the Pampa have been crucial in bringing the immense tracings down to human scale through her discovery of various functionally associated material remains. Among these are stone circles, semicircles, and arcs (Clarkson 1990: 132, 135, fig. III.11) which are found near geoglyphs. Silverman (1990a) also has observed these kinds of remains and calls them "*refugios,*" referring to their intuited function as wind-shelters for the workers making the geoglyphs; Clarkson (1990: 161) posits the same function. Clarkson also documents cairns (piles of rocks) often placed "at the end, intersection of, or beside lines" and on hill tops marking line centers; they also are present where there are no geoglyphs (Clarkson 1990: 136). Among the explanations proposed for these cairns are points of visibility, boundary markers, line markers, and water-channel markers (Aveni 1990b). In addition, Clarkson (1990: 137) has observed circular and rectangular walled enclosures, most of them located "near the edges of small pampas on the south side of the Tierras Blancas valley." Potsherds and, to a lesser degree, lithics, shell, and bone are present as artifacts on the Pampa (Clarkson 1990: 139). In addition to serving to date the geoglyphs with which they are associated, broken pottery also hints at the kinds of activities occurring on the Pampa while the geoglyphs were being made and used. Clarkson (1990: 140) suggests that pots were being ritually smashed. This is a reasonable proposition given the concentrations of potsherds that are known to occur. And, of course, it is highly likely that prior to destruction the whole pottery vessels contained food and drink. We also think that painted iconography imbued with meaning both the pots and the actions in which they were involved.

Using ethnographic and ethnohistorical data, Reinhard (1988) has cogently proposed a direct relationship between the Nazca Lines, the worship of mountain deities, rainfall, water supply, and agricultural fertility. He has identified particular mountains in the Nazca region as *huacas* (sacred places) – notably, Cerro Blanco – and he suggests that "some lines, especially the large triangles and rectangles, may well have served as symbolic connectors with water sources (rivers, mountains, the ocean) and were sacred areas where fertility rites were carried out." We are in full agreement with Reinhard (1988: 21) that:

> given the importance of the rains in the mountains and other sources of water for the agriculture of the Nazca people and the beliefs that

date at least to Inca times, it seems highly probable that worship of
water sources, including mountains (both nearby and further into
the Andes), played a very prominent role in their beliefs at the time
the geoglyphs were constructed.

Like Reinhard (1988: 24), we are much impressed with the
observation of our Peruvian avocational colleague, Josué Lancho
Rojas (personal communication, 1996), that lines appear to intersect filtration galleries at Cantalloc in the Tierras Blancas Valley.
Reinhard (1988: fig. 27) concludes that "most of the lines did not
point at anything on the geographical or celestial horizon, but
rather led to places where rituals were performed to obtain water
and fertility of crops." Again, we agree with Reinhard.

Urton (1990) and Silverman (1990a: 451–2) explain the geoglyphs
as vivifications of the Quechua concepts of *chuta* and *mit'a*: the
obligation to create tangible social space and the space of practice,
a strip of ritual and social space that was made at its proper
moment of time in the sense of fulfilling a ritual obligation by a
distinct social group (*ayllu*). The creation of the geoglyphs created
space. Borrowing from Lewis-Williams's (1982: 438) study of San
rock art, we argue that the removal of surface rock to create the
Nasca geoglyphs "was part of a symbolic and ideological practice
which dealt with the reproduction of world order and social processes of production"; the creation of the Pampa was "conscious
symbolic work."

The vast majority of the Pampa's figural geoglyphs are immediately above the Ingenio Valley between Cerro El Fraile and the
dramatic constriction of the valley at La Legua, or within a kilometer
of its edge. However, other figures (for example, Dog, Monkey) are
significantly removed from the valley rim (see, for example, Reiche
1974: 2). Furthermore, figures tend to be isolated from one another. Rarely, however, they cluster as is the case with Hands,
Lizard, and Huarango Tree. Significant line centers on the Pampa
border the Nazca Valley opposite Cahuachi (see Aveni 1986,
1990b). The vast interior of the Pampa is relatively lightly marked.

The Pampa was not executed as a unified corpus of landscape
architecture, although from the air it almost has the appearance of
a framed work. A confusing superposition of lineal geoglyphs is,
perhaps, the most dominant characteristic of the Pampa today.

Therefore, one of the most interesting issues raised by the geoglyphs on the Pampa is how the hypothesized social groups claimed drawing space on the Pampa and why certain locations were chosen and re-chosen. The stratification of lines on the Pampa stands in stark contrast to the figural geoglyphs which were, in general, traced widely spaced one from each other; occasionally, figures are damaged by later lineal geoglyphs. No overt territoriality or boundary marking appears to be operating on the Pampa beyond the notion that geoglyphs were made by and belonged to their specific groups. In the future, perhaps GIS analysis will reveal systematic spacing of geoglyphs that we do not perceive from ordinary examination of aerial photographs and maps.[2]

Rostworowski (1993: 199) plausibly interprets the superpositions as "the consequence of centuries of continuous use. It is possible that the lines were only used a few times and for this reason new lines always had to be made, thereby accounting for their great number." Silverman (1993a: 308) has also dealt with this issue of superposition. She suggests that Kosok's (1965: ch. 6) reference to the Pampa de San José as the "world's largest astronomy book" is appropriate (regardless of one's position on the astronomical hypothesis) in the sense of the Pampa being a text that was written and read. She sees the proliferation of lines on the Pampa as the cumulative result of repetitive ritual activity, perhaps calendrically organized as suggested above. Through this ritual activity on the Pampa the lines were made and in so doing the lines recorded ecological, climatological, hydrological, social, and political information necessary for social life and its prediction and scheduling. Thus, Silverman conceives of geoglyph-making as the massive storage of cultural knowledge in a graphic mnemonic system. But over time some data became obsolete. Therefore, new texts were inscribed as geoglyphs. In order to accurately read the lines (in both senses: of the text, on the Pampa):

> the text had to be clearly understandable. On the pampa some lines are more easily seen than others (they are brighter); perhaps this is because the ancient peoples swept the lines currently in use to keep them visible [see, for example, Reiche 1974: figs 118 bottom, 123 bottom] ... the lines were being kept ritually clean [i.e. ritual maintenance] ... Not only would the hypothesized sweeping of the

Nasca lines have been a religious act involving distinct social groups but, at the same time, this sweeping would have aided in the reading of the appropriate text by highlighting the relevant portion so that one would not "read between the lines" (read extraneous matter no long pertinent). (Silverman 1993a: 308)

Urton (1990) also argues that the lines were being kept ritually clean.

We think that the identity of various figural geoglyphs with creatures of the Nasca iconographic pantheon and the immensity of the geoglyphs are highly significant as well. The iconographic linkage between images on the Pampa and Nasca ceramic iconography could indicate, among other things, that these motifs were emblematic of particular social groups at the same time that they were evocative of meteorological and supernatural forces. The huge size of the geoglyphs, as well as their form (geometric, representational), must be the result of the ancient Nascas' attempt to transcend the natural by means of scale. Applying Friedberg (1993: 22), we can think in terms of an "ideology of representation" that is panoramic and that "must be placed in the context of the concurrent reconceptualization of the idea of the horizon and of perspective." Most of the entire corpus of geoglyphs on the Pampa was not being viewed from an elevated position (from hilltops); however, it was being conceived aerially. Landscape scholars have often commented on the "elevated perspective" which looks down on the landscape, as in painted landscape representations. In these views the spectator is authoritative (see Crandell 1993: 80). In the landscape of the Nazca Lines the grounded human view cannot encompass its totality. The scale of the geoglyphs on the Pampa is such that we are clearly witnessing a radical change in landscape perspective, what Friedberg (1993: 22) has called the "cult of immensity" with reference to painting and illusionist immersion. Both terrestrial use as well as aerial or immense perspective are implicated in the explanation of the Nasca geoglyphs.

At the same time, it is important to note that most of the figures are "open-ended" in the sense of not having lineal closure. Rather, they are entered and, apparently, were meant to be "maze-like" in the sense of being walked along a single line and exited by following the path which does not cross over itself. In contrast, Hands,

Huarango Tree, and Lizard are executed by a closed line, at least today. We provide this caution because Maria Reiche (1974: 118 bottom, 123 bottom) swept many of the geoglyphs; it is possible that she may have inadvertently obscured or altered original relationships between lines.

Valley perspectives

Silverman's (1990a, 1993b: 105) project in the Ingenio Valley and Browne's (1992) and Reindel and Isla's (1999) projects in the Palpa Valley explicitly sought to recover information on the manifestations of geoglyphs in the valleys and their relationship to valley settlements. It is now well documented that the geoglyphs are strongly associated with the valley populations.

In the Ingenio Valley there is an abundance of geoglyphs above the middle section of the valley where there is a dense, contemporary settlement pattern, not to mention the geoglyphs on the hillsides of the Ingenio Valley. In addition, similar pottery is found on the Pampa geoglyphs, hillside geoglyphs, and in habitation sites. Also, actual paths ascend from some of the valley settlements to the Pampa.

In addition to the dozens of geoglyphs recorded during Silverman's (1990a) survey of the Ingenio Valley, the 1944 aerial photographs reveal many more that were later destroyed. Most geoglyphs in the Ingenio Valley are trapezoids. Straight lines, cleared fields, major geoglyph complexes, and geoglyph combinations (for example, trapezoids and spirals) also were identified but no biomorphic figures.

In the Ingenio Valley, geoglyphs are found up to 525 m above sea level, although Nasca habitation sites extend many hundreds of meters further up-valley. The lack of geoglyphs above 525 m above sea level in the Ingenio Valley is not currently explicable. While it is true that most hillsides bordering the upper valley are steeper than those lower down, rendering many of these hillsides inappropriate for the elaboration of geoglyphs, nevertheless, others could have been used. Also, many upper valley *quebrada* mouths and remnant hills or terraces in these *quebradas* would have been considered ideal geoglyph locations by people living lower down valley.

Figure 7.4   Petroglyphs at Chichiktara, upper Palpa Valley (*photo*: Helaine Silverman).

Browne (1992; Silverman and Browne 1991) recorded many geoglyphs in Palpa, as have Reindel and Isla (1999) in the course of their more recent fieldwork. Reindel and Isla's new data from Palpa confirm, expand, and complicate the Ingenio geoglyph data. Their data confirm the predominant Nasca date of the geoglyph phenomenon. Like Silverman (1990a), they have recorded straight and zigzag lines and trapezoids. Unlike the Ingenio data, however, in Palpa there is significant evidence of figural geoglyphs, including human figures (Reindel and Isla 1999: fig. 181), a *tumi* (a crescent-shaped ceremonial knife with handle), and a whale (Reindel and Isla 1999: fig. 177 top right) which is readily comparable to the one on the Pampa. Furthermore, even their earliest geoglyphs appear to be made by reduction whereas the earliest geoglyphs known elsewhere (for example, on the Pampa as per figure 7.3) are made by an additive process.

Reindel and Isla make the fascinating argument that the Palpa geoglyphs have their origin in the abundant petroglyphs (rock carvings) found in the upper Palpa Valley, as seen in certain shared motifs such as stylized human figures with ray-like lines on their heads in the manner of a crown (figure 7.4). Also, other motifs on the petroglyphs are typical of Paracas and Nasca 1 pottery. Reindel and Isla suggest that:

> motifs were at first only created on the rock cliffs, mostly on places that were easily visible from the valley. Then it was discovered that one could also etch the same motifs into the surface of the desert floor. The early geoglyphs were, therefore – similar to the petroglyphs before them – placed on the valley slopes where they were easily visible to the people living in the valley. [Then] larger glyphs came into existence that became more and more abstract and took on geometric shapes. Finally, the large lines and cleared fields/campos barridos were constructed on the extensive mesas where people could no longer easily observe them.

Reindel and Isla (1999) appear to say that from an original, highly culturally significant, visible and integrated function in Nasca society of the Palpa Valley, the geoglyphs lost their meaning and became mere works of abstract land art, therefore being physically removed from the settlements of their human makers. Given the amount of coordinated effort that went into ascending to these locations and removing the surface rock with such precision, as well as the fact that the geoglyphs had symbolic content, we think we must continue to insist on their meaning and purpose to their makers, despite Reindel and Isla's proposed evolution from figural to geometric shapes.

Like Aveni (1990b: 83–7), Reindel and Isla (1999) see a relationship between the orientation of trapezoids and surface water features. They observed "long trapezoids which extend atop the flat mesas of the mountain ridge, mostly in a northeasterly to southwesterly direction . . . Because the corners almost all point to the original location of the river, it can be assumed that there exists a connection between the river and the geoglyphs."

Ethnohistoric perspectives

Rostworowski (1993) suggests that there was an intimate relationship between a coastal deity called Kón (see chapter 8) and the geoglyphs.

[I]nstead of building great temples to Kón, they had the idea of creating lines and figures on an immense plain to signal to the god that its faithful followers were awaiting him with ceremonies, rites, sacrifices, dances and festival . . . (Rostworowski 1993: 196)

There is no doubt that the geoglyphs of Nasca were conceptualized to be seen from the heavens, while the faithful were congregated on the lines and plazas. (Rostworowski 1993: 197)

The priests thought it was necessary to manifest their own presence and that of the local inhabitants, and toward this end they represented themselves in the gigantic drawings . . . The diverse lineages and specialists, such as augurs, were represented on the pampa by the drawings . . . The lines and plazas would be the places of reunion of the diverse lineages . . . The lines and biomorphic figures constituted a means of communication between the ancient Nasca and the divinity, and the drawings would be a manifestation of a religious expression . . . Maybe the spirit of the air, wind, sea and earth was present in the images. It is quite possible that the arrival of the god Kón coincided with the cresting of the rivers with water that was indispensable for life on the coast and which coincided with

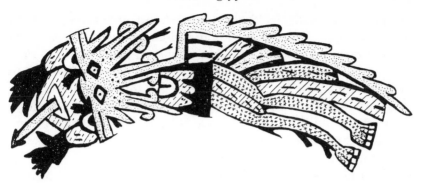

Figure 7.5   The Nasca icon identified as the god Kón by Rostworowski (1993) but actually a proliferous form of the Anthropomorphic Mythical Being.

> rain in the highlands . . . The purpose of the biomorphic figures and lines was to attract the attention of the flying divinity who had arrived on earth and whom they were awaiting . . . Possibly the principal festival was carried out during the time of the first arrival of water . . . (Rostworowski 1993: 198–9)

The problem with this argument is that the Nasca image which Rostworowski interprets as Kón (see figure 7.5) is actually a late Nasca proliferous representation of the Anthropomorphic Mythical Being, whose evolution can be traced over many Nasca ceramic phases (see Proulx 1968: figs 18–20; Roark 1965: figs 36, 37) during which time it had no relationship to flying. Furthermore, we are unconvinced that the immensity of the geoglyphs necessarily implies that they were meant to be seen from the air. It is also important to indicate that any similarity perceived between Rostworowski's theory and von Däniken's is superficial.

A New Perspective

Recently, a radical new theory about the Nazca Lines has been proposed by David Johnson, an independent investigator with a practical background in field geology and archaeology. This new hypothesis evolved over five years of fieldwork (1996–2000) and is based on Johnson's perception of a consistent association of geological faults, aquifers, filtration galleries, archaeological sites, and geoglyphs. Because of the attention this new hypothesis is attracting and because it has been published (Johnson 1999) in a respectable venue in the company of other mainstream discussions about various aspects of ancient Nasca culture and society (see Rickenbach 1999), we feel it is appropriate to summarize Johnson's theory here and the data that have been brought to bear for and against it. Specifically, Johnson argues that:

1 Water-bearing faults intersect alluvial valleys thereby providing a consistent and more reliable source of water in the form of springs and seeps than that from the river. The most productive aquifers are usually found where geological faults intersect the valleys. In addition, the most productive wells (both ancient and present) are also located at these intersections. Many of the filtration galleries seem to have their origin where these faults cross the valleys.
2 Ancient people strategically placed their filtration galleries at these locations to capture the water and redirect it to arid regions.[3]
3 Archaeological sites were located near these supplementary sources of water.
4 Some of the geometric geoglyphs mark the faults and chart the course of the subterranean aquifers from where they emerge from the foothills and cross the valleys and Pampa to the coast.[4] Johnson argues that archaeological sites are associated with faults and that faults appear to be marked by geoglyphs. Johnson says that all of these elements show a strong spatial correlation: where one element is found the other four usually are also present.

Parts 1, 2, and 3 of Johnson's hypothesis should be the least controversial since they have been preliminarily confirmed over two field seasons (1998, 1999) by geological fieldwork undertaken by Stephen Mabee of the Department of Geosciences at the University of Massachusetts in Amherst and his team of geologists, and also by archaeological survey conducted by Donald Proulx. Our position is that the data, presented below, provide enough support for parts 1, 2, and 3 of Johnson's original hypothesis as to warrant their further testing in the field. Let us look first at the water data concerning part 1.

Stephen Mabee has identified two sources of subsurface water in the Nazca region: groundwater flowing in the gravels beneath the river bed and groundwater discharging from permeable and trans- missive faults in the bedrock which intersect perpendicular to the axis of the river valleys. Mabee ascertained from field measure- ments that the faults are a few meters to several tens of meters wide. These faults show clear evidence of past fluid movement because they are usually heavily mineralized, indicating that fluids have moved through these faults in the past. In addition, Mabee has seen water seeping or weeping out of the ground in close proximity to faults at elevations that are, in some cases, more than 10 m higher than the water levels observed in the river gravels underneath the river bed. It is not uncommon to have large quant- ies of groundwater entering unconsolidated deposits from faults in the bedrock. This water can enter the gravels from below or from the valley sides. Lineament studies, geophysical investiga- tions, and analyses of the direction of groundwater flow and water chemistry have provided substantial evidence to support these observations in the Aja Valley and Nazca Valley proper.

Hydrogeological, geophysical, and geochemical analyses (includ- ing basic geological mapping; groundwater flow mapping; electro- magnetic induction, seismic refraction, resistivity and magnetometer surveys; water quality testing) performed at two sites suggest that faults do intersect the valleys or, rephrased, subterranean water enters from the sides of the valleys via faults which act as pathways for groundwater transmission; groundwater flow mapping indicates that some of the groundwater moving through the gravels beneath the river beds does have a source from the bedrock along the valley side walls. In addition, results of water-quality testing, specifically temperature, conductivity (a proxy for the dissolved solids in the water), pH, calcium, magnesium, sulfate, and chloride and stable isotope compositions (deuterium and oxygen 18), suggest that some of the groundwater from wells and springs represents a deep- seated, regional hydrological flow regime and exhibits a geochemical signature that is significantly different from the river water.

Geological data and analyses from Aja are the most compre- hensive to date. Groundwater levels from nineteen wells and three filtration galleries indicate that groundwater is moving in a south-westerly direction from the valley side walls towards the river. The water levels of wells closest to the valley sides of the Aja River are 10 m higher than the water levels in the filtration gallery closest to the riverbed. This groundwater configuration signifies a "gaining" stream scenario where groundwater from the sides of the valley is contributing water to the main trunk of the stream. Water from wells located at the valley sidewalls is slightly warmer (26.8°C versus 24.2°C), exhibits higher conductivity (106 versus 75 µS/cm), and has higher pH (7.1 versus 6.6) than the groundwater in wells adjacent to or in the riverbed.

The geochemical data are most convincing at Cerro Colorado, located at the confluence of the Grande and Nazca rivers. Here calcium, magnesium, chloride, and sulfate concentrations are significantly lower in springs emanating from a fault compared to the river. Ph levels of spring water are also higher and the temperature is about 6° warmer than the water in the rivers. These differences suggest two sources of water.

Now let us look at parts 2 and 3 of Johnson's theory. The geological fieldwork of Stephen Mabee, combined with standard archaeological survey by Donald Proulx, indicates a significant correlation between the location of filtration galleries, aquifers, and archaeological sites in the Aja and Nazca valleys. For example, both the Aja and Orcona filtration galleries are perpendicular to groundwater which enters the Nazca Valley along north–south trending faults several meters above the elevation of the riverbed; indeed, one Orcona branch appears to actually cross underneath the Aja River and head northerly, picking up water from the valley to the north. There is geological and hydrological evidence to suggest that subterranean aquifers were intercepted by ancient filtration galleries at the archaeological sites of Santo Cristo and Usaca as well. Schreiber and Lancho Rojas (1995) also argue that the arid middle stretches of the Nazca Valley were settled only when the filtration galleries were developed there.

The most controversial aspect of David Johnson's theory is part 4: that the geoglyphs functioned as a map of subsurface water resources. Johnson argues that trapezoids were laid out directly over the trace of faults and that the width of the trapezoids defined the width of the fault zone capable of transmitting groundwater as concentrated flow. Triangles (called pointers by Johnson) pointed to areas where the faults crossed the ridges or hilltops, and evidence for the fault can usually be found in the bedrock exposures. Zigzag lines mark the boundary of subterranean aquifers – areas where there is no water. As for the biomorphs, Johnson feels that they mark where aquifers change direction. Johnson has published excellent graphic examples of this summary in figs 145–8 of his 1999 article, not reproduced here because their sense is lost without his color overlays. So far, Johnson has found correlations that support his theory, but he has not tried to invalidate it which is standard procedure in scientific method.[5] Furthermore, the complex and dense superposition of geoglyphs on the Pampa must be noted (see figure 7.1), as must the frequency of geoglyphs at, but also in between and away from, habitation sites in the valleys (see Silverman 1990a). Nevertheless, the hypothesis remains intriguing and deserving of further testing.

Johnson's reading of the marked landscape is interesting, too, because independently Reinhard (1988: 34) argued that spiral and zigzag geoglyphs were used in water cults and that the spiral was derived from the ancient Peruvians' observation of shells, such as the conch, having spiral form. The conch is known ethnographically and ethnohistorically to have been used to call on the mountain gods or clouds for rain. Reinhard relates the zigzag to rivers, canals, lightning, and agricultural furrows.

Geoglyphs as Space and Synthesis

The geoglyphs indicate the centrality of spatial cognition among the Nasca people. The Nasca were literally writing their multifaceted understanding of the world at huge scale on the landscape where this knowledge could be read (retrieved), as well as modified. Silverman (1990a) argues that the Pampa as terrain was domesticated, brought within the human sphere by the social activities conducted on and around it, thereby becoming social space and sacred space. But it is important to recognize that there is no such thing as unconceived space: "the experience of space is always socially constructed" (Gupta and Ferguson 1992: 11). As Wood (1992: 78–9) puts it:

the natural content of the landscape must be culturalized *into* existence. This is a labor of culture, it is a labor of identifying, of
bounding, of naming, of inventorying . . . it is a labor of mapping.
Since these processes occur bundled up together in the living that
human occupance of the land amounts to, there is no first place
from which to launch ourselves . . . the human landscape is brought
into being historically . . . mapping is a way of making experience of
the environment shareable.

Archaeology demonstrates that there was a time when the surface
of the Pampa was unmarked. But the Pampa always must have had
a name as a meaningful concept in at least the physical geography
of the aboriginal population. Whether or not the Pampa was attributed social and sacred qualities before its engraving will never
be known. Also, the Pampa – which sits between the Ingenio and
Nazca rivers – was surely conceptualized by the ancient inhabitants
of the drainage as a *tinkuy*, an indigenous Quechua concept meaning river junction as well as a socially and supernaturally charged
place of competition, cooperation, and structural balance.

We believe that the geoglyphs on the Pampa mapped space in
the dynamic, generative sense of Wood (quoted above). We believe
that geoglyphs were associated with distinct social groups and that
the marking of the Pampa – both with figural geoglyphs and lineal
geoglyphs – brought these groups into existence and, concomitantly, reflected their existence intrinsically and with regard to
other groups with whom actual physical space on the Pampa had
to be negotiated. It is our gut feeling that the geoglyphs on the
Pampa articulated territoriality and intergroup communication,
what Rosenfeld (1997: 297) refers to as "socially constructed
identity–place relationships."

The geoglyphs were part of the larger Nasca social world. They
were part of the entire Nasca system of cultural meaning and expression, one that also was manifested by geoglyphs executed off the
Pampa. The Pampa was an important venue for civic-ceremonial
activities; the valley geoglyphs must have been similar in this
regard. The Pampa palimpsest, with its superpositions, is a diachronic record of local situations, historical contingencies, and
forgotten, new, and renewed landmarks (interestingly, we have
rarely observed superpositions among the valley geoglyphs). As

such, the Pampa was a landscape of relationships. And for hundreds of years it was a site of the Nasca people's collective memory and social identity. Geoglyphs were not just part of the Nasca landscape, they created that landscape and the landscape was, above all, social.

Most of the current theories about the Nazca Lines, in one way or another, suggest that earth-marking inscribed and vivified social identity and action on to the landscape. The making of the geoglyphs transformed the landscape and was, simultaneously, social production – the making and constituting of society. The Qoyllur R'iti pilgrimage, near Cuzco, provides an excellent contemporary example, one which readily serves as an ethnographic analogy:

[people danced into existence] a unique corridor that joins the community to the macrocosm. Each corridor incorporates a series of landmarks to guide the travelers toward their goal . . . rocks, springs, cairns, mountains, other miraculous shrines . . . and these landmarks become the more frequent and charged with greater sanctity as the shrine is neared and the various corridors converge, funneling the pilgrims into a single stream toward the center . . . Through the media of percussion, music, and dance, passive, physical features and locations are culturally appropriated and transformed into a continuous sacred topography . . . any dance routine is itself a formal, kinesthetic mapping of space . . . The ritual passage is pervaded by melody and rhythm . . . (Sallnow 1987: 201)

[on the return home from the pilgrimage site:] [T]hey reformed into moiety lines. First, they faced the sun, kneeling in silence for a few seconds . . . Suddenly they arose as a single body and proceeded to file down the hillside at a trot in two columns, led respectively by the ukukus [men dressed as bears] of each moiety with . . . flags streaming in the wind. All the musicians were playing the same tune . . . The two lines of dancers wheeled, wove and zigzagged across the landscape, successively converging, crossing and separating in a serpentine choreography that was entirely symmetrical across a vertical axis. (Sallnow 1987: 232)

As indicated above, the entrances to many of the figures on the Pampa strongly support the hypothesis that the landscape of huge, immobile geoglyphs was created by movement. Influenced by Nasca iconography (for example, the Tello plaque) and the ethnographic observation of lineal processional dancing figures across the undulating hills below the Qoyllur R'iti pilgrimage sanctuary following the descent from the glacier above Sinakara, Silverman (1990a: 453) has envisioned Nasca people similarly dancing single-file across the Pampa and the valley hillsides and then physically executing the geoglyphs at the end of that particular ceremonial episode in imitation of these danced outlines and in permanent remembrance or commemoration of the multi-faceted occasion with its many associated meanings.

Thus, in the final analysis, the geoglyphs were Mejía Xesspe's (1940) ceremonial roads, Aveni's (1986, 1990b; see also Morrison 1978) proto-*ceque* system and surface water markers, Reinhard's (1988) water/fertility cult markers, Urton's (1990) *chutas*, and Silverman's (1990a) pilgrimage routes, arenas of performance, and mnemonic and memory texts. To these many roles we cite the possibility raised by Johnson (1999) that some geoglyphs were cognitive and physical maps of the drainage's subsurface water, thereby additionally serving to create locality by graphically representing a group's relationship to the critical resources underwriting its existence and necessary for social reproduction; this suggestion would be operative for geoglyphs as surface water markers as well. And, of course, we must not forget the obvious: that the giant biomorphic figures on the Pampa, as well as some of their smaller valley cousins, may have represented the deities/supernatural beings depicted on pottery that were important to this society and the smaller groups of which it was composed as well as being emblematic of these groups. The ancient Nascas' marking of vast desert expanses and barren hillsides with tracings of animal and geometric forms is the most visible example of the integration of Nasca social, political, religious, and ecological concepts about the proper functioning and organization of the cultural world.

8

Religion and Ritual

Over the past twenty years or so archaeologists have come to view religion and ritual in ancient civilizations as key factors in sociopolitical evolution (see early statements in Coe 1981; Demarest 1984; Freidel 1981; Keatinge 1981). Monumental architecture, ritual paraphernalia, public display, and elite power can be shown to be intimately and inextricably related in many ancient societies around the world. In the Americas, the Maya and Moche come readily to mind. They are particularly susceptible to interpretation because of the narrational aspect of their art and the immense (Maya) and growing (Moche) body of field data that contextualize these ideological stories. Nasca's highly iconographic art – much of it clearly referential to the supernatural and mythological – beseeches investigators to decipher it. Cahuachi's pyramids, the geoglyphs of the Pampa and valleys, trophy heads, and full-body burials insist to us that they are critical in the interpretation of the Nasca world. In this chapter we seek to identify and reconstruct the elements and essence of the Nasca people's system of beliefs through attention to the rituals that vivified them, the cult objects used to conduct them, the iconography that represented them (Nasca people's portrayal of their own ritual activities), and the space (monumental, social, and so on) in which they were expressed and which they created.

Sources of Information

There are two primary sources of information on ancient Nasca religion: representational art and structured contexts. These primary sources implicate other classes of physical remains such as ritual attire and paraphernalia, trophy heads, geoglyphs, and cached offerings. The nature and patterning of particular activities (such as trophy-head preparation) and locales (such as certain buildings or other modifications that created a built environment) permit us to identify them as ritual in nature, or to infer ritual behavior from them, such as pilgrimage and ancestor veneration.

Some scholars argue that for Nasca and other pre-contact societies there is another, indirect source of information: our knowledge of Inca religion on the basis of what the Spanish observed (the chronicles of discovery and conquest), and our knowledge of Inca and pre-Conquest Andean beliefs on the basis of what survived into the Colonial Period and what is recoverable through the testimonies of Incas and others to the Spanish (the ethnohistory of *visitas*, law suits, extirpations of idolatries, and so on). Scholars such as Tello (1923), Carrión Cachot (1959), Zuidema (1972), Burger (1988) and Silverman (1990b, 1993a) have argued liberally back and forth in time and across space on the basis of their belief in a fundamental pan-Andean culture (and see Bennett 1948).

In contrast, others have urged caution in using Inca models for the interpretation of pre-Inca cultures (see, especially, Isbell 1995, 1997). In terms of Nasca, specifically, Donald Proulx (in press) criticizes the structuralist and unmethodical approach to Nasca religion that some scholars offer. He proposes, instead, to contextualize the study of Nasca religion within the larger framework of studies of Nasca iconography and, more generally, classic studies in the anthropology of religion such as those by Tylor and Durkheim. Proulx argues that the use of ethnographic analogy in comparing two cultures separated by long spans of time – not to mention space – must take into consideration "contextual disjunction," the possibility that beliefs alter over time and symbols can acquire new or different meanings (see, especially, Kubler 1985). For example, Zuidema's (1972) use of Inca ethnohistoric documents to interpret Nasca iconography assumes that some very specific symbolism present in Inca iconography represents a long Andean tradition that cross-cuts space and time. However, Proulx argues that Nasca culture had disappeared almost eight hundred years prior to the emergence of the Inca Empire and was separated from it by the Tiwanaku/Wari religious tradition which was quite different from earlier Nasca religion, not to mention the different political context.

As a result of the co-authors' different theoretical orientations, we have used varying perspectives in our interpretation of Nasca society; this is reflected in our previous publications. Although we have not always been in agreement with one another, we are both open-minded to alternative scenarios and, as social scientists, we keep searching for the most parsimonious explanation. In the text below we will attempt to present interpretative arguments using several models to provide the reader with what we feel are the best reasoned reconstructions of Nasca religion based on current evidence. We hope and expect that future research will augment our ideas for the better.

Kón: A Winged and Flying God of the Coast

In an important article, the great Peruvian ethnohistorian, Maria Rostworowski (1993), identifies a late Nasca image (figure 7.5) with an ethnohistorically known coastal deity called Kón (see also discussion of Kón in Tello 1923: 97–8ff). As elucidated by Rostworowski from documents, Kón did not have bones and flew in agile form, descending from the highlands to the coast. This deity peopled the world with men and women. But at some point Kón became disgusted and turned the earth into sterile deserts leaving only the rivers with which people could eke out a living. Kón was the son of the Sun and Moon and/or Kón formed the heavens, sun, moon, stars and earth and peopled the world with humans, plants, and animals. Later, the god Pachacamac appeared and replaced Kón as the focus of devotion.

Some documents indicate that Kón came from the north coast, but Rostworowski argues that the documents can be understood as indicating a southern origin. This leads Rostworowski to suggest that Kón was the principal god of the Paracas and Nasca people, in addition to the other *huacas* and divinities they had. As evidence, Rostworowski points to images on textiles and pottery that appear to show a person flying with legs extended, face covered by a mask and carrying in its extended hands plants or trophy heads. Although we are doubtful about Rostworowski's identification of Kón in Nasca, we fully accept the late pre-Hispanic existence of this god on the coast as testified in documentary sources such as the Huarochirí Manuscript (see discussion in Salomon 1991).

Ritual Performers and Ritual Practitioners

In their study of anthropological approaches to religion, Lehmann and Myers (1985: 78) indicate that individuals may engage the supernatural but that in complex societies there also are intermediaries, people who – whether part-time or full-time specialists – intervene with the "other world" on behalf of the members of their community and, in so doing, implicate social, political, economic, and other spheres of action in society. These individuals are typically called priests and shamans in the literature. Lehmann and Myers note that, cross-culturally, religious specialists are more likely to occur in societies that produce their food rather than gather it.

We distinguish priests from shamans and argue that this differentiation is significant in terms of the structure of society. Priests are full-time specialists officiating over temples and shrines. Shamans are part-time mediators between the spirit world and everyday world. We argue that Nasca religion was shamanistic with animistic rituals geared mainly toward ensuring agricultural fertility and propitiating "transhuman controlling powers" to use Victor Turner's (1985) apt phrase for the supernatural (see Proulx 1999a: 71; n.d.). In ancient Nasca society, this power appears to have been personalized and materialized in iconographically represented deities, or gods, or spirits. Although a site such as the great ceremonial center of Cahuachi was a regularly organized and permanently functioning shrine used at particular times in a traditional manner by specific social groups, we do not see evidence of Nasca religion having been a state cult in which the religious officiators were supported by the labor of others. Such temple priests would possess "a body of codified and standardized ritual knowledge [learnt] from older priests and later transmit[ted] to successors" (Turner 1985: 82). Rather, we see Nasca religion as much more fluid and flexible, more subject to innovation and modification with each celebration. Turner (1985: 84) says that the shaman "enacts his roles in small-scale, multifunctional communities whose religious life incorporates beliefs in a multitude of deities, daemons, nature spirits, or ancestral shades – societies that Durkheim might have described as possessing mechanical solidarity, low moral density, and segmental organization." While we do not like dichotomizing and static classifications in lieu of the fine-grained anthropological study of dynamic human behavior, and although we may be hair-splitting, still we think that there is an important sociological difference between religion in Nasca and, for instance, the institution of religion in the large-scale, complex Inca state. Iconographically, there is no unambiguous evidence that Nasca's religious officiators were a group of full-time occupational specialists (priests) nor is there direct archaeological evidence to that effect (unlike the Moche situation, see, for example, Alva 1994; Donnan and Castillo 1992; Strong and Evans 1947).

In the rare scenes of human interaction to which social reality might be imputed, we see Nasca ritual activity involving the participation of several to many dozens of performers, the number in part being conditioned by the medium (ceramic vessels accommodate fewer individuals than textiles). Nasca people wear masks, headdresses, fine tunics, and wings and hold agricultural products as they perform dances (see Sawyer 1979: figs 6–8). Other early Nasca ritual performers hold (and presumably took) trophy heads (Sawyer 1979: fig. 2) and are portrayed in poses so similar to those of the celebrating agriculturalists that the trophy head and agricultural products must be mutually substitutable images (and see Roark 1965: figs 54, 55, 56a for the association of Nasca 5 Harvesters with trophy heads). Nasca 5 individuals costumed in fine breechcloths, sleeved tunics, wings, turbans, and headdresses play panpipes and hold rattles (Sawyer 1979: fig. 13). Nasca 5 harvest festival textiles depict multitudes of dancing participants (Sawyer 1979: figs 14–16, 18, 20, 22). The harvest scenes are particularly interesting for their lack of noticeably differentiated individuals; the participants wear different costumes but none is much more bedecked than any other. The actors are clearly human rather than mythical. Priests are not specifically shown and it could be suggested that many individuals, upon donning the proper attire, could fulfill otherworldly roles and/or that ritual performers in AMB costume could lead the other congregants. Quilter (1999: 19) has keenly observed that "[i]mpersonating gods performing rituals of sacrifice is a religious program meant to be dramatized, for what good is donning a costume or mask if it is not to be seen?" All of these scenes are surely depicting rites similar to some of those held in the plazas of Cahuachi.

Contemporary with the florescence of Cahuachi, many religious and supernatural images are painted on pottery. Townsend (1985: 131) identifies the AMB as a masked and costumed human ritual performer engaged in ritual activities and impersonating the supernatural. He speaks of "actual performers – living, moving cult images on religious festival occasions." Silverman (1993a) has advocated Townsend's human-actor interpretation. Perhaps the existence of storage facilities for ritual paraphernalia at Cahuachi means that people took on their transcendant roles at the site through participation in ritual (see Silverman 1990a: 453, 1993a).

The Cleveland Museum of Art textile (Bennett 1954: fig. 58) portrays six elaborately costumed human figures in different ritual attire. Clearly, the textile is showing the human impersonation and personification of the supernatural beings by means of the costumes and masks inhabited by the humans. It is impossible, however, to know if these six personages are existing in synchronic time (i.e. that they are doing six distinct actions simultaneously), or if a single personage is represented diachronically (i.e. doing different actions at different times in different costumes), or if distinct personages are represented diachronically (i.e. different actors doing different things at different times), or if the action is moving from left to right or from right to left or from the middle out or the outside in.

Other painted textiles show costumed human beings impersonating the Mythical Spotted Cat. The humans wear the diagnostic tri-lobal headpiece, there are paw-print markings on the pelt suspended from the headpiece or tail, and they carry its characteristic agricultural products (see Sawyer 1979: figs 6, 7). These images must be depicting human actors rather than the Mythical Spotted

Cat *per se* because the personages are upright, wear tunics and have hands with opposable thumbs (compare to the contemporary pottery image of the Mythical Spotted Cat in Sawyer 1979: fig. 9).

Humans also dress in winged costumes (see Sawyer 1979: fig. 13), though this could refer to birds rather than overtly supernatural creatures since the humans have no other non-human referents. These costumes may have been used in fertility rites (see Yacovleff 1931).

Donald Proulx, however, argues the counter-position. While conceding that shamans did on occasion wear mouthmasks, neck-laces, and other attributes of mythical beings (Proulx 1983: 95, 1989c: 151), Proulx argues that the vast majority of the icono-graphic representations of mythical creatures in Nasca ceramic art are purely symbolic and were not meant to portray masked imper-sonators or ritual performers (Proulx 1996: 110, 1999a: 71). In other words, for Proulx, most AMB representations actually are the supernatural being, not just its human agent.

In this book we attempt to resolve our difference of opinion by proposing that ultimately it does not matter if the personage being depicted was human or not, for once the costume was donned and the ritual context entered, the being was supernatural and endowed with sacred power, a shaman able to communicate and intercede with the other supernatural forces of the Nasca pantheon such as the Killer Whale, Horrible Bird, Spotted Cat, and Serpentine Crea-ture among others. As excavations at Nasca civic-ceremonial sites continue, our different interpretations can be tested. For instance, will archaeologists find in burials the garb of the mythical creatures impersonated or vivified by humans as archaeologists have done at Moche sites such as Sipán?

The Ritual Paraphernalia of Performance and Participation

The props or settings for human ritual actions and interactions are rarely represented in Nasca art (for an example see the possible depiction of llama sacrifice atop a stepped mound, and the burial of trophy heads within or below it, in figure 8.1). This lack of spatial context in Nasca pottery contrasts notably with the ceramic art of Moche people who graphically situated the principal personage of

Figure 8.1 Roll-out from a vessel (MNAAH, C-13466) showing the ritual burial of a cache of trophy heads within a platform mound. Two shamans conduct the ceremony, possibly also involving llama sacrifice. The scene may also include ancestor worship (Proulx 1989b: fig. 15; Tello 1959: fig. 123).

their sacrifice ceremony atop a stepped pyramid, human sacrifice on mountain peaks, and captives in a sea-going raft.

Actual ritual paraphernalia is abundant in the Nasca archaeological record. Clearly, there was a rich ceremonial life in ancient Nasca society. Among the items recognized are the fancy textiles of ritual attire, hammered gold mouthmasks and forehead ornaments, fine pottery, pyro-engraved gourd containers, carved stone beakers, and musical instruments. Unfortunately, few of these have been found in context.

Musical instruments were paramount among Nasca ritual objects. Made mostly of pottery, many of these objects are richly painted with natural and supernatural imagery. Orefici (1993: 145) has written evocatively, "For the Nasca people, music was one of the indispensable means of expressing the collective religious spirit, constituting a true and proper choral language with which it was possible to communicate with the divine." The use of some of these musical instruments is shown in Nasca pottery itself. For instance, there are modeled figurines in which an individual plays panpipes, trumpet, and drum (figure 8.2). On another pot, musicians carry a trumpet that is being played by one of them (figure 8.3). The scene continues (figure 8.4) with panpipe players who are either beating a drum covered by a skin membrane, or who are going to remove a brew of San Pedro cactus from a large storage jar using a ceramic or gourd bowl.

Panpipes are very common at Cahuachi, the great early Nasca ceremonial center. Just from her small-scale excavations at the site, Silverman (1993a: table 16.6) recovered 207 panpipe fragments. Several years ago, Giuseppe Orefici (see *Life Magazine*, December 1999, pp. 96, 97) made a spectacular discovery of hundreds of broken panpipes on the floor of a storage room at Unit 2 at Cahuachi, the "Great Temple" where Strong (1957: 31) previously had recovered "an unusual amount of broken panpipes, llama remains, bird plumage, and other apparently feasting and sacrificial materials." Orefici says that the panpipes were deliberately broken and thrown into "a ruined temple as sacrificial offerings." Tracings of at least nine panpipes are present on the west wall of the Room of the Posts, a room that Silverman identifies as a temple dedicated to an ancestor cult (Silverman 1993a: 190–3, fig. 13.10). In the Ingenio Valley panpipes are found at habitation sites, cemeteries, and civic-ceremonial sites. The presence of panpipes at habitation sites suggests home rituals and portage to other ritual sites (for example, the Tello plaque). Tello recovered a cache of six matched panpipes from a Nasca 3 tomb in Las Trancas (see Bolaños 1988: 57, 60).

Even seemingly simple decoration, such as repeating *vencejos* painted on Nasca drums (see Sawyer 1975: fig. 126) and panpipes (Benson and Conklin 1981: 69), may refer to complex beliefs in which music played a major ritual role. These instruments were used in rituals that were surely concerned with propitiation of the forces of nature responsible for agricultural fertility. Nasca interest in the *vencejo* was probably due to its particular climatological cycle. The *vencejo* appears in the desert valleys of Nazca when the coastal rivers fill with water from highland rain. According to

Figure 8.2 Nasca effigy of a "one-man band" (MNAAH, C-55295; *photo*: Donald Proulx).

Figure 8.3 Nasca men carry a trumpet, played by one of them. The other side of this vessel appears in figure 8.4 (MNAAH, C-65296; *courtesy*: Patrick Carmichael).

Figure 8.4 Panpipe players; note the San Pedro cactus (MNAAH, C-65296; *courtesy*: Patrick Carmichael).

Yacovleff (1931), the ancient Nasca people associated the *vencejo* with the wet period in which seeds germinated and plants grew. Thus, the choice of the *vencejo* for "decoration" was a conscious evocation of strongly held beliefs about the life-cycle in the desert. Yacovleff also observed that Nasca mythical beings could take on attributes of the *vencejo* and that these traits could intercalate with or substitute for agricultural products such as fruit and root crops.

Sawyer (1979) plausibly suggests that many of the Nasca painted textiles functioned as ceremonial cloths and monumental hangings. Giuseppe Orefici recently discovered a cache of painted textiles at Cahuachi ("Peru's City of Ghosts": Discovery Television, 1999). We excitedly await publication of these fabulous materials and their precise context.

Sawyer (1962) illustrates and describes the miniature contents of a small textile bundle that is interpreted as a "medicine man kit" by Parsons (1962: 151). Sawyer (1962: 159) extends Parsons' functional identification of the bundle to argue that the objects were associated as fetishes or amulets used by a shaman in a fertility cult. The plainweave bag contained a modeled ceramic pepino fruit in the Nasca 2 style, which probably dates the context; a woven bag containing a unique stone sculpture of a skeletonized human holding a human trophy head in one hand and a tubular object in the other that may be conceptually related to full-size contemporary Pucara stone carvings from the northern Lake Titicaca Basin (note, too, the skeletonized humans on the early Nasca panpipe published by Bird 1962: fig. 49B); a carved stone llama head and neck; a carved stone llama wrapped in camelid fur and placed within a small plainweave pouch; and a carved wooden human head with inlaid bone eyes and teeth that had been wrapped in camelid fur. Perhaps the ritual objects were manipulated through some kind of sympathetic magic with invocations. A private rather than public ritual probably was involved because of the small size and low weight of the bundle, i.e. it is portable.

Rites of Agricultural Fertility

Proulx (1996: 110) perceptively situates the concern of Nasca religion with agricultural fertility in the context of Nasca's desert–

marine environment. He emphasizes that air (condor, falcon), earth (jaguar and puma), and water (killer whale, shark) creatures are dominant in Nasca iconography. He argues that their mythical representations (as opposed to the also occurring naturalistic ones) "should be viewed as symbolic visualizations of either nature spirits themselves or the spiritual power (*huaca* . . .) that they emit." Rituals were designed to appease a wide cadre of those nature spirits symbolizing aspects of fertility and power. Religion must have involved prediction of the annual highland rains that would bring river water for irrigation. It is interesting to note that the probable sunken court atop Unit 1 at Cahuachi looks east to the source of highland rain (Silverman 1993a: fig. 5.5).

In the situational context of rites of agricultural fertility which affected the entire social group, it is significant that the painted harvest festival textiles depict scores of farmers who are finely dressed in human garb and carry plants (Sawyer 1979: figs 14–16). Therefore, it is highly likely that the entire Nasca social entity participated or was represented in these rites.

Beliefs about Sacred Mountains and Sacred Water

Cerro Blanco (figure 8.5) and other mountains were probably of particular ritual importance to the ancient inhabitants of Nazca, just as many mountain peaks were sacred among other pre-Columbian peoples of the Andes (see Albornoz's "Instrucción" in Duviols 1967; Reinhard 1988). Rossel Castro (1977: 39–41) relates the following myth, still being told in Nazca at the time of his residency in the city (1941–50).

Illakata was the Lord of the Heights who lived in peaceful tranquility with the woman of his dreams, enjoying the beauty of the surroundings, which is to say, the fresh aroma of the wild flowers, the whistling of the vicuñas and vizcachas, the nourishment of the crystalline waters that flowed from the permanently snow-capped mountains on whose peaks condors made their nests.

In contrast, Tunga, the Lord of the Coast, was very adventurous, frolicking. During one of his accustomed runarounds, he arrived at the limits of the domain of Illakata. It was a rainy and cold afternoon, such as he had never experienced in all his life. Thunder crashed and

Figure 8.5 Cerro Blanco (background, right side), looking up-valley (east) from the modern town of Nazca (*courtesy*: David Johnson).

crossed with lightning. Tunga felt himself obligated to move close toward Illakata, supplicating him: "Oh, Lord of the Heights! I come from distant lands. My limbs, because of the intense cold, don't wish to obey me. Give me shelter." Illakata answered him, "You are welcome, oh foreigner!" "And you," (directing his speech to his wife), "prepare a heated-up chicha for this man from distant lands and climates."

Tunga became friendly with Illakata and made other visits to him as a sign of his thanks. Each time that Tunga of the Coast went to the Highlands, he took presents of gold, precious stones, cotton mantles, pieces of pottery. One night under a placid moon, Tunga seduced the wife of Illakata whom he had tricked saying to her that he came by order of the God of the Seas, the "Apu-Yaku" who lived in the immensities of the Sea, fertilizing the lands, producing animals and refreshing the hot sands. He told her to leave the horrible thunder, the icy nights and thick clouds.

The two ran hurriedly toward the Sea, taking advantage that Illakata slept. Soon Illakata awoke. He missed his companion and he called her with a potent thunder voice. The plains and hidden parts of the hills trembled with the echo of his desperate shout. Nobody replied. But his wife heard Illakata's voice from far away and she was sorry she had followed Tunga and she said this to him: "Oh, Lord of the Coastal Plain, free yourself from the ire of Illakata who is chasing us. My death in his hands is decreed. Flee! And let me die here." "But you won't die," said Tunga. "Look, I'll cover you with the maize flour of my valleys," and he left her covered.

Shortly, Illakata arrived near her with disconcerting shouts. He didn't recognize her. He left her. He returned to his cold heights disappointed, almost at the precise moment in which the rays of dawn appeared. To vent his anger Illakata sent strong cataclysms to destroy the mountains. He cursed his wife and faithless friend. They fell under the ruins of the catastrophe and were converted to inanimate objects. Truly, the maize flour that covered the body of his wife was transformed into an immense sand dune under whose weight she was buried. Since then, this hill is called Illakata. Tunga did not escape the curse of Illakata either. Rather, just as he arrived at the Sea he turned into a massive black hill of iron. Tunga is the hill of Marcona from which iron is extracted.

This myth appears to be a version of the basic story told in the Huarochirí Manuscript in which there is significant interaction between coastal and highland deities and the story's movement goes from the highlands to the coast. Zuidema (1962) emphasizes that a strong coast/highland opposition runs throughout Andean cosmology: in the highlands, the sun and the Viracocha creator god were worshiped; on the coast, Pachacamac, god of the underworld and the sea, was worshiped. As with the myth of Pariacaca in the Huarochirí Manuscript, a similar linkage of highland mountain forces of nature and coastal preoccupation with water is apparent in the Nazca myth.

Rossel Castro (1977: 39) identifies Cerro Blanco with Illakata. Reinhard (1988) distinguishes the great sand-covered Cerro Blanco from Illakata, a snow-capped mountain, also called Carhuarazo, in Soras (Lucanas, Ayacucho). Reinhard's fieldwork let him determine that there are sightlines between Illakata/Carhuarazo and Coropuna, the most powerful deities in southern Peru during the Inca Empire. Indeed, Reinhard (1988: fig. 15) publishes one of Guaman Poma's drawings which narrates that the Incas made sacrificial offerings, including children, to Coropuna. If this sacred geography existed in Nasca times, such *huacas* could have expanded Nasca's ritual territory to encompass virtually all of southern Peru (see Reinhard 1998: map on p. 130). These *huacas* also could have prefigured and conditioned the contact of Nasca society with the highland Wari Empire.

Gary Urton (1982) also recovered ethnographic testimony about the importance of Cerro Blanco. He learned that during the December solstice the sun rises from behind Cerro Blanco. This is significant because this is also the time when it begins to rain in the highlands. Also, local people told Urton that the origin of the filtration galleries is at the base of Cerro Blanco. One local legend recovered by Urton is explicit:

> In ancient times, before there were aqueducts [filtration galleries] in the valley, a great drought occurred and the people had no water for years. The people began crying out to their god, Viracocha or Con. They cried and screamed the word *nanay* [Quechua = "pain"] . . . The people went en-mass to the foot of Cerro Blanco, which was their principal *templo* or *adoratorio*; this was the place where they spoke to the gods. At that moment, Viracocha/Con descended from the sky to the summit of the mountain and heard the weeping of his people. He was so moved by their cries that he began weeping and tears flowed from his eyes. The tears ran down Cerro Blanco, penetrated the earth, and these tears were the origin of the aqueducts [filtration galleries].

In a similar vein, Reinhard (1988: 16) reports that "within recent times [it is said that] a man happened to find a cave leading into Co. Blanco. He reached a vast chamber with a waterfall and lake. Several outlets led to the subterranean canals."

Another legend collected by Urton (1982) has a man traveling to the coast at night with a jug in which to place sea foam which is then taken to a hill above Nazca and sprinkled around the summit to induce rain within the fortnight. This connection between water from the ocean and rain on top of the mountains clearly alludes to primordial Andean beliefs as illustrated by Reinhard (1985: fig. 12; and see Reinhard 1988: 19–21). García Miranda (1998: 63) is explicit that water is conceived in Andean cosmology as the mediator between the upper (sky, heaven) and lower (subterranean) worlds. Andeanist literature about water cults and the mythic-generative qualities of water (for example, as "*pacarinas*" or places of origin) is too abundant to cite (see the brief summary in García Miranda 1998: 63–4).

Some scholars have interpreted the Mythical Killer Whale as a Master of Fishes (for example, Lyon 1978; Morgan 1988). For Helaine Silverman, the importance of the sea in providing rain may explain the keen interest of the almost land-locked Nasca people in the Mythical Killer Whale. Perhaps the real creature was once seen during a trip to the sea – whether for ritual purposes or merely to fish (see, for example, Lapiner 1976: figs 511, 512) – resulting in its mythification. An initial sighting of one of the great sea mammals, either moving in the water or beached on the shore, could well have inspired a cult that sought the creature's return or beneficence. If this led to pilgrimages to the sea, though, the field evidence thus far is not forthcoming. And Carmichael's (1991) survey failed to produce evidence of significant Nasca settlement of the coastal strip.

Helaine Silverman believes that the importance of the Mythical Killer Whale lies in Andean cosmology and a connection with myths that describe the circulation of water between coast and highlands. As explained and illustrated by Reinhard (1985: 417–18, fig. 12), the Andean cosmos had tripartite organization: an upper world/ sky; mountains uniting earth and sky as an *axis mundi*, source of rivers and control of meteorological phenomena; and the under-world of craters, caves, lakes, springs, and subterranean water. Discussing the Huarochirí Manuscript, Salomon writes:

Earth's living mass was imagined rising up from the waters of the surrounding ocean . . . visualized as the green irrigable valley lands, earth is usually female. But the land's highest points, the great peaks whose ice-crusted crowns overtower the habitable earth, are usually male. One of them is Paria Caca. Roughly, the solid part of the world might be imagined as a single world mountain made of all the Andean ranges, rising from femalelike valleys to malelike snow-capped heights.

Water – rainstorms and mudslides, snow and glacial runoff, tiny irrigation canals and mighty rivers, even that astral river we call the Milky Way – is the kinetic part of the world. Water moves over pacha in a circular path. It rides up from the ocean into the sky along the Milky Way "river." . . . Then water washes down onto the heights of the earth as storm and rain, bathing and fecundating earth as it descends to the ocean. People worshiped the great snow-capped peaks "because that is where their water comes from." Water is often male, especially storm water and downward-flowing water . . . Although the Pacific Ocean plays a key part in organizing mythic space, it is not personalized in the [Huarochirí] manuscript. In modern Andean myth, the ocean [Mama Cocha, 'mother lake'] is usually female. The huaca most closely associated with the sea is Pacha Camac . . . but this great force is not clearly defined as a maritime deity.

The hydraulic embrace of moving water and enduring earth was imagined as sex. Their embrace yielded a biotic system. (Salomon 1991: 15)

Given the Mythical Killer Whale's propensity to hold human trophy heads and the trophy head's connection to concepts of fertility and regeneration, Silverman understands the bloody mouth of the Nasca 5 Mythical Killer Whale as a direct reference to trophy head-taking and propitiation of the forces of nature controlling fertility, a reasonable concern in the sixth century AD as the Central Andes suffered drought conditions (see Thompson et al. 1985: 973). Perhaps the drought caused Nasca people to focus on various emblems of fertility, such as plump women and the Killer Whale as "master/mistress of fishes," in the hope that these forces would be brought to bear on the increasingly dry landscape. The frequency of Mythical Killer Whale representations increases through time, eventually equaling, then surpassing, the number of representations of the Anthropomorphic Mythical Being.

In terms of Nasca potters' portrayal of the natural world, Proulx (1983: 103) has observed that representations of women are virtually absent from the Nasca ceramic sequence until phase 5 when they become a major theme (we note, however, that women and/or female supernaturals may appear in textiles attributed to Nasca 2: see, for example, Haeberli 1995: 127–8; Lyon 1978: 104–5). The profusion of women on Nasca 5 pottery must be related to other, interrelated changes occurring in the pottery style (for example, Blagg 1975; Roark 1965) and in society. We hypothesize that these changes are related to an increased concern with fertility under a regime of diminishing rain-supplied water due to the onset of drought conditions in the Andes.

A preoccupation with agricultural fertility also may be manifest in the Harvester, particularly the subtype in which water-related objects, such as crayfish or polliwogs, emerge from the figure's mouth (see Eisleb 1977: fig. 210). We interpret these riverine elements as a reference to irrigation water. The Harvester dies out at the end of phase 5 (Roark 1965: 26–7), perhaps at the end of the environmental crisis.

Beyond what has been offered here as speculation, we are not sure of the implications of changes in the popularity of certain mythical creatures for our understanding of the evolution of Nasca religion.

Rituals of Water: Nazca's Filtration Galleries

The Nasca filtration gallery irrigation system in the southern half of the Río Grande de Nazca drainage was composed of segmentary sections, suggesting the possibility of group control of the sections. Indeed, Urton (1990: 199) specifically says that:

> the apportionment of irrigation water in the Ingenio Valley – and in the other valleys of the Río Grande de Nazca – would have been a[n] essential . . . part of the organization of pre-Hispanic agriculture in this arid land . . . no doubt . . . based on a mit'a-like turn-taking among the ayllus of the upper and lower parcialidades ["parts" of society] within each river valley . . . the implementation of mit'a produced both spatial and temporal divisions . . . must have resulted in the partition of agricultural lands into strips, each defined by a major canal system irrigating the lands of a particular ayllu.

The actual *pukios* (natural springs) in the upper valley may have defined social groups as may the filtration galleries of the southern tributaries (see, especially, the diagram suggestive of Urton's hypothesis in Schreiber and Lancho Rojas 1995: fig. 4). Other evidence of irrigation has long since disappeared.

It would have been pragmatically necessary to clean the filtration galleries of Nazca. The occasion for doing so had to have been ritually configured and symbolically charged (for example, a *"limpia acequia"* or *"yarqa aspiy"* irrigation canal-cleaning ritual; see, for example, Isbell 1978: 138–5; Valderrama and Escalante 1988). In this context it is interesting to cite a comparative hypothesis by Gosden and Lock (1998: 6) who suggest for Britain's linear ditch systems of the Bronze Age that a "regular cycle of cleaning and refurbishment would have strengthened people's ties to a known past, reinforced the potency of that past in the present or changed the nature of attachment to that past." If ancient Andean people acquired the rights to critical resources through *ayllu* membership so, too, participation in necessary communal work projects, such as the cleaning of the irrigation canals, would have affirmed *ayllu* membership (rights and obligations), reinforced the known past, and performed locality and sense of place into existence.

Furthermore, local residents at Usaca in the lower Nazca Valley have told Donald Proulx that they hear the sound of a waterfall below them. What they are hearing is the subterranean water flowing down the river valley, falling into the Nazca fault and being redirected to the west. This aural phenomenon would have been heard in pre-Columbian times as well. Surely *pacha mama*, *pacha camac* and *mama cocha* were evident, immanent, and omnipotent for those hearing the roar of subterranean water.

If we accept that Inca, Colonial, and contemporary Andean practices are relevant to ancient Nasca society, then a new understanding of the filtration galleries may be offered. Given that Andean people conceived of water as cycling from snow-capped mountains to the surface and subsurface and into the ocean and back up again (see the Huarochirí Manuscript), then imagine the significance of piercing the earth to tap the underground water and bringing it up to the surface for irrigation. Furthermore, themes of renewal and role-gendered themes of fertility (conception, the union of male and female elements) and gestation are prominent in water rituals in traditional Andean societies today (see, for example, Isbell 1978: 143–4). Therefore, creation (and cleaning) of the filtration galleries must have been an incredibly cosmologically charged and ritually executed act.

Helaine Silverman hypothesizes that the pragmatic act of sub-surface hydraulic engineering was also a ritual re-enactment of a primordial origin myth associating water and ancestors. It was a practice whose final form was canonized a thousand years later by the Incas as seen in Jeanette Sherbondy's (1982) study of Inca irrigation and social organization.

Another aspect of the creation myth told by Molina . . . demonstrates the importance of subterranean routes for the original distribution of peoples and lands on the earth. Viracocha created the first beings of each nation and ordered them to submerge themselves and travel under the earth to the lands they were to populate. Although he does not specify that the subterranean routes were aquatic ones, the myth of Tarapaca indicates that they were. Besides, the ancestors emerged at places that were also considered important sources of water . . . Roots of trees are also associated with sources of water because old trees are usually near abundant and permanent sources of water; otherwise, they would not have survived.

. . . A modern myth from Puquio (Ayacucho) that is very similar to the myth of Viracocha in Molina, states that the ancestors traveled along subterranean aquatic routes . . . It says that the ancestors created the springs and openings in the earth. They distributed lands and waters to each people, which is exactly the same role that the ancestors played in the Viracocha myth. The ancestors of Puquio, carrying gold drums on their heads, traveled along the veins . . . of subterranean water that are the veins of the mountains, toward the source of the water. The dead, who then become ancestors, are believed to return to the lakes that had been the sources of their life.

. . . The Incas' basic explanation of how water circulates was that the waters from the Sea that is under and around the earth well up to form lakes. Lakes in turn feed underground rivers, which carry lake water to all the smaller lakes, rivers, streams and springs, thereby providing the entire earth with water sources. These waters return eventually to the Sea . . . Ultimate origins and ends are in the Sea.

. . . major lakes were thought to be directly connected to the Sea underneath, and these in turn were connected by the subterranean channels that were made and used by the original ancestors to travel to their sites of emergence. These channels are revealed to be underground rivers when we realize that most of the sites of emergence of the original ancestors were sources of water: lakes, rivers, streams and springs.

... [Inca Roca] thrust his arm into the earth to make an opening for the waters to emerge, thus replicating the actions of a founding ancestor who brings waters to the lands of his descendants and creates the opening for them to flow out. (Sherbondy 1982: 57–9, 124)

Mortuary Ritual and Ancestor Worship

It is commonplace to attribute ancestor worship to the major Andean cultures on the basis of the care with which the royal dead were disposed among the Incas; an Inca *panaca* (royal corporation) maintained the cult of a dead Inca king's mummy. An important discussion of the relationship between the living and dead is presented by Isbell (1997) in his brilliant and controversial book about *chullpas* (burial towers) and *ayllu* organization. Isbell takes a very strict approach to ancestor worship. He argues that ancestor worship is indicated only where the dead were prepared as mummies and maintained accessible in *chullpas* or other special facilities.

Speaking of the Incas and traditional Andean people overall, Sherbondy (1986: 10) states that "[t]he dead, who were transformed into ancestors, were buried in their lands and continued mediating between the living and the forces of the earth for the prosperity of the ayllu. The original ancestors, the founders of the ayllu, were the most important. They were the most powerful mediators, those who gave legitimacy to the ayllu and rights to the lands and water." Similarly, Ramírez (1996: 53–4) has argued that:

Precontact Andeans venerated their ancestors ... because they had settled the land and overseen the gradual building of the infrastructure of irrigation canals and other improvements that brought more and more of the otherwise often barren landscape into production and made it fruitful ... The ancestors had ... bequeathed the improved land to the living. For this and other legacies, the ancestors were worthy of song and praise, offerings and sacrifices.

While recognizing the validity of Isbell's tangible criteria for the recognition of ancestor worship and its attendant benefits (sustainable claims to critical resources managed communally by the ayllu on the basis of the physical existence of ancestors), Helaine Silverman believes that there are other manifestations of ancestor worship in the Central Andes and that Nasca society offers us examples. However, clearly not all of the Nasca dead were conceptualized and manipulated as ancestors. Furthermore, there is a vast difference between Nasca attention to the dead and Inca treatment of their royal mummies. Let us see, then, what can be inferred from the archaeological record for Nasca.

There is iconographic evidence at least of mortuary ritual in ancient Nasca society. The issue is whether ancestor worship is represented. Let us look at two scenes presented and interpreted by Patrick Carmichael.

> [figure 8.6] In this scenario, the large, central figures would represent ancestors, or perhaps their mummy bundles. Each of the central figures is attended by a single musician who plays a panpipe and a gourd rattle. It is interesting that the artist included a trophy head and suspension cord with one of these musicians. The presence of other trophy heads is implied by the suspension cords held by the other musicians. In these instances, the trophy head itself was omitted, perhaps to avoid crowding the design. This scene provides one of the few illustrated contexts for trophy head use . . . they are associated with ancestor worship. There is no way of knowing whether the "ancestors" in this scene were present in a real or figurative sense. If actually present the bundles may have been temporarily disinterred for renewal or revalidation ceremonies . . . but this is pure speculation. (Carmichael 1988: 379–80, plate 29)

> [figure 8.1] The vessel . . . shows a chamber containing human heads, cloth, and a pot. The material can be identified as plaid cloth by reference to other vessels which show human figurines wearing plaid garments . . . Two figures are shown outside of the chamber, one of whom wears a mask. This scene is repeated on either side of the vessel, while the end panels seem to show abbreviated versions. Note that . . . vessels are also placed on the chamber roof. [There are] three interpretations of this scene, each of which seems plausible: (1) it represents a multiple interment (in which case, it was a fairly unique occurrence); (2) a votive offering of trophy heads, cloth, and pottery is being shown; (3) it depicts ancestor worship. All

Figure 8.6   Scene of ancestor veneration or burial ritual. Two shamans flank a mummy bundle while playing panpipes, shaking rattles, and holding trophy heads (Phoebe Hearst Museum of Anthropology, University of California at Berkeley, 16-10453; *photo*: Donald Proulx).

three of these interpretations find support in the archaeological data . . . The last [may] also incorporate elements of the first two. To pursue the ancestor worship idea, it is a matter of speculation as to whether this was actually a single tomb with multiple interments, or whether the important ancestors are all figuratively represented in one scene. In either event, offering renewal appears to be taking place as shown by the vessels on the chamber roof. There are no indications that the chamber was actually re-opened . . . the figure on the right [is] the supplicant, and the masked figure on the left [is] a shaman mediator. (Carmichael 1988: 380–1, plate 28)

Proulx offers an interpretation that differs from Carmichael's. Proulx sees no empirical evidence of ancestor worship in Nasca society and argues that there is a difference between honoring one's dead relatives and true ancestor worship. Proulx interprets the scene in figure 8.1 as a ritual interment of a cache of trophy heads with a masked shaman officiating. He argues that there is no way of determining whether the trophy heads represent ancestors and that it is more likely that the heads were being buried to ensure the fertility of the crops.

Proulx would interpret the scene in figure 8.6 as representing a burial ritual, in the sense of graveside rites. An article by Anne-Marie Hocquenghem on the role of flies in Moche iconography comes to mind. In it, Hocquenghem (1981: 65) suggests that certain Moche scenes, reminiscent of the medieval *danse macabre*, are explicable as ritual dancing performed on the occasion of death commemoration ceremonies as these are known from the Huarochirí Manuscript (chapter 9, sections 127, 131, 132: see Salomon and Urioste 1991). Perhaps the vessel in figure 8.6 is showing this same custom or ritual of dancing for the dead: the mummy bundle ancestor is surrounded by the living human performers who play panpipe music and shake gourd rattles (see Carmichael 1988: 379; the Huarochirí ancestor commemorations specifically involve attendance to mummy bundles: see Salomon and Urioste 1991: nn. 246–8 for ch. 9 of the manuscript). Indeed, the early Nasca panpipe illustrated by Bird (1962: fig. 49b) appears to show just this scene with skeletal dancers.

Carmichael (1988: 377–8) also has argued for ancestor worship on the basis of tomb re-entry; that is, to renew offerings. Carmichael indicates that grave goods were, at times, placed on top of tomb roofs (*barbacoas*). He provides examples from a Nasca 1 tomb from Ica, a Nasca 3 tomb at Las Cañas (immediately east of Cahuachi), and a Nasca 4 tomb and a Nasca 5–6 tomb from Cahuachi. Carmichael interprets these rooftop goods as "another (although less direct) form of offering renewal." The physical evidence in re-entered tombs indicates disturbance: grave goods are in disarray and skeletons are missing body parts. Carmichael suggests that the hole in the north-east corner of the tomb roof of one of Ubbelohde-Doering's graves at Cahuachi and the hole in the roofs of several of Orefici's tombs (one of which had been stuffed with pieces of textiles) at Cahuachi functioned to permit re-entry. The holes are said to be large enough for a small child to pass through, perhaps to put *chicha* and other offerings, such as food, into the tombs. Alternatively, it is possible that these cases indicate pre-Columbian looting.

Carmichael (1988: 371–1) suggests that the presence of layered fill in some tombs is indicative of an entombment ritual that occurred over "a protracted period of time, perhaps requiring several days or even longer." It is clear that stages of interment were involved in these burials, but the length of time they occupied cannot be determined at present.

Carmichael (1988: 375–6) interprets the addition of later pottery to earlier assemblages as evidence of a multi-stage mortuary program with rededication to the ancestors. He recognizes Nasca 8/Loro pottery in a Nasca 7 tomb from Chaviña, and both Nasca 7 and 8/Loro pottery were recovered by Ubbelohde-Doering from a tomb he excavated at Cahuachi. In these cases, however, we may also consider the possibility of effective contemporaneity of Nasca 7 and 8/Loro pottery. Carmichael's identification of a Nasca 8/Loro vessel in one of Kroeber's Nasca 5 tombs from Ocongalla West B, however, cannot be explained away in this manner. This is a case of tomb re-entry. However, it does not necessarily indicate a protracted mortuary ritual or even rededication by descendants. But it is very interesting.

Very tentatively, Helaine Silverman would like to suggest that Tello's modeled scene (see frontispiece) may have mortuary referents in addition to those believed to refer to pilgrimage (see Silverman 1993a: 302). Perhaps the dogs are more than family pets. Anthropologists working throughout the Andes have noted an association between the souls or spirits of the dead and dogs: the dead are believed to be accompanied on their journey to the afterlife by dogs (Carter 1968: 245; Harris 1982: 62, 71).

Other archaeological data also can be interpreted as indicative of a concern with the ancestors. Silverman (1993a: 191–3) argues that the Room of the Posts at Cahuachi was a locus of ancestor worship. She suggests that huarango posts represent the ancestors. Specifically, she associates the upright huarango posts embedded in the floor of the Room of the Posts (Silverman 1993a: fig. 13.2) with the Quechua concept of *mallki* which is a cultivated tree and symbol of the ancestor of an *ayllu* (see Sherbondy 1986: 9–10). Silverman notes that Ubbelohde-Doering (1966: 142) found flat huarango posts in his Nasca 3A and Nasca 8/Loro tombs at Cahuachi. Silverman (1993a: fig. 13.43) also supports her argument with an image on Nasca pottery showing an anthropomorphic figure grasping two successively smaller human figures in one hand and a forked huarango wood post with an upturned human face in the other. She argues, following Zuidema (1972), that the image portrays a four-generational kinship system, such as that known for the Incas and that the huarango post marks the position of an ancestor. The bifurcated Horrible Bird and Trophy Head Taster that emerge from the central figure in the lower plane of the image would refer to the underworld/otherworld. On the other hand, Proulx is bothered by the lack of empirical evidence for Silverman's interpretation and says the argument suffers from selective use of an interpretation originally made for the temporally and spatially distant Incas.

Parker Pearson (1993: 204) argues that the "physical locations for activities sacred and profane form an eschatological map of practical actions and relationships linking and separating the living and the supernatural. The dead are removed from the world of the living by a series of transformations which can be detected in part through the placing and treatment of the dead." We can see Parker Pearson's argument at work in the case of the Nasca who buried their dead in the ground: the more statused or endowed the person, the deeper the tomb (see Carmichael 1988; see discussion of La Muña in Reindel and Isla 1999 and Rossel Castro 1977). Nasca burials could be located in habitation zones, at habitation sites but in separate cemeteries at these, in cemeteries apart from habitation or other sites, and in cemeteries at ceremonial centers such as Cahuachi. The Nasca also buried certain members of their society in *huacas* (for example, the mound burials discovered by Kroeber and Silverman at Cahuachi: see Kroeber and Collier 1998: 8–80; Silverman 1993a: 197–202; also see discussion of Strong's Burial 8 at Cahuachi in Silverman 1993a: 202–3).

Once buried, the Nasca dead were not easily accessed nor were they readily visible (in contrast to the situation of *chullpas* discussed by Isbell 1997). From today's perspective, Nasca cemeteries were not obviously located in highly visible locations that might readily have served as an anchor for the community burying its dead there, although the symbolism and supernatural power of a particular location may have achieved that goal (see discussion of La Muña, following). Where burials occurred within villages – as was common – they, too, may have established a community's territorial legitimacy and confirmed the kinship/lineage/*ayllu* organization underwriting it.

Exciting new data on Nasca burial ritual are provided by Reindel and Isla's (1999) recent fieldwork in the Palpa Valley at the site of La Muña, located at the junction of the Palpa and Grande rivers. In addition to the site's central burial chambers and surrounding funerary architecture, Reindel and Isla reconstruct gathering sites that could have served for cult activity held in conjunction with the burial structures. They suggest that the deceased were transported from great courtyards (appropriate for congregation) located some distance away from the center of the necropolis to be buried atop platforms. Thus, at least some individuals in post-Cahuachi times appear to have placed themselves/been placed strategically, in death, to access power as presumably they did in life.

In order to claim and manipulate an ancestor, one must know where he/she is and, presumably, whose ancestor he/she is. The tomb marker or *mira* of many Nasca tombs (see Silverman 1993a: fig. 14.4 for an example) could have functioned for this purpose.

> Nasca civilization, in its three phases of evolution, had the ancestral custom of putting over the tomb of its ancestors a marker which consisted of a conical adobe or a huarango post set upright, more or less 50 cm high. In the cemetery of Kajamarka (Paredones), almost all of the Nasca-type tombs had huarango post indicators in a perpendicular direction and set, almost always, at the entryway [to the tomb] or sometimes in the center of each tomb.
>
> Other cemeteries, also of the Nasca type, had huarango post markers set at the four corners of the tomb, from two to three meters high, with their forks in the upper part that served the purpose of supporting a cane roof, like a sun screen, or maybe, when the bodies were embalmed and funerary rites were offered to them, they were hung from the forked posts. This class of markers is seen at Estaqueria South, at Corralones, in Las Trancas, in Samaca of Callango [lower Ica Valley], in La Muña of Palpa. (Rossel Castro 1977: 268)

Helaine Silverman argues that La Muña was deliberately sited and marked so that the dead were in a direct relationship with the underworld and with primordial ancestors. This association was achieved by virtue of La Muña's location at a *tinkuy* (see chapter 7) and, possibly, as argued by David Johnson (1999), its association with geological faults, a rich subterranean aquifer and geoglyphs. The architectural complex of La Muña encompasses special mortuary architecture, civic-ceremonial features, great court-yards and platforms, a remarkable quantity of superb pottery, and the *tinkuy* location with its inherently symbolically charged water resources. Isbell (1997: 15) has demonstrated that "[w]hen com-bined with the built environment and the activities it channels, bodies of the dead become powerful symbols presencing certain meanings." The La Muña dead were in the physical, social struc-tural, and ideological position of becoming heroic ancestors with direct access to the underworld where water would emerge to the surface to cycle up to the sky and thence fall as rain that filled the descending rivers for irrigation (see Arguedas 1956; Aveni 1990b: 112; Benson 1995; Carrión Cachot 1955; Earls and Silverblatt 1976; Gelles 1984; Guillet 1992: 19; Larrea 1960; Netherly 1984; Ossio 1976; Ramírez 1996: 52–3, 135; Rostworowski 1998b: 35–6; Salomon 1991: 15, 1998: 274; Sherbondy 1982; Valderrama and Escalante 1988).

The stone statuettes described in chapter 6 (see figures 6.5, 6.6) also appear to have been mortuary in function and practice given their apparent cemetery context. Perhaps they were symbolic an-cestors of the deceased; perhaps they marked tombs on the cem-etery surface. Until archaeologists find them in place we will remain unable to securely interpret and precisely date these objects. A best guess is that they begin in Nasca 8/Loro and are used throughout the Middle Horizon. It is worth noting that the Ingenio and Grande examples share an uncanny resemblance to anthropomorphic clay figurines with secure funerary context from Lima sites on the cen-tral coast (see Amador Parodi 1998).

The Ritual Use of Hallucinogens

It is well known ethnographically that shamans use hallucinogenic drugs to induce visions, achieve or access another reality, and gain control over supernatural forces. Although most closely associated with tribal peoples (the Yanomamo are the paradigmatic case), hallucinogenic drug use is also well known in ancient complex societies. The use of psychedelic drugs in ancient Peruvian society has been well documented for Chavin and Moche (Cordy-Collins 1977; Donnan 1976: fig. 1). There appears to have been hallucinogenic drug use in Nasca society (Dobkin del Ríos 1982, 1984; Dobkin del Ríos and Cardenas 1980). The most likely source of hallucinogens was the San Pedro cactus from which mescaline can be extracted by boiling, and perhaps Floipondium (*Datura arborea*) (Sharon 1972, 1978: 2). San Pedro cactus appears painted whole on Nasca pottery (for example, figure 8.4), painted in cross-section (for example, Townsend 1985: plate 5), and modeled (for example, Lothrop 1964: 203). Valdez (1994: 677, 678) reports finding San Pedro cactus whole and as crushed seeds on Unit 8 at Cahuachi.

Coca Use

The ritual, political, economic, and social contexts of coca leaf use in the Andes are very well documented in the ethnographic (for example, Allen 1988) and ethnohistoric (for example, Murra 1972, 1980; Rostworowski 1989a) literature and in the archaeological record (for example, Donnan 1976: fig. 74; Towle 1961: 59–60, 140–2). Coca's use on the south coast is at least as early as the Cavernas occupation of the eponymous site (Towle 1961: 13). There is evidence of Nasca coca use (see chapter 3).

Prediction and Calendars

Silverman (1993a: 305) has argued that the name "Cahuachi" refers to prediction, based on the gloss of the Quechua word as "make them see, make them predict, to have bad luck." She suggests that the name of the site may refer to activities remembered to have occurred there. Furthermore, the historically known name of Cahuachi is "Cahuachipana" (Quijandría Alvarez 1961: 105). Margot Beyersdorff (personal communication, 1999), a Quechua linguist at the University of Texas at Austin, says that "-*na*" is the instrumental suffix; it points to some instrumental function, tool or place. The "-*pa*", used with *qhaway* (to look at) refers to examining or observing something (*qhawapay*).

The gloss is coherent with what we know about ancient Nasca society. The Nasca must have observed natural phenomena (the skies, the movement of heavenly bodies, animals, plants) out of their concern with agricultural fertility which, of necessity, implicated knowledge of water resources, both surface (from highland rains) and subsurface (the underground aquifer). The coordination and scheduling of agricultural activities and the religious ceremonies performed on their behalf by the social groups comprising Nasca society could have been achieved by means of a calendar. The famous Brooklyn Museum Textile, possibly attributable to Nasca 2, is said to depict such a calendar (Gundrum 2000; Haeberli 1995). Haeberli (1995) reconstructs a 30-day Nasca month divided into two 15-day portions, corresponding to the full and waning lunar cycles. He suggests that Nasca people used periods of time based on the four phases of the lunar cycle. Other scholars (for example, Kosok 1965; Reiche 1951, 1958, 1968, 1974, 1976 *inter alia*) have interpreted the Nazca Lines as an astronomical calendar, though the mechanics are not well specified (see discussion in chapter 7). On the other hand, Donald Proulx believes that a simpler calendar could have functioned based on the annual start of water coursing down the rivers. He doubts that the Nasca had the mathematical and astronomical sophistication to produce the type of calendar proposed by Haeberli.

Divination and Sacrifice

The cache of some twenty-three guinea-pigs recovered by Silverman (1993a: 168) at Unit 19 at Cahuachi may be related to divination and sacrifice. Each specimen was disarticulated; the head had been jerked off each; the stomach skin was slit open by a long incision extending to the thorax; the inner organs had been extracted. This treatment is strongly reminiscent of modern-day curing and divining practices in the Andes. Furthermore, as Sandweiss and Wing (1997) remind us, guinea-pigs were used widely in a variety of magical, religious, sacrificial, and divination rites in Colonial times and before. In these rites the guinea-pig was always cut open as was observed at Cahuachi. Thus, a strong continuity from ancient times through the present is suggested.

Pilgrimage

Building on Halbwachs (1980), Connerton (1998) has argued masterfully that memory is cultural (rather than individual) and is evoked and manipulated through ritual performances. These memory performances or "commemorative ceremonies" emphasize continuity with the past while manifesting social structure in the present. They tell a master narrative, permit reflection on it, and are the basis of "a cult enacted" through repetitive calendrical scheduling, verbal recitation, and gesture or bodily practice. For Silverman, these comments are relevant to the performance of pilgrimage and provide much insight into the nature of early Nasca religion and society.

Silverman (1988a, 1990b, 1993a, 1994b) has reconstructed the great early Nasca ceremonial center of Cahuachi as a pilgrimage shrine. On the basis of negative results in the search for large areas of permanent, domestic occupation at the site, Silverman has argued that pilgrimage filled an otherwise "empty" ceremonial center with people. In addition to ethnographic analogy from the Andes, as in the case of the Catholic shrine at Yauca studied by Silverman (1993a: 312–16, 1994b), there is ethnohistoric evidence of the existence of "vacant" pilgrimage shrines. Rostworowski (1993: 193), for instance, cites a 1572 *visita* to Chérrepe, on the north coast, which reveals that a particular village called Noquip was sparsely inhabited but "at a certain time of the year a great number of people – common as well as elite – met there to perform a great *taqui* and dances according to their ancient rites . . . After the celebrations everyone returned [home]."

Silverman argues that the Nasca social groups or *ayllus* that maintained the different mounds at Cahuachi constituted themselves *en route* to Cahuachi, on the pampas, and at Cahuachi itself (the Qoyllur R'iti pilgrimage provides a model: see Sallnow 1987). Through pilgrimage, presumably to Cahuachi and perhaps elsewhere, the Nasca people were transformed from the ordinary people they were into ritual social beings. This transformation was achieved by dressing up, dancing, trancing, and masking, for which there is ample iconographic evidence (for example, the famous modeled scene published by Tello 1931; human figures and supernatural impersonators on Nasca pots and painted textiles: see Sawyer 1979: figs 13–15; Townsend 1985) as well as modern practice (see Reinhard 1988: back cover).

Sawyer (1997: 43) argues that fancy Nasca embroidered textiles often exhibit complex groupings of agricultural and trophy head cult deities that expressed Nasca society's elaborate hierarchy of religious functionaries. Silverman argues that religious personnel may have rotated among culturally qualified individuals/groups, like cargos, within a permanent hierarchy structure. These eligible individuals are those who appear on seemingly egalitarian multi-personed textile scenes (for example, Sawyer 1979: figs 2, 7, 13–16, 22, 23). In Silverman's argument, at Cahuachi, the otherwise dormant Nasca social groups would have regaled themselves so as to recognize co-participant members of the group, express group identity in opposition to other groups, and compete for status with regard to the other social groups. At the same time, dress must have been part of the ritual symbolism of the pilgrimage which, with the iconography of early Nasca art, formed a cluster of ritual symbols, "a limited set of root metaphors or meta-ritual symbols" (Morinis and Crumrine 1991: 3). Once periodic celebrations at the ceremonial center were ended, the macro-groups would decompose into their smaller parts, returning to their distinct home villages where other principles of social group membership would exert their claims.

Although it is ostensibly undertaken for Catholic reasons, Andean pilgrimage today does not manifest the classic *communitas* of Catholic pilgrimage (Turner 1974; Turner and Turner 1978). Rather, local identities (manifested by dress and other attributes) are taken along on pilgrimage. Sallnow (1981: 180; see also Poole 1991) sees this as the cause of disharmony at contemporary Andean pilgrimage centers and, indeed, pilgrimage is a venue for the display of hierarchy. "Pilgrimage is an important means by which individuals attain prestige cargos within their community. As ritual representatives of their community, moreover, pilgrims identify throughout their journey with this local (hierarchized) group and not, as in some models of Christian pilgrimage, with a larger, theoretically 'undifferentiated' mass of pilgrims at a sanctuary" (Poole 1991: 334). Sallnow (1981) has shown that manifestations of competition and conflict characterize this kind of multi-group encounter at modern Andean pilgrimage centers; the pilgrimage center becomes the arena for the enactment of social drama (Turner 1974). In a comparison of the properties of Andean dance to the act of pilgrimage itself, Poole (1991: 333) suggests that (see also Sallnow 1987; Silverman 1990: 453):

> the use and display of these hierarchical, spatial, and transforma-
> tional principles in dance parallel and recursively reinform the im-
> portance of these same abstract principles in the pilgrimage rituals
> which present that context for dance performance. In this respect,
> the ritualized movement of Andean pilgrimage . . . derive[s] much
> of its coherence and meaning as a religious, devotional act from
> these dances in which the formal characteristics of pilgrimage are
> presented in the entertaining, emotive, anonymous (masked) and
> artistic form of dance.

The situation described by Sallnow and Poole appears to fit the Nasca case.

Nasca Religion and Ritual

Through ritual the Nasca appear to have sought to control such fundamental fertility factors as the life-giving power of water, the growth potential of seeds, and the productivity of plants. Nasca potters depicted a world of mythical creatures and rituals in which human beings participated through ceremony, costume, props, dance, and music. The abundance of all life forms was regarded as inseparably associated with fertility. The birds and creatures of the field and water were seen as beneficent spirits toward agri-culture and were so represented in art (Sawyer 1966: 122) and, conceivably, in the great ground figures of the Pampa itself (Reinhard 1988).

Following Freidel (1992: 116), we see Nasca religion and ritual as part of a "collective enterprise," involving elites, artists, farmers, and the whole "spectrum of society." Again adapting Freidel (1992: 116–17), we note the "commonality" and "redundant, replicative nature" and "integrated world view" of Nasca religion and ritual at all levels of society, as revealed in its many contexts, from simple villages (evidenced by the panpipes and fancy pottery found there) to ceremonial centers and geoglyphs. For all that Nasca art changed over time in representational form (i.e. from monumental to proliferous in style), its ideological referents (i.e. its iconographic elements) remained recognizable and perdured, even following the demise of Cahuachi. Surely this survival indicates the flexibility, adaptability, and manipulability of Nasca religion and ritual.

9

Headhunting and Warfare

A significant and influential body of archaeological literature argues that warfare is a key factor in the rise of complex society and that states are notorious for the force they are able to deploy. Carneiro's (1970) seminal theory on the origin of the state specifically argued that increasing human population pressure on limited arable resources led to a concomitant increasing importance of warfare and, ultimately, the political subordination and incorporation of conquered peoples such that the size and complexity of victorious political units increased. Carneiro saw war as the mechanism of state formation, put into action under conditions of environmental and social circumscription. Haas (1982) critically evaluated conflict and integration theories of state formation. He suggested that early leaders gained control over basic resources and with economic, military, and ideological power were able to control the populations of their societies. Earle (1997: 105) argued that "the military is perhaps the key element in the creation and retention of large-scale political institutions, such as complex chiefdoms and, later, states. The military is the immediate means of creating regional chiefdoms by defeating opposing rulers and incorporating their populace within the new polity." Yet others caution against the evolutionary role of warfare. In this chapter we examine the evidence for Nasca warfare, including its most dramatic aspect, headhunting, and the role of warfare in Nasca sociopolitical evolution.

Nasca Trophy Heads

Decapitated human heads with an artificially enlarged foramen magnum, a hole in the frontal bone, and, where preserved, a carrying cord threaded through that hole are common in the Nasca archaeo-logical record (see Silverman 1993a: figs 15.1, 15.2; figure 4.2). These heads share appearance (Nasca cranial deformation) and method of preparation (broken foramen magnum, creation of a small hole in the frontal bone, insertion of a carrying cord).

Max Uhle appears to have been the first scholar to characterize these heads as "trophies" (see Uhle 1906: 586; Uhle 1914: 11, 14; see Larrea 1960: plate 42).[1] Tello (1917: 286–7) referred to them as *"cabezas trofeos momificadas"* (mummified trophy heads) or, simply, *"cabezas trofeos"* (trophy heads). We continue that usage here even though, as explained below, there is dispute about the nature of the activity that caused the separation of the head from the body and its characteristic post-mortem treatment.

Iconographically, the Anthropomorphic Mythical Being (see Proulx 1968: 17–18, figs 18–20, plates 1–6), Mythical Killer Whale (see Proulx 1968: 19, plate 10; Townsend 1985: fig. 18), Harpy (Proulx 1983: 98, fig. 17), and Horrible Bird (see Proulx 1968: 19, plate 9b, 1983: figs 15, 16; Wolfe 1981) have strong associations with human trophy heads. The faces of the five Harvesters painted on a bowl illustrated by Townsend (1985: fig. 6) have spine-sealed mouths in the manner of trophy heads (versus the typical Secular Harvester; for example, Proulx 1968: fig. 38). Proulx (1996: plate 15) publishes a particularly interesting vessel on which a small naked human figure appears to be in the process of being devoured by a bloody-mouth Anthropomorphic Mythical Being in Mythical Killer Whale aspect from whom plants sprout. Plants often sprout from the mouths of trophy heads (Proulx 1996: 110).

This iconography strongly supports Townsend's (1985: 134) conclusion that ancient Nasca people linked animals, agriculture, and the rites of war (as evidenced by the depiction of trophy heads) to life and death. Proulx (1996: 110) observes that Nasca icon-ography "is replete with symbols of death and rejuvenation used in combination; human sacrifice is closely associated with agricul-tural fertilty." Silverman (1993a: 224–5) has specifically argued that there is a relationship between trophy heads, ancestors, and principles of cyclical death and regeneration/rebirth/fertility based on the substitutability of germinating beans and trophy heads in both Paracas Necropolis and early Nasca iconography (see, for example, Lapiner 1976: 467, 468 – a ceremonial staff depicting skeletonized/ribcage visible actors holding trophy heads) and on the basis of ethnographic analogy with contemporary fertility celebrations and homages to the dead in traditional Andean societies (see Allen 1988: 165, 182; Harris 1982: 57–8; Rasnake 1988: 242).

Scholars have contrasted the manipulation of trophy heads by priests/shamans in early Nasca times and by warriors/chiefs in late Nasca times (Browne et al. 1993; Proulx 1989b; Silverman 1993a: ch. 15). In early Nasca ceramic art, the human trophy head is a common theme, either independently or in direct association with mythical beings or humans dressed in the regalia of supernaturals (in their hands, as part of their bodies, on their costumes). In contrast, Roark (1965: 56) observes that "the frequency of Trophy Heads as independent themes increases sharply, from 4.2 percent of all Nasca 5 themes to 21.5 percent of all Nasca 6 themes. The importance of Trophy Heads is further indicated by the appearance of a new theme, the Full-bodied Trophy Head." Concomitantly, the frequency of mythical themes declines drastically in Nasca 6 and these themes lose their association with warfare and agriculture. Roark (1965: 56) concludes that the "reality which was important to the Nasca 6 potters involved warfare" and that "militarism was on the increase and . . . religion had become more remote, more isolated from the dominant concerns of society." Roark (1965: 56) believes that Nasca 6 iconography is depicting conditions of real warfare and "not simply religious sacrifice."

Late Nasca iconography leaves little doubt that the heads were taken from and subsequently manipulated by adult males. Adult males are painted or modeled in fine attire, often holding a human trophy head (figure 9.1) or they have trophy heads at the hem of their tunics (Rickenbach 1999: color plate 127; figure 4.1). These individuals appear to be chiefs and there appear to be many of them to judge from their frequency in the ceramic iconography. Iconography suggests that, after the demise of Cahuachi, non-supernaturally costumed Nasca chiefs appropriated the former role of ritual practitioners as supernatural intermediaries through their

Figure 9.1 A well-dressed adult Nasca male holds a decapitated human head (Amano Museum; *photo*: Helaine Silverman).

manipulation of trophy heads. Perhaps, too, by offering heads, these late Nasca men gained status points, so to speak, to judge from late Nasca portrait iconography that depicts them elegantly clothed and powerfully posed.

Warriors are commonly portrayed, although battles are less frequently depicted. In what is arguably the most famous Nasca combat scene, the actual act of decapitation is shown (figure 9.2). As depicted on Nasca pottery, most warriors are recognizable as Nasca men (for example, de Lavalle 1986: 147). They vary in dress from naked (see, for example, Eisleb 1977: fig. 208; Kroeber and Collier 1998: plate 24) to wearing just a loincloth (see, for example, Eisleb 1977: fig. 209) to fully and elaborately clothed (de Lavalle 1986: 174). However, on some vessels, one or more combatants

Figure 9.2 The famous Amano Museum vessel showing fierce battle and decapitation of victims (*photo*: Helaine Silverman).

are highly stylized and do not look Nasca (see, for example, Blasco Bosqued and Ramos Gómez 1991: 79; de Lavalle 1986: 174). Indeed, a Nasca 7 vase without precise provenience but said to be from Tunga (in the southernmost tributary in the Río Grande de Nazca drainage) depicts a fully clothed Nasca warrior fighting and grabbing the wild hair of a naked savage whose depiction is so "other" that he must not be Nasca (see Kroeber and Collier 1998: color plate 24). It is impossible to know, at present, if these differences in appearance are based on status, context, artists' problems with human representation, and/or if they reflect an identity constructed as foreign or unallied. By comparison, we note that the Jivaro took heads of other Jivaro with whom they were not on friendly terms (see Harner 1972).[2]

We return again to the persistent, unresolved interpretation of these heads. Were they coincidental trophies of warfare (that is, battles fought for territorial conquest and its perks)? Were they the result of explicit headhunting actions ideologized in terms of religion and its ritual? Or did late Nasca aggression result in trophy head capture, with the taking, preparation, and manipulation of human heads still being religiously charged and ritualistically performed?

Trophies of War or Ritual Heads?

Tello (1918: 57–8) observed the skulls of females and children in his sample of trophy heads. In a sample of eight early Nasca (Nasca 1–3) trophy heads excavated by A. L. Kroeber in the Nazca Valley, Williams et al. (in press) identify three adult males, two adult females, two unsexable subadults, and one child. In contrast, in the largest provenienced group of Nasca trophy heads – forty-eight from the Nasca 5 cache at Cerro Carapo in the Palpa Valley (Browne et al. 1993: figs 8, 10) – all pertain to adult males between 20 and 45 years of age save one belonging to an individual of indeterminable sex, 12–15 years old (see Browne et al. 1993: 286; Verano 1995).

Noting that some trophy heads pertained to women and children, Tello (1918) rejected their origin in warfare (though, of course, the heads could have been obtained through raiding). Instead, Tello (1917: 287) argued that the heads were used in religious or thaumaturgical ceremonies. Neira Avendaño and Coelho (1972–3: 141–2) also saw the heads as ceremonial in nature, as ritual heads, but they did not specify how they believed they were obtained except to say that they were not the result of ordinary warfare. Other scholars have interpreted Nasca trophy heads as the product of ritual battles (for example, Browne et al. 1993; Silverman 1993a: 221–5; for a discussion of these *tinkuy* see, for example, Sallnow 1991: 298–302).

Sonia Guillén (cited in Silverman 1993a: 224) emphasizes that Nasca people went to great effort to conserve the skulls they took. In preparing the head, the Nasca tried to maintain the dead person's recognizable physiognomy by means of stuffing eye sockets and cheeks with cotton to keep the face full, tying the upper and lower mandibles together so they would stay articulated, and sealing lips with spines so that they would not deform (Silverman 1993a: figs 15.1, 15.2). Guillén says the cut marks observed on various trophy heads are the result of peeling away the skin for subsequent replacement; independently, Verano (1995: 212–13) reaches the same conclusion. Guillén suggests that bloodletting evidenced by cut marks in the scalp and the removal of the brain were necessary for the process of natural mummification and that the purpose of mummification was to maintain these heads as recognizable individuals – as ancestors. Baraybar (1987) argues that the scalp cut marks are indicative of ritual bleeding. Williams et al. (in press) have observed extensive wear around the frontal perforations of some of Kroeber's Nasca trophy heads suggesting to them that the skulls had been manipulated during Nasca rituals.

Proulx (1971, 1989b, 1999b) has argued that trophy heads were procured in secular warfare or raids rather than ritual battles to be used for ritual purposes. He indicates that Nasca ceramic iconography clearly depicts warriors holding weapons (clubs, slings, spears, and spear throwers) and severed trophy heads. These heads are carried by ropes inserted through their foreheads or hang by their cords from posts (see, for example, Blasco Bosqued and Ramos Gómez 1980: fig. 47). However, Proulx believes that following these battles and the decapitation of victims, the heads were used for a variety of ritual purposes, especially as a means of propitiating the powerful forces that controlled water, agricultural fertility, and rejuvenation. Caches of trophy heads were ritually interred as offerings. An iconographic example of such an interment is depicted on a vessel showing several trophy heads beneath a mound at which two shamans conduct a ceremony (see figure 8.1). The best field evidence of this may be the Cerro Carapo cache referred to above. Verano (1995: 214) supports Proulx's interpretation and argues that the Nasca trophy heads are the result of warfare. He notes that in his sample, including the Cerro Carapo skulls, 85 percent of the trophy heads correspond to young adult men. He suggests that "Nasca trophy heads were collected from enemy combatants rather than from revered ancestors."

Carmichael (1988: 183) estimates that some 5 percent of the Nasca population, mostly men, ended up as trophy heads. Certainly, real trophy head-taking increased in Nasca 5 times (Browne et al. 1993; Silverman 1993a: 221–6, 327), perhaps a prelude to the dramatic increase in militaristic themes on Nasca 6 pottery that Roark (1965: 56) has argued was a reflection of Nasca sociopolitical reality. Yet physical–biological evidence shows that at least some Nasca skulls were obtained from long desiccated skeletons rather than from the actual act of decapitation (Patrick Carmichael, personal communication, 1993).

Schreiber and Lancho Rojas (1995) have demonstrated that the middle valleys of the southern tributaries were opened up to cultivation and, therefore, occupation in Nasca 5 times with the invention of the filtration galleries. This suggests that there was some demand on land in that part of the drainage. We hypothesize that this was because of the droughts of the sixth century AD which had consequences for the subsistence base of that resident population. We do not see evidence of population pressure exerting an effect on the Nasca 5 residents of the Ingenio–middle Grande region, however, because in the upper Ingenio Valley, where *pukios* supplemented the seasonally charged river, entire tracts of fertile agricultural lands had few or no sites in some epochs of the Early Intermediate Period and most of the lower half of the north side of the middle Ingenio Valley was unoccupied by Nasca people (a settlement pattern due only in part to destruction through modern earth-moving activities; it may be due to concentration of population at Ventilla/Site 165).

Furthermore, despite the prevalence of trophy-head iconography and actual trophy heads in Nasca society, there is no independent evidence on the ground of conflict in Nasca times. In so far as we know, Nasca habitation sites are not located strategically for defense; they do not have fortifications; remains of instruments of aggression are not associated in a meaningful way with sites. Schreiber (1999: 169), however, describes Nasca population density as "high" in late Nasca times in her survey region in the southern tributaries of the Río Grande de Nazca drainage. She sees "an increase in local warfare, *although* the cluster of smaller sites in the middle Trancas Valley does not conform to this pattern" (Schreiber 1999: 168; our emphasis).

Wilson (1988) provides compelling evidence of warfare in the Santa Valley that can serve as a comparative model for Nasca. In Wilson's Early Horizon Cayhuamarca phase, for instance, there are twenty-one citadels representing 33 percent of all defensive sites located during survey. Rock enclosure walls are massive; there are moats or ditches; there are baffled entrances, and entrances in the main wall are few and narrow; there are ramparts and parapets; there are rock bulwark walls adjacent to the upslope side of ditches; sites are remote from the irrigated valley floor (Wilson 1988: 104, 108).

A major issue is what Nasca warfare would look like on the ground. Though human interaction is uncommon in Nasca iconography, there are vivid late Nasca combat scenes. In addition to those depictions noted above, late Nasca vessels may portray hand-to-hand combat and spear wounds (see de Lavalle 1986: 174). On other vessels, warriors hold spears and spear throwers (see, for example, de Lavalle 1986: 167 bottom, 169 top; Lothrop and Mahler 1957: plate xixf). Actual spear-thrower hooks are well known (see, for example, de Lavalle 1986: 183 bottom left; Lothrop and Mahler 1957: plates xixa–e, xx) as are slings and obsidian knives (for example, Silverman 1993a: fig. 19.25).

So far, Nasca settlement pattern data do not conform to Wilson's bona-fide evidence of warfare. Rather, the Nasca data may resonate with Billman's (1997) assessment of Moche warfare, which was motivated by the status striving of an emerging elite rather than by population pressure on arable land resources. We note Demarest's (1984: 228, 229) conclusion that:

> raiding parties, captive-taking, and sacrifice were obviously endemic to Maya society, and, more importantly, they were critical to status reinforcement and political power . . . such warfare was . . . a crucial factor in the gradual development of state or proto-state political organization. Unrestricted, large-scale, and widespread warfare . . . is not the only form of conflict that has great implications. In a slow, deviation-amplifying, developmental trajectory small-scale warfare can play a critical role in the graduate increase in the power of chiefs.

Clearly, in late Nasca times, warfare and trophy headhunting were important activities. Real caches of trophy heads are known (for example, Browne et al. 1993) and elite men self-portrayed their position of status through fine garments and the possession of trophy heads (for example, Benson and Conklin 1981: 64; de Lavalle 1986: 136 top right; Rickenbach 1999: plates 127, 154). This process of self-aggrandizement through headhunting apparently began in early Nasca (see, for example, Rickenbach 1999: plate 153), though at that time the pervasive context of trophy-head manipulation was overtly ritually and supernaturally configured (see, for example, de Lavalle 1986: 134 bottom, 135; Rickenbach 1999: plates 222–4, 227–9, 232).

Clearly, significant shifts occurred from early to late Nasca times in the role and meaning of trophy heads in Nasca practice and ideology. This complex and evolving phenomenon cannot be explained by simple cause-and-effect arguments. Much more fieldwork is needed to better understand Nasca headhunting, its relationship to warfare (itself requiring further elucidation), and the sociopolitical ramifications of this activity.

10

Nasca Sociopolitical Organization

Already in 1967, Morton Fried acknowledged discontent with the word "state" and the state/non-state classification (Fried 1967: 226). But Fried argued vigorously for the validity and utility of the state concept and his masterpiece, *The Evolution of Political Society*, inspired several generations of processual archaeologists to seek to explain the evolution of the state in the various so-called pristine civilizations and to ascertain if there were regular laws determining its formation or constraining its development. The Central Andes have been a key focus of such research, from the Virú Valley Project, prior to Fried (see Steward 1948; Strong 1948; see also Armillas 1948), and forward into the present day (for example, Haas et al. 1987; Wilson 1988).

Within Andean scholarship, the nature of early Nasca socio-political complexity has been much debated (for example, Carmichael 1988; Massey 1986; Reindel and Isla 1999; Silverman 1993a; Valdez 1998). Archaeologists have categorized Nasca as a chiefdom or state – among other terms used – based on their interpretation of the geographical distribution of the exquisite pottery style, the assumption of craft specialization for pottery manufacture, complex iconography and patterns of access to it, the size and pre-eminence of Cahuachi (plus the site's former interpretation as an urban settlement), burial patterns, absence of artifacts of administration such as *quipus* and ration bowls, and so on (see discussion in Silverman 1993a: ch. 23). Like Fried, however, Silverman (1993a: ch. 23) has argued that the state/non-state debate is a flawed research question, saying that these neo-evolutionary labels are counter-productive (they say little about a society's organization and evolution) as well as inaccurate (they do not correspond to native concepts of sociopolitical organization).

Although Nasca settlement patterns can be manipulated into hierarchical rankings of site size and function (see Silverman 1993a: figs 23.3–23.10; see discussion in Isbell and Schreiber 1978; Parsons 1971; Wilson 1988), Silverman (1993a: fig. 23.11) has critiqued this procedure arguing instead for a heterarchical (see Crumley 1987) reading of the Nasca landscape. Similarly, although archaeologists use data from cemeteries to reconstruct social organization and level of sociopolitical complexity (see various papers in Brown 1971; Chapman et al. 1981), there is a significant body of literature that provides well-documented reasons for exercising caution in the typical one-to-one correlation archaeologists often make between grave wealth, status in life and level of complexity of the surrounding sociopolitical milieu (see, for example, Dillehay 1990: 233; Earle 1987; Linares 1977). These cautions also hold for Nasca.[1] In this chapter, therefore, we try to reconstruct the nature and degree of complexity of Nasca sociopolitical organization without recourse to ineffective evolutionary terms, and we consider not just the early Nasca social formation but also its later iterations. We start from the premise that Nasca was an Andean society. Using the common analytical method of ethnographic analogy, we argue that it is plausible to suggest that ethnographically and ethnohistorically known principles of Andean sociopolitical organization may have operated in Nasca times.

Andean Principles of Nasca Sociopolitical Organization

Ayllus

The *ayllu* is a kin-based landholding corporation. Within the *ayllu* there is asymmetrical dual/moiety organization (*hanan–hurin*/upper–lower) of the segmentary lineages comprising it. These lineages and their members trace descent from a common ancestor and their ranking is determined by distance from that ancestor for whom there may be a cult of remembrance and attention. As Moseley (1994: 39) succinctly points out, although the *ayllu* is communal and manages marriage, labor, land, water, camelid herds and other resources, everyone is not equal. Some individuals, households, and lineages are more affluent than others. Affluence and inequalities can be "banked." Institutions of reciprocity allow labor and goods to be "loaned" to kindred or lineage mates and then "withdrawn" in kind over the course of a generation or more. Affluent lineages reputedly descend from older, senior "brothers" or heirs of the *ayllu* founder, whereas junior siblings or heirs beget the less-affluent descent groups.

Moseley writes that communal decision-making and *ayllu* governance are vested in cargo systems of ranked offices also called prestige hierarchies. Specific hierarchical posts are responsible for particular civic, ceremonial, or religious duties. Offices are vested with authority to address dereliction of duty and crime, to mitigate disputes, and to allocate common resources, as well as to mobilize and direct work on communal projects, including the construction of canals, roads, and public buildings. Holding office is a communal service that demands very substantial private outlay of time and resources. Positions are held on a rotational basis by individuals who can afford to move up the cargo hierarchies and retire out of them with the acknowledged prestige of community service. Although individuals enter and leave, the office systems persist across generations as enduring structures of communal civic and ceremonial governance.

Importantly, Moseley (1994: 32, 33, 39) distinguishes between the cargo system of communal civic and ceremonial governance and the *curaca* class of nobility characterized by inherited status and hierarchical rank:

> ayllu and cargo governance arose before higher-order formations, such as regional religious cults or the Karaka [*curaca*] class . . . [there were certain early societies in which] communal decision-making and governance were vested in cargo-like systems of hierarchical prestige offices that were civic and religious in service. Individuals rotated through ranked offices and did not inherit them.

Furthermore, Moseley notes that cargo systems were flexible. They could deal with matters more civic-communal in nature or more religious. He observes that "cargo-like systems of corporate authority provided the templates and blueprints for the formation of multicommunal organizations. These formations were religious in guise, but fully civic in service. Similar to communal bureaucracies, authority was vested in hierarchies of ranked posts and enduring positions that rotating officeholders did not bequeath to their heirs." This is the crux of debates about level and organization of sociopolitical complexity in any society in the Andes: were principles of inherited positions of authority operative?

In a series of publications, Helaine Silverman has assumed or shown (depending on the persuasion of the reader) the existence of *ayllus* and moieties in ancient Nasca society.[2] The fullest presentation of her argument is found in *Cahuachi in the Ancient Nasca World* (Silverman 1993a: 309–12, 342–3, see also Silverman 1990b). Silverman is strongly influenced by ethnographic descriptions of the *ayllu* (for example, Allen 1988; Isbell 1978), by the ethnohistoric descriptions and archaeological interpretations of Pachacamac (for example, Jimenez Borja and Bueno Mendoza 1970), and by the ethnohistorically known sociopolitical organization of the Río Grande de Nazca drainage in late pre-Hispanic times (see Urton 1990).

Due to insufficient excavation at habitation sites, archaeologists understand little about the village level at which the *ayllu* operated. We are missing, at this stage of Nasca archaeology, "the routinized, everyday traditions of domestic and communal realms [which] are nonideological to the extent that they are not recognized in the fields of political action . . . Domestic communities are where most people exist, where most people's perceptions and dispositions are inculcated and where cultural traditions are perpetuated" (Pauketat and Emerson 1999: 302). Until Nasca archaeology generates the kind of quotidian database available elsewhere and which is necessary for fine-grained cultural interpretation, we will be arguing predominantly from the biases of great art, elite tombs, and major civic-ceremonial centers. Our understanding will remain incomplete as well as theoretically limited. In addition, only excavation will be able to provide information about the distribution and circulation of luxury goods in society, widely recognized as a key aspect of manipulated position and personhood in complex societies.

Moieties

Moore (1995) has reviewed much of the classic literature on dualism in South America. He explains that dual organization can be manifested in symmetric (i.e. equal) or diametric (ranked) societal halves. Dual organization of social units can organize kinship, residence, and the exercise of political power in terms of pairs of opposed social groups. It can organize the cosmos as well as social order in terms of dual oppositions classified as counterposed dyads (Moore 1995: 169–70). Interestingly, Moore provides compelling ethnographic data that indicate that "different forms of dualism may coexist in the same society'" and that moieties can have "fluctuating 'social visibility'" (Moore 1995: 170).

Dual organization has been considered diagnostic of ancient Andean sociopolitical organization because of the strong upper–lower moiety division in Inca society and the moiety organization ethnographically observed to characterize traditional peasant communities of the Peruvian highlands. Moore (1995: 176) indicates that the "related concepts of dualism, symmetric/diametric oppositions, moiety, exogamy and shared rule . . . are distinct social principles with different material expressions . . . dual organization embodies a class of cultural principles that may vary in their social visibility and hence in the way they are reflected in the archaeological record."

It can be suggested that the two walled areas within the central core of Cahuachi represent dualism, but it is more likely that the walls are defining functionally distinct areas of the site: a central acropolis of monumental architecture and a great plaza for the congregation of pilgrims. It seems reasonable to suppose that the Pampa was conceived as a major separation of space within the drainage with a set of rivers to the north and a set of rivers to the south; Silverman (1993a: 342) has suggested that the Pampa was conceived as a *tinkuy* and, following Urton (1990), that there were northern and southern moieties. It seems significant that the great trans-Pampa geoglyph known as the Camino de Leguia (see Silverman 1990a: 439, fig. 2) appears to connect Cahuachi and Ventilla/Site 165. Silverman (1990a: 452–3, 1993a: 326) has suggested that the two sites functioned as "dual capitals" of the early

Nasca formation. Beyond these examples, Silverman can not put forth any other data – whether site planning, site distribution, or iconography – as exemplary of dual organization in ancient Nasca society. For Silverman, the argument in favor ultimately rests in her belief in a Central Andean culture area with a deep history and, therefore, antecedents for late pre-Hispanic patterns of behavior, while Proulx remains more skeptical until additional empirical evidence is discovered.

Nasca 3 Social Formation

Working to greater and lesser degrees within a processualist paradigm and on the basis of survey in the Ica Valley and excavation at Cahuachi, Massey (1986) and Silverman (1993a), respectively, came to radically different conclusions about the early Nasca social formation as a result of their doctoral dissertation projects. Massey concluded that the disappearance of Topará influence in the upper Ica Valley at the end of EIP 2 was due to a Nasca invasion from Nazca (Massey 1986; Wallace 1986) and that Rowe (1963: 12) had been correct about the expansionist, state-based nature of early Nasca society. She argued that early Nasca was a regional state that conquered, reorganized, and administered the Ica Valley through a hierarchy of settlements led from Cerro Tortolita in the upper valley. Silverman (1993a) argued that the presence of Nasca 3 pottery in the Ica Valley cannot be considered abrupt and unprecedented given the previous existence of Nasca 1 and 2 sites there. Silverman (1993a: 321, 337) also criticized Massey's argument because of the non-correspondence of her description and dating of Cerro Tortolita to the remains observed there. In addition, she criticized Massey's lumping of Nasca 3 and Nasca 4 which impeded comparison of the settlement patterns of these two phases. Silverman concluded that Cahuachi was not a great urban settlement and she interpreted the field data as indicative of a chiefdom/paramount chiefdom/confederacy organization coordinated by Cahuachi's pilgrimage sphere of influence rather than a state-level organization.

Silverman (1990b, 1993a) argues that Nasca people were organized as independent societies in the Ica Valley and valleys of the Río

Grande de Nazca drainage. She suggests that many of the mounds of Cahuachi were built by local social groups (*ayllus*) in the drainage who maintained them as shrines and that larger groups maintained larger temple-mounds and smaller groups were able to build only lesser mounds. She interprets the abundance of ritual paraphernalia but lack of permanent domestic foci at the site during its apogee as evidence of Cahuachi's use as a pilgrimage center. The patterns of material remains at Cahuachi are readily comparable to those generated by contemporary pilgrimage in the region (see Silverman 1993a: 312–16, 1994b), and ethnohistorically and archaeologically known LIP Pachacamac provides a pre-Columbian model of how such pilgrimage could have been spatially as well as politically organized (see Silverman 1990b, 1993a: 311–12).

Morinis and Crumrine (1991: 6) emphasize that the "artistic presentation of themes of pilgrimage in the context of pilgrimage performance serves to impress upon the audience of pilgrims the meaning of the activity in which they are participating." This is true. But Silverman (1990b, 1993a) also argues that the public performances at Cahuachi were not just religious acts. They were also political acts clothed in ritual and embodying Nasca ideology. Cahuachi was a locus for status display and negotiation.

> Each celebration at Cahuachi provided the opportunity for a change in the previous hierarchy. The crucial point to remember is that there was [a] status hierarchy even if those occupying positions at the top of that hierarchy did not maintain their roles permanently. Personnel may have changed or deliberately rotated (like cargos), but a permanent hierarchy structure is posited to have existed . . . Once periodic celebrations at the ceremonial center were ended, the macrogroups would decompose into their smaller parts, returning to their distinct home villages where other principles of social group membership would exert their claims. The transient, marked social hierarchy would thus disaggregate into a less hierarchical, more permanent day-to-day social organization until the next gathering provided the opportunity for testing and reworking the hierarchy established at the previous celebration. (Silverman 1993a: 317)

Furthermore, in this book Silverman additionally suggests, following Rasnake (1986: 667), that pilgrimage could have served not only to "emphasize the structure of social groups but also to link the multiple groupings of the social order to a conception of their physical territory. This sacralization and 'socialization' of space is an aspect of ritual language quite widespread in the Andes." Similarly, Silverman is in agreement with Deborah Poole who writes:

> The link between political–economic organization and religious sanctuaries is a well known phenomenon in the history of Andean societies, and today the sanctuaries and pilgrimages maintain forms of connection with economic organization that are very similar to those which characterized their pre-Hispanic homologues. Some religious pilgrimages were directly incorporated into the economic exchange of the fairs which accompanied them. In the same way, many pre-Hispanic ceremonial centers exercised an important control over extensive routes of exchange.
>
> ... Beyond their direct participation in economic exchange, the location of the sanctuaries and the religious activities concentrated in them reproduced and delimited borders and centers of production, exchange and social organization, both contemporary and historic. The conjunction of numerous pilgrims to these religious centers reinforced the economic and social ties between the ceremonial center and the settlements within its jurisdiction, and ritually delimited the territory hegemonized by the sanctuary.
>
> In the case of the great pre-Columbian sanctuaries, the centripetal territory also implicated an internal differentiation between regions and subregions concentrated around local huacas. These ethnic or local huacas attracted pilgrims from smaller areas and demarcated social frontiers and regional economic centers. To each of these huacas was assigned a sacred status according to the territory and economy it dominated, and also in accordance to its relationship to the great ceremonial centers. The formulation of these religious hierarchies was phrased in terms of kinship and reflected political and economic relations. (Poole 1982: 80)

Silverman's pilgrimage model of early Nasca society also may be parsimonious with Elizabeth Brumfiel's discussion of factional competition.

> Monumental architecture might involve manipulation of the symbols of group unity: the ancestral or patron deity. Such symbols would be most prominent under conditions of competition at the

regional level as part of an effort to create bonds between leaders and followers that could not be easily transferred to competing leaders . . . Public architecture also suggests efforts to impress a regional audience of potential allies and rivals who use the size of the building projects to judge the size and commitment of one's following. (Brumfiel 1994: 11)

It is interesting to note again the transference of elaborate supernatural mythology from textiles to pottery in Nasca 3 times, coincident with Cahuachi's apogee. This shift in media occurred as a result of the abandonment of the time-consuming elaboration of fancy, highly iconographic textiles in Nasca 2 in favor of the massive (but not mass) production of ritual pottery vessels in Nasca 3. Silverman (1993a: 302) has suggested a positive (amplifying) effect of the Nasca cult on pottery production. This pottery was widely circulated in the drainage for the purpose of widespread participation in Nasca ritual as opposed to the fancy textiles whose use appears to have been restricted to ceremonial venues (for example, Cahuachi: see Phipps 1989; Strong 1957) and, possibly, special mortuary contexts though none of these is scientifically known.

There may be micro-stylistic variation within the Nasca pottery style from valley to valley that detailed iconographic and petrographic analysis could reveal. Still unanswered is the persistent question of who the potters were. Other classes of objects must be examined as well. These kinds of analyses, particularly ceramic, will be crucial for defining exactly who was going to Cahuachi. Once known, we can ask "why?" on a level more sophisticated than Silverman's (1990b, 1993a) pilgrimage model, for any group's relationship with Cahuachi necessarily involved issues of power, ideology, status enhancement, and negotiation.

Silverman (1990a: 439, fig. 5, 1993a: 326) has suggested that it may be appropriate to call Ventilla/Site 165 "urban" and that it may have acted as "the 'urban' capital of the early Nasca social formation" with Cahuachi being the "religious" capital. As noted earlier in this chapter, the two sites were connected to each by a trans-Pampa line that departs from above the west edge of Ventilla/Site 165 and passes by the eastern extreme of Cahuachi (Silverman 1993a: fig. 23.1). Silverman's characterization of Ventilla/Site 165 as urban may have been premature.[3] But clearly Ventilla/Site 165 had residential density. In her formulation of "dual capitals", Silverman was influenced by Urton's (1990) reconstruction of late pre-Hispanic moieties in the Río Grande de Nazca drainage that were divided by the Pampa. She also considered the very different types of irrigation agriculture to the north and south of the Pampa (typical coastal irrigation versus filtration galleries, respectively). It seemed and it still seems possible to Helaine Silverman that the Pampa was conceived as the fulcrum of pre-Hispanic social life in the drainage. Excavation is needed at the fascinating Ventilla/Site 165 in order to ascertain its nature, evolution, and relationship to Cahuachi.

Reindel and Isla (1999) have resuscitated the processualist agenda and frame their Palpa project in terms of the determination of Nasca's level of sociopolitical complexity. They interpret Los Molinos as "a type of regional governmental center of the Early Nasca Period" and the early Nasca data as indicating state-based, class-organized society. We disagree with Reindel and Isla. We think the data show that the early Nasca social formation was composed of many societies sharing a cultural tradition and participating in a cohesive religious cult. This reconstruction does not deny the existence of elites but, rather, the political centralization and social stratification (hereditary hierarchy) posited by Reindel and Isla.

Cahuachi was the prime Nasca civic-ceremonial center. We cannot explain its concentration of monumental architecture and exquisite material culture (pottery, textiles, pyroengraved gourds, carved stone beakers, and so on) other than to argue, as has Silverman (1988a, 1990a, 1993a: ch. 22, 1994b *inter alia*), that the site was recognized as having a sacred geography that led to its development as the seat of the Nasca cult and focus of pilgrimage. We assume that pilgrimage involved "calendrically based, community-focused rites that play a critical role in the resolution of cosmological discontinuities in the annual ritual sequence ... [and] are based on community-wide participation, which requires a symbolic text both highly visible and understandable to the masses" (Pauketat and Emerson 1991: 919–20). At Cahuachi that text was constituted by the sacred geography of the site, its constructed monumental architecture which must have had symbolic meaning, the geoglyphs on the Pampa opposite Cahuachi, and the highly iconographic pottery and other specialized material culture used at the site.

At the time of Cahuachi's apogee there also were "major regional centers" in the Río Grande de Nazca drainage, such as Los Molinos in Palpa, Sites 80, 165, and 552 in the middle Ingenio Valley, and Site 515 in the middle Grande Valley. For some archaeologists, such as Reindel and Isla (1999), this differentiated landscape will indicate a state-level decision-making hierarchy. For others it will support Silverman's (1993a) model of "provincial temples" at Cahuachi with independent supporting societies in the hinterland.

In the southern drainage, Schreiber (1999) has identified only two, small, early Nasca "lesser centers" consisting of "platform mound and cemetery complexes." Both of these are in the Nazca Valley proper, one at Pueblo Viejo and the other at Cantalloc. We disagree with Schreiber's classification of Cahuachi as a similar "platform mound and cemetery complex" given that most non-mound burials at Cahuachi appear to post-date its apogee (see Silverman 1993a: ch. 7) and Cahuachi played a supra-valley role rather than a solely local one in the Nazca Valley. No "centers" are reported for Taruga, Chauchilla, and Las Trancas. The apparent lack of early Nasca civic-ceremonial loci in the valleys south of Nazca may indicate a situation of sharply unequal development in the southern Río Grande de Nazca drainage just as contemporary differences of wealth and human resources existed among the Nasca 3 populations of the northern drainage. The differences of scale and complexity in the architecture of Nasca 3 Cahuachi is congruous with the differentiated Nasca 3 settlement pattern of the drainage.

Iconography and other evidence from apogee Cahuachi reveal an early Nasca society that is reminiscent of Turner's (1974) "cult of the earth" with its emphasis on communal (non-exclusionary) fertility rituals. Given the abundance of civic-ceremonial architecture, the absence (as known at present) of significant mortuary differentiation in early Nasca society, and the seeming lack of iconographic portrayal of recognizable elites, the early Nasca data appear to fit Renfrew's (1974) group-oriented chiefdom with its emphasis on pan-group monumental architecture. In societies that conform to this model, disproportionate personal accumulation of wealth is eschewed or, for reasons that must be explicated, not attainable. In early Nasca society political–ideological power and social differences were not exclusively or primarily based on the economy. As the paramount ceremonial center of early Nasca society, Cahuachi exercised centrifugal and centripetal forces on the interaction sphere and pilgrimage orbit it animated. It is at this time that Nasca people began to produce enormous amounts of ritual pottery and influence a large area of the south coast to the north and south of the Ica–Nazca Nasca heartland. Precisely because early Nasca society was composed of discrete societies participating in the Nasca cultural tradition and religious cult, each group and individuals within each group had the opportunity to interact differentially with others inside and outside the system.

The Collapse of the Nasca 3 System

Major construction at Cahuachi was not undertaken after Nasca 3 (Rowe 1963; Silverman 1988a, 1990b, 1993a; Strong 1957). Pilgrimage to the site appears to have ceased. Fewer geoglyphs were traced (Silverman 1990a). There was a major change (decline in habitation sites and ceremonial centers) in EIP 4 in settlement patterns in at least the Ingenio, middle Grande, and Palpa valleys (and beyond: in the Acarí Valley). Notably, Los Molinos was abandoned after Nasca 3, never to arise again. Site 515, which had dominated the middle Grande Valley, was permanently abandoned after Nasca 3, simultaneously with Cahuachi. In the middle Ingenio Valley, Sites 80, 165, and 552 had constituted a significant concentration of dense population and major civic-ceremonial architecture along the south bank of the river, possibly integrating that region: this nexus also collapsed after Nasca 3 (yet arose again in Nasca 5 for reasons that remain to be explained). There is no evidence of intra-site or inter-site differentiation in Nasca 4. It is appropriate to speak of the collapse of the Nasca 3 system.

Why did Cahuachi collapse? Why did the system it integrated collapse? What can the collapse tell us about Nasca 3 society? If excavation at Cahuachi continues to demonstrate a lack of significant permanent domestic occupation during the site's apogee, Cahuachi's lack of urbanism and urbanization will have to be considered in our understanding of the demise of the center and the break-up of the societies it coordinated (see Silverman 1993a: 326). Perhaps the system became overloaded, its ritual networks unable to cope with increasing complexity (demands, conflicts, contradictions, information) of the constituent groups within the system and/or the assertions of particular individuals/groups seeking to break the cultural norms of behavior to achieve individual benefit/ power in society, perhaps such as those at Los Molinos. Rather than becoming more complex (moving to a higher level of centralization, socioeconomic differentiation, and infrastructural development) which was an option, the system collapsed into a less complex configuration (the Nasca 4 social formation). If so, this outcome would have been the result of decisions and actions by the individuals and groups comprising the society.

Perhaps a worsening climate made the early Nasca fertility-dominated religious canon and rites appear inadequate and therefore participant believers stopped going to the site. The geologist, Georg Petersen (1980) has proposed desertification to explain the collapse of Cahuachi. On the other hand, architect Giuseppe Orefici (see *Life Magazine*, December 1999) argues that Cahuachi's decline was due to massive destruction through excessive rain and flooding; Silverman's (1993a) admittedly small-scale excavations at Cahuachi did not recover evidence of this inundation event. Either way, the beliefs and rituals underwriting the cult and ensuring proper balance between society, nature, and the supernaturals would have been perceived as invalidated by a climatic crisis. Consistent radiocarbon dates for each of the sequential Nasca phases at various sites in each of the valleys are desperately needed so that the occupational history of Cahuachi and the changes in settlement patterns in the Río Grande de Nazca drainage may be securely traced and interpreted and causality correctly attributed.

Nasca 4 pottery appears to be a reflection of these times. Produced after the apogee of Cahuachi, Nasca 4 pottery is characterized by increasing heterogeneity. Proulx (1968: 98) indicates that in the Ica Valley "the greatest differences in details of shape and design from those of Nasca [Nazca] took place in Phase 4." Proulx (1968: 98) interprets this situation as the result of "the loss of influence of Nasca [Nazca] and the increasing opportunity for local innovations. The decline of a centralizing influence may be responsible for the great differences in the pottery of such geographically close sites as Ocucaje and Santiago in this phase" in the Ica Valley itself. This is an important observation and a plausible hypothesis requiring further fieldwork to corroborate or amend. Also, Nasca 4 pottery is scarce in comparison to Nasca 3. Again Proulx's (1968) explanation is plausible: Nasca 4 is a seriationally valid phase of short temporal duration.

The collapse of the Cahuachi system may even be manifested macro-regionally in changes in settlement pattern beyond the Río Grande de Nazca drainage. The decline of Cahuachi is contemporary with a significant decrease in population in Acarí, this being the fact that led Rowe (1963) to posit an expansionist Nasca 3 state in the first place. We cannot fully assess what happened in Ica since Massey (1986) lumps Nasca 3 and 4.

On the other hand, the vibrant Carmen society of Pisco (Silverman 1997), which is cross-dated to Nasca 3–4 on the basis of interaction between the societies (Silverman 1991: fig. 9.2), appears to have been unaffected by the Nasca 3 collapse, assuming that the cross-dating and absolute dating are in sync. The independence of Carmen may be all the more demonstrated if the succeeding Estrella style and society developed continuously from Carmen. The problem is that the Estrella phases, and the sites to which they correspond, have not been adequately anchored to the relative chronology of EIP epochs (see Menzel 1971: 126–9; Wallace 1958). On the other hand, if Pisco Valley sites firmly dated to EIP 4, 5, and 6 cannot be identified, then we may well have to consider a systemic and domino-effect causality, and archaeologists would need to reassess the cohesiveness and linkages within and between Nasca and non-Nasca societies. Regardless, it is clear that Nasca societies were interacting with other commensurate, contemporary groups on the south coast such as Chongos in EIP 1 and Carmen in EIP 3. Thus, the Nasca 3 cultural floresence was not isolated but, rather, part of larger sphere.

The Nasca 5 Recovery and Reorganization

The demise of Cahuachi created a sociopolitical vacuum into which assertive individuals could step. After the poorly understood Nasca 4 interlude, Nasca society appears to have reconstituted itself in a context of extreme competition among human males no longer disguised as mythical beings and not acting as shamans in a unifying religious cult. These hypothesized chiefs constructed a new physical landscape of buildings, tombs, geoglyphs, special caches, and, in the southern tributaries, filtration galleries. They were not associated with any single, dominant central place as had been Cahuachi. This suggests that the landscape balkanized after the demise of Cahuachi. The new elites also consumed a portable landscape of material culture such as symbolically charged and socially situated pottery. Nasca 5 was a dynamic period, one of great experimentation and major reorganization in terms of settlement patterns, sociopolitical organization, and art style. We see these changes as systemically related as explained below.

Silverman (1993a: ch. 14) and Carmichael (1988) analyzed Nasca burial patterns from a sample of sites in the Río Grande de Nazca drainage and Ica Valley. Silverman and Carmichael independently concluded that Nasca mortuary patterns do not show rigid categories of socioeconomic differentiation and that the basis of observable ranking was gender- and age-determined with adults and males, in general, having more status/being the recipients of more attention than youths and women. Since their arguments were made more than a decade ago, however, new information on Nasca burial patterns has become available that suggests that in Nasca 5 society some individuals received markedly more attention in death than had been the case previously. Even at this early stage of the project being conducted by Markus Reindel and Johny Isla in the Palpa Valley, a plausible argument can be made that La Muña was a truly exceptional Nasca 5 burial site.

Reindel and Isla (cited in *El Comercio*, September 21, 1999, p. A10) argue that "La Muña is like a capital of the zone and a complex with monumental planned architecture that concentrated the elite of this millennial culture . . . the tombs found at La Muña demonstrate that well defined social classes existed." Although we have a stricter definition of the term "social class" than Reindel and Isla, seeing it as hereditary inequality with corresponding alienation from the means of production, we fully agree with Reindel and Isla's perception of significant socioeconomic differentiation in death in Nasca 5 society. La Muña is at the apex of a new burial pattern in which rare single tombs may be large and/or complex in their architecture and/or specially sited. Furthermore, individual burial chambers increase in number and elaboration.

The great elaboration of tombs at La Muña is strong evidence of the emergence of individual leaders and a distinct elite identity in Nasca 5 society. These individuals or members of elite groups were legitimating their rule through explicit kinship arguments/claims of descent rather than the more communal/group-oriented and ceremonial aspect of the early Nasca social formation. These actors were no longer constrained by the cult and rules of pilgrimage at Cahuachi which had maintained competition within culturally set bounds.

Based on the architecture of La Muña and the patterns of human movement that its architecture would have permitted, it is likely that staged mortuary ritual occurred there. Following Isbell's (1997) thesis about ancestor cults and mortuary monuments in the Central Andes, however, it would be highly significant that, for as elaborate as La Muña's mortuary facilities are, they are deep underground. This could be a sociopolitically meaningful contrast with burial facilities in which the dead were kept above ground and accessible for communication with the living. Nevertheless, the apparent increase of burial complexity between early Nasca and Nasca 5 times, as manifested by La Muña, must be taken as significant in the specific case of Nasca cultural evolution.

Excavation at civic-ceremonial centers and habitation sites may eventually reveal the differentiated domestic loci corresponding to the buried chiefs' residences. Conceivably, these may be marked by larger patios necessary for feasting the human labor that the chiefs mobilized. Perhaps potters will be shown to be functionally attached to these chiefly households. Perhaps archaeologists will identify structured and differentiated contexts and classes of material objects.

In addition to the opportunity created by the demise of Cahuachi, other factors played an important role in the development of Nasca society in Nasca 5 times. One of these was climate. Archaeologists know that climatic conditions deteriorated in the Central Andes throughout much of the sixth century AD: droughts occurred in AD 540–560 and AD 570–610 with the latter reaching extreme conditions (see Thompson et al. 1985). Although only one radiocarbon measurement (1430 ± 90/L–334E = ca. AD 525) has been published for Nasca 5, it suggests that Nasca 5 society could have been affected by these droughts. We furthermore suggest that the filtration galleries were constructed in response to these hyper-arid conditions (see Clarkson and Dorn 1991, 1995; Schreiber and Lancho Rojas 1995; Silverman 1993a: 327).[4] And we think that the irrigation of reclaimed lands encouraged subsequent population growth in late Nasca times in the southern half of the Río Grande de Nazca drainage (see Schreiber 1998).

The development of the filtration galleries in previously marginal areas of the southern tributaries of the Río Grande de Nazca drainage (according to Schreiber and Lancho Rojas 1995) is theoretically as well as empirically significant. A large body of important literature deals with the relationships between water control, agricultural intensification, and the rise of complex society (for example, Downing and Gibson 1974; Price 1971; Steward 1955; Wittfogel 1957 *inter alia*). Recently, Nocete (1994: 172) has argued that "rarely do . . . societies identified as chiefdoms develop any important technological advances linked with the process of subsistence production." He suggests that such an economic intensification would have made social relations more complex (Nocete 1994: 172). We believe that the Nasca 5 filtration gallery data show a significant subsistence-oriented technological advance that contributed to the increasing differentiation of Nasca society.

We hypothesize that an understanding of the complex underground hydrology of the drainage (knowledge gained through keen observations of geology, climate, and ecology) could have contributed to the emergence of elites in Nasca 5 by providing a very significant venue for the development of different roles in Nasca society. In this regard, an observation by Blanton (1995: 112) is interesting: in situations of emergent inequality, elders have a monopolizing strategy that encompasses control of knowledge in addition to other domains. We think that there were human agents in ancient Nasca society who perceived the behavior of Nazca's subsurface water and devised a culturally appropriate response to chronic water shortage. These special individuals might have actually mapped the water supply, identifying naturally occurring *pukios*, choosing the best locations for habitation sites, and conceiving of and creating the filtration gallery system. In so doing, they may have come to manipulate knowledge, thereby enhancing their position in society. We think that certain individuals were able to mobilize the labor force to tap the resource, intercede with the natural forces-cum-deities believed to provide water, and ultimately to exercise claims on the means of production (land, water, human labor).

Seen from this perspective, the filtration galleries are not just a normative aspect of an archaeological culture called Nasca, but a dynamic venue for and expression of the exercise of individual and special-interest group creativity, opportunism, and empowerment. The two irrigation regimes in the Río Grande de Nazca drainage – based on surface water in the north and subsurface water in the south (see chapter 3) – had the potential to generate different kinds of settlement patterns and social and political organization.

The appearance of voluptuous, seated, naked women figurines and the prevalence of women in Nasca 5 iconography (see figure 2.7), in comparison to their virtual absence before, may reflect an increased concern with fertility in the face of ever-worsening drought. In Nasca 5 times, too, the marking of hillsides in the Ingenio Valley with geoglyphs appears to have increased (Silverman 1990a). The increase in line-making in Nasca 5 times may have resulted from a drought-provoked, heightened concern with water if Johnson's (1999) hypothesis is correct (see chapter 7). Trophy head-taking's original concerns with death, fertility, and the regeneration of life were reworked in Nasca 5 times such that adult males now sought to take, display (as shown on modeled pottery vessels), and manipulate (as in the Cerro Carapo cache of forty-eight trophy heads) these heads to their own advantage (see Browne et al. 1993; Silverman 1993a: 221–3). Those who once conducted their most important status displays and participated in rituals at Cahuachi within a pan-Nasca communal/collective context, in Nasca 5 and later times may have deployed an agentic, individualizing strategy within their local valleys. Nasca 5 society is characterized by a shift toward personal aggrandizement and away from macro-group orientation.

We believe that environment-related tension, the social and political instability created by the demise of Cahuachi and the early Nasca social formation, and the rise of competitive and empowered elites acted together to cause the tripartite split in the Nasca 5 art style documented by Blagg (1975; see chapter 2). The three concurrent Nasca 5 substyles may be the tangible reflection of competing worldviews and ideologies following the breakdown of early Nasca cosmological hegemony.

The heterogeneous Nasca 5 pottery phase and time period are the antithesis of the apparently homogeneous symbolism of the early Nasca style and the pervasiveness of the early Nasca cult centered upon Cahuachi. The unrestricted distribution of early Nasca iconography in habitation sites of all size and complexity, the ubiquity of geoglyphs in the valleys, and the characteristic manners of creating sacred space and making burials all suggest doxa:

> the everyday, experiential, taken-for-granted arrangements of the worlds in which people live. These arrangements are neither imposed nor are they identified only with the political interests of a distinct subgroup . . . doxa is shaped during the act of living via the social and physical landscapes within which people dwell and within which they learn the meanings, beliefs, values and the like, of their world. (Pauketat and Emerson 1999: 304)

These meanings, beliefs, values, "and the like" were reiterated and reified at Cahuachi resulting, at the same time, in an orthodoxy or cultural hegemony by which the dominant worldview was naturalized and did not appear to be ideology at all (see Pauketat and Emerson 1999: 304). Orthodoxy and doxa were interlinked or in a relationship of implicit domination–subordination (see Pauketat and Emerson 1999: 304).

We believe that, beginning in Nasca 5 times, the formerly more implicit arrangements in Nasca society became explicit as particular adult men did in life that which resulted in their self-glorification on portrait pottery as well as burial in special facilities such as La Muña. Yet these men or factions thereof were not unified in belief and practice as evidenced by the distinct, contemporary substyles of the symbolically charged Nasca 5 pottery and by the different human resources of which these males disposed. Some Nasca men were more conservative, others more progressive, others radical in their approach to and understanding of Nasca culture overall. Presumably, each elite male, according to his bias and ability, was negotiating his participation in a shared culture of trophy head-taking and ancestor cult.

Furthermore, following comments by Pauketat and Emerson (1999: 309), it is fascinating to note the existence and, possibly, symbolic juxtaposition of women/fertility ideology against the pervasive scenes of masculinity and aggression. Much more excavation as well as paleobiological analysis of Nasca skeletal collections will be necessary in order to achieve a supra-iconographic understanding of gender relations and gendered politics in ancient Nasca society.

According to Blagg (1975: 43), there are more Bizarre Innovation pots in the Nazca Valley and these are more varied than elsewhere. This suggests that the Bizarre Innovation originated in Nazca. If this is so, it is stunningly important. It would strongly support the idea that when the cult led from Cahuachi collapsed, Nasca religion became subject to great examination, contestation, and reinterpretation, resulting in the break-up of the coherent monumental style into the three substyles recognized by Blagg. It is reasonable to suggest that potters who continued to express traditional Nasca iconography – the Conservative Monumental corpus – still believed in and understood the religion, despite the absence of a spectacular stage for ritual. Those who began to experiment with the iconography were more "progressive" – the Progressive Monumental corpus – with meaning/symbolism no longer so closely controlled and reinforced as was the case when Cahuachi functioned. Those who produced pots in the Bizarre Innovation style were manifesting a radically new attitude toward the status quo expressed by Nasca mythology and cosmology. The Bizarre Innovation is more than a mere reinterpretation of Monumental iconography (versus Blagg 1975: 66). Rather, "the Bizarre motifs . . . overwhelmingly stress the supernatural character of the mythical motifs . . . [this] seems to indicate a new esotericism in religion" (Blagg 1975: 67). The Bizarre Innovation shows us a dynamic, conscious, newly manipulative attitude toward cherished beliefs. The Bizarre Innovation is a reconceptualization of the relationship between humans and the supernatural as well as between humans. And although the Bizarre Innovation accounts for a minority (10 percent) of the Nasca 5 corpus, the Bizarre Innovation contributed greatly to the subsequent evolution of the late Nasca/Nasca 6–7 Proliferous style (see Roark 1965) which is the resolution of various Nasca 5 discourses.

As indicated, various internal and external factors, events, and processes provided positive opportunities for innovation and personal advancement while occurring in an environment surely perceived as destabilizing and disorienting. Applying Bentley (1987: 44) to Nasca 5 society, it may be ventured that:

> In systemic terms . . . people freed from the constraints of conventional thinking can act in ways destructive of the existing order. On the other hand, the loss of coherence between experience and the symbols through which people understand it causes feelings of discomfort and alienation, of rootlessness and anomie. Both represent powerful goads to action, hence motives for political mobilization. Mitigating these factors requires institution of new regimes of domination adapted to new realities of power. Inevitably this process involves reconfiguration of the perceived world and of one's place in it.

Michel Foucault (1972: 191, 1973: 312) used the term "epistemological breaks" to describe these perceptual and conceptual discontinuities that take place rapidly. Nasca 5 society conforms to Bentley's and Foucault's analyses.

Thus, the Nasca 5 break-up of the Nasca style involved issues of agency, factionalism, domination, resistance, and negotiation. The varied conditions of Nasca 5 times provided a milieu in which ambitious individuals could assert themselves through professed abilities to claim access to supernatural power through orthodox (for example, the Conservative Monumental Style) or unorthodox (for example, the Bizarre Innovation) manners, knowledge of hydrology, and climate (for example, the opening up of the filtration galleries), understanding of foreign societies (for example, contact with Lima society of the central coast and, possibly, with Wari), and so on.

Indeed, Blagg (1975: 65–6) was already heading in this interpretive direction when she concluded that the Bizarre Innovation was not the result of a misunderstanding of the Monumental motifs following the demise of Cahuachi given that "the new relationships found in the Bizarre motifs stem from a very subtle understanding of Nasca iconography . . . The Bizarre style could not have been created except by someone familiar with the Nasca style and aware of contemporary stylistic trends." We agree with Blagg (1975: 67) when she argues that the Bizarre Innovation's stylistic change in mythical motifs was so radical that it must have been sanctioned and initiated by the elite. "The extremely high quality of the Bizarre vessels indicates that they were special and lends further credence to this theory" (Blagg 1975: 67). This is the crux of the issue. Nasca 5 actors were consciously manipulating ceramic iconography to express certain opinions about themselves, their sociopolitical milieu, and their relationship to supernatural forces. The Bizarre Innovation maintains:

> associations of warfare and agriculture and add[s] a new concern, that of . . . fertility . . . it may also arise as a parallel development to a cultural innovation . . . the new mythical motifs speak foremost of their otherworldly appearance and only secondarily of mundane connections. The Bizarre Innovation style could have been invented to accompany a religious revolution and to spread word of it to those not living in the capital [Nazca Valley] area. No Nascan seeing a bizarre pot could fail to realize that something new had happened . . . The Bizarre Innovation must be more than an aberration in an otherwise homogeneous style . . . The reason for its being could lie with a new conception of the religion which it reflected. Its rejection [the Bizarre Innovation is short-lived and a minority aspect of the Nasca 5 ceramic corpus] reflects a choice made by a people who preferred a more "classic" iconography and who probably also rejected the esoteric cult on which the Bizarre style may have been based. (Blagg 1975: 67–9)

Blagg is clearly stating that ideology was materialized in what today is called Nasca "art" – the objects which, for the Nasca, were an expressive, contextualized material culture used in life and whose life/social histories are unknown to and unrecoverable by archaeologists until final deposition, typically in gravelots.

Change and Inter-regionalism in Late Nasca Society

The process of societal restructuration that began in Nasca 5 continued in late Nasca times. Whereas Roark (1965: 56–7) states that true portraiture was missing in Nasca art, that particular persons are not represented, we see significant individual portraiture on late Nasca pottery. Furthermore, elite status is marked in such attributes as moustaches and goatees, insignia and elaborate head-dresses, dress, feather cloaks, and earrings (in some cases made of Spondylus). This conspicuous ornamentation supports the argument that late Nasca society had become significantly more complex in sociopolitical organization than it had been in early Nasca times. The many late Nasca depictions of finely dressed human individuals in positions of power and prestige may indicate the increased role of "secular" leadership in Nasca society as compared to the earlier presumed dominant role of shamans. These human individuals are frequently depicted in positions of power, holding trophy heads in their hands, whereas in early Nasca art it was supernaturals and/or human beings costumed as supernaturals who manipulated trophy heads.

Although Nasca 6 and 7 were poorly represented in the Ingenio–middle Grande region surveyed by Helaine Silverman, Reindel and Isla (1999) and Schreiber (1999) identify several large late Nasca settlements in Palpa and the southern tributaries (respectively) that concentrated the valley populations. Schreiber (1999: 167–8; see chapter 5) says that in her Late Nasca period "most people moved from a series of closely spaced small villages into a very small number of very large sites spaced more widely apart ... There appears to have been movement out of the Nasca Valley into the valleys to the south ... The movement of settlement into the middle portions of each valley, regions in which the only source of irrigation water is tapping groundwater, also suggests the construction and use of a system of filtration galleries ... at this time."

Perhaps the limited late Nasca occupation of the Ingenio Valley also is due to people having moved (been moved?) south to take advantage of the greater possibilities for agriculture in the southern tributaries through their filtration galleries. However, since the Nazca Valley has its own filtration galleries, the reason for population decline in that valley should not be water-based.

Shady (1981, 1982, 1988; see, also, the cogent documentation in Stumer 1958) has argued that the late Early Intermediate Period was a time of significant inter-regional contact. Nasca 7 was the time of the greatest geographical distribution and influence of the Nasca ceramic style. Nasca 7 people were in contact with their contemporaries in other valleys up and down the coast. There was foreign influence on the Nasca 7 style as seen in very specific innovations of Moche origin. Proulx (1994) argues convincingly that entire major themes, notably warriors and human sacrifice, were transferred and whole manners of portrayal and vessel categories were copied; we must assume that the particular motifs were copied because they resonated with conditions in society. The Estrella style of Pisco and Chincha was influenced by the Nasca 7 ceramic style and actual Nasca 7 pottery has been found in these valleys and Estrella sherds are present in Ica (Menzel 1971: 128). Nasca 7 also is well known in the Acarí Valley (for example, Lothrop and Mahler 1957). There is Nasca 7 ceramic material at the large Cerro del Oro site in the lower Cañete Valley (Kroeber 1937). And Nasca people were in contact with highland societies (i.e. Nasca-Carahuarazo, Nasca-Huarpa: see Schreiber 1992; Knobloch 1983 and Paulsen 1983, respectively).[5] The documented inter-societal exchange of materials and intangibles must have provided the opportunity for further status enhancement by individuals or groups situated to control it.

Political Economy

Full-time craft and economic specialization have long been regarded as hallmarks of civilization (for example, Childe 1974). Beyond the cultural evolutionary aspects of the organization of craft production are many other issues that implicate the political economy such as the degree of elite involvement in/control over craft production and attached versus independent craft specialists. Moseley (1992: 73) suggests that:

> great art styles of the [Central Andes] were all corporate styles, but the nature of the organizations that underwrote them varied in terms of political, religious and social composition . . . the styles emerged well after the corporations that they identify came into existence . . . once a corporate body was established, a corporate style could be put together rapidly, either newly created or borrowed . . . critical to the creation of a corporate style was the amassing of artisans and specialized technicians. Transforming peasant farmers into skilled craftsmen was not easily done. In later

prehistoric times complicated technical expertise generally passed from parent to child and was therefore kin-based, with artisans forming guild-like kin corporations.

Stein (1998: 19) emphasizes that we must consider "the intended functions of the goods being produced, the raw materials used to produce them, the organization context of production, the structure of social demand for these goods, the organization of the exchange systems through which these goods circulate, and patterns of consumption." In his discussion of inequality in and among households, Blanton (1995: 112) says that "one dimension of emergent inequality resides in the monopolistic control, by elders, of prestige goods required for the social reproduction of junior household members." Similarly, Stein (1998: 21) observes that an "accumulating body of evidence suggests that elites in chiefdoms and states attempt whenever possible to maintain control over the production of prestige or luxury goods . . . since these are politically charged commodities . . . essential for the social reproduction of elites."

As used by archaeologists, the political economy refers to the system that creates and mobilizes the goods and services that elites use and manipulate. The political economy is an interdependent relationship between economic resources and the politically contexted strategic and strategized concentration, production, and distribution of these economic resources. The political economy can be conceived and operationalized as material spatial practices: the social production of spaces and regions, the changing spatial divisions of labor, the means by which spaces are appropriated, controlled, and regulated (Watts 1992: 118). Earle and D'Altroy (1990) argue – correctly in our opinion – that intensive and extensive household archaeology is necessary to fully recognize and interpret a political economy in terms of wealth finance and staple finance. These data are thus far lacking for Nasca. Therefore, let us examine other bodies of data and see what inferences can be made and, indeed, whether we can speak of a Nasca political economy.

In the Andes, prestige and power were manifested by control over human labor and through it the goods, services, and infrastructure that were produced. At present there is no evidence of the organization of production of goods and services by early Nasca elites for their own exclusive and exclusionary benefit. However, we do see elites – at least elite men – emerging in the archaeological record in Nasca 5 and later times. We identify them on the basis of their self-representation in ceramic portraits and increasingly more complex burial patterns in Nasca 5, most notably at La Muña.

Although archaeologists readily acknowledge the importance of craft specialization, recognizing it in the archaeological record is another matter. Stein (1998: 20) suggests that concentrated/differential distribution of production debris and homogeneous attributes of the products (such as standardized vessel morphology, mold marks, chemical composition of clay) are evidence of craft specialization. By these criteria we cannot unambiguously identify pottery craft specialization in Nasca society. This is perplexing since there was an increase in pottery consumption in Nasca 3, probably the result of the "deviation amplifying effect that ritual use has on demand" (Arnold 1985: 159, 162) and, consequently, on ceramic production itself (Silverman 1993a: 302–4).

We consider Nasca pottery to be a prestige or luxury good, potentially operative in a political economy, by virtue of the symbolic messages painted on it. It is well demonstrated in the craft workshops of Wari, Moche, Middle Sicán and Chimu (see, for example, Pozzi-Escot 1991; Russell et al. 1994a, b; Shimada and Merkel 1991; Topic 1982) that when objects bear the iconography of power and symbolize that power, the elite intervene in production and seek to control it by their proximity, resulting in production centers that are in or near the centers of corporate authority. However, survey in the various valleys of the Río Grande de Nazca drainage and in the Ica Valley demonstrates the wide and unrestricted distribution of fine Nasca pottery (including panpipes) at habitation sites. The data, as currently known, continue to support Carmichael's (1988) conclusion, based on mortuary patterns, that Nasca pottery did not have a restricted distribution among status groups.

Blanton (1995: 113) says that:

household political processes . . . are comprehended at a deeper level by reference to the behavioral and material dimension of symbolic expression. Symbols . . . are significant because they occur in "ritualized, that is, formalized communication" . . . include as formalized contexts for symbolic expression both household ritual and habitus, the latter referring to a formalization of everyday activities . . . It is precisely in ritual and habitus that an order of household inequality is made to appear powerful and holy.

The existence of symbolically charged materials in Nasca domestic contexts could have acted processually and recursively to maintain the relationship between (relatively) distant ritual and supra-communal sacred settings and the dynamic and localized social order. But this is different from a political economy as defined above.

Given the demonstrated demand for/increased production of highly iconographic pottery in Nasca 3 times, which appears to be associated with the climax of the Nasca religious cult at Cahuachi (see Silverman 1993a: 302–4, 335), it would not be surprising if significant evidence of pottery production were discovered at Cahuachi (and at other ceremonial centers as well) in addition to the pottery produced at village sites and brought in to Cahuachi for use there in ceremony and in burial. But in view of the intensity of excavations at Cahuachi and, more recently, the broad areal surveys conducted in the Nasca region, it may be that full-time Nasca craft quarters and workshops did not exist or that they were extremely rare. Indeed, the essentially unrestricted distribution of fine pottery in Nasca burials, habitation sites, and civic-ceremonial centers suggests that all members of society had more or less equal access to the medium and information contained within it. The family pilgrimage scene portrayed on the Tello modeled tablet appears to confirm this reconstruction, suggesting that each family produced its own fine ware (or was able to obtain it from more talented potters).

Proulx (1996: 118) argues that "[c]ompared to other pre-Columbian Peruvian cultures, the Nasca people produced few items of jewelry, and that which does exist seems to have been used mainly for ritual purposes rather than as symbols of status or for purposes of adornment." There is so little Spondylus and gold overall in Nasca society (see chapter 3) that it seems inappropriate to consider their monopolization and ideologically materializing and enhancing use of luxury goods by elite agents as can well be argued for the north coast Moche, Sicán, and Chimú societies.

Other Challenges

The rise of civilization is a topic that has long interested scholars. The study of ancient complex society has been undertaken from many intellectual perspectives. For instance, it has been conceptualized globally/comparatively as in the influential synthetic works by Wittfogel (1957), Service (1962), Wheatley (1971), Haas (1982), and Earle (1997), among others. And it has been investigated areally, in terms of specific civilizations such as Harappan (for example, Possehl 1998), Mesoamerican (for example, Sanders and Price 1968), Mesopotamian (for example, Adams 1966; Yoffee 1991) and Peruvian (for example, Lanning 1967; Moseley 1992; Willey 1971). Other scholars have turned their attention to particular regions or cultures within these great traditions so as to achieve a finer-grained understanding of the cultural evolutionary process. Thus, there are studies of Formative Peru (for example, Burger 1992; Moseley 1975; Silverman 1996b), Pre- and Early Dynastic Egypt (Hoffman 1991; Trigger 1983), Neolithic and Bronze Age Europe (for example, Champion et al. 1984; Renfrew 1979), Olmec in Mesoamerica (for example, Grove 1997), Shang China (Chang 1980), and Uruk in Mesopotamia (for example, Johnson 1973), among others. And scholars have interpreted the rise of civilization from all manner of theoretical positions (for example, agency/network/power relationships, cluster/peer polity interaction, conflict versus consensus, cultural ecology, cultural materialism, decision-making/information-managing, dynamic or alternating cycles, political economy, a practice paradigm, processual/systems theory, postprocessual/ideational) and prime movers (for example, environment, irrigation, population pressure, religion and ideology, trade and exchange, warfare); the literature is too vast to cite in the context of this chapter (see summaries in Dobres and Robb 2000; Johnson 1999; Pauketat in press; Preucel 1991; Whitley 1998).

For many decades, scholars have been attracted to Peru as an ideal testing ground for the study of the processes by which civilizations arise. Highland and, especially, coastal sites and material culture tend to be very well preserved. Peru has a long, unbroken record of occupation dating back more than ten thousand years and culminating in one of the greatest empires of all times anywhere, the Incas. Furthermore, although there was no writing system in pre-Columbian times, there are abundant and varied Colonial Period documents concerning the Incas and other late pre-Hispanic peoples; used judiciously, these can provide important insights into earlier societies. Indeed, Peru was the premier case study for Kosok's (1965) sweeping and comparison-directed analysis of the role of irrigation in aboriginal cultural development. And Carneiro (1970) focused on Peru in formulating his theory of the origin of the state.

But it is important to realize that there was significant variation in the nature and complexity of organization among the pre-Columbian societies of ancient Peru, both diachronically and at any one time. This variation took the form of permutations around the common theme called "Andean," itself subject to much debate (see, for example, Isbell 1995, 1997; Starn 1991). Peruvian archaeology provides the opportunity not only to study those successful behaviors that led toward statehood, but also the factors that caused the demise of certain states or inhibited their appearance.

It is in this field of inquiry that we situate Nasca archaeology. Ever since its scientific discovery in 1901, ancient Nasca culture of south coastal Peru has enjoyed a distinguished place in scholarly discussions about the rise of civilization in ancient Peru and its nature, in addition to figuring prominently in the relative chronologies that have anchored all cultural reconstructions in time and space (see, for example, Kroeber 1928; Rowe 1962c). As field investigations proceed, archaeologists working on Nasca will be able to contribute to the major theoretical problems surrounding the rise, fall, and nature of complex society worldwide. Already it appears that models of diasporic communities resulting from migration will be appropriate for understanding the Paracas antecedents of Nasca culture and society (see Silverman 1994a: 378). The growth of early Nasca society implicates the interaction of religion and politics. The identification of Cahuachi as the principal early Nasca ceremonial center and a likely pilgrimage shrine does not explain the meaning of the site for those who worshiped there. Furthermore, the dramatic decline of Cahuachi remains to be satisfactorily explained; suggested causes include climatic disaster (*Life Magazine* 1999; Petersen 1980) and the overburdening of the pilgrimage system (Silverman 1993a). And pan-Andean drought in the sixth century AD may well have played a role in culture change some time after the demise of Cahuachi (see above). Besides climate change, the role of other exogenous factors, such as political (for example, Wari), in the changing nature of Nasca society can be evaluated in terms of models of conflict and peer polity interaction. The causes and sociopolitical consequences of warfare, as this is manifested by the taking of human heads, can be studied.

Agency theory appears to be particularly appropriate for understanding the dramatic changes in Nasca art and society that resulted in a vibrant reorganization in Nasca 5 times (see above). Few projects have focused on the daily life of the ancient Nasca people. A new era of household archaeology will enable archaeologists to apply practice theory to the study of intra- and inter-site patterns of behavior and should permit far more subtle understandings and interpretations of Nasca cultural construction and culture change than currently possible.

Nasca iconography is as complex as any symbolic system developed in the Central Andes or elsewhere. The material culture on which it is deployed is amenable to study by a variety of approaches, from hermeneutics to political economy. Iconographic interpretation is in its infancy.

The geographical distribution of Nasca pottery and textiles requires consideration of the stylistic correlates of ethnicity and boundary maintenance. The engagement of Nasca people with distant societies calls into play issues of intercultural interaction, long-distance exchange and procurement networks, and the perks that may result from control of these.

Truly, the future of Nasca archaeology is bright.

11

After Nasca

The readers of this book will have grown up with the excitement of announcements about the discovery of new species, whether hominid finds in Africa or strange life forms in the depths of the oceans. Especially among paleoanthropologists, who suffer from an even more fragmentary archaeological record than prehistorians, the bio-evolutionary debates are intense and acrimonious as to where to classificatorily delineate one skeletal example or group from another. So, too, archaeologists create species through the definition of archaeological cultures. And because cultural evolution is a process, the archaeologist is faced with the decision of how (actually "when") to label and, therefore, spatially, temporally, and constituitively delimit a particular ancient society.

In previous chapters we have discussed the quintessential hallmarks of Nasca culture and society and the rise and evolution of Nasca civilization. We have also examined Nasca's fuzzy edges, so to speak, in Pisco and Acarí and valleys further removed. In this concluding chapter we chronicle the changes that occurred in the Río Grande de Nazca drainage until finally Nasca culture and society is unrecognizable as such. Our discussion, which moves chronologically, is informed by several anthropological perspectives. One of these is the study of ethnicity, here in terms of its manifestation in the archaeological record (see chapter 4). Because no ethnic group is static we feel it is productive to examine the transformation and disappearance of Nasca as an ethnic group in the final stages of ethnogenesis. Also, we seek to contextualize Nasca within the larger processes of cultural change occurring in the Central Andes; for, clearly, the older view of the major social formations of the Early Intermediate Period as insulated regional cultures is erroneous.

The Loss of "Nascaness" in Nasca 8/Loro

Following the collapse of Cahuachi and its interaction sphere, there was never again a single great cultural center in the Río Grande de Nazca drainage. Yet, as we have seen, Nasca society survived, reorganized, and thrived for several centuries more. But at some point the Nasca people ceased to be Nasca. We argue that this occurred when the cosmology underwriting their rituals ceased to be expressed in coherent iconographic form, when panpipes and double-spout-and-bridge bottles ceased to be made, when new rituals and forms of burial emerged, and more. We identify Nasca 8/Loro as the beginning of the end of Nasca cultural identity.

Nasca 8 is so divergent in form, technology, and iconography from the late Nasca style that it has been given its own style name: Huaca del Loro or Loro (see discussion in chapter 2). Furthermore, the ritual entombment of the Room of the Posts at Cahuachi (burying the temple room in clean sand and leaving offerings as the room was filled in) by some Loro group was an act as outside Nasca cultural canons as the pottery left behind. But we do not or cannot know if the act of ritual entombment was meant to annul some residual spiritual power of the place (perhaps there was still a distant memory of Cahuachi as a once great site, but any connection to it had long been broken) or whether, for reasons quite distinct ideologically, the Room of the Posts was simply viewed as appropriable for a Loro ritual of interring broken pottery (i.e. it retained its sacredness).

In addition to whole pots (Silverman 1993a: figs 13.13–13.35), broken pottery was deposited in the ritually entombed Room of the Posts (Silverman 1993a: figs 13.36, 13.39, table 13.3). This use of broken pots is reminiscent of the great Wari offering deposits documented at Pacheco, Maymi, Conchopata, and elsewhere. In the case of the Room of the Posts, we are dealing with pots already broken when deposited as well as deliberately incomplete pots, sherds, and groups of sherds left in the sand (see Silverman 1993a:

figs 13.12–13.39); they cannot be restored to complete form as at the famous Wari sites. However, whereas archaeologists are most familiar with the giant Wari pots that have been able to be reconstructed because they were deliberately smashed *in situ*, new excacavations by William H. Isbell and Anita Cook at Conchopata have documented the presence, too, of many oversize vessels that are not complete, "showing that they were not simply broken *in situ* and covered up. Either fragments were dumped . . . after being broken elsewhere, or they were broken on the spot and later some of the fragments were collected and taken away" (Isbell and Cook 2000: 5). Furthermore, the context of these newly discovered incomplete offering pots at Conchopata is a D-shaped temple building. Though that structure has no relationship to the Room of the Posts, it is nevertheless worthwhile to indicate that the Room of the Posts also was a temple. The deliberate interment of the Room of the Posts in clean sand, however, is unlike anything known from Wari sites.

In the Las Trancas Valley, there arose a dynamic, hybrid society of Wari-ized late Nasca people: Nasca 8/Loro people. They lived alongside their Wari contemporaries and in close contact with the Acarí Valley people who produced the pottery recovered by Kent and Kowta (1994) at a cemetery in Tambo Viejo. Menzel's (cited in Proulx 1994: 95) use of the term "Trancas strain" to describe the pottery was prescient in this regard. We suggest that the Nasca 8/Loro burial of the Room of the Posts is the Trancas/Loro people's adaptation of the Wari practice of ritually breaking pottery as well as their rejection/magical annulment of whatever spirit/power Cahuachi was believed to have. As wild speculation it could be proposed that those who ritually entombed the Room of the Posts were the descendants of the early Nasca people who had worshiped at that specific temple. This proposition can be tested through physical characterization of Nasca 3 and Nasca 8/Loro pottery from Unit 19 and contemporary sites in Las Trancas.

Nasca 8/Loro burial patterns show significant changes from preceding Nasca phases just as Nasca 8/Loro pottery diverges strongly from the preceding style. Most obvious is an increased frequency in multiple burials in Nasca 8/Loro times, although they are still uncommon (Carmichael 1988: 354). Some of these multiple burials may be high-status family crypts as, for instance, Orefici's Nasca 8/Loro burial at Cahuachi (see Carmichael 1988: plate 1). Multiple interments also are known from Nasca 8/Loro contexts at Tambo Viejo in Acarí, although they are not the exclusive burial pattern at this time (see Kent and Kowta 1994). These multiple burials, depending on the temporal placement of Nasca 8/Loro, could either auger or be influenced by the Middle Horizon practice of collective tombs (see, for example, Pezzia 1969: 127–8; Reiss and Stubel 1880–7). In addition, Patrick Carmichael (personal communication, 1990) has observed that in Acarí true extended burials appear for the first time in Nasca 8/Loro. These are unknown in earlier Nasca phases except as "bad-death" burials (for example, Burial 1 at Cahuachi: see Silverman 1993a: 215).

Of particular interest is the similarity between Ubbelohde-Doering's (1958) Morro burial at Cahuachi and Wari burials in the lower Ica Valley. Ubbelohde-Doering (1958: 82–4, fig. 13) reports that the Cahuachi tomb was rectangular and covered with a fine *barbacoa*. The walls of the tomb were hung with textiles and two huarango posts were upright in the tomb, alongside the seat of the mummy bundle. This seat was wrapped in beautiful colored cloth and was made out of many layers of vegetal material tied together with black strips of cloth that were wound around in a sort of spiral technique, like a basket. Ubbelohde-Doering indicates that the head of the mummy was missing when he located the burial. During her survey of the lower Ica Valley, Anita Cook recorded Wari mummy bundle remains at elite residential Wari sites and cemeteries. At these, the "deceased is usually seated on one or more coils of worked cloth stuffed with raw cotton, wrapped in a bale or bundle, and topped with a false head and face mask" (Cook 1992b: 357).

Interestingly, trophy head-taking appears to continue in Nasca 8/Loro times though we do not know if it had the same function and symbolism as before. Ubbelohde-Doering (1958) reports nine trophy heads in his Morro grave at Cahuachi. Two of these had been placed on a bed of coca leaves on the floor of the chamber and under each head were several maize cobs. For Ubbelohde-Doering, the complex of trophy heads and maize confirmed the "magical use" of the heads which he related to the fertility of the fields.

The Wari Intrusion

The Wari state coalesced in the highlands north-east of the Ica–Nazca region around AD 550 (Isbell 1983: table 1; Isbell and Cook 2000: 1, 6, 8; Menzel 1977: chronological table; Rowe and Menzel 1967: chronological table). Wari either conquered or strongly influenced Nasca people of the south coast of Peru.

Schaedel (1993) has been particularly insightful in distinguishing Wari's transitory features in the Central Andes from those resulting in a "transformation of the affected culture continuum" in terms of iconographic clusters relating contemporary styles, technology, architecture, settlement planning, and the systemic features of state control based on analogy with the Incas. The issue is what agency or agencies were responsible for the diffusion of the phenomena called "Middle Horizon" (Schaedel 1993: 245). Schaedel argues for a range of behaviors within the Middle Horizon, a position that is reasonably isomorphic with Shady's (1981, 1982, 1988) multiple polities model yet supportive of the state/empire reality of Wari.

In her article assessing the impact of Wari in northern Peru, coast and highlands, Topic (1991) suggests a series of features that could indicate conquest. She notes that the "presence of foreign administrative centers has long been regarded as a key to understanding the process of conquest and administrative change in subject areas" (Topic 1991: 234). Usually, she says, the administrative center is associated with a military conquest and accompanied by significant reorganization of the landscape in terms of settlement patterns, storage facilities, roads, and so forth (Topic 1991: 235). But, as Menzel (1959) has so clearly illustrated with the Incas, a military conquest *per se* is not the only way to gain control of a foreign people: coercion and co-option also may work quite nicely. Also, Menzel demonstrated that new, canonical administrative centers are not necessarily established among subject peoples. Under a conquest situation:

> goods produced by the conquerors, whether manufactured in their home center and imported or produced locally by imported artisans, would be prestigious and would occur most frequently in high-status contexts controlled by the invaders. Some imported goods might be distributed to conquered elites, and the prestigious exotic styles might be imitated by local craftsmen. (Topic 1991: 235)

McEwan (1990), on the other hand, recognizes an important difference between Wari influence and Wari invasion and argues for their practical decoupling in addressing the issue of Wari remains outside Ayacucho.

Rectangular enclosure compounds are the hallmark of Wari administrative rule in the highlands (Isbell and McEwan 1991). For Schreiber (1992: 107), Wari-style architecture and pottery constitute the baseline requirement for associating a site with the eponymous highland capital. Such architecture exists on the coast but is rare (see, for example, Isla and Guerrero 1987) and, where present, is far smaller in scale than the Wari enclosures known in the highlands.

In the Río Grande de Nazca drainage two sites (thus far) appear to be candidates for the status of Wari rectangular enclosure compounds. One of these sites was discovered by Katharina Schreiber (1999) at Pataraya, located at an elevation of 1325 m above sea level in the Tierras Blancas Valley. She refers to it as an "imperial Wari site."

> The Wari enclosure is tiny, only about 40 by 50 m, but the architecture is unmistakably of Wari style. Associated Wari ceramics date to Middle Horizon 2. The site is located near the lower end of the environmental zone termed chaupiyunga . . . It is likely that in prehistoric times this zone was used for the production of coca leaves . . . Immediately adjacent to the Wari enclosure is a small sector of domestic architecture: round houses, some with attached round tombs. This architecture is typical of the sierra, not the coast, and the associated ceramics are mostly highland types, suggesting that Wari brought with it a highland village that was relocated here. And a small cluster of above-ground, stone-slab tombs was found nearby; such tombs are typically found associated with Wari sites. (Schreiber 1999: 169)

In the middle Ingenio Valley, at an elevation of 410 m above sea level, Helaine Silverman recorded a major architectural complex with a trapezoidal layout (figure 11.1). She believes that this site may be a Wari rectangular enclosure compound despite the lack of confirming surface pottery.

Wari did not impact the south coast uniformly; significant differences existed among the valleys. Intrusive rectangular enclosure compounds are not the only manifestation of Wari on the coast.

Figure 11.1 Sketch plan of Site 459 in the middle Ingenio Valley, a possible Wari administrative center.

Pottery, in fact, was the material culture trait that was first used to postulate a Wari conquest of the Central Andes on the basis of its rapid replacement of local styles (see Kroeber 1925: 208, 211–12, 1928: 15; Larco Hoyle 1948: 37–45; Menzel 1964; Stumer 1956). In the Río Grande de Nazca drainage, Nasca 9 pottery occurs as grave goods either with other pottery styles (see Menzel 1964: 25, plate vi/figs 14–16) or exclusively (for example, at Cantalloc according to Menzel 1964: 25 versus actual pieces published in Kroeber and Collier 1998: 253). It is also present in ritual context at Huaca del Loro in the Las Trancas Valley (Paulsen 1983).

The most dramatic evidence of Wari presence on the south coast is the great offering deposit at Pacheco, a site only some 7 km east of the early Nasca ceremonial center of Cahuachi in the Nazca Valley. At Pacheco, in 1927, Julio C. Tello's project recovered nearly three tons of broken pottery vessels. By 1932, "23 oversize vessels, including 3 urns ornamented with mythical figures, 14 urns with plant designs, 3 tumblers, and 3 modeled llamas" had been wholly or partly reconstructed (Menzel 1964: 24); in the years since, yet more vessels have been reconstructed. Ronald Olson recovered more spectacular pottery at Pacheco in 1930 (see Menzel 1964: 24). The Pacheco pottery includes the Robles Moqo, Chakipampa B and Nasca 9 styles of the early Middle Horizon (Menzel 1964: 25).

Other early Middle Horizon pottery offering deposits are known on the south coast in addition to Pacheco (see Menzel 1964). At Maymi, in the lower Pisco Valley, Anders (1990; Anders et al. 1998) discovered a pottery production site for the manufacture of exquisite polychrome pottery with similarities to Wari pottery from Pacheco. Maymi vessel forms are both emblematic of Wari and innovative. The similarities are not just stylistic but cultural. As at Pacheco and Conchopata, Anders documented offering pits full of deliberately smashed spectacular pottery. Anders (1990: 27, 29) dated this material to MH 1 and also noted the occurrence of "Nasca 8" and "Nasca 9" pottery which she called "late Nasca."

There are many documented sources of MH 2 pottery in the Río Grande de Nazca drainage, such as Chiquerillo, Jumana, Coyungo, Tunga, and the Atarco ravine which gave its name to the type-style of the epoch (see Menzel 1964: 46). Menzel (1964: 46) indicates that almost two hundred MH 2 vessels are known to come from sites near the confluence of the Grande and Ingenio rivers and she publishes five vessels said to have been recovered in a single MH 2B gravelot at San José in Ingenio (Menzel 1964: plate vii, plate viii/ fig. 22). The Atarco style appears to be found only in burial contexts (Menzel 1964: 47).

Unlike Nasca burial patterns, Atarco tombs include oblong rectangular chambers lined with rectangular adobes with roofs made of clay plaster and tool-cut huarango posts (Nasca huarango posts were burnt off: see Menzel 1964: 46). Furthermore, these tombs have a specific orientation (east–west, with the entrance to the west) and the bodies are prepared as mummy bales with elaborate false heads (Menzel 1964: 46–7). This alteration of burial patterns in the former Nasca heartland is another indication of the dramatic culture changes caused by Wari.

In the course of his fieldwork in Ica and the Río Grande de Nazca drainage, Strong (1957: 41) did not find "living sites where the colorful Tiahuanaco A style was dominant." Helaine Silverman's survey in Ingenio, and Browne's (Browne 1992; Browne and Baraybar 1988) survey in Palpa, produced almost identical results (see Silverman 1993b: 118). In his survey of the lower Río Nasca and Grande in 1998, Proulx (1999c) recorded only one Middle Horizon habitation site, but pottery of this period was found on the surface of eighteen separate cemeteries, including several with underground chambers having painted plaster walls and niches in the walls. Similarly, Silverman found early MH pottery significantly represented at more than fifty cemeteries and ceremonial sites. Unfortunately, the nature of the early MH occupation at about one-quarter of the sites with Middle Horizon pottery on their surfaces could not be determined because of surface ambiguity due to bulldozing, looting, and insufficient representation.

In contrast to these data, Schreiber (1992: 107, 1999: fig. 11.9) reports that she found Wari ceramics:

> on local habitation sites dating to the Middle Horizon, as well as two hilltop redoubts with Wari ceramics. These latter sites have irregular rectilinear architecture, and are located high on a ridge top without direct access to agricultural land or water. They provide an excellent vantage point from which to observe any movement into or out of the adjacent highlands.

Was there an actual abandonment of some valleys as Schreiber (1999: 168) suggests for the Nazca Valley? Were Nasca people moving south to avoid Wari or because Wari was physically transplanting them? Were they moving because of better prospects for agriculture in the southernmost tributaries (though this seems problematic given the presence of filtration galleries in the Nazca Valley)? Or both? These questions cannot be answered at present.

Paulsen (1983) has argued that the field-stone construction and circular layout of a stone building at Huaca del Loro, which Strong (1957) identified as a temple, is indicative of highland influence. Strong (1957: 36–40, table 1) discovered a similar circular, plastered, stone temple at Tres Palos II in the middle Grande Valley, associated with the same kind of pottery as at Huaca del Loro. Ronald Olson recorded a circular structure at Pacheco in 1930 (see illustration in Paulsen 1983: fig. 1b). Paulsen (1983) hypothesizes that Huaca del Loro was built by a highland colony from Ayacucho prior to the emergence of the Wari state. Although Schreiber (1989; see also Schreiber 1992: 107) has correctly pointed out the existence of circular field-stone dwellings in the southern tributaries of the drainage long before Nasca 8/Loro and Wari, and Silverman has documented them in Ingenio, Paulsen is correct that circular floor plans do not characterize Nasca civic-ceremonial architecture whereas circular civic-ceremonial architecture is well known at Wari (see Isbell et al. 1991: figs 3, 4, 6, 8, 17) where it may be associated with the EIP–MH transition (Isbell et al. 1991: 25–7).

The Round Temple at Huaca del Loro almost appears to be framed within a square (see Strong 1957: fig. 16). William Duncan Strong's field notes of October 19, 1952 suggest that the circle-in-a-square pattern existed at Tres Palos II. The similarity of architectural plan between the Round Temple at Huaca del Loro, which is appendaged off a rectilinear compartmentalized complex (see Strong 1957: fig. 16), and Wari's circular buildings, which are immediately adjacent to (see Isbell et al. 1991: fig. 6) or within (see Isbell et al. 1991: fig. 4 [Robles Moqo sector]) rectilinear compartmentalized architecture, is striking. A direct relationship may be evidenced. Either the pattern developed in Nasca and somehow spread to Wari or the pattern developed in Wari and was taken to the coast where it influenced Nasca society.

Most exciting is Helaine Silverman's re-identification of Strong's (1957) Tres Palos I site in the middle Grande Valley, though the site is now in significantly worse condition than when Strong recorded it on October 19, 1952. In his field notes, Strong described it as:

> a main right angle platform, upon which are the major portion of the stakes, and an outer more irreg. shaped terrace roughly rounded and looks like natural terrace which has been reshaped to fit into building pattern. Loaf shaped adobe walls outline the platform and probably outer terrace also. Other rooms of same type adobe walls also present at site. There are 13 rows of stakes running in an E–W direction and there is from 1–12 remaining stakes in each row. No row has all its stakes – must have been more than 12 stakes in each row. There is c. 1.5 mts between each stake and there are 51 remaining stakes on the platform area to the east of the road. Only complete stake at the site is 3.5 m high and 50 cms in diameter.

Site 395, in the middle Ingenio Valley, is particularly intriguing. It consists of a single square room built of double-faced angular field stones set in mud mortar; there are traces of other walls. The room has been devastated by looting. In it were incomplete fragments of at least sixty MH 2 pots. There were no bones, textiles, or roofing material on the surface, though if this room was a tomb the mummy bundle might have been removed by looters for unwrapping elsewhere in order to conserve the textiles for sale. The quantity and high quality of the pottery, and its obvious direct relationship to Wari through its iconography, suggest that if this was a tomb, it was elite in nature. Excavation is required to determine the function of the architecture.

In the Ica Valley, "authentic Nasca 9 pottery and a local variant of it have been found at several sites" (Menzel 1964: 26), neither mortuary nor ritual. Also, at Site 28L-11K05, in the upper valley, Williams León and Pazos Rivera (1974) reported a Wari/MH 1 cemetery with collective tombs of fine funerary chambers of field-stone walls and stone-slab roofs, in association with a group of five terraces on which small habitation structures were present. At Site 28L-14I06, Wari/MH 2 pottery was found in association with a small area of destroyed walls that are undescribed. Wari/MH 2 pottery was present at several other sites but its association is unclear. Cemeteries with Wari/MH 2 pottery also are known.

Finally, we note the presence of Nasca pottery in a Wari area, not just Wari materials in the Nasca region. McEwan (1996: fig. 12) illustrates sherds from a Nasca 6 bowl which he recovered in excavated context in a midden at Pikillacta, the great Wari administrative center in the Cuzco Valley.

The Post-Wari Restructuration

The collapse of the Wari Empire at the end of MH 2B had a major effect on the inhabitants of the Río Grande de Nazca drainage, seen most dramatically in the end of the fancy Atarco pottery style with its Wari-related iconography and in the end of the Middle Horizon's widespread stylistic exchanges (Menzel 1964: 62). Thus, the post-Wari Soisongo style of the Río Grande de Nazca drainage lacks mythical designs (see Menzel 1964). In Ica, the fall of Wari appears to have ended the close relationship that had developed between that valley and the great ceremonial center of Pachacamac as had been manifested by the distinct Ica–Pachacamac style of MH 2B (see Menzel 1964). The post-Wari Pinilla style of Ica lacks the mythical and representational iconography of Ica–Pachacamac (Lyon 1968; Menzel 1964; Paulsen 1968).

The Soisongo and Pinilla styles were followed by Uhle's Epigonal (MH 4) styles. These are simplified and reduced derivatives of Soisongo and Pinilla with no new elements (Menzel 1964: 65; see studies by Robinson 1957 and Kroeber and Strong 1924: plate 30, respectively). Thus far, no researcher has concentrated on these post-Wari/pre-Ica people. Yet this interregnum or "in-between" period should be fascinating in terms of the major stresses and opportunities created by the demise of the Wari-influenced sociopolitical and economic arrangements and the comparisons and contrasts that will be possible to make with other coastal areas impacted by Wari.

Lyon (1968: 11) has assessed the situation in Ica and Nazca in these terms. She says "there was an active rejection on the part of the previously subjected peoples of those symbols which they associated with their erstwhile overlords, and that with the withdrawal of the representatives of empire, there was a conscious effort made to change the decorative style." It is fascinating that the indigenous people of Ica and Nazca did not reach back in time to the pre-Wari Nasca style once they were free of Wari. This lack of Nasca archaism and revival strongly suggests that the south coast belief system and society had irrevocably changed and that the "old ways" were not remembered, understood, or appreciated.

The Late Intermediate Period

Based on survey data, it is clear that there was a dense LIP occupation of the Río Grande de Nazca drainage. LIP habitation sites can be quite large and significantly agglutinated (for example, Ciudad Perdida de Huayurí in the Santa Cruz Valley; the spectacular Cerro Colorado site at the junction of the Grande and Nazca rivers). Some of these sites are located on hilltops in a defensible position. Others, such as Ciudad Perdida de Huayurí, are hidden in a protected position between hills. Perhaps their locations reflect competition for scarce resources in the drainage. Certainly, Menzel (1959) was correct in her assessment of a lack of political centralization. The picture currently available of LIP society in the Río Grande de Nazca drainage supports the image of late pre-Hispanic "warring tribes" ("fourth age of the *auca pacha runa*") related and portrayed by Guaman Poma de Ayala (1980: 60–1). Clearly, there were socioeconomic differences among this population to judge from the ordinary and exceptional remains found at looted cemeteries.

Nevertheless, the Late Intermediate Period was a time of significant cultural elaboration. These Río Grande de Nazca people engaged in significant interaction with other societies to judge from the quantity of fine Ica–Chincha trade wares among the indigenous Poroma-style pottery on the surface of LIP sites in the Nazca drainage (see Robinson 1957; see also Menzel 1976). Long-distance connections between the north coast, central coast, and south coast are manifested by close stylistic similarities in Chimú, Chancay, and Chincha textiles (a readily portable medium).

Public space existed at many of the LIP sites in the Río Grande de Nazca drainage but, until recently, post-Wari ceremonial architecture was unreported. Therefore, the discovery of a "Painted Temple" in the Ingenio Valley is most interesting (see Kauffmann Doig and Chumpitaz 1993). Also, at a site in the Taruga Valley, Christina

Conlee (1999) has documented an area of civic-ceremonial architecture consisting of a plaza and small mound.

Urton (1990) has provided new insights into late pre-Hispanic Nazca based on his interpretation of the 1593 *Visita de Acarí*. He presents ethnohistoric evidence to show that there were two hereditary lines of *curacas* in the drainage in the late pre-Hispanic period. The principal *cacique* came from the Nazca Valley and belonged to the Nasca or Nanasca family. The other *cacique* was from Ingenio, home of the Ylimanga line. Furthermore, Urton (1990: 195, fig. iv.13) reconstructs the existence of four *parcialidades* in addition to the two moieties straddling the Pampa. These four groups were called Nasca, Cantad, Poromas, and Collao and were territorially manifested in the drainage in the lower Nazca Valley, upper Nazca Valley/Tierras Blancas, Las Trancas Valley, and Ingenio Valley, respectively. In turn, these *parcialidades* were composed of *ayllus*. Urton suggests that each river in the drainage had an upper and lower *parcialidad*, not just the ones named in his ethnohistoric source.

The sociopolitical configuration in the Ica Valley also was complex. Guillén Guillén's (1963) discussion of a 1594 document reveals that Ica's upper valley (*yunga*) macro-ethnic group controlled the intake canals in the late pre-Hispanic period. Ethnohistoric documents clearly indicate that the Ica Valley was organized into two moieties called Hanan Ica and Lurin Ica (Quijandría Alvarez 1961: 145–6; Rostworowski 1996: 127–8). Within each moiety, rulership was shared between a pair of higher-ranking and lower-ranking *curacas* (Rostworowski 1996: 128). The Ica Valley appears to have been unified in LIP times from a site known today as Ica La Vieja, located in the middle valley (Menzel 1976: maps 1–3). Menzel (1976: 12, 16) calls it an administrative and ceremonial center, the "capital of the native Ica state before the Inca conquest." *Huacas*, though badly damaged, still stand and await excavation.

The Inca Conquest

According to the traditional chronology, the Incas conquered the south coast of Peru in the second half of the fifteenth century (Menzel 1959). There is incontrovertible evidence of the Incas in

Figure 11.2   Victor von Hagen's aerial photograph of the Inca administrative center of Tambo de Collao at La Legua in the Ingenio Valley, prior to its destruction (*courtesy*: Adriana von Hagen).

the various valleys of the south coast. In the Río Grande de Nazca drainage the Incas established two administrative centers, one in the Nazca Valley at Paredones (see photo in Bridges 1991: 49) and the other in Ingenio at Tambo de Collao/La Legua (figure 11.2). At Paredones, excavations by the Instituto Nacional de Cultura have revealed imperial Inca stone masonry (Herrera 1997), niches, and the characteristic trapezoidal plaza. The Inca center in Ica may have been "Old Ica." The Incas established themselves in Pisco at Lima La Vieja and Tambo Colorado. The Incas set themselves up in Chincha at La Centinela. And in Acarí they built a center at Tambo Viejo. Menzel (1959) argued persuasively that the Incas tailored their rule and its physical manifestation to the circumstances of the native LIP societies of each valley.

In Ingenio there may be dramatic evidence of the Inca conquest. At Site 207, which is a huge geoglyph field at La Legua (see Silverman 1990a: fig. 17), elaboration of the geoglyphs appears to have ceased abruptly as a result of the intrusion of the Incas into the valley: many of the geoglyphs are incomplete, unfinished. Remains of hundreds of LIP decorated pots, possibly broken *in situ*, were observed on the site surface. The geoglyph field is at the base of a large LIP hillside settlement, Site 201, which controlled the west end of the narrow constriction (*angostura*) between the middle and lower valley. The Incas laid out their administrative center, Tambo de Collao, at the base of this hill, also facing west, and in front (north) of the geoglyph field. Furthermore, in the middle Ingenio Valley Helaine Silverman recorded a small architectural unit built of angular and square field stones on which only Inca sherds are present. The site is intrusive in an ordinary 2.5-ha LIP habitation site and conforms to the *tambos* discussed by Hyslop (1984: ch. 19). Urton (1990: 203) cites a 1620 ethnohistorical document that states there was an Inca road passing eastward through the Ingenio Valley to the highland province of Lucanas.

The Final Transformation of Native Life

Following the arrival of the Spaniards, the native population of the Ica–Nazca region declined precipitously as it did elsewhere on the coast. It is well known that Andean people succumbed massively to a host of European diseases (smallpox, measles, influenza, typhus, others: see Cook and Lovell 1992; Verano and Ubelaker 1992). Spanish impact also was felt through the *encomienda* system, the vice-regal government, the establishment of the colonial towns of Ica and Nazca, the extirpation of idolatries (see, especially, García Cabrera 1994: 122–38), and the missionization and landholdings of the Jesuits till their explusion from Peru in 1767. Interestingly, the Jesuits owned land ("*valiosos fundos*" [valuable farms]) at Pangaraví, Bisambilla, Matará, Llicuas, Curve, and La Gobernadora. It is surely not coincidental that ancient filtration galleries (i.e. accessible water) exist on the territory of these *fundos* (see Rossel Castro 1977: 171).

Nevertheless, for decades into the Colonial Period there still was a significant native presence in the Ica–Nazca region. Archival documents concerning the Jesuits make reference to various "*caciques*" and their names, as recorded in a series of wills bequeathing their land to the Church or contesting Jesuit claims, show native ancestry despite the deceased's conversion or birth into the Catholic faith (see Quijandría Alvarez 1961; Rostworowski 1996: 127–8; Urton 1990: 194–5).

The principal *cacique* whom the Spaniards found in Nazca at the time of their entry was Nanasca who was called Santiago García (after his *encomendero*, García de Salcedo) following his baptism. At this time the greatest population lived around what today is Nazca, called "Santiago de Caxamarca del Valle de la Nanasca" and later "Villa de Nasca del Valle de la Nanasca" by the Spanish (Quijandría Alvarez 1961). Eventually the name was corrupted to Nasca. When Nanasca died in 1589 one of the landholdings that he bequeathed to the Church was Cahuachipana, today Cahuachi. The early date of his will suggests that Cahuachipana was the name of the area of the archaeological site of Cahuachi at least as far back in time as the late pre-Hispanic period.

The ethnohistoric documents also tell us that Nanasca was married to Beatriz Illacucuchi (also a baptized Indian), the daughter of Alonso Huamán Aquije, the principal *cacique* of Lurinica who was one of the three principal *caciques* whom the Spanish found in Ica upon their arrival (Quijandría Alvarez 1961). Quijandría Alvarez (1961) argues that the name of the Ica Valley derives from this *cacique* (Huamán Aquije or "Huamanica"). This marriage alliance between Ica and Nazca may reflect the close late pre-Hispanic relationship between the valleys as evidenced by abundant Ica Valley tradewares in Nazca.

In 1623, the Spanish extirpators of idolatries complained that in Nazca idolatries were still being practiced. However, by this time aboriginal religion was physically, materially, spatially, and organizationally impoverished from what it had been centuries before. Just as memory is socially formed (for example, Halbwachs 1980), it is socially unformed – deliberately and coincidentally backgrounded and ultimately forgotten. Smith (1987) argues that ritual enables society to "take place." So, too, the absence of or radical change in ritual must affect the sense of place and the locality or anchoring of people previously created there.

> [M]any Indians showed lots of rocks that they say they worshiped in their fields . . . there aren't any idols of major importance, only these rocks which ordinarily are found in the rivers . . . (García Cabrera 1994: 124)

[T]here isn't a formal shrine in this town but, rather, the hills, the springs of water and the rocks that the Indians brought . . . (García Cabrera 1994: 131)

[T]here wasn't in this town a shrine to tear down because the people went to the mountain of sand called Moich [Cerro Blanco] and another mountain called Uracancana and to springs and the idols were rocks . . . (García Cabrera 1994: 135)

Interestingly, one of the witnesses called to give sworn testimony during the idolatries investigation was "*Diego Nanasca, governador deste repartimiento indio principal ladino y entendido en nuestra lengua castellana*" (García Cabrera 1994: 134). Despite the almost one hundred years that had transpired since the coming of the Spaniards, indigenous power still remained within the Nanasca family, though this Nanasca, as the scribe indicates, was Catholic and fluent in Spanish.

Ethnogenesis and Morphogenesis

Tainter (1988: 4) has explicitly defined *collapse* as the rapid, significant loss of an established level of sociopolitical complexity. Yoffee (1991) has modified Tainter's formulation to carefully distinguish *political* collapse, which is the collapse of *states*, from *cultural* collapse, which is the collapse of a *civilization*. The latter precludes the possibility that another characteristic manifestation of the fallen suite of behaviors and beliefs will emerge from the decomposed predecessors.

Our review of the trajectory of cultural evolution on the south coast reveals that there was no implosion of Nasca society so much as its repeated morphogenesis. From its emergence in Nasca 1 times, marked by the establishment of monumental construction at Cahuachi and associated ritual paraphernalia, Nasca evolved as a civilization and sociopolitical formation. In early Nasca times Cahuachi was the prime site and it grew over time. But there were other Nasca contemporary centers of prestige and ritual as well as major domestic settlements in various of the valleys of the Río Grande de Nazca drainage such as Palpa and Ingenio. The local societies participating in the early Nasca world orchestrated by/at

Cahuachi shared a wide range of material culture and behavior such as fancy pottery with its expressed cosmology and ritual functions, geoglyph-making, and burial patterns, to name the most obvious.

For reasons still to be fully explained, construction at and use of Cahuachi largely ceased in Nasca 4 times. A vibrant, reorganized Nasca civilization emerged in Nasca 5 and evolved in Nasca 6 and 7, manifesting itself differently on the landscape (for example, lack of emphasis on monumental construction as had been most notable at Cahuachi, increase in geoglyph-making, increase in trophy head-taking), yet with the hallmarks of Nasca culture still recognizable (for example, ceramic iconography, pottery style, cranial deformation, method of preparing trophy heads, construction techniques, burial patterns) and new ones added (for example, the filtration galleries, elite tombs, changes in textile technology). It is so-called Nasca 8 or Loro that marks the truly divergent aspect of Nasca civilization and the beginning of its end.

After the collapse of the Wari Empire, with its associated influence or control over the Nasca area, there appears to have been no possibility for a return to Nasca civilization nor was there ever again a single prime site as Cahuachi had been. In turn, the Incas put an end to the last surviving material feature of Nasca cultural life: the geoglyphs. By the time the Spanish conquerors arrived, Nasca society and culture had long since disappeared.

Thanks to the ethnographic fieldwork of a local parish priest, Alberto Rossel Castro, in the 1940s, and anthropologist Gary Urton in the early 1980s, the few remaining native beliefs of Nazca have been rescued from obscurity and permanent loss (see also Arguedas 1956: 199). Today, other than the occasional legend that seems miraculously to have survived the centuries, and the use of water brought to the surface by refurbished filtration galleries, there is little left of native life in the Río Grande de Nazca drainage.

Notes

Chapter 2   Emergence and Evolution of the Nasca
Ceramic Tradition

1   In the future, DNA studies will allow us to make even more precise connections between groups in separate tributaries or to identify members of the same family groups.

2   Also recovered with the Nasca 6 pottery at Pikillacta were five Cajamarca-style sherds (McEwan 1996: 181). We know from their association in the "Tomb of the Priestess" at San José de Moro that the Moche V, Cajamarca, and Nievería styles are contemporary and date to the early Middle Horizon, "sometime after AD 550" (Donnan and Castillo 1992: 42). The Pikillacta context seems to establish the contemporaneity of Cajamarca and Nasca 6. However, at the San José de Cordero site in the upper Ica Valley, Menzel (1964: 26) recorded "Nasca 9 refuse covering an older structure associated with a refuse deposit of Nasca Phase 7."

Chapter 4   We, the Nasca

1   Williams et al. (in press) emphasize that the term "cranial deformation" encompasses a "heterogeneous category" that varies classificatorily according to researcher.

2   It is interesting that males in Nasca society do not wear ear spools as a sign of rank. Ear spools are known in various other complex societies of ancient Peru including Moche, contemporary with Nasca, and, of course, among the Inca whom the Spanish called "*orejones*" meaning

"big ears" in recognition of the distension of the ear lobe through use of ear spools.

3 Carmichael (1992: 5) offers a somewhat different chronology from Valdez. Carmichael proposes an Amato Phase (EIP 1–2), Monte Grande Phase (EIP 3–5/6), and Chaviña Phase (EIP 7–8; "if Nasca 8 is still included in the EIP").

4 Indeed, the interaction that existed between Nazca and Acarí in the Early Intermediate Period may anticipate that which is historically documented in the early Colonial Period. Citing the 1593 Visita de Acarí, Urton (1990: 194) suggests that the frequency of early Colonial Period ties (including marriage ties) between the populations of the two valleys reflects the pre-Hispanic situation and that the Incas built on existing practice. Neira Avedaño (1990: 74) raises the possibility that the section of Inca royal highway between Nazca and Acarí incorporated earlier routes of communication.

5 Nor is this textile material the earliest evidence of contact between the south coast and far south coast. Gayton (1961) published five Ocucaje-style textiles collected by Uhle in Yauca in 1905 and Garaventa (1981) identifies another Yauca textile in the Uhle collections at Berkeley as Ocucaje 8 in style.

6 Many Peruvian river valleys change names between the coast and high-lands. Camaná is lower down than Majes, which itself is below Colca. Forming a "Y," the Sihuas River on the north and the Vitor River on the south unite to form the Quilca River which exits to the sea.

7 Haeberli has established the appropriate orthographic convention of writing the river, river valley, and region as "Sihuas" with an "h" and the archaeological material of the late Early Horizon and early Early Intermediate Period as "Siguas" with a "g."

Chapter 6   Symbolic Expressions of the Natural and Supernatural World

1 And today we know that fishing never constituted the basis of the Nasca economy (see, e.g., Carmichael 1991). Rather, Yacovleff was influenced by the depiction of fishermen on early Nasca pots.

2 Peters (1991) calls these "deliberate ambiguities."

3 This makes for a very interesting comparison with McClelland (1990), who recognizes a shift to maritime iconography in Moche art at this time.

4 Furthermore, we must pay attention to the larger folk or non-elite corpus.

Chapter 7 The Geoglyphs of the Río Grande de Nazca Drainage

1 By way of comparison, Cook (1992a) observes that in the lower Ica Valley there are both subtractive and additive geoglyphs. She dates these geoglyphs to Ocucaje 9 through the late Middle Horizon and early Late Intermediate Period.

2 We have not ground surveyed the Pampa geoglyphs.

3 Part 2 of Johson's hypothesis largely contradicts Schreiber and Lancho Rojas's (1995) reconstruction of Nazca hydrology and the filtration galleries. Schreiber and Lancho Rojas (1995: 231, 232) argue that the "valley alluvium has a moderate to high infiltration capacity that results in a substantial transmission loss in river volume" and that the "underground water filters into" the filtration galleries. Johnson says that while some river water may go into some filtration galleries as runoff during the summer flood season, especially into those filtration galleries located lower down and near the river, the filtration galleries that are upslope are unlikely to gather water from the river because they are significantly above the river itself. Dr Stephen Mabee, of the Department of Geosciences at the University of Massachusetts in Amherst, suggests that contributions from the faults to the valleys are an important source of water and this water augments the existing groundwater in the main river valleys. However, he cautions, until a detailed water budget can be performed (a very difficult task), it cannot be determined precisely how much water each of these sources provides to the valley and which one is the greater source.

4 Part 4 stands in direct contradiction to one of Aveni's (1990b: 105–6) observations which associates geometrical markings with the general direction of the flow of surface (not subsurface) water across the Pampa; Horkheimer (1947) also had observed an association of trapezoids with the direction of water flow (see also Reindel and Isla 1999, cited above).

5 Graduate students from the Department of Geosciences at the University of Massachusetts, under the direction of Stephen Mabee, are currently plotting the location of all the geoglyphs recorded by Johnson. Their objective is to determine what percentage of the geoglyphs is correlated with faults and subterranean aquifers and what percentage is random or unassociated. This correlation will provide another test of Johnson's hypothesis.

Chapter 9   Headhunting and Warfare

1   Silverman (1993: 218) is incorrect when she says that Uhle coined the
     term "trophy head" in 1901, obviously impossible since that is the
     year in which Uhle discovered the Nasca style at Ocucaje. This care-
     less error also appears in Browne et al. (1993: 274). Rather, on p. 586
     of his 1906 publication Uhle briefly talks about representations of
     human trophy heads and shows examples from both Nasca and Moche
     iconography. This publication is the written version of the paper Uhle
     presented in 1904 at the International Congress of Americanists in
     Stuttgart. Uhle also clearly describes and names Nasca trophy heads
     on pp. 11 and 14 of his 1914 publication.

2   We note, too, that chapter 9 of the Huarochirí Manuscript says that
     "all the Yunca shared one single way of life" (Salomon and Urioste
     1991: 71) yet the Manuscript names discrete communities and ethnic
     groups. We bring this up to highlight the very real possibility that
     recoverable material culture – such as a shared pottery style – may be
     inadequate for recognizing the distinctions drawn by Nasca people for
     the purpose of trophy headhunting.

Chapter 10   Nasca Sociopolitical Organization

1   For instance, a sherd from a fine black pattern-burnished Nasca 1
     bowl and a cylindrical lapis lazuli bead – the latter one of the few
     exotics for any time period encountered on survey in the Ingenio
     Valley – were recovered at a site consisting merely of three looters'
     holes on a possibly artificially leveled terrace on a hillside. Similarly,
     sherds of excellent quality Nasca 1 pottery in addition to a modeled
     step-fret-shaped panpipe fragment and a piece of chrysacolla were
     recovered at a site consisting of five looters' holes. Seemingly ordinary
     Nasca burials – without any architectural elaboration – contained
     luxury goods of limited distribution in society. Concomitantly,
     Carmichael (1988) has shown that pottery had an unrestricted distri-
     bution in Nasca mortuary society, a conclusion echoed by the wide
     distribution of Nasca pottery at habitation sites.

2   Isbell (1995, 1997) has criticized archaeologists for basing many of
     their interpretations more on what they think the past was like than
     on what can actually be demonstrated in the archaeological record.
     That notion of "what the past was like" is based overwhelmingly on
     ethnohistoric knowledge of the Incas recursively filtered through the
     knowledge of ethnographic fieldwork among contemporary peasant

farming communities of the Peruvian highlands. In addition to the assumption of Inca-like *mit'a* labor tax tribute for all pre-Inca state-level societies, archaeologists also widely assume the existence of *ayllu* organization, *ayni* and *minka* forms of labor reciprocity, and *curaca* authority in the ancient past. Isbell (1995: 6–7) criticizes many of us for working from a "conflated idealization" of "Andean Culture" that is "timeless and homogeneous."

3   Actually, it was an over-enthusiastic reaction to the major agglutination of habitation terraces there in contrast to Cahuachi's unexpected lack of such residential foci.

4   We note, however, the criticism recently levied at Dr Dorn's rock varnish dating procedures (see Beck et al. 1998; Malakoff 1998). Dorn's absolute dating appears to be supported by Schreiber and Lancho Rojas's (1995) relative chronological inference that the filtration galleries were constructed in the middle Nazca Valley during Nasca 5 based on the onset of domestic settlements during this phase. Only future testing will be able to determine if the Clarkson and Dorn chronology for the filtration galleries is correct or flawed.

5   Suggestive evidence of a meaningful contact between Nasca and Huarpa–Wari peoples is the possibility that the Nasca 7 Mythical Monkey with its sinuous body and long curled tail, first identified by Seler (1923: fig. 254; see also Schlesier 1959: figs 201–5; see Proulx 1989a), was transformed into the Nasca 9/Chakipampa Humped Animal in the highlands and returned to the coast as a supernatural feline (Menzel 1964: 29). In Seler's (1923: fig. 254) example the creature already has the fleur-de-lys and circular space fillers that would characterize Nasca 9 (see Menzel 1964: plates ii, iii) and was painted on a bottle with a long spout and handle which is a form foreign to Nasca.

Bibliography

Adams, Robert McC. (1966) *The Evolution of Urban Society*. Aldine-Atherton, Chicago.

Allen, Catherine (1981) The Nasca creatures: some problems of iconography. *Anthropology*, 5 (3): 43–69.

— (1988) *The Hold Life Has*. Smithsonian Institution Press, Washington, DC.

Allison, Marvin (1979) Paleopathology in Peru. *Natural History*, 88 (2) (February): 74–82.

— and Pezzia, Alejandro (1976) Treatment of head wounds in pre-Columbian and colonial Peru. *Medical College of Virginia Quarterly*, 12 (2): 74–9.

Alva, Walter (1994) *Sipán*. Cervecería Backus y Johnston SA, Lima.

Amador Parodi, Augusto (1998) Figurinas funerarias de la cultura Lima. *Arqueología y Sociedad*, 12: 29–35.

Anders, Martha (1990) Maymi: un sitio del Horizonte Medio en el valle de Pisco. *Gaceta Arqueológica Andina*, 17: 27–39.

—, Arce, Susana, Shimada, Izumi, Chang, Victor, Tokuda, Luis, and Quiroz, Sonia (1998) Early Midde Horizon pottery production at Maymi, Pisco Valley, Peru. *MASCA Research Papers in Science and Archaeology*, 15 (suppl.): 233–51.

Anonymous (1934) Notas necrológicas: Eugenio Yacovleff. *Revista del Museo Nacional*, 3 (3): 323–6.

Anton, Ferdinand (1987) *Ancient Peruvian Textiles*. Thames and Hudson, New York.

Arguedas, José María (1956) Puquio: una cultura en proceso de cambio. *Revista del Museo Nacional*, 25: 184–232.

Armillas, Pedro (1948) A sequence of cultural development in Meso-America. *A Reappraisal of Peruvian Archaeology*, ed. Wendell C.

Bennett, pp. 105–11. Memoir no. 4, Society for American Archaeology, Menasha.

Arnold, Dean (1985) *Ceramic Theory and Cultural Process*. Cambridge University Press, New York.

Aveni, Anthony F. (1986) The Nazca lines: patterns in the desert. *Archaeology*, 39 (4): 32–9.

— (1990a) An assessment of previous studies of the Nazca Lines. *The Lines of Nazca*, ed. Anthony F. Aveni, pp.1–40. The American Philosophical Society, Philadelphia.

— (1990b) Order in the Nazca Lines. *The Lines of Nazca*, ed. Anthony F. Aveni, pp. 41–114. The American Philosophical Society, Philadelphia.

— (1990c) *The Lines of Nazca*, ed. Anthony F. Aveni. The American Philosophical Society, Philadelphia.

Baraybar, José Pablo (1987) Cabezas trofeo nasca: nuevas evidencias. *Gaceta Arqueológica Andina*, 15: 6–10.

Barnes, Monica and Fleming, David (1991) Filtration-gallery irrigation in the Spanish New World. *Latin American Antiquity*, 2: 48–68.

Barth, Frederick (1969) Introduction. *Ethnic Groups and Boundaries: The Social Organization of Culture Difference*, ed. Frederick Barth, pp. 1–38. Little, Brown, Boston.

Baumann, Max Peter (1996) Music, symbolism and duality in Andean cosmology. *Cosmología y música en los Andes*, ed. Max Peter Baumann. Bibliotheca Ibero-Americana, 55. Ibero-americana, Vervuert.

Bawden, Garth (1996) *The Moche*. Blackwell, Oxford.

Beck, W., Donahue, D. J., Jull, A. J. T., Burr, G., Broecker, W. S., Bonani, G., Hajdas, I. and Malotki, E. (1998) Ambiguities in direct dating of rock surfaces using radiocarbon measurements. *Science*, 280: 2132–5.

Benavides Calle, Mario (1971) Analisis de la cerámica Huarpa. *Revista del Museo Nacional*, 37: 63–88.

Bennett, Wendell C. (1948) The Peruvian co-tradition. *A Reappraisal of Peruvian Archaeology*, ed. Wendell C. Bennett, pp.1–7. Memoir no. 4, Society for American Archaeology, Menasha.

— (1954) *Ancient Arts of the Andes*. The Museum of Modern Art, New York.

— and Bird, Junius B. (1964) *Andean Culture History*. The Natural History Press, Garden City, New York.

Benson, Elizabeth P. (1995) Art, architecture, warfare and the guano islands. *Andean Art: Visual Expression and its Relation to Andean Beliefs and Values*, ed. Penny Dransart, pp. 245–64. Avebury, Hampshire, England.

— and Conklin, William (1981) *Museums of the Andes*. Newsweek, New York.

Bentley, G. Carter (1987) Ethnicity and practice. *Comparative Studies in Society and History*, 29 (1): 24–55.

Billman, Brian (1997) Population pressure and the origins of warfare in the Moche Valley, Peru. *Integrating Archaeological Demography: Multidisciplinary Approaches to Prehistoric Population*, ed. Richard R. Paine, pp. 285–309. Center for Archaeological Investigations, Occasional Paper no. 24. Southern Illinois University, Carbondale, IL.

Bird, Junius B. (1962) *Art and Life in Old Peru: An Exhibition*. The American Museum of Natural History, New York.

Blagg, Mary Margaret (1975) The bizarre innovation in Nazca. Unpublished MA thesis, Department of Art History, University of Texas at Austin.

Blanton, Richard E. (1995) The cultural foundations of inequality in households. *Foundations of Social Inequality*, ed. T. Douglas Price and Gary M. Feinman, pp. 105–27. Plenum, New York.

Blasco Bosqued, Concepción and Ramos Gómez, Luis J. (1980) *Cerámica Nazca*. Seminario Americanista de la Universidad de Valladolid, Valladolid.

— and — (1986) *Catálogo de la cerámica Nazca, 1*. Ministerio de Cultura, Dirección de los Museos Estatales, Madrid.

— and — (1991) *Catálogo de la cerámica Nazca, 2*. Ministerio de Cultura, Dirección de los Museos Estatales, Madrid.

Bolaños, Cesar (1988) *Las antaras Nasca*. Programa de Arqueomusicología del Instituto Andino de Estudios Arqueológicos, Lima.

Bridges, Marilyn (1986) *Markings: Aerial Views of Sacred Landscapes*. Aperture, New York.

— (1991) *Planet Peru: An Aerial Journey through a Timeless Land*. Aperture, New York.

Browman, David (1998) Lithic provenience analysis and emerging material complexity at Formative Period Chiripa, Bolivia. *Andean Past*, 5: 301–24.

Brown, James A. (ed.) (1971) *Approaches to the Social Dimensions of Mortuary Practices*. Memoir no. 25. Society for American Archaeology, Menasha.

Browne, David M. (1992) Further archaeological reconnaissance in the Province of Palpa, Department Ica, Peru. *Ancient America: Contributions to a New World Archaeology*, ed. Nicholas J. Saunders, pp. 77–116. Oxbow Monograph 24. Oxbow Books, Oxford.

— and Baraybar, José Pablo (1988) An archaeological reconnaissance in the Province of Palpa, Department of Ica, Peru. *Recent Studies in Pre-Columbian Archaeology*, ed. Nicholas J. Saunders and Olivier de Montmollin, pp. 299–325. BAR International Series 421, Oxford.

—, Silverman, Helaine and García, Rubén (1993) A cache of 48 trophy heads from Cerro Carapo, Peru. *Latin American Antiquity*, 4 (3): 359–82.

Brugnoli, P. and Hoces, S. (1991) Análisis de un textíl pintado Chavín. *Boletín del Museo Chileno de Arte Precolombino*, 5: 67–80.

Bruhns, Karen Olsen (1976) The Moon Animal in northern Peruvian art and culture. *Ñawpa Pacha*, 14: 21–40.

Brumfiel, Elizabeth (1994) Factional competition and political development in the New World: an introduction. *Factional Competition and Political Development in the New World*, ed. Elizabeth M. Brumfiel and John W. Fox, pp. 1–13. Cambridge University Press, Cambridge.

Bueno Mendoza, Alberto and Orefici, Giuseppe (1984) Nuevas investigaciones arqueológicas en el sur medio: avances preliminares del Proyecto Nasca. *Boletín de Lima*, 36: 29–37.

Burger, Richard L. (1981) The radiocarbon evidence for the temporal priority of Chavín de Huantár. *American Antiquity*, 46: 592–602.

— (1984) Archaeological areas and prehistoric frontiers: the case of Formative Peru and Ecuador. *Social and Economic Organization in the Prehistoric Andes*, ed. David L. Browman, Richard L. Burger and Mario A. Rivera, pp. 33–71. BAR International Series 194, Oxford.

— (1988) Unity and heterogeneity within the Chavín horizon. *Peruvian Prehistory*, ed. Richard W. Keatinge, pp. 99–144. Cambridge University Press, New York.

— (1992) *Chavin and the Origins of Andean Civilization*. Thames and Hudson, New York.

— and Asaro, Frank (1977) Análisis de rasgos significativos en la obsidiana de los andes centrales. *Revista del Museo Nacional*, 43: 281–325.

— and Glascock, Michael D. (2000) Locating the Quispisisa obsidian source in the Department of Ayacucho, Peru. *Latin American Antiquity*, 11 (3): 258–68.

—, Asaro, Frank, Salas, Guido, and Stross, Fred (1998a) The Chivay obsidian source and the geological origin of Titicaca Basin type obsidian artifacts. *Andean Past*, 5: 203–24.

—, —, Trawick, Paul, and Stross, Fred (1998b) The Alca obsidian source: the origin of raw material for Cusco type obsidian artifacts. *Andean Past*, 5: 185–202.

—, Schreiber, Katharina, Glascock, Michael D., and Ccencho, José (1998c) The Jampatilla obsidian source: identifying the geological source of Pampas type obsidian artifacts from southern Peru. *Andean Past*, 5: 225–40.

Buse, Hermann et al. (n.d.) *La Pesca en el Perú Prehispánico*. Editoriales Unidas, SA, Lima.

Carmichael, Patrick (1986) Nasca pottery construction. *Ñawpa Pacha*, 24: 31–48.

— (1988) Nasca mortuary customs: death and ancient society on the south coast of Peru. Unpublished PhD dissertation, Department of Archaeology, University of Calgary.

— (1991) Prehistoric settlement of the Ica–Grande Littoral, Southern Peru. Research Report to the Social Sciences and Humanities Research Council of Canada.

— (1992) Local traditions on the south coast of Peru during the Early Intermediate Period. *Willay*, 37–8: 4–6.

— (1994) The life from death continuum in Nasca imagery. *Andean Past*, 4: 81–90.

— (1998) Nasca ceramics: production and social context. *Andean Ceramics: Technology, Organization and Approaches*, ed. Izumi Shimada, pp. 213–32. MASCA Research Papers in Science and Archaeology, suppl. to vol. 15, Philadelphia.

Carneiro, Robert (1970) A theory of the origin of the state. *Science*, 169: 733–8.

Carrión Cachot, Rebeca (1955) *El culto al agua en el antiguo Perú*. Lima.

— (1959) *La religión en el antiguo Perú*. Lima.

Carter, William (1968) Secular reinforcement in Aymara death ritual. *American Anthropologist*, 70: 238–63.

Castillo, Luis Jaime (1989) *Personajes míticos, escenas y narraciones en la iconografía mochica*. Fondo Editorial, Pontificia Universidad Católica del Perú, Lima.

— and Donnan, Christopher B. (1994) Los Mochica del norte y los Mochica del sur. *Vicús*, ed. Krzysztof Makowski, pp. 143–81. Banco del Crédito del Perú, Lima.

Cazeau, Charles J. and Scott, Stuart D. (1979) *Exploring the Unknown: Great Mysteries Reexamined*. DaCapo/Plenum, New York.

Champion, Timothy, Gamble, Clive, Shennan, Stephen, and Whittle, Alasdair (1984) *Prehistoric Europe*. Academic Press, New York.

Chang, Kwang-Chih (1980) *Shang Civilization*. Yale University Press, New Haven, CT.

Chapman, R., Kinnes, I., and Randsborg, K. (eds) (1981) *The Archaeology of Death*. Cambridge University Press, New York.

Chávez, Sergio and Chávez, Karen Mohr (1975) A carved stela from Taraco, Puno, Peru and the definition of an early style of stone sculpture from the altiplano of Peru and Bolivia. *Ñawpa Pacha*, 13: 45–84.

Childe, V. Gordon (1974) The urban revolution. *The Rise and Fall of Civilizations*, ed. Jeremy A. Sabloff and C. C. Lamberg-Karlovsky, pp. 6–14. Cummings Publishing Co., Menlo Park (first published 1950).

Cieza de León, Pedro (1973) *La crónica del Perú*. Biblioteca Peruana, PEISA, Lima.

Clarkson, Persis (1990) The archaeology of the Nazca pampa: environmental and cultural parameters. *The Lines of Nazca*, ed. Anthony F. Aveni, pp. 117–72. American Philosophical Society, Philadelphia.

— and Dorn, Ronald (1991) Nuevos datos relativos a la antiguedad de los geoglifos y pukios de Nazca, Perú. *Boletín de Lima*, 78: 33–45.

— and — (1995) New chronometric dates for the puquios of Nasca, Peru. *Latin American Antiquity*, 6: 56–69.

Coe, Michael D. (1981) Religion and the rise of Mesoamerican states. *The Transition to Statehood in the New World*, ed. G. D. Jones and R. R. Krautz, pp. 157–71. Cambridge University Press, Cambridge.

Coehlo, Vera Penteado (1972) Enterramentos de cabeças da cultura Nasca. Unpublished doctoral dissertation, Departamento de Comunicações e Artes da Escola de Comunicações e Artes, Universidade de São Paulo.

Conkey, Margaret and Hastorf, Christine (eds) (1990) *The Uses of Style in Archaeology*. Cambridge University Press, New York.

Conlee, Christina (1999) Sociopolitical complexity in the Late Intermediate Period in Nasca: new evidence from the site of Pajonal Alto. Paper presented at the 64th Annual Meeting of the Society for American Archaeology, Chicago.

Connerton, Paul (1998) *How Societies Remember*. Cambridge University Press, Cambridge.

Cook, Anita (1992a) The Lower Ica Valley ground drawing on the south coast of Peru. Paper presented at the 11th Annual Northeast Andeanist Conference, Hamilton, New York.

— (1992b) The stone ancestors: idioms of imperial attire and rank among Huari figurines. *Latin American Antiquity*, 3 (4): 341–64.

— (1999) Asentamientos paracas en el valle bajo de Ica, Peru. *Gaceta Arqueológica Andina*, 25: 61–90.

Cook, Noble David and Lovell, W. George (1992) *Secret Judgments of God: Old World Disease in Colonial Spanish America*. University of Oklahoma Press, Norman.

Cordy-Collins, Alana (1976) An iconographic study of Chavín textiles from the south coast of Peru: the discovery of a Pre-Columbian catechism. Unpublished PhD dissertation, Department of Archaeology, UCLA.

— (1977) Chavín art: its shamanic/hallucinogenic origins. *Pre-Columbian Art History: Selected Readings*, ed. Alana Cordy-Collins and Jean Stern, pp. 353–62. Peek Publications, Palo Alto.

Craig, Alan and Psuty, Norbert (1968) *The Paracas Papers: Studies in Marine Desert Ecology*. Occasional Publication no. 1, Department of Geography, Florida Atlantic Univerity, Boca Raton.

Crandell, Gina (1993) *Nature Pictorialized: "The View" in Landscape History*. Johns Hopkins University Press, Baltimore, MD.

Crumley, Carole (1987) A dialectical critique of hierarchy. *Power Relations and State Formation*, ed. Thomas C. Patterson and Christine W. Gailey, pp. 155–69. American Anthropological Association, Washington, DC.

Davidson, Judith (1982) Ecology, art and myth: a natural approach to symbolism. *Pre-Columbian Art History: Selected Readings*, ed. Alana Cordy-Collins, pp. 331–43. Peek Publications, Palo Alto.

Dawson, Lawrence E. (1964) Slip casting: a ceramic technique invented in ancient Peru. *Ñawpa Pacha*, 2: 107–12.

— (1979) Painted cloth mummy masks of Ica, Peru. *The Junius B. Bird Pre-Columbian Textile Conference*, ed. Ann Pollard Rowe, Elizabeth P. Benson and Anne-Louise Schaffer, pp. 83–104. The Textile Museum and Dumbarton Oaks, Washington, DC.

DeLeonardis, Lisa (1991) Settlement history of the Lower Ica Valley, Peru, fifth to first centuries, BC. Unpublished MA thesis, Department of Anthropology, The Catholic University of America, Washington, DC.

— (1997) Paracas settlement in Callango, Lower Ica Valley, first millennium BC, Peru. Unpublished PhD dissertation, Department of Anthropology, The Catholic University of America, Washington, DC.

Della Santa, Elisabeth (1962) *Les vases Peruviens de la collection de LL MM le Roi Albert et la Reine Elisabeth de Belgique*. Musées Royaux d'Art et d'Histoire, Brussels.

Demarest, Arthur (1984) Overview: Mesoamerican human sacrifice in evolutionary perspective. *Ritual Human Sacrifice in Mesoamerica*, ed. Elizabeth H. Boone, pp. 227–47. Dumbarton Oaks, Washington, DC.

Dillehay, Tom D. (1990) Mapuche ceremonial landscape, social recruitment and resource rights. *World Archaeology*, 22 (2): 223–41.

Disselhoff, Hans Dietrich (1966) *Daily Life in Ancient Peru*. McGraw-Hill, New York.

— (1969) Früh-Nazca im äuBersten Süden Perus, Provincia de Camaná (Dep. Arequipa). *Verhandlungen des XXXVIII Internationalen Amerikanisten Kongress*, 1: 385–91.

— (1972) *Das Imperium der Inka und die Indianischen Frühkulturen der Andenländer*. Safari-Verlag, Berlin.

Dobkin de Rios, Marlene (1982) Plant hallucinogens, sexuality and shamanism in the ceramic art of ancient Peru. *Journal of Psychoactive Drugs*, 14 (1–2): 81–90.

— (1984) The Nazca fishermen of coastal Peru. *Hallucinogens: Cross-cultural Perspectives*, ed. Marlene Dobkin del Rios, pp. 59–79. University of New Mexico Press, Albuquerque.

— and Cardenas, Mercedes (1980) Plant hallucinogens, shamanism and Nazca ceramics. *Journal of Ethnopharmacology*, 2: 233–46.

Dobres, Marcia-Anne and Robb, John (eds) (2000) *Agency in Archaeology*. Routledge, London.

Donnan, Christopher (1976) *Moche Art and Iconography*. UCLA Latin American Center Publications, Los Angeles.

— (1992) *Ceramics of Ancient Peru*. Fowler Museum of Cultural History, UCLA.

— and Castillo, Luis Jaime (1992) Finding the tomb of a Moche priestess. *Archaeology*, 45 (6): 38–42.

Dorn, Ronald, Clarkson, Persis, Nobbs, Margaret, Loendort, Lawrence, and Whitley, D. S. (1992) New approach to the radiocarbon dating of rock varnish, with examples from drylands. *Annals of the Association of American Geographers*, 82 (1): 136–51.

Downing, Theodore and Gibson, McGuire (eds) (1974) *Irrigation's Impact on Society*. Anthropological Papers of the University of Arizona, no. 25. University of Arizona Press, Tucson.

Duviols, Pierre (1967) Un inédit de Cristóbal de Albornoz: La Instrucción Para Descubrir Todas Las Guacas del Pirú Y Sus Camayos Y Haziendas. *Journal de la Société des Américanistes*, 56 (1): 7–39.

Dwyer, Jane P. (1971) Chronology and iconography in Late Paracas and Early Nasca textile designs. Unpublished PhD dissertation, Department of Anthropology, University of California at Berkeley, CA.

Earle, Timothy R. (1987) Chiefdoms in archaeological and ethnohistorical perspective. *Annual Review of Anthropology*, 16: 279–308.

— (1997) *How Chiefs Come to Power: The Political Economy in Prehistory*. Stanford University Press, Stanford.

— and D'Altroy, Terence N. (1990) The political economy of the Inka empire: the archaeology of power and finance. *Archaeological Thought in America*, ed. C. C. Lamberg-Karlovsky, pp. 183–204. Cambridge University Press, Cambridge.

Earls, John and Silverblatt, Irene (1976) La realidad física y social en la cosmología andina. *Actes du XLII Congres International des Americanistes*, 4: 299–325. Paris.

Eisleb, Dieter (1975) *Altperuanische Kulturen I*. Museum für Völkerkunde, Berlin.

— (1977) *Altperuanische Kulturen II: Nazca*. Museum für Völkerkunde, Berlin.

Emberling, Geoff (1997) Ethnicity in complex societies: archaeological perspectives. *Journal of Archaeological Research*, 5 (4): 295–344.

Engel, Frederic (1957) Early sites in the Pisco Valley of Peru: Tambo Colorado. *American Antiquity*, 23 (1): 34–45.

— (1966) *Paracas: cien siglos de cultura peruana*. Editorial Juan Mejía Baca, Lima.

— (1981) *Prehistoric Andean Ecology. Man, Settlement and Environment in the Andes: The Deep South*. Humanities Press and Hunter College/CUNY, New York.

— (1991) *Un desierto en tiempos prehispánicos: Río Pisco, Paracas, Río Ica*. Centro de Investigacion de Zonas Aridas and Department of Anthropology, Hunter College, CUNY, Lima and New York.

Fagan, Brian (1999) *Floods, Famines and Emperors: El Niño and the Fate of Civilizations*. Basic Books, New York.

Feder, Kenneth (1990) *Frauds, Myths and Mysteries: Science and Pseudoscience in Archaeology*. Mayfield, London.

Ferris, H. B. (1916) The Indians of Cuzco and the Apurimac. *Memoirs of the American Anthropological Association*, 3 (2): April–June.

Forbes, Henry (1913) Peruvian pottery from Nasca. *Illustrated London News*, 6 December.

Foucault, Michel (1972) *The Archaeology of Knowledge*. Harper Colophon, New York.

— (1973) *The Order of Things: An Archaeology of the Human Sciences*. Random House, New York.

— (1980) Questions on geography. *Power/Knowledge: Selected Interviews and Other Writings, 1972–1977*, pp. 63–77. Pantheon Books, New York.

Freidel, D. A. (1981) Civilization as a state of mind: the cultural evolution of lowland Maya. *The Transition to Statehood in the New World*, ed. G. D. Jones and R. R. Kautz, pp. 188–227. Cambridge University Press, Cambridge.

— (1992) The trees of life: *ahau* as idea and artifact in classic lowland Maya civilization. *Ideology and Pre-Columbian Civilizations*, ed. Arthur A. Demarest and Geoffrey W. Conrad, pp. 115–33. School of American Research Press, Santa Fe.

Fried, Morton H. (1967) *The Evolution of Political Society*. Random House, New York.

Friedberg, Anne (1993) *Window Shopping: Cinema and the Postmodern*. University of California Press, Berkeley, CA.

Garaventa, Donna (1981) A discontinuous warp and weft textile of Early Horizon date. *Ñawpa Pacha*, 19: 167–76.

García Cabrera, Juan Carlos (1994) Transcription of "Averiguación que se hizo de la conducta observada por los Visitadores durante el tiempo que les tocó ver las causas de idolatries, Nazca, 1623." *Ofensas a Diós: pleitos e injurias: causas de idolatrías y hechicerías. Cajatambo*, vols 17–19, pp. 122–38. Centro de Estudios Regionales Andinos "Bartolomé de las Casas", Cuzco. García Miranda, Juan José (1998) Los santuarios en los andes centrales. *Historia, religión y ritual de los Pueblos Ayacuchanos*, ed. Luis Millones, Hiroyasu Tomoeda, and Tatsuhiko Fujii, pp. 51–85. National Museum of Ethnology, Osaka.

García Soto, Rubén and Pinilla Blenke, José (1995) Aproximación a una secuencia de fases con cerámica temprana de la región Paracas. *Journal of the Steward Anthropological Society*, 23: 43–81.

Gayton, Anna H. (1961) Early Paracas textiles from Yauca, Peru. *Archaeology*, 14 (2): 117–21.

— and Kroeber, A. L. (1927) The Uhle pottery collections from Nazca. *University of California Publications in American Archaeology and Ethnology*, 24 (1): 1–46.

Gelles, Paul (1984) *Agua, faenas y organización comunal en los Andes: el caso de San Pedro de Casta*. Pontificia Universidad Católica del Perú, Lima.

Goldstein, Paul S. (2000) Exotic goods and everyday chiefs: long-distance exchange and indigenous socio-political development in the south central Andes. *Latin American Antiquity*, 11 (4): 335–61.

González García, M. Francisco (1978) Los acueductos incaicos de Nazca. *Tecnología Andina*, ed. Roger Ravines, pp. 129–56. Instituto de Estudios Peruanos and CONCYTEC, Lima.

Gosden, Chris and Lock, Gary (1998) Prehistoric histories. *World Archaeology*, 30 (1): 2–12.

Grodzicki, Jerzy (1990) Las catastrofes ecológicas en la Pampa de Nazca a fines del Holoceno y el fenómeno "El Niño." *El fenómeno El Niño a traves de las fuentes arqueológicas y geológicas*, ed. Jerzy Grodzicki, pp. 64–102. Misión Arqueológica Andina, Instituto de Arqueología, Universidad de Varsovia, Warsaw.

Grove, David C. (1997) Olmec archaeology: a half century of research and its accomplishments. *Journal of World Prehistory*, 11 (1): 51–101.

Guaman Poma de Ayala, Felipe (1980) *El primer nueva corónica y buen gobierno*. Critical edition by John V. Murra and Rolena Adorno. Quechua translations and analysis by Jorge L. Urioste. Siglo Veintiuno, Mexico City.

Guillén Guillén, Edmundo (1963) Un documento para la historia social y económica de Ica (1594). *Revista del Archivo Nacional del Perú*, 27: 88–103. Lima.

Guillet, David (1992) *Covering Ground: Communal Water Management and the State in the Peruvian Highlands*. University of Michigan Press, Ann Arbor.

Gundrum, Darrell (2000) Fabric of time. *Archaeology*, 53 (2): 46–51.

Gupta, Akhil and Ferguson, James (1992) Beyond "culture": space, identity and the politics of difference. *Cultural Anthropology*, 7 (1): 6–23.

Haas, Jonathan (1982) *The Evolution of the Prehistoric State.* Columbia University Press, New York.

—, Pozorski, Shelia, and Pozorski, Thomas (eds) (1987) *The Origins and Development of the Andean State.* Cambridge University Press, New York.

Haberland, Wolfgang (1958) Some wooden figures from Peru in the Hamburg Ethnographical Museum. *Proceedings of the 32nd International Congress of Americanists, 1956,* pp. 346–52. Copenhagen.

Hadingham, Evan (1987) *Lines to the Moutain Gods.* Random House, New York.

Haeberli, Joerg (1979) Twelve Nasca panpipes. *Ethnomusicology,* 23 (1): 57–74.

— (1995) The Brooklyn Museum textile no. 38.121: a mnemonic and calendrical device, a huaca. *Journal of the Steward Anthropological Society,* 23 (1–2): 121–51.

Halbwachs, Maurice (1980) *The Collective Memory.* Harper-Colophon Books, New York.

Hardman de Bautista, Martha J. (1978) Jaqi: the linguistic family. *International Journal of American Linguistics,* 44: 146–53.

Harner, Michael (1972) *The Jivaro: People of the Sacred Waterfall.* Doubleday/Natural History Press, Garden City, NY.

Harris, Olivia (1982) The dead and the devils among the Bolivian Laymi. *Death and the Regeneration of Life,* ed. Maurice Bloch and Jonathan Parry, pp. 45–73. Cambridge University Press, Cambridge.

Harrold, Francis and Eve, Raymond (1987) *Cult Archaeology and Creationism: Understanding Pseudoscientific Beliefs about the Past.* University of Iowa Press, Iowa City.

Hawkins, Gerald S. (1969) Ancient lines in the Peruvian desert. Final Scientific Report for the National Geographic Society Expedition, Smithsonian Institution, Astrophysical Observatory, Cambridge.

Helms, Mary W. (1979) *Ancient Panama: Chiefs in Search of Power.* University of Texas Press, Austin.

— (1988) *Ulysses' Sail: An Ethnographic Odyssey of Power, Knowledge, and Geographical Distance.* Princeton University Press, Princeton, NJ.

Herrera, Fernando (1997) Trabajos preliminares en Paredones en el valle de Nazca. *Tawantinsuyo,* 3: 119–26.

Hocquenghem, Anne Marie (1981) Les mouches el les morts dans l'iconographie mochica. *Ñawpa Pacha,* 19: 63–9.

Hoffman, Michael (1991) *Egypt before the Pharaohs.* University of Texas Press, Austin.

Horié, Donna (1990–1) A family of Nasca figures. *Textile Museum Journal,* 29–30: 77–92.

Horkheimer, Hans (1947) Las plazoletas, rayas y figuras prehispánicas en las pampa y crestas de la Hoya del Río Grande. *Revista de la Universidad Nacional de Trujillo*, 2 (1): 47–63.

Hrdlicka, Ales (1911) Some results of recent anthropological exploration in Peru. *Smithsonian Miscellaneous Collections*, vol. 56, no. 16.

— (1914) Anthropological work in Peru in 1913, with notes on the pathology of the ancient Peruvians. *Smithsonian Miscellaneous Collections*, vol. 61, no. 18.

Hyslop, John (1984) *The Inka Road System*. Academic Press, New York.

Isbell, Billie Jean (1978) *To Defend Ourselves: Ecology and Ritual in an Andean Village*. Institute of Latin American Studies, University of Texas, Austin.

Isbell, William H. (1978) The prehistoric ground drawings of Peru. *Scientific American*, 239 (4): 140–53.

— (1983) Shared ideology and parallel political development: Huari and Tiwanaku. *Investigations of the Andean Past: Papers from the First Annual Northeast Conference on Andean Archaeology and Ethnohistory*, ed. Daniel H. Sandweiss, pp. 186–208. Latin American Studies Program, Cornell University, Ithaca, NY.

— (1995) Constructing the Andean past or "as you like it." *Journal of the Steward Anthropological Society*, 23 (1–2): 1–12.

— (1997) *Mummies and Mortuary Monuments*. University of Texas Press, Austin.

— and Cook, Anita (2000) Reinterpreting the Middle Horizon: implications of recent excavations at Conchopata, Ayacucho, Peru. Manuscript in the possession of the authors.

— and McEwan, Gordon (eds) (1991) *Huari Administrative Structure: Prehistoric Monumental Architecture and State Government*. Dumbarton Oaks, Washington, DC.

— and Schreiber, Katharina J. (1978) Was Huari a state? *American Antiquity*, 43: 372–89.

—, Brewster-Wray, Christine, and Spickard, Lynda E. (1991) Architecture and spatial organization at Huari. *Huari Administrative Structure: Prehistoric Monumental Architecture and State Government*, ed. William H. Isbell and Gordon McEwan, pp. 19–53. Dumbarton Oaks, Washington, DC.

Isla, Elizabeth and Guerrero, Daniel (1987) Socos: un sitio Wari en el valle del Chillón. *Gaceta Arqueológica Andina*, 14: 23–8.

Isla, Johny (1990) La Esmeralda: una ocupación del período arcaíco en Cahuachi, Nasca. *Gaceta Arqueológica Andina*, 20: 67–80.

— (1992) La ocupación nasca en Usaca. *Gaceta Arqueológica Andina*, 22: 119–51.

—, Ruales, Mario, and Mendiola, Andrés (1984) Excavaciones en Nasca: Pueblo Viejo, sector X3. *Gaceta Arqueológica Andina*, 12: 8–11.

Jackson, Margaret Ann (2000) Notation and narration in Moche iconography: Cerro Mayal, Perú. Unpublished PhD dissertation, Department of Art History, University of California, Los Angeles.

Jimenez Borja, Arturo and Bueno Mendoza, Alberto (1970) Breves notes acerca de Pachacamac. *Arqueología y Sociedad*, 4: 13–25. Universidad Nacional Mayor de San Marcos, Lima.

Johnson, David (1999) Die Nasca-Linien als Markierungen für unterirdische Wasservorkommen. *Nasca: Geheimnisvolle Zeichen im Alten Peru*, ed. Judith Rickenbach, pp. 157–64. Museum Rietberg Zürich, Switzerland.

Johnson, Gregory (1973) *Local Exchange and Early State Formation in Southwestern Iran*. Anthropological Papers, 51. Museum of Anthropology, University of Michigan.

Johnson, Matthew (1999) *Archaeological Theory: An Introduction*. Blackwell, Oxford.

Jones, Sian (1997) *The Archaeology of Ethnicity: Constructing Identities in the Past and Present*. Routledge, London.

Joyce, Thomas A. (1912) *South American Archaeology*. G. P. Putnam's Sons, New York.

— (1913a) On an early type of pottery from the Nasca Valley, Peru. *The Burlington Magazine*, 22 (119): 249–55.

— (1913b) The clan-ancestor in animal form as depicted on ancient pottery of the Peruvian coast. *Man*, 13: 112–17.

Kauffmann Doig, Federico (1981) *Sexualverhalten Im Alten Peru*. Kompaktos, SCRL, Lima.

— and Chumpitaz, Evaristo (1993) Exploración del Templo Pintado, de El Ingenio, Nasca (Perú). *Baessler-Archiv: Beiträge Zur Völkerkunde*, new series, 41: 39–72. Berlin.

Keatinge, R. W. (1981) The nature and role of religious diffusion in the early stages of state formation: an example from Peruvian prehistory. *The Transition to Statehood in the New World*, ed. G. D. Jones and R. R. Kautz, pp. 172–87. Cambridge University Press, Cambridge.

Kent, Jonathan and Kowta, Makoto (1994) The cemetery at Tambo Viejo, Acarí Valley, Peru. *Andean Past*, 4: 109–40.

Knobloch, Patricia (1983) A study of the Andean Huari ceramics from the Early Intermediate Period to the Middle Horizon Epoch 1. Unpublished PhD dissertation, Department of Anthropology, State University of New York at Binghamton.

Kosok, Paul (1965) *Life, Land and Water in Ancient Peru*. Long Island University Press.

— and Reiche, Maria (1947) The mysterious markings of Nazca. *Natural History*, 56: 200–7, 237–8.

— and — (1949) Ancient drawings on the desert of Peru. *Archaeology*, 2 (4): 206–15.

Kowta, Makoto (1987) *An Introduction to the Archaeology of the Acarí Valley in the South Coast Region of Peru*. California Institute for Peruvian Studies, Sacramento.

Kroeber, A. L. (1925) The Uhle pottery collections from Moche. *University of California Publications in American Archaeology and Ethnology*, 21 (5): 191–234.

— (1928) Cultural relations between North and South America. *Proceedings of the 23rd International Congress of Americanists*, pp. 5–22.

— (1937) *Archaeological Explorations in Peru, Part IV, Cañete Valley*. Anthropology, Memoirs, vol. II, no. 4. Field Museum of Natural History, Chicago.

— (1944) *Peruvian Archaeology in 1942*. Viking Fund Publications in Anthropology, 4. Wenner-Gren Foundation for Anthropological Research, New York.

— (1956) Toward definition of the Nazca style. *University of California Publications in American Archaeology and Ethnology*, 43 (4): 327–432.

— (1960) Introduction. *The Archaeology and Pottery of Nazca, Peru: Alfred L. Kroeber's 1926 Expedition* by Alfred L. Kroeber and Donald Collier, pp. 25–7. Altamira, Walnut Creek (1998).

— and Collier, Donald (1998) *The Archaeology and Pottery of Nazca, Peru: Alfred L. Kroeber's 1926 Expedition*. Altamira Press, Walnut Creek.

— and Strong, William Duncan (1924) The Uhle pottery collections from Ica. *University of California Publications in American Archaeology and Ethnology*, 21 (5): 95–133.

Kubler, George (1948) Towards absolute time: guano archaeology. *A Reappraisal of Peruvian Archaeology*, ed. Wendell C. Bennett, pp. 29–50. Memoir no. 4, Society for American Archaeology, Menash.

— (1962) *The Shape of Time: Remarks on the History of Things*. Yale University Press, New Haven, CT.

— (1985) History – or anthropology – of art? *Studies in Ancient American and European Art: The Collected Essays of George Kubler*, ed. Thomas F. Reese, pp. 406–12. Yale University Press, New Haven, CT.

— (1990) *The Art and Architecture of Ancient America*. Penguin Books, London.

Lanning, Edward P. (1960) Chronological and cultural relationships of early pottery styles in ancient Peru. Unpublished PhD dissertation, Department of Anthropology, University of California at Berkeley, CA.

— (1967) *Peru before the Incas.* Prentice-Hall, Englewood Cliffs, NJ.

Lapiner, Alan (1976) *Precolumbian Art of South America.* Harry N. Abrams, New York.

Larco Hoyle, Rafael (1948) *Cronología arqueológica del norte del Perú.* Hacienda Chiclín, Trujillo.

— (1966) *Peru.* Archaeologia Mundi. The World Publishing Company, Cleveland and New York.

Larrea, Juan (1960) Pakcha. *Corona Incaica* by Juan Larrea, pp. 231–7. Facultad de Filosofía y Humanidades, Universidad Nacional de Cordoba, Argentina.

de Lavalle, José Antonio (1986) *Nazca.* Colección Arte y Tesoros del Perú, Banco de Crédito del Perú, Lima.

— and Lang, Werner (1978) *Arte Precolombino. Segunda parte: escultura y diseño.* Colección Arte y Tesoros del Perú. Banco de Crédito del Perú, Lima.

— and — (1980) *Arte Precolombino. Primera parte: arte textil y adornos.* Colección Arte y Tesoros del Perú, Banco de Crédito del Perú, Lima.

Lechtman, Heather (1984) Andean value systems and the development of prehistoric metallurgy. *Technology and Culture,* 25 (1): 1–36.

Lehmann, Arthur and Myers, James (1985) Shamans, priests and prophets. *Magic, Witchcraft, and Religion,* ed. Arthur Lehmann and James Myers, pp. 78–80. Mayfield Publishing Co., Palo Alto.

Lewis-Williams, J. D. (1982) The economic and social context of southern San rock art. *Current Anthropology,* 23 (4): 429–49.

Life Magazine (1999) Abandoned by the gods. *Life Magazine,* pp. 94–101, December.

Linares, Olga (1977) *Ecology and the Arts in Ancient Panama: On the Development of Social Symbolism in the Central Provinces.* Studies in Pre-Columbian Art and Archaeology 17, Dumbarton Oaks Research Library and Collection, Washington, DC.

Lothrop, S. K. (1937) Gold and silver from southern Peru and Bolivia. *Journal of the Royal Anthropological Institute,* 67: 305–25 (plus plates).

— (1964) *Treasures of Ancient America.* Skira, New York.

— and Mahler, Joy (1957) *Late Nazca Burials at Chaviña, Peru.* Papers of the Peabody Museum of Archaeology and Ethnology, vol. 50, no. 2. Peabody Museum of Archaeology, Cambridge, MA.

Lumbreras, Luis et al. (1975) *Guía para museos de arqueología peruana.* Editorial Milla Batres, Lima.

Lyon, Patricia (1968) A redefinition of the Pinilla style. *Ñawpa Pacha,* 6: 7–14.

— (1978) Female supernaturals in ancient Peru. *Ñawpa Pacha,* 16: 95–140.

McClelland, Donna (1990) A maritime passage from Moche to Chimu. *The Northern Dynasties: Kingship and Statecraft in Chimor*, ed. Michael E. Moseley and Alana Cordy-Collins, pp. 75–106. Dumbarton Oaks, Washington, DC.

McEwan, Gordon F. (1990) Some formal correspondences between the imperial architecture of the Wari and Chimu cultures of ancient Peru. *Latin American Antiquity*, 1 (2): 97–116.

— (1996) Archaeological investigations at Pikillacta, a Wari site in Peru. *Journal of Field Archaeology*, 23 (2): 169–86.

Macharé, José and Ortlieb, Luc (1993) Registros del fenómeno El Niño en el Perú. *Bulletin de l'Institut Français d'Etudes Andines*, 22 (1): 35–52.

Makowski, Krzysztof (1994) Los señores de Loma Negra. *Vicús*, ed. Krzysztof Makowski, pp. 83–141. Banco de Crédito del Perú, Lima.

Malakoff, David (1998) Rock dates thrown into doubt, researcher under fire. *Science*, 280: 2041–2.

Marcus, Joyce (1987) *Late Intermediate Period Occupation at Cerro Azúl, Perú: A Preliminary Report*. Technical Report 20. University of Michigan Museum of Anthropology, Ann Arbor.

Mason, J. Alden (1926) Dr Farabee's last journey. *Museum Journal*, 17 (2): 128–65.

Massey, Sarah A. (1986) Sociopolitical change in the Upper Ica Valley: BC 400 to 400 AD: regional states on the south coast of Peru. Unpublished PhD dissertation, Department of Anthropology, University of California at Los Angeles. University Microfilms, Ann Arbor.

— (1992) Investigaciones arqueológicas en el valle alto de Ica: Período Intermedio Temprano 1 y 2. *Estudios de Arqueología Peruana*, ed. Duccio Bonavia, pp. 215–36. FOMCIENCIAS, Lima.

Matos, Ramiro (1980) Las culturas regionales tempranas. *Historia del Perú*, ed. Juan Mejía Baca, vol. 1, pp. 353–524. Editorial Juan Mejía Baca, Lima.

Mayer, Enrique (1985) Production zones. *Andean Ecology and Civilization*, ed. Shozo Masuda, Izumi Shimada, and Craig Morris, pp. 45–84. University of Tokyo Press, Tokyo.

Mejía Xesspe, Toribio (1940) Acueductos y caminos antiguos de la hoya del Río Grande de Nazca. *Actas y Trabajos Científicos del 27 Congreso Internacional de Americanistas* 1: 559–69.

— (1976) Sitios arqueológicos del valle de Palpa, Ica. *San Marcos*, 17: 23–48. Revista de Artes, Ciencias y Humanidades, Universidad Nacional Mayor de San Marcos, Lima.

Menzel, Dorothy (1957) The disjunctive Nasca styles. Unpublished manuscript in possession of the co-authors.

— (1959) The Inca conquest of the south coast of Peru. *Southwestern Journal of Anthropology*, 15 (2): 125–42.

— (1964) Style and time in the Middle Horizon. *Ñawpa Pacha*, 2: 1–105.

— (1971) Estudios arqueológicos en los valles de Ica, Pisco, Chincha y Cañete. *Arqueología y Sociedad*, 6.

— (1976) *Pottery, Style and Society in Ancient Peru: Art as a Mirror of History in the Ica Valley, 1350–1570.* University of California Press, Berkeley, CA.

— (1977) *The Archaeology of Ancient Peru and the Work of Max Uhle.* R. H. Lowie Museum of Anthropology, University of California, Berkeley, CA.

— and Riddell, Francis A. (1986) *Archaeological Investigations at Tambo Viejo, Acarí Valley, Peru, 1954.* California Institute for Peruvian Studies, Sacramento.

—, Rowe, John H., and Dawson, Lawrence E. (1964) The Paracas pottery of Ica: a study in style and time. *University of California Publications in American Archaeology and Ethnology*, 50.

Moore, Jerry D. (1991) Cultural responses to environmental catastrophes: post-El Niño subsistence on the prehistoric north coast of Peru. *Latin American Antiquity*, 2 (1): 27–47.

— (1995) The archaeology of dual organization in Andean South America: a theoretical review and case study. *Latin American Antiquity*, 6 (2): 165–81.

— (1996) *Architecture and Power in the Ancient Andes.* Cambridge University Press, New York.

Morgan, Alexandra (1988) "The Master or Mother of Fishes": an interpretation of Nasca pottery figurines and their symbolism. *Recent Studies in Pre-Columbian Archaeology*, ed. Nicholas J. Saunders and Olivier de Montmollin, pp. 327–61. BAR International Series 421, Oxford.

Morinis, Alan and Crumrine, N. Ross (eds) (1991) *Pilgrimage in Latin America.* Greenwood Press, Westport, CT.

Morris, Craig and von Hagen, Adriana (1993) *The Inka Empire and its Andean Origins.* Abbeville Press and American Museum of Natural History, New York.

Morrison, Tony (1978) *Pathways to the Gods.* Andean Air Mail and Peruvian Times, Lima.

— (1987) *The Mystery of the Nasca Lines.* Nonesuch Expeditions Ltd, Suffolk, England.

Moseley, Michael E. (1975) *The Maritime Foundations of Andean Civilization.* Cummings, Menlo Park.

— (1987) Punctuated equilibrium: searching the ancient record for El Niño. *The Quarterly Review of Archaeology*, 8 (3): 7–10.

— (1992) *The Incas and their Ancestors*. Thames and Hudson, New York.

— (1994) New light on the horizon. *The Review of Archaeology*, 15 (2): 26–41.

— (1997) Climate, culture and punctuated change: new data, new challenges. *The Review of Archaeology*, 18 (1): 19–27.

—, Tapia, Jorge, Satterlee, Dennis, and Richardson III, James B. (1992) Flood events, El Niño events, and tectonic events. *Paleo ENSO Records. International Symposium: Extended Abstracts*, ed. Luc Ortlieb and José Macharé, pp. 207–12. ORSTOM-CONCYTEC, Lima.

Murra, John V. (1972) El control "vertical" de un máximo de pisos ecológicos en la economía de las sociedades andinas. *Visita de la Provincia de León de Huánuco en 1562*, vol. 2, ed. John V. Murra, pp. 429–76. Universidad Nacional Hermilio Valdizán, Huánuco.

— (1975) El tráfico de mullu en la costa del Pacífico. *Formaciones económicas y políticas del mundo andino* by John V. Murra, pp. 255–67. Instituto de Estudios Peruanos, Lima.

— (1980) *The Economic Organization of the Inka State*. JAI Press, Greenwich (originally published 1955).

National Geographic Society (1992) *Mysteries of Mankind: Earth's Unexplained Landmarks*. National Geographic Society, Washington, DC.

Neira Avendaño, Máximo (1990) Arequipa prehispánica. *Historia general de Arequipa*, ed. Máximo Neira Avedaño et al., pp. 5–234. Fundación M. J. Bustamante de la Fuente, Arequipa.

— and Coelho, Vera Penteado (1972–3) Enterramientos de cabezas de la cultura nasca. *Revista do Museu Paulista*, n.s. 20: 109–42.

Netherly, Patricia (1984) The management of late Andean irrigation systems on the north coast of Peru. *American Antiquity*, 49 (2): 227–54.

Neudecker, Angelika (1979) *Archäologische Forschungen Im Nazca-Gebiet, Peru. Das Tal des Rio Santa Cruz in praespanischer Zeit aus der Sicht der Forschungen Professor Dr Ubbelohde-Doerings in Jahre 1932*. Münchner Beiträge zur Amerikanistik. Klaus Renner Verlag, Hohenschäftlarn.

Nials, Fred, Deeds, Eric, Moseley, Michael, Pozorski, Shelia, Pozorski, Thomas, and Feldman, Robert (1979) El Niño: the catastrophic flooding of coastal Peru. *Bulletin of the Field Museum of Natural History*, 50 (7): 4–14, 50 (8): 4–10.

Nocete, Francisco (1994) Space as coercion: the transition to the state in the social formations of La Campiña, Upper Guadalquivir Valley, Spain, ca. 1900–1600 BC. *Journal of Anthropological Archaeology*, 13: 171–200.

O'Neale, Lila M. (1937) Archaeological explorations in Peru, part III: textiles of the Early Nazca Period. *Field Museum of Natural History, Anthropology, Memoirs*, 2 (3): 118–253.

— and Whitaker, Thomas W. (1947) Embroideries of the Early Nazca Period and the crop plants depicted on them. *Southwestern Journal of Anthropology*, 3: 294–321.

ONERN (Oficina Nacional de Evaluación de Recursos Naturales) (1971a) *Inventario, evaluación y uso racional de los recursos naturales de la costa: Cuenca del Río Grande (Nazca)*. ONERN, Lima.

— (1971b) *Inventario, evaluación y uso racional de los recursos naturales de la costa: Cuenca del Río Ica*. ONERN, Lima.

Orefici, Giuseppe (1987) *Hacia la antigua Nasca: una contribución Italiana*. Exhibit guide. Galería de Exposiciones Banco Continental, Miraflores, Lima.

— (1988) Una expresión de arquitectura monumental Paracas–Nasca: El Templo del Escalonado de Cahuachi. *Atti convegno internazionale: archeologia, scienza y societa nell'America Precolombiana*, pp. 191–201. Centro Italiano Studi e Ricerche Archeologiche Precolombiane, Brescia.

— (1990) Evidencias arqueológicas de la influencia de los cambios climáticos en la evolución de la cultura nazca. *El fenómeno El Niño a traves de las fuentes arqueológicas y geológicas*, ed. Jerzy Grodzicki, pp. 103–20. Misión Arqueológica Andina, Instituto de Arqueología, Universidad de Varsovia, Warsaw.

— (1992) *Nasca: archeologia per una ricostruzione storica*. Jaca Books, Milan.

— (1993) *Nasca: arte e societá del popolo dei geoglifi*. Jaca Books, Milan.

— (1996) Nuevos enfoques sobre la transición Paracas–Nasca en Cahuachi (Perú). *Andes*, 1: 173–89. Boletín de la Misión Arqueológica Andina, Warsaw.

Ossio, Juan (1976) El simbolismo del agua y la representacion del tiempo. *Actes du XLII Congres International des Americanistes*, 4: 377–96. Paris.

Panion, Tonya (1997) The Carmen style: an analysis of Early Intermediate Period ceramics from the Pisco Valley, Peru. Unpublished MA thesis, Department of Anthropology, University of Massachusetts, Amherst.

Panofsky, Erwin (1955) Iconography and iconology: an introduction to the study of Renaissance art. *Meaning in the Visual Arts* by Erwin Panofsky, pp. 26–54. Doubleday Anchor, New York.

Parker Pearson, Michael (1993) The powerful dead: archaeological relationships between the living and the dead. *Cambridge Archaeological Journal*, 3 (2): 203–29.

Parrish, Nancy and Cook, Anita (1999) Gardens in the desert: macro-botanical analysis from the lower Ica Valley, Peru. Paper presented at the 64th Annual Meeting of the Society for American Archaeology, Chicago.

Parsons, Jeffrey R. (1971) *Prehistoric Settlement Patterns in the Texcoco Region, Mexico*. Memoirs of the Museum of Anthropology, no. 3. University of Michigan, Ann Arbor.

Parsons, Lee (1962) Peruvian mortuary art: the Malcolm K. Whyte Collection at Milwaukee. *Archaeology*, 24 (4): 316–21.

Patterson, Thomas C. (1966) *Pattern and Process in the Early Intermediate Period Pottery of the Central Coast of Peru*. University of California Publications in Anthropology, vol. 3. University of California Press, Berkeley, CA.

Pauketat, Timothy (1998) Refiguring the archaeology of greater Cahokia. *Journal of Archaeological Research*, 6: 45–89.

— (in press) Practice and history in archaeology: an emerging paradigm. *Anthropological Theory*, 1.

— and Emerson, Thomas E. (1991) The ideology of authority and the power of the pot. *American Anthropologist*, 93: 919–41.

— and — (1999) Representations of hegemony as community at Cahokia. *Material Symbols: Culture and Economy in Prehistory*, ed. John E. Robb, pp. 302–17. Occasional Papers no. 26. Center for Archaeological Investigations, Southern Illinois University, Carbondale, IL.

Paul, Anne (1979) *Paracas Textiles: Selected from the Museum's Collections*. Etnologiska Studier 34, Göteborgs Etnografiska Museum.

— (1990) *Paracas Ritual Attire: Symbols of Authority in Ancient Peru*. University of Oklahoma Press, Norman.

— (1991) Paracas: an ancient cultural tradition on the south coast of Peru. *Paracas Art and Architecture: Object and Context in South Coastal Peru*, ed. Anne Paul, pp. 1–34. University of Iowa Press, Iowa City.

Paulsen, Allison C. (1968) A Middle Horizon tomb, Pinilla, Ica Valley, Peru. *Ñawpa Pacha*, 6: 1–6.

— (1974) The thorny oyster and the voice of God: Spondylus and Strombus in Andean prehistory. *American Antiquity*, 39 (4): 597–607.

— (1983) Huaca del Loro revisited: the Nasca–Huarpa connection. *Investigations of the Andean Past*, ed. Daniel H. Sandweiss, pp. 98–121. Latin American Studies Program, Cornell University, Ithaca, NY.

Peters, Ann (1987–8) Chongos: sitio Paracas en el valle de Pisco. *Gaceta Arqueológica Andina*, 16: 30–4.

— (1991) Ecology and society in embroidered images from the Paracas Necrópolis. *Paracas Art and Architecture: Object and Context in South Coastal Peru*, ed. Anne Paul, pp. 240–314. University of Iowa Press, Iowa City.

— (1997) Paracas, Topará and Early Nasca: ethnicity and society on the South Central Andean coast. Unpublished PhD dissertation, Department of Anthropology, Cornell University, Ithaca, NY.

Petersen, Georg (1980) *Evolución y desaparición de las altas culturas Paracas–Cahuachi (Nasca)*. Lima.

Pezzia, Alejandro (1968) *Ica y el Perú Precolombino. Vol. 1: Arqueología de la Provincia de Ica*. Empresa Editora Libreria Imprenta Ojeda SA, Ica.

— (1969) *Guía al mapa arqueológico-pictográfico del Departamento de Ica*. Editorial Italperu, Lima.

Phipps, Elena (1989) Cahuachi Textiles in the W. D. Strong Collection: cultural transition in the Nasca Valley, Peru. Unpublished PhD dissertation, Department of Art History, Columbia University.

Pitluga, Phyllis (1999) Die Nasca-Figuren als Abbilder der Milchstrasse. *Nasca: Geheimnisvolle Zeichen im Alten Peru*, ed. Judith Rickenbach, pp. 153–5. Museum Rietberg Zurich, Switzerland.

Poole, Deborah (1982) Los santuarios religiosos en la economía regional andina (Cusco). *Allpanchis Phuturinqa*, 19: 79–116.

— (1991) Rituals of movement, rites of transformation: pilgrimage and dance in the highlands of Cuzco, Peru. *Pilgrimage in Latin America*, ed. Alan Morinis and N. Ross Crumrine, pp. 307–38. Greenwood Press, Westport, CT.

Possehl, Gregory (1998) Sociocultural complexity without the state: the Indus civilization. *Archaic States*, ed. Gary M. Feinman and Joyce Marcus, pp. 261–91. School of American Resarch Press, Santa Fe.

Pozzi-Escot, Denise (1991) Conchopata: a community of potters. *Huari Administrative Architecture: Prehistoric Monumental Architecture and State Government*, ed. William H. Isbell and Gordon McEwan, pp. 81–92. Dumbarton Oaks, Washington, DC.

Preucel, Robert W. (ed.) (1991) *Processual and Postprocessual Archaeologies: Multiple Ways of Knowing the Past*. Occasional Paper no. 10, Center for Archaeological Investigations, Southern University University, Carbondale, IL.

Price, Barbara J. (1971) Prehispanic irrigation agriculture in Nuclear America. *Latin American Research Review*, 6 (3): 3–60.

Proulx, Donald A. (1968) *Local Differences and Time Differences in Nasca Pottery*. University of California Publications in Anthropology, vol. 5. University of California Press, Berkeley, CA.

— (1970) *Nasca Gravelots in the Uhle Collection from the Ica Valley, Peru*. Research Reports no. 5, Department of Anthropology, University of Massachusetts, Amherst.

— (1971) Headhunting in ancient Peru. *Archaeology*, 24 (1): 16–21.

— (1983) The Nasca style. *Art of the Andes: Precolumbian Sculptured and Painted Ceramics from the Arthur M. Sackler Collections*, ed. Lois Katz, pp. 87–105. AMS Foundation, Washington, DC.

— (1989a) Monkeys in Nasca art and society. Paper presented at the 8th Northeast Conference on Andean Archaeology and Ethnohistory, Yale University.

— (1989b) Nasca trophy heads: victims of warfare or ritual sacrifice? *Cultures in Conflict: Current Archaeological Perspectives*, ed. Diana C. Tkaczuk and Brian C. Vivian, pp. 73–85. Proceedings of the 20th Annual Chacmool Conference, University of Calgary Archaeological Association.

— (1989c) A thematic approach to Nasca mythical iconography. *Faenz: Bollettino del Museo Internazionale delle Ceramiche in Faenza*, 75 (4–6): 141–58, plus figures.

— (1991) L'iconographie nasca. *Inca–Perú: 3000 ans d'histoire*, ed. Sergio Purin, pp. 384–99. Imschoot, uitgevers s.a., Gent (Belgium).

— (1994) Stylistic variation in proliferous Nasca pottery. *Andean Past*, 4: 91–107.

— (1996) Nasca. *Andean Art at Dumbarton Oaks*, ed. Elizabeth Hill Boone, pp. 107–22. Dumbarton Oaks, Washington, DC.

— (1999a) Die Nasca-Kultur Ein Überblick. *Nasca: Geheimnisvolle Zeichen im Alten Peru*, ed. Judith Rickenbach, pp. 59–77. Museum Rietberg Zurich, Switzerland.

— (1999b) Kopfjagd und rituelle Verwendung von Trophäenköpfen in der Nasca-Kultur. *Nasca: Geheimnisvolle Zeichen im Alten Peru*, ed. Judith Rickenbach, pp. 79–87. Museum Rietberg Zurich, Switzerland.

— (1999c) Settlement patterns and society in south coastal Peru. Unpublished report to the H. John Heinz III Charitable Fund.

— (in press) Nasca religion and ritual. *Encyclopedia of Andean Religions*, vol. 1, ed. Henrique Urbano and Daniel Arsenault. Centro de Estudios Regionales Andinos "Bartolomé de las Casas," Cuzco.

— (n.d.) Nasca ceramic iconography. Unpublished manuscript in possession of the co-authors.

Pulgar Vidal, Javier (1996) *Geografía del Perú*. PEISA, Lima.

Purin, Sergio (ed.) (1990) *Inca–Perú: 3000 ans d'histoire*. Imschoot, uitgevers s.a., Gent (Belgium).

Putnam, Edward K. (1914) The Davenport collection of Nazca and other Peruvian pottery. *Proceedings of the Davenport Academy of Sciences*, 13: 17–46.

Quijandría Alvarez, Cornelio (1961) *Orígen y fundación del Colegio e Iglesia de San Luis Gonzaga de los Jesuítas de Ica*. Tip. Cultura, Ica.

Quilter, Jeffrey (1999) Representing Moche: continuity and change in public art in early Peru. Paper presented at the symposium "Moche: Art and Political Representation in Ancient Peru," CASVA, National Gallery of Art, Washington, DC.

Ramírez, Susan (1996) *The World Upside Down: Cross-cultural Contact and Conflict in Sixteenth-century Peru*. Stanford University Press, Stanford.

Ramos Gómez, Luis Javier and Blasco Bosqued, María Concepción (1977) Las representaciones de "Aves Fantásticas" en materiales Nazcas del Museo de América de Madrid. *Revista de Indias*, 37 (147–8): 265–76.

Rasnake, Roger (198) Carnaval in Yura: ritual reflections on ayllu and state relations. *American Ethnologist*, 13 (4): 662–80.

— (1988) *Domination and Cultural Resistance*. Duke University Press, Durham.

Reiche, Maria (1951) Orientación y medidas en los dibujos antiguos de las Pampas de Nazca. *Homenaje al IV centenario de la fundación de la universidad, Conferencia de Ciencias Antropológicas*, pp. 219–27. Universidad Nacional Mayor de San Marcos, Lima.

— (1958) Interpretación astronómica de la figura del Mono en la Pampa al sur del Río Ingenio. *Actas y trabajos del II Congreso Nacional del Perú, Epoca Prehispánica*, 1: 285–6. Centro de Estudios Históricos-Militares del Perú, Lima.

— (1968) Giant ground drawings on the Peruvian desert. *Proceedings of the 27th International Congress of Americanists*, 1: 379–84. Stuttgart.

— (1973) How the Nazca lines were made. *Peruvian Times*, pp. 9–13 (13 April).

— (1974) *Peruanische Erdzeichen. Peruvian Ground Drawings*. Kunstraum München E. V., Munich.

— (1976) *Geheimnis der Wüste. Mystery on the Desert. Secreto de la Pampa*. Heinrich Fink GmbH and Co., Stuttgart.

Reindel, Markus and Isla, Johny (1999) Das Palpa-Tal: Ein Archiv der Vorgeschichte Perus. *Nasca: Geheimnisvolle Zeichen im Alten Peru*, ed. Judith Rickenbach, pp. 177–98. Museum Rietberg Zurich, Switzerland.

Reinhard, Johan (1985) Chavín and Tiahuanaco: a new look at two Andean ceremonial centers. *National Geographic Explorer*, 1 (3): 395–422.

— (1988) *The Nazca Lines: A New Perspective on their Origin and Meaning*, 4th edn. Editorial Los Pinos, Lima.

— (1992) Interpreting the Nazca Lines. *The Ancient Americas: Art from Sacred Landscapes*, ed. Richard F. Townsend, pp. 291–301. The Art Institute of Chicago, Chicago.

— (1998) Research update: new Inca mummies. *National Geographic*, 194 (1): 128–35 (July).

Reiss, Wilhelm and Stübel, Alphons (1880–7) *Peruvian Antiquities: The Necropolis of Ancón in Peru. A Series of Illustrations of the Civilisation and Industry of the Empire of the Incas. Being the Results of Excavations by W. Reiss and A. Stübel*, 3 vols. A. Ascher, London and Berlin.

Renfrew, Colin (1974) Beyond a subsistence economy: the evolution of social organization in prehistoric Europe. *Reconstructing Complex Societies: An Archaeological Colloquium*, ed. Charlotte B. Moore, pp. 69–85. Supplement to the Bulletin of the American Schools of Oriental Research, no. 20.

— (1979) *Before Civilization*. Cambridge University Press, Cambridge.

Richardson III, James B. (1994) *People of the Andes*. Smithsonian Institution Press, Washington, DC.

Rickenbach, Judith (ed.) (1999) *Nasca: Geheimnisvolle Zeichen im Alten Peru*. Museum Rietberg Zurich, Switzerland.

Riddell, Francis (1985) *Report of Archaeological Fieldwork: Tambo Viejo, Acarí Valley, Peru, 1984*. California Institute for Peruvian Studies, Sacramento.

— (1986) *Report of Archaeological Fieldwork: Acarí and Yauca Valleys, Arequipa, Peru, 1985*. California Institute for Peruvian Studies, Sacramento.

— (1989) *Archaeological Investigations in the Acarí Valley, Perú: A Field Report*. California Institute for Peruvian Studies, Sacramento.

— and Valdez, Lidio (1988) *Prospecciones arqueológicas en el Valle de Acarí, Costa Sur del Perú*. California Institute for Peruvian Studies, Sacramento.

Roark, Richard P. (1965) From monumental to proliferous in Nasca pottery. *Ñawpa Pacha*, 3: 1–92.

Robinson, David A. (1957) An archaeological survey of the Nasca Valley, Peru. Unpublished MA thesis, Department of Anthropology, Stanford University.

Rodman, Amy Oakland (1992) Textiles and ethnicity: Tiwanaku in San Pedro de Atacama, North Chile. *Latin American Antiquity*, 3 (4): 316–40.

Rodríguez de Sandweiss, María del Carmen (1993) Malacological analysis. *Cahuachi in the Ancient World*, ed. Helaine Silverman, pp. 294–9. University of Iowa Press, Iowa City.

Rosenfeld, Andrée (1997) Archaeological signatures of the social context of rock art production. *Beyond Art: Pleistocene Image and Symbol*, ed. Margaret Conkey, Olga Soffer, Deborah Stratmann, and Nina Jablonski, pp. 289–300. Memoirs of the California Academy of Sciences, vol. 23. San Francisco.

Rossel Castro, Alberto (1977) *Arqueología Sur del Perú*. Editorial Universo, SA, Lima.

Rosselló Truel, Lorenzo (1960) Sobre el estilo nasca. *Antiguo Perú: espacio y tiempo*, pp. 47–88. Editorial Juan Mejía Baca, Lima.

— (1978) Sistemas astronómicas de campos de rayas. *El hombre y la cultura Andina*, ed. Ramiro Matos, pp. 521–30. Secretaría General de III Congreso Peruano "El Hombre y La Cultura Andina", Lima.

Rostworowski, María (1978) *Señoríos indígenas de Lima y Canta*. Instituto de Estudios Peruanos, Lima.

— (1982) Comentarios a la Visita de Acarí de 1593. *Historica*, 6 (2): 227–54.

— (1989a) Las etnías del valle de Chillón. *Costa Peruana Prehispánica* by María Rostworowski de Diez Canseco, pp. 23–69. Instituto de Estudios Peruanos, Lima.

— (1989b) Plantaciones prehispánicas de coca en la vertiente del Pacífico. *Costa Peruana Prehispánica* by María Rostworowski de Diez Canseco, pp. 239–61. Instituto de Estudios Peruanos, Lima.

— (1993) Origen religioso de los dibujos y rayas de Nasca. *Journal de la Société des Américanistes*, 79: 189–202.

— (1996) *Estructuras Andinas del poder*. Instituto de Estudios Peruanos, Lima.

— (1998a) Sistemas hidráulicos de los señoríos costeños prehispánicos. *Ensayos de historia Andina II* by Maria Rostworowski, pp. 125–49. Instituto de Estudios Peruanos, Lima.

— (1998b) The coastal islands of Peru: myth and natural resources. *The Spirit of Ancient Peru: Treasures from the Museo Arqueológico Rafael Larco Herrera*, ed. Kathleen Berrin, pp. 33–9. Fine Arts Museums of San Francisco and Thames and Hudson, New York.

Rowe, Ann Pollard (1972) Interlocking warp and weft in the Nasca 2 style. *Textile Museum Journal*, 3 (3): 67–78.

— (1986) Textiles from the Nasca Valley at the time of the fall of the Huari Empire. *The Junius B. Bird Conference on Andean Textiles*, ed. Ann Pollard Rowe, pp. 151–82. The Textile Museum, Washington, DC.

— (1990–1) Nasca figurines and costume. *Textile Museum Journal*, 29–30: 93–128.

Rowe, John H. (1956) Archaeological explorations in southern Peru, 1954–55: preliminary report of the Fourth University of California Archaeological Expedition to Peru. *American Antiquity*, 22 (2): 135–51.

— (1959) Archaeological dating and cultural process. *Southwestern Journal of Anthropology*, 15 (4): 317–24.

— (1960) Nuevos datos relativos a la cronología relativa del estilo nasca. *Antiguo Perú: espacio y tiempo*, pp. 29–45. Editorial Juan Mejía Baca, Lima.

— (1961) Stratigraphy and seriation. *American Antiquity*, 26: 324–30.

— (1962a) Alfred Louis Kroeber, 1876–1960. *American Antiquity*, 27 (3): 395–414.

— (1962b) *Chavín Art: An Inquiry into its Form and Meaning*. Museum of Primitive Art, New York.

— (1962c) Stages and periods in archaeological interpretation. *Southwestern Journal of Anthropology*, 18 (1): 40–54.

— (1963) Urban settlements in ancient Peru. *Ñawpa Pacha*, 1: 1–27.

— (1967) An interpretation of radiocarbon measurements on archaeological samples from Peru. *Peruvian Archaeology: Selected Readings*, ed. John H. Rowe and Dorothy Menzel, pp. 16–30. Peek Publications, Palo Alto.

— (1971) The influence of Chavín art on later styles. *Dumbarton Oaks Conference on Chavín*, ed. Elizabeth P. Benson, pp. 101–24. Dumbarton Oaks, Washington, DC.

— and Menzel, Dorothy (eds) (1967) *Peruvian Archaeology: Selected Readings*. Peek Publications, Palo Alto.

Russell, Glenn S., Leonard, Banks L., and Rosario, Jesús Briceño (1994a) Cerro Mayal: nuevos datos sobre la producción de cerámica moche en el valle de Chicama. *Moche: propuestas y perspectivas*, ed. Santiago Uceda and Elias Mujica, pp. 181–206. Travaux de l'Institut Français d'Etudes Andines, 79. Lima.

—, —, and — (1994b) Producción de cerámica a gran escala en el valle de Chicama, Perú: el taller de Cerro Mayal. *Tecnología y organización de la producción de cerámica prehispánica en los Andes*, ed. Izumi Shimada, pp. 201–27. Fondo Editorial, Pontificia Universidad Católica del Perú, Lima.

Sackett, James (1990) Style and ethnicity in archaeology: the case for isochrestism. *The Uses of Style in Archaeology*, ed. Margaret Conkey and Christine Hastorf, pp. 32–43. Cambridge University Press, New York.

Salguero Jara, Eduardo (1989) Excavations at La Oroya. *Archaeological Investigations in the Acarí Valley, Peru: A Field Report*, ed. Francis A. Riddell, pp. 14–32. California Institute for Peruvian Studies, Sacramento.

Sallnow, Michael J. (1981) Communitas reconsidered: the sociology of Andean pilgrimage. *Man*, n.s. 16: 163–82.

— (1987) *Pilgrims of the Andes: Regional Cults in Cusco*. Smithsonian Institution Press, Washington, DC.

— (1991) Dual cosmology and ethnic division in an Andean pilgrimage cult. *Pilgrimage in Latin America*, ed. Alan Morinis and N. Ross Crumrine, pp. 281–306. Greenwood Press, Westport, CT.

Salomon, Frank (1991) Introduction. *The Huarochiri Manuscript*, ed. Frank Salomon and George Urioste, pp. 1–38. University of Texas Press, Austin.

— (1998) Collquiri's dam: the colonial re-voicing of an appeal to the archaic. *Native Traditions in the Postconquest World*, ed. Elizabeth H. Boone and Tom Cummins, pp. 265–93. Dumbarton Oaks, Washington, DC.

— and Urioste, George (eds) (1991) *The Huarochirí Manuscript*. University of Texas Press, Austin.

Sanders, William T. and Price, Barbara J. (1968) *Mesoamerica: The Evolution of a Civilization*. Random House, New York.

Sandweiss, Daniel (1992) The archaeology of Chincha fishermen: specialization and status in Inka Peru. *Bulletin of the Carnegie Museum of Natural History*, no. 29. Pittsburgh.

— and Wing, Elizabeth (1997) Ritual rodents: the guinea pigs of Chincha, Peru. *Journal of Field Archaeology*, 24 (1): 47–58.

Sawyer, Alan R. (1962) A group of early Nazca sculptures in the Whyte Collection. *Archaeology*, 24 (4): 152–9.

— (1964) Paracas and Nazca iconography. *Essays in Pre-Columbian Art and Archaeology*, ed. Samuel K. Lothrop, pp. 269–98. Harvard University Press, Cambridge.

— (1966) *Ancient Peruvian Ceramics: The Nathan Cummings Collection*. Metropolitan Museum of Art, New York.

— (1968) *Mastercraftsmen of Ancient Peru*. Solomon R. Guggenheim Foundation, New York.

— (1975) *Ancient Andean Arts in the Collections of the Krannert Art Museum*. Krannert Art Museum, University of Illinois, Urbana–Champaign.

— (1979) Painted Nasca textiles. *The Junius B. Bird Pre-Columbian Textile Conference*, ed. Ann Pollard Rowe, Elizabeth P. Benson and Anne-Louise Schaffer, pp. 129–50. Textile Museum and Dumbarton Oaks, Washington, DC.

— (1997) *Early Nasca Needlework*. Laurence King Publishing, London.

Schaedel, Richard P. (1993) Congruence of horizon with polity: Huari and the Middle Horizon. *Latin American Horizons*, ed. Don Stephen Rice, pp. 225–61. Dumbarton Oaks, Washington, DC.

Schlesier, K. H. (1959) Stilgeschichtliche Einordnung der Nazca-Vasenmalereien: Beitrag zur Geschichte der Hochkulturen des Vorkolumbischen Peru. *Annali Lateranensi*, vol. 23. Pontificio Museo Missionario Ethnologico, Vatican City.

Schreiber, Katharina J. (1989) On revisiting Huaca del Loro: a cautionary note. *Andean Past*, 2: 69–79.

— (1992) *Wari Imperialism in Middle Horizon Peru*. Anthropological Papers, no. 87. Museum of Anthropology, University of Michigan, Ann Arbor.

— (1998) Afterword: Nasca research since 1926. *The Archaeology and Pottery of Nazca, Peru: Alfred L. Kroeber's 1926 Expedition*, ed. Alfred L. Kroeber and Donald Collier, pp. 261–70. Altamira Press, Walnut Creek.

— (1999) Regional approaches to the study of prehistoric empires: examples from Ayacucho and Nasca, Peru. *Settlement Pattern Studies in the America: Fifty Years since Virú*, ed. Brian R. Billman and Gary M. Feinman, pp. 160–71. Smithsonian Institution Press, Washington, DC.

— and Lancho Rojas, Josué (1995) The puquios of Nasca. *Latin American Antiquity*, 6 (3): 229–54.

Seler, Eduard (1923) Die buntbemalten Gefässe von Nazca in sudlichen Peru und die Hauptelemente ihrer Verzierung. *Gesammelte Abhandlungen zur Amerikanischen Sprach und Altertunskunde*, 4: 160–438. Verlag Behrend u. Co., Berlin.

Service, Elman (1962) *Primitive Social Organization*. Random House, New York.

Shady, Ruth (1981) Intensificación de contactos entre las sociedades andinas como preludio al movimiento Huari del Horizonte Medio. *Boletín del Museo Nacional de Antropología y Arqueología*, 7: 7–9. Lima.

— (1982) La cultura Nievería y la interacción social en el mundo andino en la época Huari. *Arqueológicas*, 19: 7–108. Museo Nacional de Antropología y Arqueología, Lima.

— (1988) La época Huari como interacción de las sociedades regionales. *Revista Andina*, 6: 67–99.

Sharon, Douglas (1972) The San Pedro cactus in Peruvian folk healing. *Flesh of the Gods: The Ritual Use of Hallucinogens*, ed. Peter Furst, pp. 114–35. Praeger, New York.

— (1978) *Wizard of the Four Winds*. The Free Press, New York.

Shennan, S. J. (ed.) (1989) *Archaeological Approaches to Cultural Identity*. Unwin Hyman, London.

Sherbondy, Jeanette (1982) The canal systems of Hanan Cuzco. Unpublished PhD dissertation, Department of Anthropology, University of Illinois at Urbana–Champaign.

— (1986) Mallki: ancestros y cultivo de árboles en los andes. Proyecto FAO-Holanda/INFOR-GCP/PER/027/NET. Documento de Trajabo, 5. Lima, Peru.

Shimada, Izumi (1981) The Batán Grande–La Leche archaeological project: the first two seasons. *Journal of Field Archaeology*, 8: 405–46.

— and Merkel, John F. (1991) Copper-alloy metallurgy in ancient Peru. *Scientific American*, 265 (1): 80–6.

Shimada, Melody and Shimada, Izumi (1985) Prehistoric llama breeding and herding on the north coast of Peru. *American Antiquity*, 50: 3–26.

Silverman, Helaine (1977) Estilo y estado: el problema de la cultura nasca. *Informaciones Arqueológicas*, 1: 49–78.

— (1988a) Cahuachi: non-urban cultural complexity on the south coast of Peru. *Journal of Field Archaeology*, 15 (4): 403–30.

— (1988b) Nasca 8: a reassessment of its chronological placement and cultural significance. *Multidisciplinary Studies in Andean Anthropology*, ed. Virginia J. Vitzthum, pp. 23–32. Michigan Discussions in Anthropology, vol. 8, University of Michigan, Ann Arbor.

— (1990a) Beyond the pampa: the geoglyphs of the valleys of Nazca. *National Geographic Research*, 6 (4): 435–56.

— (1990b) The Early Nasca pilgrimage center of Cahuachi: archaeological and anthropological perspectives. *The Lines of Nazca*, ed. Anthony F. Aveni, pp. 209–44. American Philosophical Society, Philadelphia.

— (1991) The Paracas problem: archaeological perspectives. *Paracas Art and Architecture: Object and Context in South Coastal Peru*, ed. Anne Paul, pp. 349–415. University of Iowa Press, Iowa City.

— (1992a) The Nazca Lines: sacred geography and cult archaeology. *Broken Images*, photographs by David Parker, texts by Helaine Silverman and Gerry Badger, pp. 7–13. Cornerhouse, Manchester.

— (1992b) Sobre la antiguedad de los geoglifos de Nazca: observaciones a Clarkson y Dorn. *Boletín de Lima*, 83: 5–10.

— (1993a) *Cahuachi in the Ancient Nasca World*. University of Iowa Press, Iowa City.

— (1993b) Patrones de asentamiento en el valle de Ingenio, cuenca del río Grande de Nazca: una propuesta preliminar. *Gaceta Arqueológica Andina*, 23: 103–24.

— (1994a) Paracas in Nazca: new data on the Early Horizon occupation of the Río Grande de Nazca Drainage, Peru. *Latin American Antiquity*, 5 (4): 359–82.

— (1994b) The archaeological identification of Cahuachi as a pilgrimage site. *World Archaeology*, 26 (1): 1–18.

— (1996a) *Ancient Peruvian Art: An Annotated Bibliography*. G. K. Hall, New York.

— (1996b) The Formative Period on the south coast of Peru. *Journal of World Prehistory*, 10 (2): 95–146.

— (1996c) Musicians of the desert. *Birds on a Drum: Conservation of a Pre-Columbian Musical Instrument*, pp. 8–12. Krannert Art Museum, University of Illinois, Urbana–Champaign.

— (1997) The first field season of excavations at the Alto del Molino site, Pisco Valley, Peru. *Journal of Field Archaeology*, 24 (4): 441–57.

— and Browne, David M. (1991) New evidence for the date of the Nazca Lines. *Antiquity*, 65: 208–20.

Smith, Jonathan Z. (1987) *To Take Place*. University of Chicago Press, Chicago.

Spielbauer, Judith (1972) Nazca figurines from the Malcolm Whyte Collection. *Archaeology*, 25 (1): 20–5.

Stark, Miriam T. (ed.) (1998) *The Archaeology of Social Boundaries*. Smithsonian Institution Press, Washington, DC.

Starn, Orin (1991) Missing the revolution: anthropologists and the war in Peru. *Cultural Anthropology*, 6: 63–91.

Stein, Gil J. (1998) Heterogeneity, power and political economy: some current research issues in the archaeology of Old World complex societies. *Journal of Archaeological Research*, 6 (1): 1–44.

Steward, Julian H. (1948) A functional-developmental classification of American high cultures. *A Reappraisal of Peruvian Archaeology*, ed. Wendell C. Bennett, pp. 103–4. Memoir no. 4, Society for American Archaeology, Menasha.

— (ed.) (1955) *Irrigation Civilizations: A Comparative Study*. Pan American Union, Washington, DC.

Stierlin, Henri (1983) *La clé du mystére*. Albin Michel, Paris.

Strong, William Duncan (1948) Cultural epochs and refuse stratigraphy in Peruvian archaeology. *A Reappraisal of Peruvian Archaeology*, ed. Wendell C. Bennett, pp. 93–102. Memoir no. 4, Society for American Archaeology, Menasha.

— (1957) *Paracas, Nazca and Tiahuanacoid Cultural Relationships in South Coastal Peru*. Memoir no. 13, Society for American Archaeology, Menasha.

— and Evans, Clifford (1947) Finding the tomb of a warrior-god. *National Geographic Magazine*, April, pp. 453–82.

Stumer, Louis M. (1956) Development of Peruvian coastal Tiahuanacoid styles. *American Antiquity*, 22 (1): 59–69.

— (1958) Contactos foráneos en la arquitectura de la costa central. *Revista del Museo Nacional*, 27: 11–30.

Tainter, Joseph A. (1988) *The Collapse of Complex Societies*. Cambridge University Press, Cambridge.

Tello, Julio C. (1917) Los antiguos cementerios del valle de Nazca. *Proceedings of the Second Pan American Scientific Congress*, 1: 283–91.

— (1918) *El uso de las cabezas humanas artificialmente momificadas y su representación en el antiguo arte peruano*. Casa Editora de Ernesto R. Villarán, Lima.

— (1923) Wira Kocha. *Inca*, 1 (1): 93–320, 1 (3): 583–606. Lima.

— (1928) Los descubrimientos del Museo de Arqueología Peruana en la península de Paracas. *Proceedings of the Twenty-second International Congress of Americanists (Rome, 1926)*, 1: 679–90.

— (1931) Un modelo de escenografía plástica en el arte antiguo peruano. *Wira Kocha*, 1 (1): 87–112.

— (1940) Vaso de piedra de Nasca. *Chaski*, 1 (1): 27–48.

— (1959) *Paracas: Primera parte*. T. Scheuch, Lima and Institute of Andean Research, New York.

— and Mejía Xesspe, Toribio (1967) Historia de los Museos Nacionales del Perú, 1822–1946. *Arqueológicas*, 10.

— and — (1979) *Paracas. Segunda parte: cavernas y necropolis*. Universidad Nacional Mayor de San Marcos, Lima.

Thompson, Lonnie G., Mosley-Thompson, E., Bolzan, J. F., and Koci, B. R. (1985) A 1500-year record of tropical precipitation in ice cores from the Quelccaya Ice Cap, Peru. *Science*, 229: 971–3.

Topic, John (1982) Lower-class social and economic organization at Chan Chan. *Chan Chan: Andean Desert City*, ed. Michael E. Moseley and Kent C. Day, pp. 145–75. University of New Mexico Press, Albuquerque.

Topic, Theresa (1991) The Middle Horizon in northern Peru. *Huari Administrative Structure: Prehistoric Monumental Architecture and State Government*, ed. William H. Isbell and Gordon McEwan, pp. 233–46. Dumbarton Oaks, Washington, DC.

Torero, Alfredo (1975) Linguistica e historia de la sociedad andina. *Linguistica e indigenismo moderno de America: Proceedings of the Thirty-ninth International Congress of Americanists*, 5: 221–59. Lima.

Towle, Margaret (1961) *The Ethnobotany of Pre-Columbian Peru*. Aldine, Chicago.

Townsend, Richard F. (1985) Deciphering the Nazca world: ceramic images from ancient Peru. *Museum Studies*, 11 (2): 117–39. The Art Institute of Chicago.

Trigger, B. G. (1983) The rise of Egyptian civilization. *Ancient Egypt: A Social History*, ed. B. G. Trigger, B. J. Kemp, D. O'Connor, and A. B. Lloyd, pp. 1–70. Cambridge University Press, Cambridge.

Turner, Victor (1974) *Dramas, Fields and Metaphors*. Cornell University Press, Ithaca, NY.

— (1985) Religious specialists. *Magic, Witchcraft and Religion: An Anthropological Study of the Supernatural*, ed. Arthur C. Lehmann and James E. Myers, pp. 81–8. Mayfield Publishing Co., Palo Alto.

— and Turner, Edith (1978) *Image and Pilgrimage in Christian Culture*. Columbia University Press, New York.

Ubbelohde-Doering, Heinrich (1925–6) Alt Peruanische Gefässmalerein. *Marburger Jahrbuch für Kunstwissenschaft*, vol. 2. Verlag des Kunstgeschichtlichen Seminar der Universität Marburgan der Lahn, Marberg.

— (1931) Altperuanische Gefässmalereinen II. *Marburger Jahrbuch für Kunstwissenschaft*, vol. 6. Verlag des Kunstgeschichtlichen Seminar der Universität Marburgan der Lahn, Marberg.

— (1958) Bericht über archäologische Feldarbeiten in Perú. *Ethnos*, 2–4: 67–99.

— (1966) *On the Royal Highways of the Incas*. Praeger, New York.

Uhle, Max (1906) Aus meinem Bericht über die Ergebnisse meiner Reise nach Südamerika 1899–1901. Uber die historische Stellung der feinen bunten Gefässe von Ica unter den übrigen prähistorischen Resten von Peru. *Internationaler Amerikanisten-Kongres, Vierzehnte Tagung, Stuttgart 1904*, part II, pp. 581–92.

— (1913) Zur chronologie der alten Culturen von Ica. *Journal de la Société des Américanistes*, n.s. 10 (2): 341–67.

— (1914) The Nazca pottery of Ancient Peru. *Proceedings of the Davenport Academy of Sciences*, 13: 1–16.

— (1924) Ancient civilizations of Ica Valley. *University of California Publications in American Archaeology and Ethnology*, 21 (5): 128–32 (Appendix C in Kroeber and Strong 1924).

— (1998) Las ruinas de Moche. *Max Uhle y El Perú Antiguo*, ed. Peter Kaulicke, pp. 205–27. Fondo Editorial, Pontificia Universidad Católica del Perú, Lima (originally "Die Ruinen von Moche," published in 1913 in *Journal de la Société des Américanistes de Paris*, n.s. 10, pp. 95–117).

— and Stübel, Alphons (1892) *Die Ruinenstaette von Tiahuanaco im Hochlande des alten Perú*. Verlag von Karl W. Hiersemann, Leipzig.

Urton, Gary (1981) *At the Crossroads of the Earth and the Sky: An Andean Cosmology*. University of Texas Press, Austin.

— (1982) Report of fieldwork in Nazca Peru. Unpublished manuscript in the possession of Helaine Silverman.

— (1990) Andean ritual sweeping and the Nazca Lines. *The Lines of Nazca*, ed. Anthony F. Aveni, pp. 173–206. American Philosophical Society, Philadelphia.

Valcárcel, Luis E. (1932) El gato de agua. *Revista del Museo Nacional*, 1 (2): 3–27.

Valderrama, Ricardo and Escalante, Carmen (1988) *Del Tata Mallku a la Mama Pacha: riego, sociedad y ritos en los Andes Peruanos*. DESCO, Centro de Estudios y Promoción del Desarrollo, Lima.

Valdez, Lidio (1988) Los camélidos en la subsistencia Nasca: el caso de Kawachi. *Boletín de Lima*, 57: 31–5.

— (1989) Excavaciones arqueológicas en Gentilar (PV74–5). *Archaeological Investigations in the Acarí Valley, Peru: A Field Report*, ed. Francis A. Riddell, pp. 42–55. California Institute for Peruvian Studies, Sacramento and Universidad Católica de Santa María, Arequipa.

— (1990) *Informe de los trabajos de campo de la temporada de 1990 del "Proyecto Arqueológico Acarí, Yauca, Atiquipa y Chala."* California Institute for Peruvian Studies, Sacramento.

— (1994) Cahuachi: new evidence for an early Nasca ceremonial role. *Current Anthropology*, 35 (5): 675–9.

— (1998) The Nasca and the valley of Acarí: cultural interaction on the Peruvian south coast during the first four centuries AD. Unpublished PhD dissertation, Department of Archaeology, University of Calgary, Alberta.

Vaughn, Kevin (1999) Early Intermediate Period complexity on the south coast of Peru: new perspectives from Marcaya, an early Nasca domestic site. *Abstracts of the 64th Annual Meeting of the Society for American Archaeology*, pp. 293–4. Society for American Archaeology, Chicago.

— and Neff, Hector (2000) Reconsidering Nasca ceramic production: new evidence from Marcaya. *Abstracts of the 65th Annual Meeting of the Society for American Archaeology*, p. 342. Society for American Archaeology, Philadelphia.

Verano, John (1995) Where do they rest? The treatment of human offerings and trophies in ancient Peru. *Tombs for the Living: Andean Mortuary Practices*, ed. Tom D. Dillehay, pp. 189–228. Dumbarton Oaks, Washington, DC.

— and Ubelaker, Douglas (1992) *Disease and Demography in the Americas*. Smithsonian Institution Press, Washington, DC.

Von Däniken, Erich (1969) *Chariots of the Gods? Was God an Astronaut?* Souvenir Press, Great Britain.

— (1970) *Chariots of the Gods? Memories of the Future: Unsolved Mysteries of the Past.* G. P. Putnam's Sons, New York.

— (1972) *Gods from Outer Space?* Bantam, New York.

— (1980) *Chariots of the Gods?* Berkley Books, New York.

— (1998) *Arrival of the Gods: Revealing the Alien Landing Sites of Nazca.* Element, Boston.

Wallace, Dwight (1958) Early Intermediate Period ceramics of the south-central Peruvian coast. Unpublished manuscript in the possession of the co-authors.

— (1962) Cerrillos, an early Paracas site in Ica, Peru. *American Antiquity*, 27 (3): 303–14.

— (1971) Sitios arqueológicos del Perú (segunda entrega): Valles de Chincha y de Pisco. *Arqueológicas*, 13. Museo Nacional de Antropología y Arqueología, Lima.

— (1986) The Topará tradition: an overview. *Perspectives on Andean Prehistory and Protohistory: Papers from the Third Annual Northeast Conference on Andean Archaeology and Ethnohistory*, ed. Daniel H.

Sandweiss and D. Peter Kvietok, pp. 35–47. Latin American Studies Program, Cornell University, Ithaca, NY.

— (1991) A technical and iconographic analysis of Carhua painted textiles. *Paracas Art and Architecture: Object and Context in South Coastal Peru*, ed. Anne Paul, pp. 61–109. University of Iowa Press, Iowa City.

Watts, Michael J. (1992) Space for everything (a commentary). *Cultural Anthropology*, 7 (1): 115–29.

Wegner, Steven (1976) A stylistic seriation of Nasca 6 painted pottery designs. Unpublished manuscript in the possession of the co-authors.

Weiss, Pedro (1953) Las trepanaciones peruanas estudiadas como técnica y en sus relaciones con la cultura. *Revista del Museo Nacional*, 22: 17–34.

— (1958) *Osteología cultural. Prácticas cefálicas. Primera parte: cabeza trofeos-trepanaciones-cauterizaciones.* Lima.

— (1962) Tipología de las deformaciones cefálicas de los antiguos peruanos, según la osteología cultural. *Revista del Museo Nacional*, 31: 15–42.

— (1972) Las deformaciones cefálicas intencionales como factores de la arqueología. *Proceedings of the Thirty-ninth International Congress of Americanists*, pp. 165–80. Lima.

Wheatley, Paul (1971) *The Pivot of the Four Quarters*. Aldine, Chicago.

Whitley, David S. (ed.) (1998) *Reader in Archaeological Theory: Postprocessual and Cognitive Approaches*. Routledge, London.

Whitten, Dorothea S. and Whitten Jr, Norman E. (1988) *From Myth to Creation: The Art of Amazonian Ecuador*. University of Illinois Press, Urbana, IL.

Wiessner, Polly (1990) Is there a unity to style? *The Uses of Style in Archaeology*, ed. Margaret Conkey and Christine Hastorf, pp. 105–12. Cambridge University Press, New York.

Willey, Gordon R. (1953) *Prehistoric Settlement Patterns in the Virú Valley, Perú*. Bulletin 155, Bureau of American Ethnology, Smithsonian Institution, Washington, DC.

— (1971) *An Introduction to American Archaeology* Vol. II: *South America*. Prentice-Hall, Englewood Cliffs, NJ.

— (1974) *Das Alte Amerika*. Propyläen Kunst Geschichte, vol. 18. Propyläen Verlag, Berlin.

Williams, Sloan R., Forgey, Kathleen, and Klarich, Elizabeth (in press) An osteological study of Nasca trophy heads collected by A. L. Kroeber during the Marshall Field Expedition to Nazca, Peru. *Fieldiana*.

Williams León, Carlos (1980) Arquitectura y urbanismo en el antiguo Perú. *Historia del Perú*, 8: 389–585. Editorial Juan Mejía Baca, Lima.

— and Pazos Rivera, Miguel (1974) *Inventario, catastro, y delimitación del patrimonio arqueológico del Valle de Ica*. Instituto Nacional de Cultura, Lima.

Wilson, David (1988) *Prehispanic Settlement Patterns in the Lower Santa Valley, Peru*. Smithsonian Institution Press, Washington, DC.

Wittfogel, Karl (1957) *Oriental Despotism*. Yale University Press, New Haven, CT.

Wolfe, Elizabeth Farkass (1981) The Spotted Cat and the Horrible Bird: stylistic change in Nasca 1–5 ceramic decoration. *Ñawpa Pacha*, 19: 1–62.

Wood, Denis (1992) *The Power of Maps*. The Guilford Press, New York.

Woodman, Jim (1997) *Journey to the Sun. Nazca: Exploring the Mystery of Peru's Ancient Airfields*. Pocket Books, New York.

Yacovleff, Eugenio (1931) El vencejo (*Cypselus*) en el arte decorativo de Nasca. *Wira Kocha*, 1 (1): 25–5.

— (1932a) La deidad primitiva de los Nasca. *Revista del Museo Nacional*, 1 (2): 103–60.

— (1932b) Las falcónidas en el arte y en las creencias de los antiguos peruanos. *Revista del Muso Nacional*, 1 (1): 33–111.

— (1933) La jíquima, raíz comestible extinguida en el Perú. *Revista del Museo Nacional*, 2 (1): 49–66.

— and Muelle, Jorge (1932) Una exploración en Cerro Colorado: informe y observaciones. *Revista del Museo Nacional*, 1 (2): 31–59.

— and — (1934) Un fardo funerario de Paracas. *Revista del Museo Nacional*, 3 (1–2): 63–153.

Yoffee, Norman (1991) The collapse of ancient Mesopotamian states and civilization. *The Collapse of Ancient States and Civilizations*, ed. Norman Yoffee and George L. Cowgill, pp. 44–68. University of Arizona Press, Tucson.

Ziólkowski, Mariusz S., Pazdur, Mieczyslaw F., Krzanowski, Andrzej, and Michczynski, Adam (1994) *Andes: Radiocarbon Database for Bolivia, Ecuador and Peru*. Andean Archaeological Mission of the Institute of Archaeology, Warsaw University and Gliwice Radiocarbon Laboratory of the Institute of Physics, Silesian Technical University, Warsaw–Gliwice.

Zuidema, R. Tom (1962) The relationship between mountains and coast in ancient Peru. *Mededelingen van het Rijksmuseum voor Volkekunde*, 15: 156–65. Leiden.

— (1964) *The Ceque System of Cuzco*. E. J. Brill, Leiden.

— (1972) Meaning in Nazca art. *Artstryck 1971*: 35–54. Göteborgs Etnografiska Museum.

— (1977) The Inca kinship system: a new theoretical view. *Andean Kinship and Marriage*, ed. Ralph Bolton and Enrique Mayer, pp. 240–81. Special publication, no. 7, American Anthropological Association, Washington, DC.

— (1982) Bureaucracy and systematic knowledge in Andean civilization. *The Inca and Aztec States, 1400–1800: Anthropology and History*, ed. George Collier, Renato Rosaldo, and John Wirth, pp. 419–58. Academic Press, New York.

— (1983) The lion in the city: royal symbols of transition in Cuzco. *Journal of Latin American Lore*, 9 (1): 38–100.

Index

Notes: All references, unless otherwise indicated, are to the Nasca. Illustrations are signified by page numbers in *italics*. There may be information in print on the same page. Information in notes is signified by "n" after the page number.